African-American Holidays, Festivals, and Celebrations

SECOND EDITION

African-American Holidays, Festivals, and Celebrations

SECOND EDITION

The History, Customs, and Symbols Associated with Both Traditional and Contemporary Religious and Secular Events Observed by Americans of African Descent

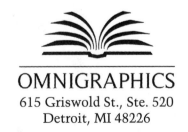

OMNIGRAPHICS
615 Griswold St., Ste. 520
Detroit, MI 48226

OMNIGRAPHICS

Angela L. Williams, *Managing Editor*

Copyright © 2019 Omnigraphics

ISBN 978-0-7808-1605-3
E-ISBN 978-0-7808-1606-0

Library of Congress Control Number:2019947964

This book is printed on acid-free paper meeting the ANSI Z39.48 Standard. The infinity symbol that appears above indicates that the paper in this book meets that standard.

Printed in the United States of America.

Table of Contents

vii

Preface

*A*frican-American Holidays, Festivals, and Celebrations, Second Edition presents the history, customs, symbols, and lore of Americans of African descent and people of the African diaspora who have immigrated to the United States from slavery times to today. The heritage, cultures, and milestones of this group are celebrated in myriad ways: through celebrations; concerts; events celebrating African-American artistic expression; events marking important moments in history, such as **Buffalo Soldiers commemorations** and **Emancipation Day**; feasts; festivals; historical reenactments; national holidays and observances, such as **Martin Luther King Jr's Birthday**; parades; religious events; special days that honor various African Americans, such as **Harriett Tubman Day**, **Rosa Parks Day**, and **Jackie Robinson Day**; special observances of communal and domestic importance, such as **Kwanza** and **Umoja Karamu**; and more. Religious observances include those of various Christian denominations as well as those of Santería and other African-based faiths.

Special events such as these offer an inspirational and educational space where people can increase their knowledge of the traditions and customs that influence and inspire them. They provide context for the ways that Americans of African descent find meaning in traditions and historical milestones unique to the group, and offer a space where attendees can learn more about their history and heritage through displays and exhibits; sample food and fare at culinary booths and stands; enjoy drama, dance, and musical performances unique to these traditions; and spend time immersed in the culture and fellowship of their group. The events also serve as an ideal place to initiate children into the culture, customs, foods, and traditions of their ancestors, while offering an ideal climate for making vital connections.

African-American Holidays, Festivals, and Celebrations is a primary source for information about holidays, festivals, and other events of importance to Americans of African descent. This new and expanded edition is a key resource for teachers and students, religious organizations, community groups, and anyone who seeks reliable information about events of importance to this ethnic group.

Entries in this book are intended for both a general audience of educators, librarians, researchers, and scholars, and for people who plan vacations around celebratory events that focus on African-American heritage. Entries range from slave observances to Kwanza and are arranged alphabetically by the name of the event. Each entry opens with (1) the name of the celebration, (2) the date on which the event is observed, and (3) the location of the event. The main body of each entry then introduces and outlines who or what the event commemorates and the kind of event the celebration is. The balance of the entry is organized by

- **Historical background:** This section provides an overview of the event or person commemorated.
- **Creation of the event:** This section provides information about the process by which the event was created.
- **Observance:** This section details what is being observed.

Contact information, event descriptions, and websites for each event are included, provide suggestions for further reading, and direct travelers to the communities where the celebrations are planned as well as to African-American cultural centers, historic sites, and museums.

Cross References

Within each entry, terms set in boldface type and as see-also references guide the reader to holidays and festivals featured in other entries in the book.

Hyphenation

Hyphenation of the term "African American" differs in the text depending on usage and the formal names of events. The term is generally not hyphenated in its noun form ("African Americans") but is hyphenated in its adjectival form ("African-American holidays").

Other Features
Appendix 1: Chronology

This appendix lists significant events in the history of African-American events covered in this book and includes the date of the first observance as well as significant dates related to the historical events or people memorialized during the event. This format offers an at-a-glance guide to the history of African-American holidays, festivals, and celebrations. Historical events are included as well, but the chronology is not intended to serve as a comprehensive list of all events in African-American history.

Appendix 2: Calendar of Holidays, Festivals, and Celebrations

This appendix lists each currently observed event in calendar order. Events that occur annually on the same fixed date are listed first within each month, followed by events that occur throughout the month or events that take place during the month on varying dates each year.

Appendix 3: Geographical List of Holidays, Festivals, and Celebrations

This appendix lists each currently observed event by the state(s) in which the event takes place. Events that are official state holidays or observances are listed first, followed by events observed in cities within the states.

Bibliography

The bibliography offers a complete list of books and articles consulted in the preparation of this book.

Organizations—Contact Information and Websites

The organizations section provides a comprehensive list of organizations represented in the book listed in alphabetical order, along with their contact information and websites addresses.

Index

The index includes an alphabetical listing of the people, places, customs, symbols, foods, musical and literary works, and other subjects mentioned in the entries.

The Sankofa symbol, shown above and appearing throughout the book is an illustration of a bird with its head facing backward. The symbol comes from the pictorial writing system of the Akan people of Ghana. The term "sankofa" means "one must return to the past in order to move forward." The symbol is also associated with an Akan proverb that translates as "go back and fetch it" or "return to the source and fetch [learn]."

Acknowledgments

We would like to acknowledge early work on this book by author and editor Kathlyn Gay and advisors Jean Currie Church (Chief Librarian, Moorland-Spingarn Research Center, Howard University) and Jessie Carney Smith (University Librarian and William and Camille Cosby Professor in the Humanities, Fisk University). Thanks also to the event organizers and institutions who responded to our requests for additional information.

Comments and Suggestions

We welcome your comments on *African American Holidays, Festivals, and Celebrations*, including suggestions for topics that you would like to see covered in future editions. Please address correspondence to:

Managing Editor
African-American Holidays, Festivals, and Celebrations
Omnigraphics
615 Griswold St., Ste. 520
Detroit, MI 48226

African-American Holidays, Festivals, and Celebrations

*A dance group from New York performs at the Odunde Festival
in Philadelphia, Pennsylvania.*

The African American Cultural Festival of Raleigh and Wake County

Date Observed: Labor Day weekend
Location: Raleigh, North Carolina

Held over the Labor Day weekend since 2010, this annual festival, which celebrates Raleigh's African American Culture, has become an important calendar event in North Carolina that connects people and artists of diverse cultures and artistic backgrounds through art, music, food, and fellowship.

Historical Background

African-American festivals have been taking place on a widespread scale in the United States since the 1980s. Many of these festivals have been initiated to connect the past with the present in black communities and to foster understanding of the African diaspora and the contributions people of African descent have made worldwide. Festivals also provide opportunities for local black communities to display their talents and highlight their accomplishments.

Creation of the Festival

Raleigh, N.C.'s capital city, boasts several cultural markers of African-American excellence, determination, and struggle, and is located near Durham, N.C., whose Hayti neighborhood was once referred to as "Black Wall Street." The festival is organized each year to celebrate and commemorate African-Americanculture and lend support to small businesses in the community.

The festival developed under the aegis of the African American Cultural Festival (AACF) Governing Board, an organization appointed by the Wake County Board of Commissioners and the Raleigh City Council. When the festival debuted in 2010, Artsplosure, a nonprofit art and cultural events production studio based in Raleigh, was contracted to provide planning and organizational expertise. By 2013, the AACF governing board acquired its own nonprofit status and went on to assume complete responsibility for organizing the festival. That year, the festival curated a vibrant African American cultural experience in downtown Raleigh featuring over 70 juried artists; traditional and contemporary village arts and crafts; and family entertainment, attracting unprecedented crowds.

Observance

Since its inception, volunteers and attendees from diverse communities have arrived year after year to learn about the history and cultural heritage of African Americans and to soak up the local culture. Local, national, and international artists, including musicians, dancers, and storytellers, showcase their work on the main stage on City Plaza. Playwrights, authors, and artisans hold educational workshops, and chefs offer different kinds of cuisines. The vendor marketplace is a crowd pleaser and rows of stalls are set up on either side of Fayetteville Street to display a wide choice of clothing, accessories, beauty products, arts and crafts work, and services. Some of the past editions of the festival have remained relatively alcohol-free in view of the family-centric theme envisioned by the board.

Contacts and Websites

The African American Cultural Festival of Raleigh and Wake County
5 W. Hargett St., Rm. 310
Raleigh, NC 27601
919-977-4027 or 919-813-0977
E-mail: info@aacfestival.org
http://www.aacfestival.org

City Plaza
400 Fayetteville St.
Raleigh, NC 27601
919-832-1231
E-mail: info@aacfralwake.org

Further Reading

Linda Simmons-Henry, Linda Harris Edmisten. *Culture Town: Life in Raleigh's African American Communities.* Raleigh Historic Districts Commission, 1993.

African American Day Parade

Date Observed: Third Sunday in September
Location: Harlem, New York

T he African American Day Parade held in Harlem in New York City in September is considered one of the largest black parades in the United States. Held since 1969, the parade's primary purpose is to display African-American achievement and pride.

Historical Background

New York has had a significant African-American population since the 18th century. It was a concentrated center for abolitionist activities, harboring numerous Underground Railroad stops and groups, such as the New York Manumission Society, that worked to abolish slavery, free slaves, and educate young African Americans. As a state, New York passed laws granting freedoms and rights to blacks much more progressively than many others in the United States. In a 1799 Act, children of slaves born after July 1799 were granted freedom. And the state of New York abolished slavery in the state in 1827, 38 years before the nation did so in 1865.

In the early 20th century blacks began to flock to New York in large numbers to escape the extreme poverty and racism of the South and to explore the burgeoning chances for economic opportunity. Harlem is considered the center of New York City's black culture. But Harlem actually began as Nieuw Haarlem, named by the Dutch, who initially established a farming community on the site (*see also* **Pinkster**). By the beginning of the 20th century, however, black New Yorkers had begun moving uptown into Harlem's apartment buildings and townhouses.

Harlem came to international prominence during the 1920s through a cultural movement known as the "Harlem Renaissance." This golden era

Adam Clayton Powell Jr.

The main thoroughfare of the African American Day Parade route is named for another notable New York: Adam Clayton Powell Jr. (1908-1972). Powell was a civil rights leader, minister, publisher, and politician. He came to prominence during his years as a U.S. congressman, first elected in 1944 and serving until 1970. He was the first black congressman from New York City's Harlem district.

During his years in the U.S. House of Representatives, Powell worked to end racial segregation in schools, the military, and the U.S. Capitol, where House rules prohibited blacks from using dining rooms, barbershops, and other facilities. He also succeeded in making changes in the House press gallery, bringing in black journalists for the first time. Powell was so consistent and adamant about overturning racial segregation that he became known as "Mr. Civil Rights." He also was known for a tactic that congressional members called the "Powell Amendment," which was attached to spending bills and, when successful, forbade federal funds to any government agencies that engaged in racial discrimination.

Additional accomplishments included a House chairmanship of the Education and Labor Committee. Under Powell, the committee helped pass such legislation as the Minimum Wage Bill of 1961, the Vocational Education Act, the Elementary and Secondary Education Act, and anti-poverty bills. Powell was a powerful congressman, but he was also a controversial figure. He was accused of tax fraud, taking kickbacks from former employees, and misuse of public funds, along with other charges. His numerous court cases eventually affected his political clout and the House expelled him for his excesses. The U.S. Supreme Court ruled against the action, however, and Powell was reinstated. Nevertheless, his political career was over. When he ran for office in 1970, he was defeated by Charles Rangel. Powell died two years later of cancer. Although Powell is not revered nationwide like some other civil rights leaders, he is honored in Harlem with an office building and boulevard bearing his name.

A woman carries the Ethiopian flag in the 1997 African American Day Parade.

propelled local writers, such as W. E. B. Du Bois, Ralph Ellison, Langston Hughes, and Zora Neale Hurston, and artists, such as Aaron Douglas, Lois Mailou Jones, and Jacob Lawrence, into the limelight. The Renaissance cast a spotlight on Harlem itself, which was, at the time, quite prosperous. However, in the 1930s, the Great Depression hit hard, and its impact was felt strongly for years afterward. By the turn of the 21st century, an economic renaissance appeared to be taking place, with a renewed effort to celebrate the culture and history of Harlem's past and present (*see also* **Harlem Week**).

Creation of the Festival

In 1969 a group of community members, led by Abe Snyder, organized the first African American Day Parade. Their goal was to celebrate the achievements of the black community, as well as to provide a positive venue in which to bring people together in a joyful demonstration of unity and culture.

Observance

The African American Day Parade is held on the third Sunday of September each year. Celebrating its 50th year in 2019, it kicks off with a documentary highlighting the 50-year legacy followed by the parade, which starts mid-afternoon in Harlem at 111th Street and proceeds to 136th Street, traversing along Adam Clayton (Powell,) Jr. Boulevard. Participating in the event are various local officials, celebrities, and other community leaders, who march along the entire distance of the parade route waving and sometimes interacting with those gathered to watch the festivities. "Interspersed among these notables are parade favorites, such as marching bands and dance groups. Each year AADP selects a theme from the following sectors: Health, Business, Education, Politics/Government, and Arts/Culture. This year, the theme for the parade is *Integrity and Transparency = Good Government*" and will see the honoring of individuals and organizations that have made significant contributions to the growth of the African-American community.

Contacts and Websites

African-American Day Parade, Inc.
P.O. Box 1860
Manhattanville Stn.
New York, NY 10027
917-294 8107
E-mail: info@africanamericandayparade.org
https://africanamericandayparade.org

Greater Harlem Chamber of Commerce
200A W. 136th St.
New York, NY 10030-7200
212-862-7200
https://www.greaterharlemchamber.com

Further Reading

Hamilton, Charles V. *Adam Clayton Powell, Jr.: The Political Biography of an American Dilemma.* Lanham, MD: Rowman & Littlefield/Cooper Square Press, 2001.

Hill, Laban Carrick. *Harlem Stomp!: A Cultural History of the Harlem Renaissance.* 2009. Reprint. New York: Little, Brown/Megan Tingley, 2014. (young adult)

African American Heritage Festival

Date Observed: Last week in March
Location: Ohio State University, Columbus, Ohio

The Multicultural Center at Ohio State University in Columbus holds an annual African American Heritage Festival over the last week in March. The purpose of the festival is to share a celebration of African-American culture and history within the university.

Historical Background

Ohio State University opened in 1873 with 24 students, none of whom were black. Fewer than 20 years later, however, the first African-American students were enrolled. The university established its Black Studies Department

---

Stepping

For decades African-American fraternities and sororities have developed and performed stepping performances that are rooted in African and African-American cultures. The tradition has been passed on for generations, and step shows are part of many African-American festivals and celebrations in the United States. Step shows also have become popular worldwide.

Stepping involves synchronized movements, such as high steps, hand clapping, arm crossing, and shoulder tapping. This complex performance also is mixed with singing and chanting.

---

in 1972. During the 1970s black enrollment had increased to the point at which African-American student services became necessary. The umbrella Multicultural Center, which organizes the festival, was created during the mid-1990s.

Creation of the Festival

The African American Heritage Festival has its origins in an informal block party held by students in the 1970s. Each year the event was repeated and grew in size. By the 1980s, students began efforts to instead create an event that would focus on cultural awareness. In 2001 they named the celebration the African American Heritage Festival. Organizers also began to use a different Swahili term each year as part of the festival's theme. *Heshima*, a Swahili word for respect, is adopted as an integral part of the Heritage Festival.

Observance

The African American Heritage Festival begins with a parade of student groups and marching bands. During the week, events include forums that address the year's theme. The theme for the year 2019 is "Aspire to Inspire" and the university incorporated the theme throughout the academic year to prepare for the festival. A step show, basketball tournament, food market, music, art, poetry, and dancing are part of this annual festival as well. In addition, volunteers read stories and poems to young schoolchildren throughout the week to encourage them to read. The week-long festival features talent and poetry showcases, cultural-awareness programs, public-health talks, and an annual Gospel Festival, and culminates with the Mahogany Moments dinner and dance.

Contact and Website

Office of Student Life Multicultural Center
The Ohio Union
1739 N. High St.
Columbus, OH 43210
614-688-8449
E-mail: aahf@osu.edu
http://heritagefestival.osu.edu

Further Reading

Fine, Elizabeth C. *Soulstepping: African American Step Shows.* 2003. Reprint. Champaign: University of Illinois Press, 2007.

African American Women in Cinema Film Festival

Date Observed: Last week of March
Location: New York, New York

The African American Women in Cinema, Inc. holds an annual film festival in New York City. The event aims to expand, explore, and create career opportunities for minority women filmmakers within the entertainment industry.

Historical Background

Although blacks have been involved in filmmaking ever since motion pictures were first produced, white males have dominated the industry. Not surprisingly, then, African-American women have struggled not only to be recognized as filmmakers, but also to attain the funds needed to produce motion pictures. Usually, they have produced independent films or videos for specific audiences and, for the most part, have not been known by the general movie-going public—or, for that matter, by major studios.

Black women directed and produced movies from about 1920 to 1930, when white men took over the industry, forcing nearly all women into the background. One of the early filmmakers was the famed author Zora Neale Hurston, according to *Sisters in the Cinema*, a documentary written, directed, produced, and narrated by Yvonne Welbon (*see also* **Zora Neale Hurston Festival of the Arts and Humanities**). Welbon's film was the result of a search for other black women filmmakers. Premiering in 2004, the documentary traces the history of black women in filmmaking and has been widely and favorably reviewed.

In January 1992, Julie Dash's *Daughters of the Dust* opened in Chicago. It was the first feature-length film by an African-American woman to receive a wide theatrical release. The film is the story of three generations of African Americans who meet on a Sea Island in 1902 (*see also* **Georgia Sea Island Festival, Hilton Head Island Gullah Celebration,** *and* **Penn Center Heritage Days**).

Creation of the Festival

The African American Women in Cinema Festival began in 1998 in an effort to develop opportunities for African-American women in filmmaking. The non-profit African American Women in Cinema (AAWIC), which incorporated in 2000, focuses on supporting minority female filmmakers, particularly by providing resources that might not otherwise be readily accessible to them.

Julie Dash's groundbreaking film, Daughters of the Dust *(1992), was released as a DVD in 2000.*

Observance

The festival is a combination of film screenings, workshops, seminars, social events, and award ceremonies.

The films screened at the festival aspire to achieve AAWIC's mission: to improve cultural understanding and overall social welfare through the promotion of diversity in dramatic and documentary media content. All other activities support the organization's belief that the tools of enlightenment, empowerment, entertainment, education, and enterprise can be used by women, for the betterment of women, to break barriers in the black filmmaking arena.

12

Contacts and Websites

African American Women in Cinema Organization, Inc.
545 Eighth Ave., Ste. 401
New York, NY 10018
212-769-7949
http://www.aawic.org

Sisters in Cinema, a resource guide provided by Yvonne Welbon's Our Film Works, Inc.
http://www.sistersincinema.com

Further Reading

Dash, Julie, with Toni Cade Bambara and bell hooks. *Daughters of the Dust: The Making of an African American Woman's Film.* New York: The New Press, 1992.

Ellerson, Beti. *Sisters of the Screen: Women of Africa on Film, Video and Television.* Lawrenceville, NJ: Africa World Press, 2000.

Foster, Gwendolyn Audrey. *Women Filmmakers of the African and Asian Diaspora: Decolonizing the Gaze, Locating Subjectivity.* 1997. Reprint. Carbondale: Southern Illinois University Press, 2008.

Moss, Marilyn. "Sisters in Cinema." *Hollywood Reporter,* February 6, 2004.

Williams, John. "Re-creating Their Media Image: Two Generations of Black Women Filmmakers." *Black Scholar,* Spring 1995.

African Film Festival

Date Observed: April through May
Location: New York, New York

T he African Film Festival is an annual two-month, noncompetitive cinematic celebration held in New York City. The festival runs from the beginning of April until the end of May and showcases both short- and feature-length films produced by African directors in the diaspora.

Historical Background

Since the 1950s Africans have been creating films that depict the diverse cultures of the continent. The films have covered such topics as colonialism, corruption in independent nations, and traditional ways of life. Over the years, the films have served as vehicles of cultural exchange.

A Global Impact

D irector Mbye B. Cham describes "A significant development in African film culture, in the last two decades, especially, . . . the turn toward the subject of history. Since its inception in the 60s and 70s, a significant portion of African cinema has focused and continues to focus on issues of racism, colonial exploitation and injustice, tradition and modernity, hopes, betrayals and disaffections of independence, immigration and many other social-justice issues. Historicizing these issues, as well as creating narratives based primarily on events, figures, and subjects of history, has emerged in recent years as a prominent trait of African film culture, as a cursory glance at African film production in the past two decades will demonstrate."

In the late 1980s a committee of African and American artists and scholars banded together to find a way to use African cinema to promote and increase knowledge and understanding of African arts, literature, and culture. The goals were to develop a non-African audience for African films and to expand the opportunities for the distribution of African films in the United States. Ultimately, the committee formed a non-profit organization in 1990, the African Film Festival, Inc. (AFF), to sponsor a festival.

Creation of the Festival

The African Film Festival was established in 1993. The festival has grown both in terms of attendance and respect among critics. The AFF also has expanded the festival's impact by adding a traveling film series, a young adults' education program, summer outdoor screenings, and community outreach.

Observance

During the festival, an impressive array of African films are available for viewing. AFF's commitment to bridging the divide between postcolonial Africa and the American public through the medium of film is reflected by the diverse selection. Panel discussions and post-screening events have also been added over the years to broaden both educational and film-distribution opportunities.

In recent years, a wider embrace of the festival has been demonstrated by the recurring commitment of the festival's hosts: the Film Society of Lincoln Center and the Brooklyn Academy of Music.

Contacts and Websites

"African Cinema" a resource of the Media Resources Center, University of California at Berkeley, provides synopses of movies by African filmmakers
http://www.lib.berkeley.edu/taxonomy/term/371/all

African Film Festival, Inc.
154 W. 18th St., Ste. 2A
New York, NY 10011
212-352-1720
E-mail: info@africanfilmny.org
http://www.africanfilmny.org

Further Reading

Armes, Roy. *Postcolonial Images: Studies in North African Film*. Bloomington: Indiana University Press, 2005.

Gugler, Joseph. *African Film: Re-Imagining a Continent*. Bloomington: Indiana University Press, 2003.

Pfaff, Francoise. *Focus on African Films*. Bloomington: Indiana University Press, 2004.

Ukadike, Nwachukwu Frank. *Black African Cinema*. Berkeley: University of California Press, 1994.

African Street Festival

Date Observed: Third weekend in September
Location: Nashville, Tennessee

The African Street Festival is held each year in Nashville, Tennessee, on the main campus of Tennessee State University and extends into the nearby community. Sponsored by the African American Cultural Alliance, the festival promotes increased awareness of the culture and history of people of African descent.

Historical Background

In the early 1980s, a small group of African Americans founded the African American Cultural Alliance in Nashville, Tennessee. The original mission of the Alliance was to recognize and promote positive aspects of African cultures, raise awareness of the heritage of people of African descent, and create opportunities to demonstrate African cultures. By doing so, the Alliance hoped to instill a collective sense of pride in African Americans.

Yvette Brunson and Helen Shute-Pettaway were two of the founding members of the Alliance. Believing that African heritage and history had been largely ignored by American mainstream society, Brunson and Shute-Pettaway wanted the Alliance to create a festival celebrating Africa and its diverse cultures and stories. The two hoped that giving African Americans reasons to be proud of their heritage would generate positive self-esteem and motivate the community to learn more.

Creation of the Festival

In 1983 the Alliance created the African Street Festival as a public showcase for positive images of African nations, people of African descent, and African ways of life. The festival's primary goals include increased education about

17

and understanding of the unique creative aspects of African cultures as well as continued support of the African/African-American community.

Observance

The African Street Festival has grown to become one of Nashville's largest cultural events. It includes a wide variety of activities of interest to people of all ages such as the Children's Pavilion, which features arts and crafts, dance, and storytelling; and drumming and a mix of live music for adults. This family-oriented festival attracts thousands of people and includes cultures of the Caribbean; North, South, and Central America; and other places throughout the world where Africa is also represented in its people and cultures. The theme of the 2019 festival is "UBUNTU" (I am because we are).

Contact and Website

African American Cultural Alliance
1215 Ninth N. Ave., Ste. 210
P.O. Box 22173
Nashville, TN 37202
615-942-0706; hotline: 329-521-4038
E-mail: info@aacanashville.org
http://www.aacanashville.org

African World Festival in Detroit

Date Observed: Third weekend in August
Location: Detroit, Michigan

The African World Festival celebrates the richness, diversity, and world-wide influence of African cultures through music, art, and food. The festival is produced by the Charles H. Wright Museum of African American History and is held in downtown Detroit on the third weekend of August each year.

Historical Background

The city of Detroit has a rich African-American history spanning as far back as the 1800s. Although it is unknown exactly when the first African Americans came to Detroit, the U.S. Census of 1820 reported that African Americans made up 4.7 percent of the city's population. By 1837, Detroit had become an important stop along the Underground Railroad, with city residents helping multitudes of slaves escape across the Detroit River to Canada. Black Bottom, Detroit's first African-American community, was established in the mid-1800s on the banks of the Detroit River. Black Bottom soon became an African-American cultural center with the founding of social and political organizations, educational and recreational societies, and churches and schools. During the Civil War, many southerners moved north, and by 1870 the city's African-American population had increased dramatically.

To meet the military demands of World War I, the industrial manufacturing factories in Detroit recruited southern African Americans by advertising high-paying jobs for able-bodied workers. This triggered a massive migration of African Americans to Detroit that continued through the 1930s. A second

A dancer instructs a festivalgoer at the 1999 African World Festival.

influx of African Americans occurred during World War II as southerners again moved north looking for work. Detroit's African-American population doubled during the 1950s and 1960s, and the city again became an important cultural center. The Motown Record Corporation launched the careers of many popular African-American superstars such as Aretha Franklin, Diana Ross and the Supremes, and the Jackson Five. During these years Detroit also became a focal point of the U.S. Civil Rights Movement, making national news when violence erupted throughout the city in the 1967 riots. After this period of extreme racial tension, African Americans in Detroit focused on political activism and worked to elect African Americans to public office. By 1975, African Americans made up the majority of Detroit's population, and by 1990 Detroit was among the 10 U.S. cities with the largest percentage of African Americans. The 2018 U.S. Census Bureau reported Detroit's population as 79.1% African American, a 3.9% decrease from the 2000 Census Report.

Creation of the Festival

The Charles H. Wright Museum of African American History (formerly known as the Afro-American Museum of Detroit) has produced the African World Festival since 1983. The African World Festival is modeled after the Festival of African Culture, an international event that was last held in Nigeria in 1977. More than a celebration of African-American culture, the African World Festival honors all of the cultures that have evolved in the African diaspora— the descendants of African people who are now scattered all over the world. The festival promotes the ideals of the Pan-African movement that began in the 1920s. Championed by Jamaican civil rights pioneer Marcus Garvey, the Pan-African movement encourages the descendants of African nations to learn about the customs and cultures of their homeland (*see also* **Marcus Garvey's Birthday**). The African World Festival provides opportunities for people to see the connections between African people all over the world.

Observance

The African World Festival has grown to be Detroit's largest ethnic festival and one of the largest festivals of its kind in the United States. More than 150,000 visitors attend this free outdoor event each year.

The festival celebrates the music, art, and food of Africans and those of African descent, and features arts and crafts, film screenings, poetry readings, lectures, and storytelling in African traditions. Local musicians as well as performers from around the world provide live entertainment focusing on African and African-influenced music from various eras, including blues, jazz, gospel, reggae, soul, and folk. African-American fraternities and sororities perform elaborately choreographed step shows, and African touring groups showcase traditional dances of Africa. Like the busy open-air markets found throughout Africa, the marketplace area gives visitors a chance to explore the wares of hundreds of vendors, many of whom travel to Detroit from Africa to participate in the three-day festival each year.

Contact and Website

Charles H. Wright Museum of African American History
315 E. Warren Ave.
Detroit, MI 48201
313-494-5800
E-mail: awf@thewright.org
http://thewright.org

Further Reading

Bates-Rudd, Rhonda. "Rhythms of the African World: Detroit Brings Out the Best of Art, Music, Clothing and Food to Celebrate Cultures." *The Detroit News*, August 18, 1999.

Heron, W. Kim. "A World of Africa in Detroit." *Detroit Free Press*, August 26, 1983.

Rich, Wilbur C. "Detroit, Michigan." In *The African-American Experience: Selections from the Five-Volume Macmillan Encyclopedia of African-American Culture and History*, edited by Jack Salzman. New York: Macmillan, 1998.

Sutter, Mary. "Black Fest Picks 'One' (American Black Film Festival 'On the One')." *Daily Variety*, July 18, 2005.

African World Festival in Milwaukee

Date Observed: First weekend in August
Location: Milwaukee, Wisconsin

The African World Festival in Milwaukee is celebrated during the first weekend in August. It highlights African-American culture and its many contributions to the world, both past and present. Participants learn about life and rituals in Africa and the variety of African-American experiences.

Historical Background

One aspect of the African World Festival is West African history, particularly that of the great Benin Empire in what is modern-day Nigeria. The logo for the festival depicts a mask that Oba (King) Esigie, who ruled the Benin Empire from about 1504 to 1550, created to honor his mother, whom he designated first Iy'Oba, or Queen Mother. During Esigie's reign, Benin artists produced numerous works in copper and brass and refined casting techniques that had been passed on since the 13th century. King Esigie and other powerful and wealthy leaders became patrons of artists, helping to establish the tradition of casting bronze heads and ivory masks and possibly the first brass plaques. Such works of art that have survived are preserved in museums worldwide and have influenced later art.

Creation of the Festival

The African World Festival began in 1982 when four members of Milwaukee's African-American community—a population of about 200,000—met to initiate an event that would focus on the heritage and culture of Africa and members of the diaspora. Since the inception of the African World Festival, its leadership has grown to a board of directors with 17 members as well as a 20-member advisory board. Each year some 500 volunteers contribute their time and efforts to making sure the festival is a success.

Observance

The African World Festival draws as many as 80,000 attendees each year. The opening ceremonies for the festival include a traditional African libation: pouring a liquid on the ground to honor and give thanks to ancestors and to remember the struggles and trials of African Americans. The designated festival Queen Mother, King, and Elders Council are recognized during the ceremony, and African drummers and dancers perform. Participants also may learn about African ways of life by visiting a replica of a village and listening to African storytellers present traditional tales.

Other venues during the weekend celebrate African-American music—gospel, blues, hip hop, and rhythm and blues. There are sports events and youth activities. A marketplace offers such goods as fried plantains, peanut stew, barbecued ribs, fried chicken, catfish, seafood gumbo, Mississippi mud pie, peach cobbler, and funnel cakes. African jewelry, artwork, and clothing are also for sale at the marketplace. The African World Festival in Milwaukee has ceased to exist now, but other Africa-themed festivals continue in Milwaukee.

Contacts and Websites

African World Festival
315 E. Warren Ave.
Detroit, MI 4820
313-494-5800
E-mail: awf@thewright.org
http://thewright.org/african-world-festival

Greater Milwaukee Convention and Visitors Bureau
648 N. Plankinton Ave., Ste. 425
Milwaukee, WI 53203-2926
800-231-0903 or 414-273-3950; fax: 414-273-5596
www.visitmilwaukee.org

Further Reading

Giblin, James. "Introduction: Diffusion and Other Problems in the History of African States." *Art & Life in Africa Project of the School of Art and Art History,* University of Iowa. Revised March 7, 1999.

African-American History Month

Date Observed: February
Location: Communities Nationwide

African-American History Month is celebrated each February to honor prominent African Americans of the past as well as present-day leaders and others who have made significant contributions to the nation and world. It began in 1926 as Negro History Week. Since 1976, the president of the United States has issued a proclamation calling on Americans to observe African American History Month with appropriate programs and events. Each February communities, schools, libraries, and other institutions across the United States pay tribute to African-American achievements in numerous ways.

Historical Background

Until the early part of the 1900s, few if any U.S. history books contained information about African-American accomplishments. References to blacks nearly always depicted the low status forced on them by the dominant white society. Because of the vision of Carter Goodwin Woodson (1875–1950) and others, the historical contributions and roles of African Americans were largely accepted as integral to American history by the end of the century.

Woodson was the son of former slaves and one of nine children in the family. When the Woodsons moved to West Virginia, Carter found work in the coal mines and also enrolled in high school at age 20, and went on to graduate in two years. He later earned a degree from the University of Chicago and a doctorate from Harvard, becoming the second African American to earn a Ph.D. in history. For 10 years he taught high-school history in Washington, D.C., and began his study of African-American history, believing that educating people about black history would promote racial pride and harmony.

> ## "Black History Month Matters"
>
> ### By Carter G. Woodson
>
> "Historian Carter G. Woodson realized that black people were underrepresented in the history books while he was pursuing a Ph.D. in history from Harvard. He also said that, 'if a race does not have a history—it will not have valuable traditions, it becomes a negligible factor in the world's thought, and it is in the risk of being exterminated." The movie *Hidden Figures* explains how black history remains forgotten. So the celebration is necessary because African-American history remains mainly unknown and unappreciated and it is associated with America's growth, and evolution—politically, economically, and culturally."

In 1915, Woodson and a few colleagues in Chicago organized the Association for the Study of Negro Life and History (ASNLH), now called the Association for the Study of African American Life and History (ASALH). Under the auspices of the association but with his own funds, Woodson founded the *Journal of Negro History,* and published the first issue in January 1916. To further his mission of publishing black perspectives on history (as opposed to those by white scholars), he established the Associated Negro Publishers in the 1920s.

Creation of the Observance

In 1926 Woodson and the Association for the Study of Negro Life and History launched Negro History Week after first announcing the event in 1925. Woodson and the other leaders chose the second week in February for the celebration because the birth dates of Frederick Douglass and Abraham Lincoln are observed around that time (*see also* **Frederick Douglass Day**). Negro History Week eventually became Black History Week. In 1976 Gerald Ford was the first president to call for Americans to observe February as Black History Month. Since then each president of the United States has done the same, though in recent years the observance is better known as African-American History Month.

African-American Achievements

From colonial times through the U.S. Civil Rights era—and, sometimes, to the present day—African Americans often have been prevented from entering occupations and professions dominated by whites. Once someone broke the color barrier that person became known as an "African-American First." Today there are so many "firsts" that their lives and achievements fill hundreds of books, and their success stories are part of African-American History presentations. Out of thousands of people, a variety in diverse fields may be featured during the month.

As a public service, the U.S. Census Bureau sponsors features for a radio program called "Profile America." All year long "Profile America" offers vignettes of important observances, commemorations, or people. The first day of February was dedicated to Black History Month and February 19, 2019, saw a slot that talked about "Notable Blacks in Law." Over the past few decades, the radio program featured many people in detail. Highlighted below are a few people:

- Robert Pelham, who worked for the U.S. Census Bureau from 1900 to 1930, patented two devices that mechanically totaled statistical tables.

- Evelyn Ashford, one of the world's fastest sprinters, won five Olympic medals—four gold and one silver—during the 1980s and 1990s.

- Maurice Ashley became the first African American to achieve the distinction of international grandmaster in chess in 1999.

- Dorothy West, associated with the Harlem Renaissance of the 1920s, was a magazine publisher and author of short stories and books such as *The Living Is Easy* and *The Wedding: A Novel.*

- Sarah Goode, a former slave who was freed after the Civil War, opened a furniture store in Chicago, invented a fold-up cabinet bed, and in 1885 became the first African-American woman to hold a patent for an invention.

- Fannie Lou Hamer organized voter registration drives in the 1960s and, at the 1964 Democratic National Convention, led an effort to unseat the all-white delegation from Mississippi.

- Captain Frederick Branch became the first African American to be commissioned as an officer in the Marine Corps in 1945.

Among others featured were pianist and vocalist Bobby Short; Army officer, physician, and judge Martin Robinson Delany; U.S. Secretary of State Condoleezza Rice; publisher John Johnson; National Football League coach Tony Dungy; award-winning playwright Lorraine Hansberry; traditional jazz saxophonist Sidney Bechet; inventor Miriam Benjamin, who received a patent in 1888 for a hotel "signal chair" that lit up when a guest wanted service; cell scientist Ernest Just; poet Arna Bontemps; Dr. George Grant, a dentist who created the first golf tee, which he patented in 1899; Vietnam veteran Sherian Cadoria, an African-American woman who retired as a brigadier general; and former slave Lewis Temple, who developed a whaling harpoon in 1848.

Others profiled were Harriet Tubman, who led slaves from the South to freedom in the North (*see also* **Harriet Tubman Day**); famed photojournalist, film director, and poet Gordon Parks; civil-rights worker C. DeLores Tucker, Pennsylvania's first African-American secretary of state; inventor George Edward Alcorn Jr., whose expertise is nuclear and molecular physics at the Goddard Space Flight Center; George Washington Bush, a pioneer who went West by wagon train in 1844; and Edward Davis of Detroit, a 1996 inductee in the Automotive Hall of Fame as the first African-American new car dealer.

Historic Sites

During African American History Month, many individuals and tour groups visit National Park Service historic sites that commemorate African Americans, although people visit these places throughout the year as well. One of the sites is in Boston, Massachusetts, where there is a Black Heritage Trail that links 15 historic buildings, such as the African-American Meeting House and an African-American church dating back to pre-Civil War times.

In Topeka, Kansas, the Monroe Elementary School, once a segregated school, is now a historic site maintained by the U.S. National Park Service. The site commemorates *Brown v. Board of Education of Topeka*, the 1954 U.S. Supreme Court decision that struck down "separate but equal" educational facilities, declaring them unconstitutional.

The Tuskegee Institute National Historic Site in Tuskegee, Alabama, welcomes visitors to the home of George Washington Carver, founder of the Tuskegee Institute, and the Carver Museum. Also located on the site are original buildings designed by Robert R. Taylor, the first African American to graduate from the Massachusetts Institute of Technology. Tuskegee students constructed the buildings (*see also* **George Washington Carver Day**).

Educator Booker T.
Washington

Activist Mary
Church Terrell

Writer and educator
W. E. B. Du Bois

Abolitionist
Sojourner Truth

Labor leader
A. Philip Randolph

Activist Roy Wilkins

Educator Mary
McLeod Bethune

U.S. Supreme Court
Justice Thurgood Marshall

U.S. Representative
Barbara Jordan

Diplomat Ralph Bunche

Leaders in African-American History

African-American National Park Sites

The U.S. National Park Service provides links to the following African-American National Park Sites at http://www.cr.nps.gov/aahistory/parks/parks.htm:

Booker T. Washington National Monument (Virginia)

Boston African American National Historic Site (Massachusetts)

Brown v. Board of Education National Historic Site (Kansas)

Cane River National Historic Area (Louisiana)

Cane River Creole National Historic Park (Louisiana)

Central High School National Historic Site (Arkansas)

Colonial National Historic Park, "African Americans at Jamestown" (Virginia)

Dayton Aviation Heritage National Historic Park, Dunbar House (Ohio)

Frederick Douglass National Historic Site (Washington, D.C.)

Fort Donelson National Battlefield, "African Americans at Fort Donelson" (Tennessee)

Fort Donelson National Cemetery (Tennessee)

Fort Scott National Historic Site, "First to Serve: African-American Soldiers" (Kansas)

Fort Smith National Historic Site, "From Slavery to Parker's Court" (Arkansas)

George Washington Birthplace National Monument, "Slavery at Pope's Creek Plantation" (Virginia)

George Washington Carver National Monument (Missouri)

Guadalupe Mountains National Park, "Buffalo Soldiers" (Texas)

Gulf Islands National Seashore, "Louisiana Native Guards on Ship Island 1863–1870" (Mississippi)

Hampton National Historic Site (Maryland)

Harpers Ferry National Historic Site, "Frederick Douglass at Harpers Ferry" (West Virginia)

In Richmond, Virginia, the Maggie L. Walker National Historic Site was once the home of a prominent African-American woman. Walker was the first woman in the United States to establish a bank and serve as its president. Guided tours of the house are provided at the site, and a video illustrates her life as a civic leader and businesswoman.

The National Register of Historic Places lists numerous sites that have significant ties to African-American history and are recognized during the month.

African-American National Park Sites *continued*

Hopewell Furnace National Historic Site, "African Americans at Hopewell Furnace" (Pennsylvania)

Independence National Historical Park, "The Robert Morris Mansion" (Pennsylvania)

Jean Lafitte National Historical Park and Preserve (Louisiana)

Jefferson National Expansion Memorial (Missouri)

Lincoln Memorial (Washington, D.C.)

Maggie L. Walker National Historic Site (Virginia)

Martin Luther King Jr. National Historic Site (Georgia)

Mary McLeod Bethune Council House National Historic Site (Washington, D.C.)

Manassas National Battlefield Park, "The Robinson House" (Virginia)

Natchez National Historic Park (Mississippi)

New Orleans Jazz National Historic Site (Louisiana)

Nicodemus National Historic Site (Kansas)

Perry's Victory and International Peace Memorial, "African American Seamen" (Ohio)

Petersburg National Battlefield, "African Americans at Petersburg" (Virginia)

Port Chicago Naval Magazine National Memorial (California)

Richmond National Battlefield Park (Virginia)

San Francisco Maritime Park, "African American History" (California)

Selma to Montgomery National Historic Trail (Alabama)

Timucuan Ecological and Historic Preserve, "Kingsley Plantation" (Florida)

Tuskegee Institute National Historic Site (Alabama)

Virgin Islands National Park (Virgin Islands)

In Indianapolis, Indiana, for example, there are several historic places, among them the Madame C. J. Walker Building, a National Historic Landmark. This museum documents the life of successful businesswoman Madame Walker, who developed, manufactured, and sold formulas for hair care and other beauty products for black women. She was also the first African-American millionaire.

Baltimore, Maryland, touts its numerous African-American historical sites of interest to visitors during Black History Month as well as at other times of the year. The National Great Blacks In Wax Museum houses lifelike African-American wax figures that represent various periods in black history. The museum also has a replica of a slave ship. At the Eubie Blake National Jazz Institute and Cultural Center, memorabilia and artifacts honor the life of Blake. Other historic sites in Baltimore include buildings where Frederick Douglass lived and worked; headquarters of the National Association for the Advancement of Colored People (NAACP); and St. Francis Academy, a black educational institution established in 1828 and still in operation.

The Monroe School in Washington, D.C., once served as the National Trade and Professional Training School for Women and Girls, providing vocational training to African-American females. The name was later changed to Nannie Helen Burroughs School to honor Dr. Nannie Helen Burroughs, the African-American educator, orator, businesswoman, and religious leader who founded the school in 1909. The 1928 Trades Hall building, a portion of the current school, was declared a National Historic Landmark in 1991.

Many other cities across the United States also call attention to markers, monuments, museums, schools, and other buildings associated with African-American heritage. These structures provide physical context for notable African Americans featured in educational programs offered during the month.

Observance

As with other national holidays and observances, the U.S. president issued a proclamation calling on Americans to mark the occasion with appropriate programs and activities designed to honor African Americans' contributions to the nation.

Throughout February, books, magazine articles, newspaper features, Internet sites, television documentaries, videos, and other materials feature scholars, explorers, civil-rights leaders, authors, poets, journalists, musicians, artists, sports and film stars, and many others of African descent. Print and electronic materials frequently explain how African American History Month should be celebrated. But there is no single "correct" way. Observances may involve the celebration of a potpourri of individuals and events, or they may be designed around a specific theme or field of interest.

As this month-long observance takes place each year, people from diverse backgrounds pay tribute to African-American heritage and achievements in many fields. For example, in Los Angeles, California, the **Pan African Film & Arts Festival** is billed as the largest African-American History Month event in the nation.

At religious institutions a common practice is to reflect on the lives of such historical figures as Richard Allen, the founder of the African Methodist Episcopal Church (*see also* **Founder's Day/Richard Allen's Birthday**); Peter Spencer, founder of the African Union Methodist Protestant Church (*see also* **August Quarterly**); and prominent abolitionists and civil-rights pioneers such as Frederick Douglass, Martin Luther King Jr., and Rosa Parks (*see also* **Frederick Douglass Day; Martin Luther King Jr.'s Birthday;** *and* **Rosa Parks Day**).

Libraries mark African American History Month with tables and showcases displaying titles about African Americans or by African-American authors. Some libraries also participate in the annual African-American Read-In, sponsored by the Black Caucus of the National Council of English Teachers (NCET). The yearly event, which is also designed to encourage literacy, takes place in elementary and secondary schools, on university campuses, and in bookstores and churches. Local celebrities, community leaders, and students read from works by their favorite African-American writers or African-American authors read from their works.

Along with reading, writing is usually emphasized in schools during the observance. Many states have school essay contests with specific themes for Black History Month. Rewards for such essay contests range from savings bonds to college scholarships. In Florida, for example, the state sponsors an annual essay contest that is just one of numerous events during the month to commemorate Florida's African-American heritage. The theme for 2019 is "Celebrating Public Service."

African-American athletes are often the subjects of tributes during Black History Month. Some popular figures are Jackie Robinson (1919–1972), the first black man to break the color barrier in the modern era of major league baseball (*see also* **Jackie Robinson Day**); Hank Aaron (1934-), a MLB player; Jack Johnson (1878–1946), the first black heavyweight boxing champion; boxers Joe Louis (1914–1981) and Muhammad Ali (1942–2016); Jessie Owens (1913–1980), famous track star and winner of Olympic gold medals; James

"Jim" Brown (1936-), a football legend inducted into the Professional Football Hall of Fame; John Carlos (1944-) and Tommie Smith (1945-), whose black power salute during the 1968 Summer Olympics spotlighted racial injustices in America; basketball great Michael Jordan (1963-); tennis stars Arthur Ashe (1943–1993), Althea Gibson (1927–2003), Serena Williams (1981-) and Venus Williams (1980-); track star and Olympic medal winner Jacqueline "Jackie" Joyner-Kersee (1962-); golfers Charles Luther Sifford (1922–2015), Eldrick Tont "Tiger" Woods (1975-); and many more.

Contacts and Websites
"African-American History Month"
https://www.africanamericanhistorymonth.gov

"The African-American Mosaic: A Library of Congress Resource Guide for the Study of Black History & Culture"Association for the Study of African-American Life and History
https://www.loc.gov/exhibits/african/afam001.html

Association for the Study of African-American Life and History
301 Rhode Island Ave., N.W.
Washington, DC 20059
202-238-5910
http://www.asalh.org

Eubie Blake National Jazz Institute and Cultural Center
847 N. Howard St.
Baltimore, MD 21201
410-225-3130
E-mail: info@eubieblake.org
http://www.eubieblake.org

The HistoryMakers
1900 S. Michigan Ave.
Chicago, IL 60616
312-674-1900; fax: 312-674-1915
https://www.thehistorymakers.org

Madam C. J. Walker Building
617 Indiana Ave.
Indianapolis, IN 46202
317-236-2099
E-mail: info@madamwalkerlegacycenter.com
https://madamwalkerlegacycenter.com

National Civil Rights Museum
450 Mulberry St.
Memphis, TN 38103
901-521-9699
https://www.civilrightsmuseum.org

National Great Blacks in Wax Museum
1601-03 E. North Ave.
Baltimore, MD 21213
410-563-3404; fax: 410-563-7806
http://www.greatblacksinwax.org

Further Reading

Cantor, George. *Historic Landmarks of Black America*. Detroit: Gale Research, 1991.

Curtis, Nancy C. *Black Heritage Sites: The South*. New York: The New Press, 1996.

Muwakkil, Salim. "Black History Month Matters." *In These Times*, January 2006. http://inthesetimes.com/article/2476/black_history_month_matters

Savage, Beth. *African American Historic Places*. Hoboken, NJ: John Wiley & Sons, 1994.

Smith, Jessie Carney. *Black Firsts: 4,000 Ground-Breaking and Pioneering Historical Events*. 2nd ed., revised and expanded. Canton, MI: Visible Ink Press, 2003.

Webster, Raymond B. *African American Firsts in Science & Technology*. Farmington Hills, MI: Gale, 1999.

West, Cornel. *Race Matters*. 2001. Reprint. Boston: Beacon Press, 2017.

Woodson, Carter. *The Mis-Education of the Negro*. Independently Published, 2019.

African/Caribbean International Festival of Life

Date Observed: Five days, including July 4
Location: Chicago, Illinois

The African/Caribbean International Festival of Life (IFOL) is a multi-cultural family event held each year over the Fourth of July weekend in Chicago, Illinois. Since 1993 the festival has presented African and Caribbean music and foods to a diverse audience.

Historical Background

Chicago is home to people from a great variety of ethnic groups, including European, Latinx, Caribbean, and African Americans, as well as people of Asian and Native American descent.

To celebrate this city's richness, Ephraim M. Martin—an entrepreneur, publisher, and TV personality, established Martin's Inter-Culture, Ltd., a company that has produced festivals in Chicago since the 1980s. In addition to the African/Caribbean Festival of Life, Martin also produces The Chicago Reggae Music Awards and International Reggae and World Music Awards (IRAWMA).

Creation of the Festival

Martin's Inter-Culture presented the first African/Caribbean International Festival of Life in 1993. Now it attracts an estimated 50,000 people per year. Martin's objective has been to attract a diversity of people from Chicago to experience African, Caribbean, and African-American music, food, arts, and more.

Observance

The festival is held at Washington Park, where three stages provide live entertainment daily. One is typically devoted to music. Genres include reggae, calypso, salsa, blues, rhythm and blues, highlife (West African music that is described as a fusion of indigenous dance rhythms and melodies and Western influences), soukous (modern Zairean dance music), hip hop, and rap. The second stage is more often geared to gospel and educational undertakings.

There are numerous children's activities available during the festival, in keeping with its family orientation. An international marketplace is open daily and has something for every taste and temptation. Between 200 and 300 vendors offer food, arts and crafts, jewelry, and clothing. At the food booths participants can sample Caribbean, African, Asian, Mexican, Indian, Middle Eastern, and American dishes. Local business merchants and companies also have booths to showcase their area services. Each year the event has a specific theme but, typically, it follows along the lines of IFOL founder Martin's belief that "Out of the Many, We Are One People."

Contact and Website

International Festival of Life
c/o Martin's International
1325 S. Wabash Ave., Ste. 307
Chicago, IL 60605
312-427-0266; fax: 312-427-0268
E-mail: festoflife@gmail.com
https://www.internationalfestivaloflife.com

AfroSolo Arts Festival

Date Observed: February
Location: San Francisco

The festival provides a forum to give an authentic voice to diverse experiences of the people of African descent and nurtures the cultural heritage of the African-American diaspora by presenting performances of artists from the Bay area and around the world.

Historical Background

The AfroSolo Arts Festival can be traced back to 1991, when actor, writer, director, and producer Thomas Robert Simpson hosted his birthday party. His artist friends were invited to the party to perform, and the gathering was such a huge success that it was decided that the tradition must continue. The following two birthday celebrations also turned out to be as resounding a success as the one in 1994, and Simpson decided to launch an annual arts festival to showcase local and international talent and transform the cultural landscape of the Bay area. Thus was born the AfroSolo Arts Festival.

Simpson was born and raised in a predominantly black neighborhood in Nashville. He graduated with a degree in psychology from Lipscomb University, Nashville, and began work as a psychologist. But his leaning toward theater and the arts had begun at a very young age: as a child he used to perform on stage at church pageants. In 1984, he moved to the Bay area, which is known for its vibrant art scene. There he signed up for a theater workshop with Cultural Odyssey, a famous touring ensemble in San Francisco that is committed to presenting solo creations of artists of diverse cultures. Growing up during the Civil Rights Movement, he regarded art as a medium for lending voice to the black experience in the country.

Creation of the Festival

Thomas Robert Simpson decided to invite some artist friends over to celebrate his 39th birthday. He rented a space, organized food, and sold tickets for a performance which included music, dance, and spoken word poetry. The shindig was a huge success and his friends urged him to do it again on his following birthdays: two in a row. Inspired by the success of his birthday parties Simpson went on to found and direct the AfroSolo Arts Festival in 1994. He set up an advisory board and obtained sponsors. The festival debuted at Diego Rivera Theatre, City College, San Francisco. Since its inception, the festival has been using art to explore personal, social, and political issues. One of their influential projects is "Black Voices: Our Stories, Our Lives," which includes solo shows which lend voice to the black experience. The festival also presents professional-development programs and workshops on creating and marketing solo performances.

Simpson went on to make a name for himself in community services and the art scene. He is the winner of the coveted Bay Area Jefferson Award for Public Service. He was the recipient of the Certificate of Honor from the San Francisco Board of Supervisors. He has also been honored with many other awards for his valuable contributions toward community service. In 2014, he founded "Project Empowerment: The Audacity to Succeed—Young Black Men and Boys Soaring into the Future," whose mission has been to support the transition of black youth to adulthood.

Observance

The festival repertoire features performances of dance, music, visual arts, and literature; and exhibits that showcase various genres in the visual arts and cartoons. The festival also promotes contemporary art and culture by collaborating with other black arts organizations. Each festival has a specific theme and Simpson has collaborated with community leaders and medical professionals to organize health camps as part of the festival agenda since 1999. The festival has focused on health disparities experienced by blacks. Panel discussions and health camps are held to raise awareness of breast cancer, prostate cancer, diabetes, and HIV with a view toward improving the health and well-being of the community.

Contact and Website

AfroSolo Theatre Company
762 Fulton St., Ste. 303
San Francisco, CA 94102
E-mail: info@afrosolo.org
417-771-2376; fax: 415-771-2312
events.afrosolo.org

Further Reading

https://northcarolinahistory.org/encyclopedia/civil-rights-movement/
Hill, Shirley A. *Inequality and African-American Health: How Racial Disparities Create Sickness.* Policy Press, 2016.

American Black Film Festival

Date Observed: Five days in July
Location: Miami/South Beach, Florida

The American Black Film Festival (ABFF), formerly known as the Acapulco Black Film Festival, is an annual five-day retreat and international film market held in Miami/South Beach, Florida. It aims to provide the most prestigious platform for Pan-African films garnered from around the world, competitively screening features, shorts, and documentaries from black artists..

Historical Background

In 1997, three men cofounded the Acapulco Black Film Festival. Jeff Friday (president and CEO of Film Life, Inc.), Byron E. Lewis (chairman and CEO of UniWorld Group, Inc.), and Warrington Hudlin (president of the Black Filmmakers Foundation) united for a common purpose: to create a forum that would provide a springboard for black cinematic achievement while simultaneously broadening public perception of their accomplishments.

Creation of the Festival

The festival was held in Acapulco for its first five years. In 2002, Film Life, Inc. acquired sole rights to the festival, which was then renamed the American Black Film Festival. Until 2007 the festival has been held in the South Beach area of Florida. Then it was moved to Los Angeles, California, to attract more attendees. However, the change in the venue resulted in a decline in attendance, so it again moved to Florida in 2010. Since then, the festival has been held in the South Beach/Miami area of Florida.

Observance

Since its inception, ABBF has shown more than 1,000 films, including full features, shorts, web originals, and documentaries.

This festival has been a platform for emerging black performers for over two decades. It attracts approximately 7,000 to 10,000 people each year.

This five-day festival features independent film screenings, celebrity talks, live entertainment, and a variety of networking and hospitality events. In 2017, the ABFF introduced its Greenlighters Academy, a student pipeline program for those who are interested in pursuing corporate careers in the film industry and entertainment media. During the 23rd annual ABFF festival (In 2019), it launched *About Women*, a panel to inspire and unite women of color in the film and television industry. ABFF also began showcasing films based on cause-related topics impacting communities of color.

The festival ends with the award presentation of the "BEST OF ABFF," showcasing the hard work of filmmakers throughout the festival. In 2019, the film *CAP*, written and directed by Marshall Tyler, won a cash prize of $10,000.

Contacts and Websites

American Black Film Festival
http://www.abff.com

Black Hollywood Education & Resource Center
1875 Century Park E, Sixth fl.
Los Angeles, CA 90067-2199
323-957-4656; fax: 310-284-3169
http://bherc.org

Further Reading

"Filmmaker Spike Lee and Actress Rosario Dawson Honored at American Black Film Festival." *Jet*, August 16, 2004.
"Russell Simmons and Gabrielle Union Saluted at American Black Film Festival." *Jet*, August 4, 2003.

August Quarterly

Date Observed: Third weekend of August
Location: Wilmington, Delaware

T he August Quarterly is a meeting of the African Union Methodist Protestant (AUMP) Church held each year at the end of August in Wilmington, Delaware. This religious festival, also known as the Big Quarterly, commemorates the founding of the church in 1813. It has served as an opportunity to conduct yearly church business as well as a reunion celebration.

Historical Background

The African Union Methodist Church (AUMC) was the first independent black church to be established in the United States. Although the African Methodist Episcopal (AME) Church in Philadelphia began earlier, it did not separate from the predominantly white Methodist Episcopal denomination.

Peter Spencer was born a slave in Kent County, Maryland, in 1782 and was freed when his owner died. During the 1790s, he moved to Wilmington. There he eventually became known as "Father Spencer" because of his strong faith, teaching abilities, and knowledge of the law. He not only taught people to read and write but also offered legal advice. Spencer believed that the combination of education and religion would empower and liberate African Americans.

Soon after he arrived in Delaware, Spencer became active in the white-dominated Asbury Methodist Episcopal Church, called the" Mother of Methodism" in the state. Although accepted into the church, black congregants were not considered equal to whites and were segregated—required to sit in the church balcony rather than on the main floor. During worship, black congregants would praise the Lord out loud when they felt the presence of the Holy Spirit, and white church members disapproved, insisting that the African Americans

A Spencer Obituary

On July 28, 1843, three days after Peter Spencer's death, *The Delaware State Journal* published the following obituary:

"Died in this City on Tuesday last, Rev. Peter Spencer (colored) aged 61 years, and six months. He bore an excellent character, and was extensively known as the most active and influential minister of the Union Church (colored) in this City, branches of which are spread throughout several of the surrounding states. His death has produced a vacancy, and it will be difficult to find any person who will fill his station with the industry, ability and influence which he did."

From "Diamonds of Delaware and Maryland's Eastern Shore: Seven Black Men of Distinction" by James E. Newton, Professor, University of Delaware Black American Studies Program.

should worship quietly. Spencer believed that was an unfair request, and he and another layman, William Anderson, left the church.

Nearly 40 people followed Spencer and Anderson out of the church and formed the Ezion Methodist Episcopal Church, which was still part of the Asbury denomination. But neither Spencer nor Anderson was ordained, so in 1812 the Asbury church appointed a white minister to lead the new church. Spencer and his followers were not allowed to control their church finances or other business affairs. By 1813 they were so dissatisfied that they withdrew entirely from the Asbury Methodist Episcopal Church and founded the Union Church of Africans. This was the first African-American-controlled church in America.

With the help of Delaware's Quaker community, Spencer built a church on land near an Underground Railroad station. This new and independent church was recorded under the title of the Union Church of Africans. In 1813 Peter

Spencer founded the church, originally called the Union Church of Africans, in Wilmington, Delaware. The legal document clearly stated that the church, also called the "African Union Church," was for "African Brethren and their descendants," which secured African-American control of church administration and worship.

The church name was changed to the African Union Methodist Protestant Church in 1867. Under Spencer's leadership, 31 churches were established in several more states. As of 2019, there are about 40 AUMP congregations in Delaware, New York, New Jersey, Pennsylvania, Maryland, and the District of Columbia.

Creation of the Observance

After the church was established, Spencer created the August Quarterly in 1814. The church held four meetings during the year, and the August Quarterly became the annual conference. Also known as the "Big Quarterly," the meeting, or conference, was held in Wilmington on the last Sunday of every August. At that time of year, the harvest was usually completed and enslaved and free African-American workers were given time off to attend. The Quarterly was the first major church festival for African Americans and has long symbolized African-American religious freedom.

Observance

Since 1814, the Big Quarterly has been held annually (except for during the Civil War years) on the last weekend in August. During the early years of the event, pastors were assigned to the churches they would serve during the upcoming year. Other church business, such as reports from trustees, also took place at the Quarterly.

African-American congregants came to the Quarterly from several surrounding states, reuniting with relatives and friends and celebrating their religious independence (*see also* **Church Homecomings**). Sermons were the major features of the Big Quarterly festivals and involved call-and-response elements—a back-and-forth conversation between the preacher and the congregants. Along with preaching, the festival included singing, dancing, testimonies, and faith healing.

The Ring Dance Ceremony

Religious or holy dances at the Quarterly were known as ring dances, which had their roots in Africa and at the August festival were usually performed by men. In his book *"Invisible" Strands in African Methodism*, historian Lewis Baldwin includes a description of the dance which was published in the *Delaware State Journal*:

> In the basement of the church a hundred or more men formed a circle and swayed to and fro, sometimes fast and sometimes slow, according to the meter of the hymn sung. Those who formed the inner line of the human ring were the most violent in their movements and most of the time perspired so freely that they could not have been more wet if a hose had been turned upon them. Frantically, they urged one another to more violent feats of gymnastic devotion, clapping their hands, jumping and shouting, and occasionally groaning. When they grew weary they dropped upon their knees and prayers were offered. The women were modest and did not help form the rings. Instead, they sang and watched the proceedings with interest.

The August festival also provided an opportunity for runaway slaves to escape via the Underground Railroad. Spencer, along with Quaker Thomas Garrett, Wilmington's station master, helped escapees.

Over the years, the Big Quarterly brought together African Americans across denominational lines. Baptist and Methodist attendees took part, affirming their unity as Christians. The Quarterly also was an opportunity for participants to express themselves through singing and dancing and to share traditional foods at a feast.

Attendance at the Quarterly dropped after the original AUMP church was torn down in 1969 to provide space for a city center plaza that became the Peter Spencer Plaza. The church found another location in Wilmington, and by the 1980s the Quarterly had been rejuvenated somewhat. It is considered the oldest African-American church festival in the nation.

Former U.S. Senator and Vice President Joseph R. Biden Jr. of Delaware frequently recognize the festival on the floor of the Senate, noting that "the history and spirit represented by the Big Quarterly are important to our identity and character as a community and as a nation. It is an event that both reminds us of what has been overcome, and challenges us to complete the journey."

Contacts and Websites

The August Quarterly Festival
http://augustquarterly.org

Delaware Historical Society
505 N. Market St.
Wilmington, DE 19801
302-655-7161; fax: 302-655-7844
https://dehistory.org/august-quarterly

Further Reading

Baldwin, Lewis V. *"Invisible" Strands in African Methodism: A History of the African Union Methodist Protestant and Union American Methodist Episcopal Churches, 1805-1980*. Metuchen, NJ, and London: The American Theological Library Association and The Scarecrow Press, 1983.

———. *The Mark of a Man: Peter Spencer and the African Union Methodist Tradition*. Lanham, MD: University Press of America, 1987.

McNeil, Lydia. "Peter Spencer." *The Encyclopedia of African American Culture and History*, edited by Jack Salzman, David Lionel Smith, and Cornel West. Vol. 5. New York: Macmillan, 1996.

Newton, James E., and Harmon Carey. "Diamonds of Delaware and Maryland's Eastern Shore: Seven Black Men of Distinction." In *A History of African Americans of Delaware and Maryland's Eastern Shore*, edited by Carole Marks. Newark: University of Delaware, 1997. http://www.udel.edu/BlackHistory/diamonds.html.

Russell, Daniel James. *History of the African Union Methodist Protestant Church*. 2001. Reprint. CreateSpace Independent Publishing Platform, 2017.

Battle of Olustee Reenactment

Date Observed: Mid-February
Location: Olustee Battlefield Historic State Park, Florida

The Civil War Battle of Olustee was fought on February 20, 1864, and since 1977 an annual reenactment has taken place in mid-February. The commemoration in North Central Florida features reenactors of the Massachusetts 54th Regiment, one of the most famous African-American regiments. Popularized in the 1989 movie *Glory*, the 54th took part in Florida's largest Civil War battle.

Historical Background

At the beginning of the Civil War, many free blacks in the North attempted to serve in the Union forces, but they were not accepted. In fact, a 1792 law prohibited people of color from serving in the military. Some northern officials believed that if African Americans took up arms, they would try to kill slave owners. Others insisted, based on widespread prejudice, that black soldiers were cowardly and did not have the intellect for military service. During the first year of the war, African Americans were only permitted to do manual labor such as build trenches, unload supplies from wagons, and bury the battle dead, for the army.

Nevertheless, African-American men formed companies and regiments so they would be ready if called. By 1862, Union forces had lost a series of battles, and white recruits were hard to find. As a result, the U.S. Congress was forced to take action, repealing the 1792 law and passing the Confiscation Act on July 17, 1862, which freed all slaves who were able to cross into Union lines. Congress also passed the Militia Act, which allowed African Americans to serve in the armed forces, and the War Department created the United States Colored Troops.

Portraits of Massachusetts volunteers who served in the 54th regiment at the Battle of Olustee.
Top: 1st Sergeant Jeremiah Rolls (left) and Corporal Abram C. Simms (right)
Center: Corporal George Lipscomb (left) and Sergeant Thomas Bowman (right)
Bottom: Private Isom Ampey (left) and Sergeant Major John H. Wilson (right)

In January 1863 Massachusetts Governor John Andrew signed up a voluntary regiment composed primarily of free African Americans, including two sons of the great black abolitionist leader Frederick Douglass (*see also* **Frederick Douglass Day**). Colonel Robert Gould Shaw, a young white man in his twenties and a strong abolitionist, trained the regiment, which became the 54th.

In June 1863 the 54th, as it was commonly known, was sent to South Carolina to battle Confederates at Fort Wagner. After that battle, there was no doubt about the bravery of the regiment. Colonel Shaw led 600 soldiers in an assault on the fort. More than 100 soldiers of the 54th were killed, and the remaining troops were compelled to withdraw. Several members of the regiment, some of them former slaves, were awarded the Medal of Honor, the highest military award in the U.S.

The 54th eventually captured Fort Wagner and went on to fight with other Union soldiers in Florida. The Union had launched an operation to occupy Jacksonville in order to disrupt transportation links and deprive the Confederacy of food and other supplies. They also hoped to move west to eventually capture the state capital at Tallahassee.

The Confederate strategy was to stage an offense west of Jacksonville at Olustee, Florida, where there was a lake (Ocean Pond) on one side and a treacherous swamp on the other. Five thousand Confederate soldiers, who defended their post against 5,500 Union soldiers and 16 cannons, forced the Union army to retreat. The Olustee battle resulted in 1,861 Union and 946 Confederate casualties.

Creation of the Observance

Since its inception in 1977, the commemoration of the battle at Olustee Battlefield Historic State Park has become the largest annual Civil War reenactment in the southeastern United States. In the beginning, a festival focusing on the battle took place in nearby Lake City, and two years later the reenactment began. Since then, more than 1,700 Civil War reenactors (men, women, and children) participate in the reenactment each year, with some 15,000 spectators in attendance. In 2003 Olustee Battlefield Historic State Park received the prestigious U.S. Congressional Black Caucus Veterans' Braintrust Award for its recognition of African-American veterans. General Colin Powell established the award in 1990 to recognize outstanding national and community commitment to black veterans.

Observance

When the observance gets under way, reenactors portraying southern troops create a charge formation, and opposite them across the field, Union reenactors set up a line of defense. A cannon roars and the Union troops start to fall. The battle continues with officers shouting to their men. As the Union soldiers begin their retreat, they dodge "dead" and "dying" men, depicting the bloody battle and chaos on the Olustee Battlefield in 1864.

During the commemoration weekend, other activities include a parade at Lake City, arts and crafts sales, food booths, Civil War-period music, concert, medical demonstration, educational exhibitions, fashion shows and programs, and artillery night-firing demonstrations. Visitors can tour authentic Civil War campsites and Sutler's Row, where merchants sell period items. Volunteers also provide living-history presentations for school groups and medical units.

Contacts and Websites

Battle of Olustee Home Page, sponsored by the Florida Park Service, the Olustee Battlefield Citizen Support Organization
https://battleofolustee.org/what_is_cso.htm

Olustee Battlefield Citizens Support Organization
P. O. Box 382
Glen St. Mary, FL 32040
https://battleofolustee.org/what_is_cso.htm

Olustee Battlefield Historic State Park Citizens Support Organization
C/O Stephen Foster FCC State Park
11016 Lillian Saunders Dr.
White Springs, FL 32096
https://www.floridastateparks.org

Company B, 54th Massachusetts Volunteer Infantry Regiment
54th Mass
P. O. Box 116
Kensington, MD 20895-0116
http://www.54thmass.org

Further Reading

Adams, Virginia M., ed. *On the Altar of Freedom: A Black Soldier's Civil War Letters from the Front.* University of Massachusetts Press, 1999.

Blatt, Martin Henry, Thomas J. Brown, and Donald Yacovone, eds. *Hope and Glory: Essays on the Legacy of the 54th Massachusetts Regiment* 2001. Reprint. Amherst: University of Massachusetts Press, 2009.

Burchard, Peter. *One Gallant Rush: Robert Gould Shaw and His Brave Black Regiment.* 1965. Reprint. New York: St. Martin's Press, 1989.

Cox, Clinton. *Undying Glory: The Story of the Massachusetts 54th Regiment.* 1993. Reprint. iUniverse, 2007.

Emilio, Luis F. *A Brave Black Regiment: The History of the Fifty-Fourth Regiment of Massachusetts Volunteer Infantry, 1863–1865.* 1894. Reprint. Cambridge, MA, and New York: Da Capo Press, 1995.

Kashatus, William C. "54th Massachusetts Regiment: A Gallant Rush for Glory." *The Black Phalanx: A History of the Negro Soldiers of the United States in the Wars of 1775–1812, 1861–'65.* 1890. Reprint. Manchester, NH: Ayer, 1992.

Bessie Smith Strut

Date Observed: Third Monday in June
Location: Chattanooga, Tennessee

The Bessie Smith Strut is an evening event held as part of the annual Riverbend Festival in Chattanooga, Tennessee. The Strut was named in homage to one of the most important women in the history of American music. Though unofficial, residents and businesses in Chattanooga, Tennessee, plan to re-brand the Festival into the Big 9 Roots Festival and stage it in early October 2019.

Historical Background

Bessie Smith was born into impoverished circumstances on April 15, 1892, and began her musical journey by singing on the street corners of Chattanooga, a gritty, industrial railroad hub in the southeastern United States. Her professional career began onstage as a dancer, not a singer, in the famed Atlanta "81" Theatre around 1913. Ten years later, she had secured a contract with Columbia Records.

Smith's soulful blues and jazz performances earned her the title "Empress of the Blues." She had a larger-than-life persona, on and off stage, belting out moving lyrics. Notably, at one time, she was the highest paid African-American singer in the United States, earning over $2,000 per week. "Downhearted Blues," her first record, was a runaway hit in 1923, selling more than 750,000 records in its first 6 months of release. In the winters, she performed in theaters; the remainder of the year, she did tent shows, traveling in her personal railroad car.

Like other performers of her era, Smith's career was affected by the Great Depression, which crippled the recording industry. However, she never stopped performing or attempting new ventures. In 1929 Smith appeared in *Pansy*, a

Broadway show, in which critics acclaimed her as the production's only redeeming asset. That same year, she also made her only cinematic appearance in *St. Louis Blues*, singing the title song as well. Her final recordings, in 1933, show a transition from her accomplished blues stylings into swing-era tempos and tunes. Few doubt that she would have continued to evolve with the changing times.

On September 26, 1937, Bessie Smith suffered fatal injuries in an automobile accident. For years, rumors flourished about the cause of her death, with some purporting that Smith was refused admittance to a whites-only hospitals, with the resultant delay causing or contributing to her demise. These tales seem to have been adequately put to rest over the years.

Jazz great Bessie Smith in 1936.

Regardless, the loss of Smith was tragic enough without further embellishment.

Bessie Smith performed with the greats while she was alive: Louis Armstrong, James P. Johnson, Joe Smith, Charlie Green, and Fletcher Henderson, to name a handful. Her legacy lives on in the artistry of those she has inspired, from Ella Fitzgerald, Dinah Washington, Billie Holiday, and Mahalia Jackson to the likes of Janis Joplin, and many more whom she has yet to inspire.

Creation of the Observance

The Bessie Smith Strut has been part of the Riverbend Festival since its beginning. The festival, initially named "Five Nights in Chattanooga," started in 1981 with the dual goals of drawing diverse community elements together via the common language of music and bringing economic development to Chattanooga's downtown and riverfront.

Chattanooga has also remembered Smith with the 264-seat Bessie Smith Performing Arts Hall and a museum to preserve and share the contributions to history of local African Americans.

Observances

The Bessie Smith Strut might best be described as a gigantic block party. Headliners perform on Coca-Cola Stage, and the more than 100,000 attendees can also find barbecue and blues on every corner. The Strut is the sole Riverbend Festival event for which no admission fee was charged initially, but a nominal entrance fee of $10 was introduced in 2018. Multiple musical acts are booked and perform throughout the night.

The Riverbend Festival is a nine-night observance, drawing a capacity 350,000 crowd, marshaled by over 1,000 volunteers. It is considered one of the top 10 American festivals, offering something for everyone: a variety of music, arts and crafts exhibits, fireworks, aerial skydiving artists, a 5k and 10k run, and a children's village.

Contacts and Websites

Chattanooga African-American Museum
200 E. Martin Luther King Blvd.
Chattanooga, TN 37403
423-266-8658; fax: 423-267-1076
http://www.bessiesmithcc.org

Chattanooga Chamber of Commerce
811 Broad St., Ste. 100
Chattanooga, TN 37402
423-756-2121
http://www.chattanoogachamber.com

Chattanooga Convention & Visitors Bureau
736 Market St., 18th Fl.
Chattanooga, TN 37402
423-756-8687 (or) 800-322-3344
http://www.chattanoogafun.com

Riverbend Festival Friends of the Festival
200 Riverfront Pkwy.
Chattanooga, TN 37402
423-756-2211; fax: 423-756-2719
http://www.riverbendfestival.com

Further Reading

Albee, Edward. *The American Dream, The Death of Bessie Smith and Fam &*
  Yam. 1962. Reprint. New York: Dramatists Play Service Inc., 2009.
Albertson, Chris. *Bessie.* New Haven, CT: Yale University Press, 2003.
Albertson, Chris, and Gunther Schuller. *Bessie Smith: Empress of the Blues.*
  New York: Schirmer Books, 1975.
Davis, Angela Y. *Blues Legacies and Black Feminism: Gertrude 'Ma' Rainey,*
  Bessie Smith, and Billie Holiday. New York: Random House, 1998.
Kofskey, Frank. *Black Music, White Business: Illuminating History and*
  Political Economy of Jazz. 1998. Reprint. New York: Pathfinder Press, 2003.
Lomax, Alan. *The Land Where the Blues Began.* New York: Delta Book, 1993.
Moore, Carman. *Somebody's Angel Child: The Story of Bessie Smith.* New
  York: Thomas Y. Crowell Co., 1969.

Bill Pickett Invitational Rodeo

Date Observed: November through February
Location: Varies

The Bill Pickett Invitational Rodeo, the nation's only touring black rodeo, is on the road from November through February. Named after the renowned cowboy, the Rodeo celebrates the contributions that African-American cowboys and cowgirls made to America's western frontier and showcases the talents of their modern-day counterparts. It is a living proof of the history of blacks in the American West.

Historical Background

William "Bill" Pickett was born on December 5, 1870, into a family of African American, Cherokee, and white lineage. He spent his formative years in Texas and worked with four of his brothers (B. W., J. J., C. H., and B. F.) in the family business, Pickett Brothers Bronco Busters and Rough Riders Association.

The exact date and place of Pickett's claim to fame is unknown, but it earned him a lifelong nickname—Bull Dogger—and created a rodeo event called Bulldoggin' that remains popular today. According to an October 11, 1931, article in the *Tulsa* (Oklahoma) *World* newspaper:

> The steer lunged into the arena . . . [Pickett's] horse plunged full speed after it . . . the rider leaped from the saddle. He turned a complete somersault along the length of the steer's back, flying out and down over the curved horns to fasten his teeth in the side of the steer's mouth.

> With sheer strength he dragged the running behemoth's head to the tanbark, thrust its horn in the ground, and forward momentum threw the steer hocks over horns in a somersault of its own.

In 1923 the Norman Film Company produced a movie about Bill Pickett.
This poster was created to advertise the film.

Pickett's fame led the Miller Brothers to hire him. He and his family relocated to Oklahoma and the 101 Ranch where he joined their traveling Wild West Show, billed as the "Dusky Demon." When not on the road, Pickett worked as a farmhand, handling such chores as cotton picking, fence mending, corral building, and horse gentling.

On December 9, 1971, nearly 40 years after his death resulting from "an altercation with a bronco," William "Bulldog" Pickett earned the distinction of being the first black man to be inducted into the Rodeo Hall of Fame in Oklahoma City. In 1987 a bronze statue of Pickett—posed in his infamous bulldogging sneer—was unveiled at the Fort Worth Cowtown Coliseum. The U.S. Postal Service issued a commemorative stamp in his honor in 1994, although the first issue had to be recalled as it mistakenly portrayed one of his brothers.

Having traveled from Texas to Madison Square Garden to England and performed with the likes of Tom Mix and Will Rogers as his assistants, Bill Pickett has earned his place in history for his notable achievements—and for that bulldogging.

"Old Bill Pickett"

by Mark Ross

Songwriter Mark Ross wrote this song about Bill Pickett around 1971. According to Ross, "I came across this poem by Zack Miller, Pickett's boss, written as an epitaph. The story struck me so hard, I had to jump out of bed and grab my guitar. The whole thing took about 20 minutes to throw together. I changed the rhyme scheme slightly and threw on a bunch more verses and a chorus borrowed by Lead Belly." Ross added, "It was a story that needed to be told. Having grown up on a steady diet of western movies, songs, and TV shows, it was surprising to learn that at least half the drovers who rode in the Old West were African American, Native American, and maybe even some Jews. You see, I grew up in the Mysterious East (New York, to be precise), and, like I said, I was surrounded by this imagery and wanted to grow up to be like that."

"Old Bill Pickett" *continued*

Old Bill Pickett's gone away,
Over the great divide
To the place where all the preachers say
Both saint and sinner abide
If they check his brand like I think
  they will
It's a runnin' hoss they'll give to Bill
Some good wild steers 'till he gets his
  fill
And a great big crowd to watch him ride

Chorus:
Old Bill Pickett's a long time gone
Left me here to sing this song
Old Bill Pickett's a long time gone
Left me here to sing this song

Old Bill Pickett was a mighty black man
And he rode for the One-O-One
Way down yonder in the Cherokee
  Land
Around when the West was won
He'd jump a steer from a runnin' hoss
And throw him down with a mighty toss
He worked for many, but he had no boss
He's the last of the great cowhands

Chorus

Way down south in Mexico
He took a great big dare
To try and hold a fightin' bull
To see how he would fare
He grabbed Old Toro by the horns
Grabbed the bull's nose in his jaws
That crowd never seen such a thing
  before
For an hour and a half they cheered

Chorus

With the great Will Rogers and Wild
  Tom Mix
He rode in the rodeo
For all who paid their fifty cents
They gave a great big show
For all who paid to come and see
Bill wrestled steers with his teeth
We've never seen such a mighty feat
'Cause he left us long ago

Chorus

Way down on the Miller ranch
In the year of thirty two
Bill Pickett roped a sorrel stud
To see what he could do
That sorrel stomped and jumped and
  bucked
And tromped Bill's body in the dust
At seventy-three, Bill was out of luck
He took eleven days to die
There was nothin' they could do

Chorus

They laid him down in a six-by-three
Beneath the land he knew
And they left a cross for the world to
  see
Said, "Of his kind we've seen few"
That night for Bill they drank some
  wine
And old Zack Miller wrote these lines
And left "em here for me to find
To put to music and sing to you

Chorus

Creation of the Rodeo

The rodeo was founded in 1984 by promoter Lu Vason, a special-events producer in Denver, Colorado. He developed the idea after he attended Cheyenne Frontier Days in Wyoming and noted the lack of black cowboys at this pre-eminent rodeo event. Vason learned of Bill Pickett during a visit to Denver's Black American West Museum. In 1984 the first Rodeo drew crowds numbering into the thousands. In recent years, annual attendance has easily topped the hundred thousand mark.

Observance

The Rodeo is a traveling event conducted annually from November through February. The Rodeo is entertaining and exciting, but it also has an educational aspect. Each performance is dedicated to the black cowboys and cowgirls who played an integral part in shaping the West, as well as those of today who help to keep the spirit of the West alive (*see also* **Black Cowboy Parade**).

Participants are attired in full western regalia and compete in the following events: bareback riding, junior breakaway roping, relay racing, ladies' steer undecorating, tie down roping, junior barrel racing, bull riding and—of course—bulldogging.

Since 1987, the pioneers in the sport of rodeo have been remembered by the Bill Pickett Memorial Scholarship Fund (BPMSF), which is dedicated to enrich and enhance the lives of African Americans and the legacy contributed by African Americans to the West and the arts. The 2019 theme of this event is "Kickin' It in the Dirt!"

Contacts and Websites

Bill Pickett Invitational Rodeo
5829 S Quintero Cir.
Centennial, CO 80015
303-373-1246
http://www.billpickettrodeo.com

Black American West Museum and Heritage Center
3091 California St.
Denver, CO 80205

720-242-7428
https://bawmhc.org

National Cowboy and Western Heritage Museum
1700 N.E. 63rd St.
Oklahoma City, OK 73111
405-478-2250
E-mail: info@nationalcowboymuseum.org
http://www.nationalcowboymuseum.org

National Multicultural Western Heritage Museum
2029 N Main St.
Ft. Worth, TX 76164
817-922-9999 (or) 817-534-8801; fax: 817-923-9304
www.cowboysofcolor.org

Further Reading

Hanes, Bailey C. *Bill Pickett, Bulldogger: The Biography of a Black Cowboy.* 1977 Reprint. Norman: University of Oklahoma Press, 1989.

Landau, Elaine. *Bill Pickett: Wild West Cowboy.* Berkeley Heights, NJ: Enslow Publishers, 2004. (young adult)

Pinkney, Andrea Davis. *Bill Pickett—Rodeo Ridin' Cowboy.* New York: Harcourt Children's Books, 1999. (young adult)

Black Arts Fest MKE

Date Observed: 1st weekend in August
Location: Milwaukee

Ethnic festivals are a conscious construction of ethnic identity. Every summer, the city of Milwaukee, a mosaic rich in tradition and heritage, comes out of its hibernation to celebrate its ethnic diversity through folk festivals. The festival grounds in the city play host to these ethnic festivals over the weekends. One such festival is the Black Arts Fest MKE, a celebration of Milwaukee's African-American culture, which aims to connect people and artists of diverse cultures and artistic backgrounds through art, music, food, and fellowship.

Historical Background

African American festivals have been taking place on a widespread scale in the United States since the 1980s. Many of these festivals have been initiated to connect the past with the present in black communities and to foster understanding of the African diaspora and the contributions people of African descent have made worldwide. Festivals also provide opportunities for local black communities to display their talents and highlight their accomplishments.

Creation of the Festival

The Black Arts Festival MKE, which debuted in 2018, showcases African and African-American culture through art, live music and dance, and food and drinks. Founded to fill the void left by the famed African World Festival, the inaugural event attracted over 9,000 people and hosted Blues legends such as MC Lyte, Bobby Rush, and Tony! Toni! Tone. The festival board comprises top African-American professionals and businessmen from Milwaukee and the festival receives funding through sponsorship from the community. The event is ticketed, but exempts veterans and children under seven.

Observance

The Henry Maier Festival Park, set along the Lake Michigan shoreline in downtown Milwaukee, is the festival venue. A fine-arts pavilion set in a temperature-controlled building allows budding artists to showcase and sell their visual artwork. Vendors arrive from far and wide to sell a variety of merchandise at the festival marketplace. Kids areas are designated for a variety of recreational activities. The festival also offers children an opportunity to learn African heritage activities, including tribal masks and body art. They also get to paint murals and create wearable art among other interesting activities. Artists workshops provide a platform for both artists and students to learn and exchange ideas.

Contact

Henry Maier Festival Park
200 N. Harbor Dr.
Milwaukee, WI 53202

Black August Benefit Concert

Date Observed: August
Location: New York, New York

The Black August Benefit Concert has been held since 1998 in New York City. A project of the Malcolm X Grassroots Movement (MXGM), the concert celebrates "hip hop and freedom fighters"— African Americans jailed because of their activism on behalf of people of color—and remembers the death of George L. Jackson and others considered political prisoners by the group. The event was last celebrated in 2018 and is no longer celebrated.

Historical Background

George L. Jackson was incarcerated from 1964 until his death in 1971. He had been convicted of armed robbery. During the first years of his imprisonment, Jackson earned a reputation for being violent. At some point, however, he was drawn to reading Communist works, such as those by Mao Zedong, Fidel Castro, Karl Marx, and others. He drew prison authorities' concern when he began to organize fellow prisoners to demand better conditions as well as encourage the revolutionary aims of the Black Panther Party, which he had joined.

In 1970 Jackson became nationally known as one of the Soledad Brothers after he and two fellow inmates were charged with killing a guard at the prison. Activists staged protests, arguing that he was accused because of his political activities. Educator and political activist Angela Davis led the movement to support the Soledad Brothers. Some scholars have agreed that the evidence in the case against them was unclear. But, on August 21, 1971, shortly before Jackson's trial, prison guards killed him during an apparent escape attempt.

Creation of the Observance

In August 1998, the MXGM sponsored its first Black August Benefit Concert to call attention to black political prisoners and to aid in their release, as well as to highlight the social and political issues which affect inner-city youth.

The MXGM formed in 1992 when a group of young people in Brooklyn, New York, organized campus activities designed to create public awareness of black political prisoners and police brutality in New York's inner-city communities. A non-profit volunteer organization, MXGM also has created community programs to address the needs of the homeless and indigent, such as legal services, youth development and leadership, and soup kitchens.

The group chose to hold the concerts in August because of the many significant historical events that have taken place during the month. In addition to the anniversary of Jackson's death, August is also the month that marks the arrival of the first enslaved Africans to Jamestown in Virginia, a general strike by enslaved New Africans led by Henry Highland Garnett (the "Watts rebellion"), the bombing of the MOVE family by Philadelphia police, the Haiti slave revolt, abolishment of slavery in the West Indies, the Nat Turner rebellion, Marcus Garvey's birth month, and the month in which Rev. Martin Luther King Jr. led the famous March on Washington (*see also* **Haitian Flag Day**; **Marcus Garvey's Birthday**; **Martin Luther King Jr.'s Birthday**; *and* **West Indies Emancipation Day**).

Observance

The Black August Benefit Concert is not just about performances. Audiences are reminded by some hip-hop performers and MXGM directors that the purpose of the Benefit Concert is to help finance campaigns to free political prisoners. Concertgoers learn about protesters who have been jailed and others who were killed while involved in political activities opposing the oppression of people of color. There also has been an emphasis on HIV/AIDS awareness.

While most Black August Concerts have been held in New York City, where the MXGM is based, the organization also produced concerts in Cuba during the annual Cuban Rap Festival, and in South Africa, South America, Venezuela, Haiti, Tanzania, and Brazil.

Contact and Website

Malcolm X Grassroots Movement
https://www.mxgm.org

Further Reading

"Jackson, George Lester." In *Africana: The Encyclopedia of the African and African American Experience, A Concise Reference*, edited by Kwame Anthony Appiah and Henry Louis Gates Jr. Philadelphia: Running Press, 2003.

Kelley, Robin D. G. "Into the Fire: 1970 to the Present." In *To Make Our World Anew: A History of African Americans*, edited by Robin D. G. Kelley and Earl Lewis. New York: Oxford University Press, 2000.

Lee, Chisun. "Taking the Rap." *The Village Voice*, September 5, 2000. https://www.villagevoice.com/2000/09/05/taking-the-rap/.

Black Cowboy Parade

Date Observed: First Saturday in October
Location: Oakland, California

T he Black Cowboy Parade in Oakland, California, celebrates the legacy of African-American cowboys—and cowgirls. It seeks to recognize and heighten awareness of African-American contributions to the development of the western states.

Historical Background

It is not widely known that between one-quarter and one-third of the pioneer settlers of the western U.S. plains were of African-American heritage. After the Civil War, there were 8,000–9,000 African-American cattle trail drivers. Between drives, they made significant contributions to the cattle industry, working on ranches throughout the western territories.

Blacks in the west were considerable not just in number but also in talent; many were top cooks, ranch hands, riders, and ropers. In fact, historians have noted that blacks held every job that whites held with the exception of trail boss. Many trail drives consisted solely of blacks, save the trail boss.

The demand for talent decreased the amount of discrimination and segregation commonly experienced by blacks elsewhere in the country. In those days, in cattle country, blacks often ate, worked, played, fought, and slept side-by-side with whites. Abilities and courage could—and would—merit admiration and respect. The possibility of earning a decent, if not always equal, wage existed. While black cowboys were not seen as white cowboys' equals per se, some were viewed as superiors, in terms of job skills and abilities, and were recognized as such. And they were often treated on a fraternal level, regardless of ability rankings, based upon commonalities of life experiences and other factors. For a short time in American history, fairly large numbers of whites and blacks coexisted in relative peace, on a more or less equal terms, than had ever been possible before in the United States, or would ever be possible again for quite some time.

Cowboys of the West, as is known today, were not the stuff of movies and folklore. The passage of time has turned fact into fiction and vice versa. White men were portrayed as the romanticized cowboys on the range. Indians were depicted as red-skinned savages. Mexicans were shown as marauding bandits. Blacks were seen in subservient positions. Such stereotyped representations reflected the widespread prejudices of the time.

Actually, African Americans have a long heritage of "cowboy-ing." For example, Gambia and other African countries had large cattle lands, and many black men were skilled herders—work that required similar abilities as those of cowboys.

"Deadwood Dick"

One of the most famous black cowboys was Nate "Nat" Love, who was born a slave in Tennessee in June 1854. After he gained his freedom at the end of the Civil War, Love set out for the American Southwest and found work on a ranch in Texas, where many black cowboys were employed as horsebreakers or performers in rodeos.

After three years in Texas, Love went to southern Arizona and worked for 18 years as a cowboy on a huge ranch. He herded cattle between Texas and Montana and reportedly encountered extremely harsh weather as well as unfriendly Indian tribes. During one trip to deliver cattle in Deadwood City in the Dakota Territory, he took part in a roping contest set up by miners and others in the area. In his autobiography, Love claimed that in nine minutes he roped, tied, and saddled a wild mustang—three minutes faster than the next closest competitor. As the winner, Nat Love was given prize money as well as the moniker "Deadwood Dick," the name of a character in a popular novel of the 1870s. In telling stories about his exploits, Love continued to call himself "Deadwood Dick," enhancing his reputation as a fearless cowboy who was able to outperform anyone on the range. He died in 1921.

A cowboy and his horse posed for this photo sometime between 1890 and 1920.

In the United States, southern slave owners with large cattle plantations were interested in acquiring slaves from African cattle lands. In the South, these slaves worked herds in the tall grasses, pine barrens, and marshes. Some rode horses, but most used dogs and bullwhips to manage the cattle. At first, they were concentrated in Alabama, the Carolinas, Florida, Georgia, Louisiana, Mississippi, and Texas.

As more and more cattle farmers moved westward with their herds and slaves, an increasing number of slaves escaped into the northern states. Some ex-slaves swapped skills with *vaqueros* (Spanish for "cowboys"), who were often American Indians trained by the Spanish. Black cowboys taught vaqueros how to control cattle, and, in turn, learned horseback riding and roping.

71

Creation of the Observance

The first Black Cowboy Parade was held in 1975. A Brooklyn-born Jew, George Rothman, along with other Oakland businessmen raised the funds for this initial event. Soon thereafter, Rothman, along with recognized local activist Booker T. Emery, founded the Black Cowboy Association that has been sponsoring the event. The parade has continued annually ever since.

Observance

At 10 A.M. on the first Saturday of every October, thousands of people line the downtown streets of West Oakland to view the start of the Black Cowboy Parade. Horse-borne participants wear authentic western attire: cowboy hats, vests, chaps, boots, and spurs. Also joining in are youth groups, dance troupes, color guards, and drill teams. Parade entrants compete for trophies based on various yearly categories. Along with the parade itself, there are information booths, food vendors, and entertainment events. Activities last until the early evening hours.

Contacts and Websites

Black American West Museum and Heritage Center
3091 California St.
Denver, CO 80205
720-242-7428
https://bawmhc.org

National Cowboy and Western Heritage Museum
1700 N.E. 63rd St.
Oklahoma City, OK 73111
405-478-2250
E-mail: info@nationalcowboymuseum.org
http://www.nationalcowboymuseum.org

Oakland Black Cowboy Association
P.O. Box 4889
Oakland, CA 94605-6889
http://www.blackcowboyassociation.org

Convention information bureau in Oakland
481 Water St.

Oakland, CA 94607
510-839-9000
https://www.visitoakland.com

Real Cowboy Association
1010 Maledon Dr.
Longview, TX 75602
903-753-3165

Further Reading

Katz, William Loren. *The Black West*. New York: Broadway Books, 2005.

Love, Nat. *The Life and Adventures of Nat Love, Better Known in the Cattle Country as "Deadwood Dick," By Himself*. 1968. Reprint. New York: DocSouth Book, 2017.

Mugleston, William F. "Love, Nat." In *African American Lives*, edited by Henry Louis Gates Jr. and Evelyn Brooks Higginbotham. New York: Oxford University Press, 2004.

Reed, Ishmael. *Blues City: A Walk in Oakland*. New York: Crown Publishing Group, 2003.

Richman, Josh. "A Lone Cowboy Rides Roughshod Over Racism." *Forward* (New York, NY), October 17, 2003.

Schlissel, Lillian. *Black Frontiers: A History of African-American Heroes in the Old West*. New York: Simon & Schuster Books for Young Readers, 1995. (young adult)

Slatta, Richard W. *The Cowboy Encyclopedia*. New York: W. W. Norton, 1996.

Taylor, Quintard. *In Search of the Racial Frontier: African Americans in the American West, 1528-1990*. New York: W. W. Norton, 1998.

Wheeler, B. Gordon. *Black California, A History of African-Americans in the Golden State*. New York: Hippocrene Books, 1993.

Black History Month

See **African-American History Month**

Black Music Month

Date Observed: June
Location: Communities nationwide

B lack Music Month is observed each June to celebrate African-American influences on American music. Since its creation in the late 1970s, radio, television, electronic media, music publishing, and recording industries, schools, libraries, and other institutions have marked the month with gospel, jazz, rhythm and blues, soul, rap, hip hop, reggae, and many other musical genres that have their roots in African and African-American cultures.

Historical Background

Enslaved Africans brought their music and dance traditions with them to the Americas and West Indies during the 1600s and 1700s. They incorporated these traditions into such early festivals as **Pinkster** celebrations and **Negro Election Days and Coronation Festivals** in New England.

Slaves also created work songs in call-and-response form that had roots in tribal chants and were related to religious beliefs. Early on, however, they generally were not allowed to follow their religious rituals, chant in their own languages, or use drums. Many plantation owners feared these practices would help slaves plan and carry out rebellions. Thus, the work songs became a way to share stories of their lives and preserve their history.

When white colonists decided that black slaves should become Christians, slaves learned Protestant hymns, which they adapted and which evolved into spirituals and, eventually, gospel music. During the American Revolutionary War period, black drummers, fifers, and trumpet players were part of military units, and black performers played the fiddle and other instruments at society dances.

In 1865 the 13th Amendment to the Constitution abolished slavery, but many whites continued to obstruct African Americans' new rights (*see* **National Freedom Day**). The trials and tribulations of the late 1800s led many blacks to develop the musical genre known as the blues, which expressed their frustration, sadness, and despair.

From the early 1900s, the blues influenced ragtime and jazz, and, later, rhythm and blues, rock and roll, hip hop, rap, and other genres. In short, black music is the origin of much of today's popular music.

Creation of the Observance

In 1978 producer and composer Kenny Gamble and broadcast executive Ed Wright created Black Music Month. Previously, Gamble had founded the Black Music Association, which established Black Music Month to support and advance black music worldwide. On June 7, 1979, as a result of their efforts, President Jimmy Carter declared the first Black Music Month, and the month has been proclaimed in succeeding years by later presidents.

In the late 1980s, Philadelphia disc jockey Dyana Williams (Gamble's ex-wife) and music executive Sheila Eldridge founded the International Association of African American Music Foundation, which became a powerful advocate for the national observance of Black Music Month. In 2000, they succeeded in persuading Pennsylvania Representative Chaka Fattah to introduce a resolution to the House of Representatives to officially recognize Black Music Month.

Observance

A great variety of events mark Black Music Month across the United States. In Washington, D.C., the president of the United States usually hosts a reception and concert at the White House, as well as issued a proclamation calling for Americans to observe the month by recognizing the contributions of black musical artists.

In Harlem, New York, there are conferences and performances in honor of Black Music Month. Awards ceremonies salute jazz, rhythm and blues, and hip hop.

The Jefferson Street United Merchants Partnership in Nashville, Tennessee, has produced the Jefferson Street Jazz and Blues Festival to mark the month since 2000. During the mid-20th century Jefferson Street's music clubs, and other businesses, flourished, hosting artists such as Ray Charles, Fats Domino, Memphis Slim, and Jimi Hendrix.

At Downtown Disney Pleasure Island at the Disney World Resort in Buena Vista, Florida, a Black Music Month Concert is held. The Charles H. Wright Museum of African American History in Detroit, Michigan, celebrates Black Music Month with musical performances, workshops, and films.

Media observances include radio and TV programs devoted to all types of black music and African-American musicians, singers, lyricists, and composers. Film and sound departments of libraries nationwide promote videocassettes and DVDs to celebrate Black Music Month, and museums of African-American history present programs that honor black music from the past and the present.

Contacts and Websites

Charles H. Wright Museum of African American History
315 E. Warren Ave.
Detroit, MI 48201
313-494-5800
E-mail: awf@thewright.org
http://thewright.org

Greater Harlem Chamber of Commerce
200A W. 136th St.
New York, NY 10030-7200
212-862-7200
https://www.greaterharlemchamber.com

International Association of African American Music
413 S Broad St.
Philadelphia, PA 19147
215-664-1677

Jefferson Street United Merchants Partnership, Inc.
1215 9th Ave. N., Ste. 201
Nashville, TN 37208
615-726-5867; fax: 615-726-2078
http://www.jumpnashville.com

Further Reading

Floyd, Samuel A., Jr. *The Power of Black Music: Interpreting Its History from Africa to the United States.* New York: Oxford University Press, 1995.

"Music." In *Encyclopedia of Black America*, edited by W. Augustus Low and Virgil A. Clift. New York: McGraw-Hill Book Company, 1981.

Ramsey, Guthrie P., Jr. *Race Music: Black Cultures from Bebop to Hip-Hop.* Berkeley: University of California Press, 2003.

Southern, Eileen. *The Music of Black Americans: A History.* 3rd ed. New York: W. W. Norton and Company, 1997.

Black Poetry Day

Date Observed: October 17
Location: U.S. Schools and Libraries

Black Poetry Day is celebrated on October 17, the birthday of Jupiter Hammon, considered to be the first African American to publish his own verse. The day recognizes not only Hammon but also the contributions of other black poets who are commemorated in elementary and secondary schools, colleges, and libraries across the United States. This Black Poetry Day is considered the time to celebrate both past and present black authors like Paul Laurence Dunbar, Phillis Wheatley, and Langston Hughes.

Historical Background

Before West Africans were brought to the Americas as slaves, they had long traditions in literature and storytelling. The slavery system suppressed education, yet a small number of slaves managed to read and write in English and became pioneers in African-American literature. Among them was Jupiter Hammon, who was born a slave on October 17, 1711, on Long Island, New York.

A slave his entire life, Hammon first served Henry Lloyd, a merchant, and then the next two generations of Lloyds. He was allowed to attend school, and his education as well as his Christian beliefs and the religious revivals of the 1700s influenced his development as a poet. His first published poem was titled "An Evening Thought. Salvation by Christ with Penitential Cries: Composed by Jupiter Hammon, a Negro belonging to Mr. Lloyd of Queen's Village on Long Island, the 25th of December 1760."

Following Hammon's publication, Phillis Wheatley (one of the first female black poets), another early African-American poet, published a slim volume of poetry. In 1778 Hammon wrote *An Address to Miss Phillis Wheatley, Ethiopian Poetess, in Boston, who came from Africa at eight years of age, and*

> ## African-American Poets Laureate of the United States
>
> During the 20th century, three African-American poets were appointed to the honorary office of Poet Laureate by the Librarian of Congress:
>
> Robert Hayden (1913–1980) served from 1976 to 1978
> Gwendolyn Brooks (1917–2000) served from 1985 to 1986
> Rita Dove (1952-) served from 1993 to 1995
>
> When Hayden and Brooks served, the position was still known as the Consultant in Poetry to the Library of Congress. In 1985 Congress passed an act changing the title to Poet Laureate and the act took effect in 1986. Poets Laureate receive monetary compensation in return for performing such duties as an annual public lecture and reading of their poetry.

soon became acquainted with the Gospel of Jesus Christ. He also wrote tracts about African-American religion and protest pieces against slavery, although he did not demand freedom for himself but instead wanted enslaved youth to be free. Hammon is believed to have died around 1806.

Creation of the Observance

Stanley A. Ransom, a folk musician and former director of the Huntington Public Library in New York, edited a book of the complete writings of Jupiter Hammon, which was published in 1970. From that time on, Ransom promoted a national observance of Black Poetry Day on October 17 because of his concern that African-American literary accomplishments would not be recognized. Although there is not yet an official national day proclaimed as Black Poetry Day, elementary and secondary schools, colleges, and libraries across the United States focus on African-American poetry on October 17 or a day around that time, depending on when the institutions are open.

Observance

To observe Black Poetry Day, instructors and librarians usually focus on books and websites that highlight the works of African-American poets both past and present, such as Paul Laurence Dunbar, W. E. B. Du Bois (who wrote free verse as well as scholarly works), James Weldon Johnson, Langston Hughes, Gwendolyn Brooks, Sonia Sanchez, Nikki Giovanni, Maya Angelou, Audre Lorde, Danez Smith, and many others. Students and patrons are encouraged to express themselves through poetry.

Many universities have diversity programs and speakers bureaus that bring in well-known black poets to read and discuss their poetry. On some campuses, students compete in contests, reading their original works or those by African-American poets.

Contact and Website

Dunbar-Jupiter Hammon Public Library, the largest African-American book collection in southwest Florida
3095 Blount St.
Fort Myers, FL 33916
239-533-4150; fax: 239-485-1194
https://www.leegov.com/library/branches/db

Further Reading

"Black Poetry Day." In *Holidays, Festivals, and Celebrations of the World Dictionary*, edited by Helene Henderson. 3rd ed. Detroit: Omnigraphics, 2005.

Rampersad, Arnold, ed. *The Oxford Anthology of African-American Poetry*. 2005. Reprint. New York: Oxford University Press, 2006.

Ransom, Stanley A. *1970. Reprint. America's First Negro Poet*. Port Washington, NY: Associated Faculty Press, 1983.

Smith, Jessie Carney. *Black Firsts: 4,000 Ground-Breaking and Pioneering Historical Events*. 2nd ed., revised and expanded. Canton, MI: Visible Ink Press, 2003.

Bridge Crossing Jubilee

*Date Observed: Four days including the
first weekend in March*
Location: Selma, Alabama

T he Bridge Crossing Jubilee commemorates "Bloody Sunday"—the brutal halt of the Selma to Montgomery voting rights march on March 7,
1965—and the successful march two weeks later. Held near the anniversary of the historic event, the Jubilee is an annual celebration of the struggle
to improve the voting rights of African Americans.

Historical Background

The 15th Amendment to the Constitution, ratified in 1870, declared that "The
right of citizens of the United States to vote shall not be denied or abridged
by the United States or by any State on account of race, color, or previous
servitude." Male African Americans were thus legally entitled to vote. But
particularly in the South, after the Civil War, blacks faced huge obstacles when
they tried to register to vote or to cast a ballot. White registration boards used
every imaginable legal trick to prevent blacks from voting. Registrars would
tell blacks that they had arrived on the wrong day or that they would have
to take a literacy test. A person might be deemed ineligible because he could
not recite the entire U.S. Constitution or just because the board arbitrarily
decided the black person was not qualified. Other more brutal measures, such
as threats on their lives, loss of jobs, physical attacks, and the inability to
pay poll taxes, also kept African Americans from voting. Acts of race-based
disenfranchisement were finally outlawed in 1964 with ratification of the
24th Amendment.

Without federal enforcement, the 24th Amendment guaranteeing black voting
rights had little effect in the South. In Alabama, very few African Americans

Alabama Voter Registration Form Used Before 1965

APPLICATION FOR REGISTRATION

I, _____ , do hereby apply to the Board of Registrars of
_____ County, State of Alabama, to register as an elector under the
Constitution and laws of the State of Alabama, and do herewith submit answers to the inter-
roratories propounded to me by said board.

_____

(Applicants Full Name)

QUESTIONNAIRE

1. State your name, the date and place of your birth, and your present address
    _____

2. Are you single or married? _____ (a) If married, give name, resident and place
    of birth of your husband or wife, as the case may be: _____
    _____

3. Give the names of the places, respectively, where you have lived during the last five
    years; and the name or names by which you have been known during the last five years:
    _____
    _____

4. If you are self-employed, state the nature of your business: _____
    _____

A. If you have been employed, by another during the last five years, State the nature of your
    employment and the name or names of such employer or employers and his or their
    addresses: _____

5. If you claim that you are a bona fide resident of the State of Alabama, give the date on
    which you claim to have become such bona fide resident: _____ (a) When did you
    become a bona fide resident of _____ County: _____ (b) When did you
    become a bona fide resident of _____ Ward or Precinct _____

6. If you intend to change your place of residence prior to the next general election, state
    the facts: _____

7. Have you previously applied for and been denied registration as a voter? _____ (a) If so,
    give the facts: _____

8. Has your name been previously stricken from the list of persons registered? _____

9. Are you now or have you ever been a dope addict or a habitual drunkard? _____
    (A) If you are or have been a dope addict or habitual drunkard, explain as fully as you can:
    _____

10. Have you ever been legally declared insane? _____ (a) If so, give details: _____

11. Give a brief statement of the extent of your educaiton and business experience: _____ _____

12. Have you ever been charged with or convicted of a felony or crime or offense involving moral turpitude? _____ (a) If so, give the facts: _____

13. Have you ever served in the Armed Forces of the United States Government? _____ (a) If so, state when and for approximately how long: _____ _____

14. Have you ever been expelled or dishonorable discharged from any school or college or from any branch of the Armed Forces of the United States, or of any other Country? _____ If so, state facts: _____

15. Will you support and defend the Constitution of the United States and the Constitution of the State of Alabama? _____

16. Are you now or have you ever bene affiliated wiht any group or organization which advocates the overthrow of the United States Government or the government of any State of the United States by unlawful means? _____ (a) If so, state the facts: _____

17. Will you bear arms for your county when called upon it to do so? _____ If the answer is no, give reasons: _____

18. Do you believe in free elections and rule by the majority? _____

19. Will you give aid and comfort to the enemies of the United States Government or the Government of the State of Alabama? _____

20. Name some of the duties and obligations of citizenship: _____ _____ _____

(A) Do you regard those duties and obligations as having priority over the duties and obligations you owe to any other secular organization when they are in conflict? _____ _____

21. Give the names and post office addresses of two persons who have present knowledge of your bona fide residence at the place as stated by you: _____ _____ _____ _____

Insert Part III (5)

(The following questions shall be answered by the applicant without assistance.)

1. What is the chief executive of Alabama called? ___Governor___

2. Are post offices operated by the state or federal government? _Federal Government_

3. What is the name of the president of the United States? ___Lyndon B. Johnson___

4. To what national lawmaking body does each state send senators and representatives?
   ___Congress___

Instructions "A"

The applicant will complete the remainder of this questionnaire before a Board member and at his instructions. The Board member shall have the applicant read any one or more of the following excepts from the U. S. Constitution using a duplicate form of this Insert Part III. The Board member shall keep in his possession the application with its inserted Part III and shall mark thereon the words missed in reading by the applicant.

EXCERPTS FROM THE CONSTITUTION

1. "The right of the people to be secure in their persons, houses, papers, and effects, against unreasonable searches and seizures, shall not be violated, and no warrants shall issue, but upon probable cause supported by oath or affirmation, and particularly describing the place to be searched, and the person or things to be seized."

2. "Representatives shall be apportioned among the several states according to their respective numbers, counting the whole number of persons in each state, excluding Indians not taxed."

3. "Treason against the United States, shall consist only in levying war against them, or in adhering to their enemies, giving them aid and comfort."

4. "The senators and representatives before mentioned, and the members of the several legislatures, and all executive and judicial officers, both of the United States and of the several states, shall be bound by oath or affirmation, to support this constitution."

INSTRUCTIONS "B"

The Board member shall then have the applicant write several words, or more if necessary to make a judicial determination of his ability to write. The writing shall be placed below so that it becomes a part of the application. If the writing is illegible, the Board member shall write in parentheses beneath the writing the words the applicant was asked to write.

HAVE APPLICANT WRITE HERE, DICTATING WORDS FROM THE CONSTITUTION

Signature of Applicant _____

Source: Alabama Department of Archives and History, Montgomery, Alabama.

Marching from Selma to Montgomery, Alabama, in March 1965.

were registered to vote because of white intimidation and repression. In one county, 78 percent of the population was black and in another 81 percent was black, but not one African American in either county was registered to vote. The actual voter registration form used in Alabama before 1965 is reproduced on the following three pages. White officials often required blacks to complete this daunting form.

During the 1960s, such organizations as the Congress of Racial Equality (CORE), the Southern Christian Leadership Conference (SCLC), and the Student Nonviolent Coordinating Committee (SNCC) staged marches to compel the federal government to protect African-American voting rights. Activists also conducted voter registration drives and made numerous attempts to help African Americans vote. Part of that effort in early 1965 took place in Selma, Alabama, with a campaign led by Martin Luther King Jr. King and hundreds of others were arrested (*see also* **Martin Luther King Jr.'s Birthday**). During one demonstration, state troopers fatally shot Jimmie Lee Jackson, a black man who was trying to protect his mother from being beaten by police.

In March 1965, about 15,000 people in Harlem, New York, participated in a march supporting the Alabama marchers.

The Marches

Protesters planned to march from Selma to Montgomery, the state capital, on Sunday, March 7. Since King was out of town, civil-rights leaders John Lewis (who was later elected a U.S. representative) and Hosea Williams organized the 50-mile march of 525 participants. At the Edmund Pettus Bridge over the Alabama River, police met the marchers with clubs, cattle prods, chains, and tear gas. At least 50 marchers were beaten and hospitalized, among them John Lewis, whose skull was fractured.

Television images and newspaper photographs of the attack, which became known as Bloody Sunday, incensed much of the American public, who called on the federal government to stop the police brutality. More activists quickly headed for Selma.

Another march was planned even though a federal judge issued an order to stop it. King, who had come back to Selma, first agreed to lead the marchers across the bridge, but then asked them to turn around and return to Selma because he had never defied a judge's order. Nevertheless, another murder was committed that evening. A white northern minister who was with the demonstrators was killed by a group of Selma whites, which created a wave of protests across the United States—a reaction quite different from the listless public response to Jackson's death.

On March 15, in a televised address, President Lyndon B. Johnson asked Congress to pass a voting rights bill. Afterward he persuaded the federal judge to lift the ban on the Selma marchers. Johnson also gave notice to Alabama Governor George Wallace that federal troops would be on hand for the march from Selma to Montgomery, which began on March 21. By March 25, an estimated 3,200 marchers had arrived in Montgomery. Five months later—in August—the U.S. Congress passed the Voting Rights Act of 1965, which banned literacy tests and provided for federal examiners to register voters and oversee elections in counties where voter eligibility was determined by testing.

Creation of the Observance

Since 1996 the National Voting Rights Museum and Institute in Selma has organized the Bridge Crossing Jubilee, which draws more than 50,000 visitors each year. The event serves as an annual reminder of the sacrifices made to improve voting rights, as well as an occasion to gather and honor the original marchers.

Observance

The Jubilee begins with a welcome reception and a mass meeting featuring a keynote speaker. On the following days, events include a remembrance ceremony for martyrs of the voting rights movement, a program urging people to vote, a Miss Jubilee Pageant, a Jubilee Festival with music and storytelling, a black-tie awards dinner, and a bridge-crossing reenactment at the Edmund Pettus Bridge.

National leaders who have attended past Jubilees have included Rosa Parks, Ethel and Max Kennedy, Jack Kemp, Roy Jones, Congressman John Lewis, Reverend Jesse Jackson, Coretta Scott King, Congresswomen Sheila

Jackson-Lee and Maxine Waters, former Senator Bill Fritz, and former presidents Bill Clinton, George W. Bush, and Barack Obama. (*see also* **Rosa Parks Day**). Every five years, the celebrants continue all the way to Montgomery.

Contact and Website

National Voting Rights Museum and Institute
P.O. Box 1366
Selma, AL 36702-1366
334-526-4340; fax: 334-418-1991
http://nvrmi.com

Further Reading

Christian, Charles M., ed. *Black Saga: The African American Experience—A Chronology.* Washington, DC: Counterpoint, 1999.

Horton, James Oliver, and Lois E. Horton, eds. *A History of the African American People: The History, Traditions & Culture of African Americans.* Detroit: Wayne State University Press, 1997.

Powledge, Fred. *Free At Last? The Civil Rights Movement and the People Who Made It.* 1991. Reprint. Boston: HarperPerennial, 1992.

Williams, Juan, with the Eyes on the Prize Production Team. *Eyes on the Prize: America's Civil Rights Years, 1954–1965. A Companion Volume to the PBS Television Series.* 2002. Reprint. New York: Penguin Books, 2013.

Bud Billiken Parade and Picnic

Date Observed: Second Saturday in August
Location: Chicago, Illinois

The annual Bud Billiken Parade and Picnic is held on the second Saturday in August. The event, held since 1929, is named after a fictional character featured in the pages of the *Chicago Defender* newspaper. The annual celebration is a salute to the community's youth and a gigantic back-to-school rally. This Bud Billiken Day Parade is the largest African-American parade in the United States of America.

Historical Background

On May 5, 1905, Robert S. Abbott established the *Chicago Defender*, which became one of the most important African-American newspapers in the nation. The paper spoke out against racist practices, advocated for civil rights, and encouraged black migration to the city. The paper also listed contacts for churches and other groups that would assist newcomers with housing, employment, and acclimation to the city (from 1910 to 1930, Chicago's African-American population grew from 44,000 to 235,000).

In 1923 Abbott added a special page for children. The *Chicago Defender* was the first newspaper in the U.S. to include such a feature. It was called the Bud Billiken page, which also served as a forum for the Bud Billiken Club, complete with membership cards and buttons.

Bud Billiken is not a real person; Abbott and his managing editor Lucious Harper made up the name. According to some accounts, "Bud" was Harper's nickname, and "Billiken" came from the name of a Buddha-like good-luck figurine popular during the early 1900s. The Bud Billiken character was intended to be a protector of children.

The purpose of the Bud Billiken Parade and Picnic is to celebrate children, including those who sell and deliver the paper—such as this boy, photographed in Chicago in 1942.

Creation of the Observance

By 1929 the Bud Billiken character and club were so popular that Abbott decided to organize an event for children. The idea was to show appreciation for the young people who delivered the paper and also to delight and inspire young African-American children by creating a venue where they would have a chance to be in the spotlight. The first parade was held on August 11, 1929. Abbott kicked off the parade riding in his Rolls Royce, and children in costumes followed. The *Chicago Defender* Charities took over organizing the event and has managed it ever since.

Observance

The Bud Billiken Parade and Picnic is a much-anticipated annual event in Chicago. As such, even though official festivities do not begin until the parade starts at 10 A.M., people begin staking out prime spots along Martin Luther King Jr. Drive in the early hours each second Saturday in August. Every year over 500,000 people take part in the parade, with spectators estimated at well over a million and television viewers reaching in excess of 1.2 million (the parade receives both local and national cable coverage).

The Bud Billiken Parade is chock-full of typical parade fare, but on a fairly grand scale; it is promoted as the largest of its kind in the country. Over 200 floats and vehicles take part, as do countless marching bands and various other types of entertainers. Each year, a King and Queen are announced and they preside over the festivities. National figures also take part. Past parades have hosted Oprah Winfrey, Spike Lee, Bozo the Clown, Jesse Jackson, Muhammad Ali, Duke Ellington, Michael Jordan, and then-U.S. Senator Barack Obama.

After the excitement of the parade has ended and the second half of the day begins, people get down to the serious business of eating at the Bud Billiken

Picnic. Other events include drill team and drum corps competitions, entertainment by local performers, and lots of activities planned to keep young people occupied and happy on their special day.

Contacts and Websites

Chicago Convention and Tourism Bureau
301 E. Cermak Rd.
Chicago, IL 60616
312-567-8500
http://www.choosechicago.com

Chicago Defender
4445 S. Martin Luther King Dr.
Chicago, IL 60653
312-225-2400; fax: 312-225-9231
http://www.chicagodefender.com

Chicago Defender Charities, Inc.
700 E. Oakwood Blvd., 5th Fl.
Chicago, IL 60616
773-536-3710
http://www.budbillikenparade.org

Encyclopedia of Chicago, an online cooperative effort of the Chicago Historical Society, the Newberry Library and Northwestern University
http://www.encyclopedia.chicagohistory.org

Further Reading

Adero, Malaika. *Up South: Stories, Studies, and Letters of This Century's African American Migrations.* New York: The New Press, 1994.

Arnesen, Eric J. *Black Protest and the Great Migration: A Brief History with Documents.* 2002. Reprint. Boston: Bedford Book/St. Martin's, 2018.

Ottley, Roi. *The Lonely Warrior: The Life and Times of Robert S. Abbott.* Chicago: H. Regnery, 1955.

Reed, Christopher Robert. *Black Chicago's First Century, Volume 1, 1833–1900.* Columbia: University of Missouri Press, 2005.

Simmons, Charles A. *The African American Press: A History of News Coverage During National Crises, with Special Reference to Four Black Newspapers, 1827–1965.* Jefferson, NC: McFarland and Company, 2006.

Buffalo Soldiers Commemorations

Date Observed: July 28
Location: Communities nationwide

In 1992, the U.S. Congress designated July 28 as Buffalo Soldiers Day to commemorate the date in 1866 when Congress created six regular Army regiments composed of African-American enlisted soldiers. These segregated units, who adopted the name Buffalo Soldiers, were sent to fight Native Americans in the military campaigns of the Southwest. Even though July 28 became a national day to remember these soldiers, various U.S. states and communities have honored the soldiers on other days.

Historical Background

African Americans have served in all of America's wars, including the Civil War, when they were assigned to the U.S. Colored Troops. After the end of the war, in 1866, the U.S. Army formed the first regular African-American regiments. These were the 9th and 10th Cavalry, and the 38th, 39th, 40th, and 41st Infantry. In 1869 the four infantry regiments combined to form the 24th and 25th Infantry. These regiments fought alongside the cavalry and became known collectively as Buffalo Soldiers.

No one is certain how the name originated. Some historians say tribal warriors nicknamed the regiments Buffalo Soldiers because they fought as fiercely as the buffalo, and African Americans considered the name an honorary title. But, during the 1990s, some Native Americans voiced their disagreement. Members of the American Indian Movement (AIM) declared that Plains Indians used the term "Buffalo Soldier" disparagingly to indicate soldiers with dark skin who help kill their people. In 1994 AIM protested when the U.S. Postal Service issued a stamp honoring Buffalo Soldiers, and they demonstrated at museums and other exhibits on Buffalo Soldier history.

In 1890 these Buffalo Soldiers of the 25th Infantry were photographed at Fort Keogh, Montana.

The original Buffalo Soldiers were stationed mainly in Kansas, Texas, and New Mexico, where they had to face the prejudice of many white settlers and Army officials. They were given old horses, inadequate rations and ammunition, and faulty equipment. Nevertheless, they fought against Native Americans in what has been called "The Plains War" or "The Indian Campaigns" on a western frontier that extended from Montana and the Dakotas to Texas, New Mexico, and Arizona. Buffalo Soldiers also participated in armed conflicts against Mexican revolutionaries, outlaws, and cattle rustlers. They protected stagecoaches and crews building railroads and helped string telegraph lines, build outposts on the frontier, and map areas of the Southwest.

For their bravery and heroism, 18 Buffalo Soldiers received the Congressional Medal of Honor, the nation's highest honor, over a 20-year period. On July 9, 1870, First Sergeant Emanuel Stance became the first African American in the post-Civil War period to receive this award for his valor in the Battle of Kickapoo Springs, Texas.

Buffalo Soldiers took part in combat during the Spanish-American War in Cuba in 1898. When the United States entered World War I in 1917, no cavalry units served, but the Buffalo Soldier tradition of heroic service continued with the 92nd Infantry, another African-American regiment. In 1941, the 9th and 10th Cavalry became the 4th Cavalry Brigade, led by General Benjamin O. Davis, the first African-American general in the regular army. Horse cavalry units disbanded in 1944, and members transferred to other units of the armed forces;, with some serving in World War II.

Creation of the Observance

In early 1992, the U.S. Congress designated July 28 as Buffalo Soldiers Day. On July 25, 1992, General Colin L. Powell, a black four-star army general, dedicated a statue of a mounted Buffalo Soldier at Fort Leavenworth, Kansas, on a site where Buffalo Soldiers camped during the late 19th and early 20th centuries. At the dedication Powell said he considered himself "the descendent of those Buffalo Soldiers ... and all the black men and women who have served the nation in uniform." In the audience were African-American veterans of the segregated army and reenactors in the uniforms of Buffalo Soldiers.

The congressional designation and the commemoration in Kansas were widely publicized, prompting numerous events in the following years. Some states set aside their own days to honor the Buffalo Soldiers. In 1998 the Maryland General Assembly signed a citation marking February 20 of each year as Buffalo Soldiers Day. Other states and localities conduct ceremonies on Memorial Day. In all the military commitments of this country, African Americans have battled with distinction. Some of their most significant contributions and sacrifices, however, came during the Civil War. Over 180,000 African Americans wore the Union Army blue during that conflict. Another 30,000 served in the Navy, and 200,000 served as labor, engineering, hospital, and other projects of military assistance. For the sake of freedom and their country, more than 33,000 of these gallant soldiers gave their lives.

Observances

The events that honor Buffalo Soldiers vary by location, but nearly all include a recitation of the combined mythology and history of the African-American 9th and 10th Cavalry and the 24th and 25th Infantry. Honorary observances

94

include special museum displays, documentaries, and performances by reenactment societies.

One group of horseback riders in Michigan formed a horseback riding club in 1992 in honor of the Buffalo Soldiers. They named their group the "Washtenaw County Buffalo Soldiers, 10th Cavalry," and they participate in local parades, rodeos, and educational presentations.

Another group is the National Association of Buffalo Soldiers Motorcycle Clubs, which is headquartered in Chicago and has chapters across the United States. Comprised of African-American men and women, the club members participate in numerous rides on "iron horses" to promote the history of the African-American regiments. On one ride in 2004, the association staged a ride to Fort Leavenworth, Kansas, to honor the history of the troopers of the 9th and 10th Cavalry.

Contacts and Websites

Buffalo Soldier Monument
290 Stimson Ave.
Fort Leavenworth, KS 33027
913-682-4113
http://kansastravel.org/buffalosoldiermonument.htm

Buffalo Soldiers National Museum
713-942-8920
http://www.buffalosoldiermuseum.com

"Buffalo soldiers" online exhibit at the International Museum of the Horse
Kentucky Horse Park
4089 Iron Works Pkwy.
Lexington, KY 40511
859-233-4303 or 800-678-8813; fax: 859-254-0253
http://imh.org/exhibits/online/legacy-of-the-horse/buffalo-soldiers
https://kyhorsepark.com/contact

Captain Buffalo, website of author Frank Schubert, offers presentations on the Buffalo Soldiers
http://www.captainbuffalo.com

The National Association of Buffalo Soldiers & Troopers Motorcycle Club
http://www.buffalosoldiersnational.com

Further Reading

Bellecourt, Vernon. "The Glorification of Buffalo Soldiers Raises Racial Divisions between Blacks, Indians." *Indian Country Today*, May 4, 1994.

Billington, Monroe Lee. *New Mexico's Buffalo Soldiers, 1866–1900*. 1991. Reprint. Boulder: University Press of Colorado, 1994.

Butler, Ron. "The Buffalo Soldier, A Shining Light in the Military History of the American West." *Arizona Highways*, March 1972.

Leckie, William H. *The Buffalo Soldiers: A Narrative of the Negro Cavalry in the West*. Norman: University of Oklahoma Press, 1967.

Brooks, Christopher A., ed. *The African American Almanac*. 11th ed. Detroit: Gale, 2011.

Schubert, Irene, and Frank Schubert. *On the Trail of the Buffalo Soldier 2: New and Revised Biographies of African Americans in the U.S. Army, 1866–1917*. Lanham, MD: Scarecrow Press, 2004.

Charlie Parker Jazz Festival

Date Observed: A weekend in late August
Location: New York, New York

The festival, held in lower Manhattan and Harlem every August, features both Charlie Parker contemporaries and youthful jazz musicians who keep shaping and driving the art form. The annual Charlie Parker Jazz Festival celebrates the legendary music master and impresario for whom it is named. Two New York City public parks are opened up on two consecutive days at the end of August so that citizens and visitors can appreciate the genius that is credited with changing the face of modern jazz.

Historical Background

Charlie Parker's brief life, from 1920 to 1955, had a gigantic impact on the American music scene and the jazz world in particular. As an African American born to modest circumstances in the Midwest, he achieved his successes in what might be viewed as somewhat unconventional ways. Parker left an impressive legacy, despite more than a few stumbling blocks and hurdles.

His early childhood and teenage years were spent in Kansas City, Missouri, where there are varied stories of a largely absent father whose background was in the black vaudeville circuit. Parker's mother was of African-American and Choctaw descent (the source of much theorizing with regard to *Cherokee* and *Ko-Ko*, two of Parker's significant works). Her work hours are said to have allowed young Parker's free reign of the "Paris of the Plains," as Kansas City was then called. His introduction to vice came early; his dual addictions to heroin and alcohol were established by the time he was 15. That was also the year he married his first wife. Three others followed, and when he passed away, Parker had fathered at least three children.

Charlie Parker playing his saxophone around 1940.

The little formal music education that Parker received was obtained via the Kansas City public schools. His first instrument was a baritone horn, of which he quickly tired. Parker then moved on to what would become his passion, the alto sax. He played in a high-school group for a brief time before dropping out in 1935 to pursue music full time. Before long, and with the involvement of two hawked instruments, Parker made his way to New York City. He stayed there a year, working a stint as a dishwasher in order to be near musicians he admired. It was during this time that Parker began to formulate his sound, although it would be years before he would actualize it musically. In the meantime, he honed his basic music abilities and worked toward his creative goals, playing first with the Jay McShann Band and then Earl Hines's group, teaming up with the likes of Dizzy Gillespie and other young modernists. These "hep cats" spent off hours in jam sessions in such renowned Harlem hotspots of the day as Minton's Playhouse and Monroe's Uptown House.

By the mid-1940s, Parker's career was ready to take off. He was grounded in the fundamentals and knew the sound he was after. He and Gillespie set out and did a string of Hollywood engagements. Parker then went to Los Angeles on his own where a reported effort to kick his drug habit landed him in Camarillo State Hospital for six months. Afterward, he worked in Los Angeles for three months, then returned to New York to form a quintet with whom he recorded some of his most famous works.

For Parker, though, this productive period had its ups and downs; ultimately, his lifestyle choices took their toll. In mid-1951, New York's Narcotics Squad curtailed his ability to earn a living locally by having his cabaret license revoked. Constantly forced to be on the road—or broke and begging—Parker's

98

mental and physical health increasingly suffered. Although he did get his license back within two years or so, Parker tried to commit suicide twice in 1954 and he voluntarily committed himself to Bellevue Hospital.

Parker made his final public appearance on March 5, 1955. His death was announced on March 12, 1955.

No one argues Parker's technical mastery of the saxophone or his influence. While some question his character, and others still are challenged by the complexity of his compositions, the very longevity of Parker's work has given credence to his stature and the stamina of his place in the halls of music.

Much recognition of the jazz legend occurred posthumously during the last decade of the 20th century. In 1994 efforts to have Parker's one-time New York home on Avenue B placed on the U.S. National Register of Historic Places came to fruition. At the end of the decade, the building also was granted New York City landmark status. Easier to achieve was the renaming of Avenue B as "Charlie Parker Place" in 1993. In Kansas City, Missouri, the Charlie Parker Memorial Statue was dedicated in 1999.

Creation of the Festival

The first Charlie Parker Jazz Festival was held in 1993. The original organizers ran the event until its 10th year, at which time the City Park Foundation took over and has managed it since. The month of August was selected to honor Parker's birthday.

Observance

The festival is held over the course of two days, Saturday and Sunday, at two different venues, both in areas where Parker lived and worked: Marcus Garvey Park in Harlem and Tompkins Square

"Yardbird"

Several accounts purport to explain how Charlie Parker got the nickname "Yardbird," often shortened to "Bird." One popular story, recounted on the official Charlie Parker website, has it that while Parker was traveling to a gig with Jay McShann, the car hit a chicken—also known as a yardbird—and Parker insisted on stopping the car and retrieving it to cook for dinner.

Plaza in the East Village, near Parker's home on what was then Avenue B. The events start at midday, allowing attendees the chance to spend an afternoon, or two, inspired by Parker's intricate compositions and twists on old standards.

Each year the festival brings together some of the most talented jazz musicians from all corners of the globe. The aim is to exemplify the individuality and innovation that Parker himself intensely idealized. Admission on both dates is free of charge. The event is one to which jazz aficionados eagerly look forward, considering Parker's works to be as provocative today as they were more than a half century ago. The City Parks Foundation will present the 27th edition of the Charlie Parker Jazz Festival in 2019, a vibrant–and free–celebration of jazz in New York, bringing together stories, veteran players and the next generation of jazz artists.

Contact and Website

City Park Foundation
830 Fifth Ave.
New York, NY 10021
212-360-1399
https://cityparksfoundation.org

Further Reading

"Charlie Parker Memorial Issue." *Down Beat*, March 11, 1965.

Hodeir, Andre, and Jean-Louis Pautrot, eds. *Andre Hodeir Jazz Reader.* Ann Arbor: University of Michigan Press, 2006.

Priestly, Brian. *Chasin' the Bird: Life & Legend of Charlie Parker.* New York: Oxford University Press, 2005.

Ward, Geoffrey C., and Ken Burns. *Jazz: A History of America's Music.* New York: Knopf, 2000

Chicago Gospel Music Festival

Date Observed: First weekend in June
Location: Chicago, Illinois

The Chicago Gospel Music Festival, sponsored by the Mayor's Office of Special Events since 1984, is held each year on the first weekend in June. The festival celebrates the history of gospel music in Chicago and people gather each year to pay tribute to the musical art form. Chicago plays a vital role in keeping gospel music alive, and the festival features the mesmerizing backdrop of Millennium Park and the Chicago Cultural Center. This festival reveals the various music genres, spanning traditional and contemporary, lively choral groups, extraordinary vocalists, dynamic duos, and more.

Historical Background

Gospel music has a long history in Chicago's African-American community, but elements of the genre come from slave songs, spirituals, folk songs, hymns, and blues. Its roots go back even further to Africa and rhythms and chants that captured people brought to the Americas.

During the 1700s many enslaved people on plantations became Christianized and went to church services, staying afterward to sing and dance in "praise houses." Slaves also sang to bolster their spirits during back-breaking work in the fields, while logging, and on prisoner chain-gang construction sites. Some songs were related to runaway slaves and the Underground Railroad, such as the spirituals "Wade in the Water" (referring to walking in streams to avoid detection by dogs) and "Swing Low, Sweet Chariot" (escaping by wagon).

Protestant hymns also played a role in the development of gospel music, particularly when Richard Allen, founder of the African Methodist Episcopal Church, published collections of hymns that he considered suitable for African-American churches (*see also* **Founder's Day/Richard Allen's Birthday**).

But the hymns were undemonstrative, and a lighter, less restrained style of singing began to take hold in the 1800s. By the end of the century, Pentecostal churches were influencing gospel music with clapping, foot stomping, and shouting, as were common in praise houses. In addition, African-American composers were contributing to gospel music by arranging spirituals in new ways and publishing their work.

Not until the 1920s did "gospel music" become an accepted term for this genre of music. In 1921 the **National Baptist Convention, USA** met in Chicago and officially acknowledged the sacred spirit of gospel music. At the time, Rev. Thomas A. Dorsey, a honky-tonk piano player and composer who accompanied blues singer, such as Ma Rainey, attended the convention and liked the music he heard. But he wanted to change the rhythms "to get the feeling and the moans and the blues into the songs," according to the *Chicago Tribune.* Dorsey said he "modified some of the stuff from way back in the jazz era, bashed it up and smoothed it in. It had that beat, that rhythm. And people were wild about it."

However, when Dorsey attempted to introduce the music to black church congregations on Chicago's South Side, elders did not welcome his style. Although discouraged, Dorsey began to compose his own songs, which totaled more than 1,000 during his lifetime; about half were published. In 1926 he coined the term "gospel music," publishing his first two gospel songs "Someday, Somewhere" and "If You See My Savior."

Dorsey eventually found a home for his compositions at Pilgrim Baptist Church, considered the birthplace of gospel music. As choir director at Pilgrim Baptist, Dorsey trained gospel singers, including the great Mahalia Jackson and many others who gained fame. (Tragically, on January 6, 2006, the historic church was severely damaged in a fire that destroyed priceless artifacts, including some of Dorsey's original compositions.)

Sallie Martin (1896–1988) was instrumental in spreading gospel music through the Midwest and the South. As a young hospital worker with an interest in the genre, Martin joined Dorsey's choir in 1932 "and gradually earned a reputation as a charismatic artist. Also in 1933, she cofounded, with Dorsey, the National Convention of Gospel Choirs and Choruses and remained its first vice president until her death. In 1940 Martin started a gospel publishing company in Chicago with songwriter Kenneth Morris. Martin and Morris, Inc.,

Thomas A. Dorsey (1899–1993)

Known as the "Father of Gospel Music," Thomas Andrew Dorsey was born in 1899 in Villa Rica, Georgia. His father was a minister, and Thomas heard spirituals and Baptist hymns at church and at home. As a child his life was also filled with secular music—the blues were then emerging. Although the Dorsey family had limited income, they managed to buy an organ, which Thomas learned to play at about six years old. He also received some musical education from an uncle.

When the Dorsey family moved to Atlanta in 1908, Thomas frequented a vaudeville theater, where he watched pianists at work. He himself became a paid performer, playing blues in clubs and for parties and dances while he was still a teenager.

In 1916, Dorsey went to Chicago looking for better-paying jobs. For the next few years, he traveled between Atlanta and Chicago trying to improve his income. By the mid-1920s, he was touring the country. He also began publishing some of his songs.

Married in 1925, Dorsey's wife died seven years later while giving birth to their only child. Their infant son died the next day. Dorsey became deeply depressed and after some months began to recover by composing the famous song "Take My Hand, Precious Lord." From then on, he was devoted to gospel music, which he promoted in Chicago and across the nation. He also continued to compose and publish his work, including "There'll Be Peace in the Valley," "Ev'ry Day Will Be Sunday By and By," and "I'll Be Climbing Up the Rough Side of the Mountain." His song "Precious Lord" was played at the funerals of both Dr. Martin Luther King and President Lyndon B. Johnson. He remained a resident of the National Convention of Gospel Choirs and Choruses until 1983 and was laid to rest ten years later.

grew to be the most prominent publisher of gospel music in the nation. Until the 1950s, she and her Sallie Martin Singers toured and performed in Europe as well as in the United States. For these contributions Martin is known as "the Mother of Gospel Music."

Creation of the Festival

The first Chicago Gospel Music Festival was held in 1984 in Grant Park on the shores of Lake Michigan. The Chicago Department of Cultural Affairs and Special Events (DCASE) organized the event for the year 2019.

Observance

During the June weekend of the annual Chicago Gospel Music Festival, performers include local, national, and international gospel artists. There is also a gospel art fair.

Each year the DCASE selects festival performers based on applications. Applicants submit biographical sketches, tapes, CDs, photographs, and other materials for consideration. Appearing at the festival have been such gospel music favorites as Bryon Cage, the Williams Brothers, and Solomon Burke, called the "King of Rock and Soul." A Grammy winner, Burke is known for creating soul music by applying gospel techniques to rhythm and blues. Other past performers include the Mississippi Mass Choir, the Canton Spirituals, Mary Mary, Yolanda Adams, Daryl Coley, Men of Standard, John P. Kee & New Life Community Choir, Fred Hammond & Radical for Christ, Bobby Jones & New Life, Sounds of Blackness, Richard Smallwood & Vision, Take 6, Dottie Peoples & The Peoples Chorale, Dorothy Norwood, Shirley Caesar, Albertina Walker, The Winans, Smokie Norful, Smokey Robinson, D. J. Rogers, Israel & New Breed, and Tye Tribbett & GA.

In 2019 the 34th annual gospel event was staged at the Chicago Cultural Center and Millennium Park with performances on its main stage at the Jay Pritzker Pavilion and its North Promenade. The festival draws tens of thousands of gospel lovers.

Contact and Website

Mayor's Office of Special Events
City Hall
901 Bagby, First Fl.
Houston, TX 77002
832-393-0868
E-mail: specialevents@houstontx.gov
https://www.houstontx.gov/specialevents

Further Reading

Boyer, Horace Clarence. "Gospel Music." In *The African-American Experience: Selections from the Five-Volume Macmillan Encyclopedia of African-American Culture and History*, edited by Jack Salzman. New York: Macmillan, 1998.

Darden, Robert. *People Get Ready: A New History of Black Gospel Music.* 2004. Reprint. Chicago: Continuum International Publishing Group, 2005.

Harris, Michael W. *The Rise of Gospel Blues: The Music of Thomas Andrew Dorsey in the Urban Church.* 1992. Reprint. New York: Oxford University Press, 1994.

Jackson, Jerma A. *Singing in My Soul: Black Gospel Music in a Secular Age.* Chapel Hill: University of North Carolina Press, 2004.

Lornell, Kip. "Dorsey, Thomas Andrew." In *African American Lives*, edited by Henry Louis Gates Jr. and Evelyn Brooks Higginbotham. New York: Oxford University Press, 2004.

Reich, Howard. "Gospel Music Loses Its Storied Birthplace." *Chicago Tribune*, January 8, 2006.

Church Homecomings

Date Observed: Varies
Location: Churches nationwide

Annual homecomings have a long tradition among African-American church congregations and families. Depending on the congregation, homecomings may have one or more of several purposes: commemorating a church's anniversary, honoring its deceased, celebrating its members and encouraging those who have moved away to return for a reunion. Homecomings tend to be scheduled from Memorial Day on through the autumn, when the weather is pleasant for outdoor events. Although many of these gatherings have taken place every year for decades, some have discontinued because a church no longer exists or because church members and families are too widely scattered.

Historical Background

From the time the first black churches were built, homecomings have been common annual events. Some occur when large denominational churches mark such anniversaries as **Founder's Day/Richard Allen's Birthday**, celebrating the founding of the African Methodist Episcopal Church (AME) in the late 1700s, and the **August Quarterly**, marking the beginning of the African Union Methodist Protestant Church. Although not as well known, many African-American churches have held homecomings and "decoration days" for many years. Some homecomings mark a church anniversary. One example is the Tynes Chapel AME Zion Church in Dry Fork, Virginia, built in 1901 with donated lumber and the labor of the small black community. As Dry Fork residents moved away, the church's anniversary drew them back for a homecoming held each summer. They came from Pennsylvania, Ohio, New Jersey, and other states for reunions and for sermons, singfests, and picnics.

Some homecomings have been held on the weekend of Memorial Day, which originated in 1868 as Decoration Day to honor American Civil War veterans and to decorate the graves of those who died in that war. Other homecomings have occurred during the spring and summer months when flowers were plentiful for decorating the graves. Summer also was a good time to have "dinner-on-the-grounds," a picnic after a church service.

Creation of the Observance

No specific date marks the beginning of church homecomings; individual churches set their own schedules for such events. In St. John, Kansas, for example, an African-American church held homecomings on Memorial Day, when black families gathered and shared a potluck meal, then took part in a group sing. In Boone County, Kentucky, the First Baptist Church in Burlington held homecomings on the church's anniversary in April; the church was organized in 1881. Sometimes **Juneteenth**, which celebrates June 19, 1865, when slaves in Texas were notified of their freedom, is selected as church homecoming time. July and August, though, are the months when most church homecomings occur.

Observance

A church homecoming generally includes preaching, singing, and dinner on the grounds. The church pastor usually begins the homecoming with prayer, followed by the congregation singing hymns. After a sermon, it is time for dinner. Members of the congregation set up tables and fill them with platters of food. Traditional dishes include fried chicken, chicken and dumplings, ham, potato salad, green beans with fatback, deviled eggs, macaroni and cheese, candied yams, cornbread, and plenty of pies, cobblers, and cakes.

If a cemetery is associated with the church, tending to graves is also part of the observance. Many families who get together at black church homecomings take the opportunity to clean up old burial sites and to preserve genealogical records and the history of a community.

At historic Asbury United Methodist Church in Washington, D.C. (founded in 1836), homecoming events take place in late September and may span an entire weekend. Some years the Asbury homecoming kicks off with a concert of gospel or other sacred music. Outdoor activities, including games

Men prepare food for this benefit dinner-on-the-grounds held in August 1940 at St. Thomas's Church near Bardstown, Kentucky.

for children and young people, are held on the street in front of the church, and the homecoming worship service traditionally features a guest preacher. Occasionally, homecoming has been augmented by a revival (*see also* **Church Revivals**). Asbury's homecoming in 2000 included a theatrical production titled *Escape on the Pearl*. The play dramatizes the story of more than 70 enslaved people, including members of Asbury, who attempted to escape to freedom in 1848 aboard the *Pearl*, which was to take them to a stop on the Underground Railroad. But they were soon captured, and the incident added fuel to the national debate on slavery.

A church called "Roberts Chapel," in a small Indiana community known as "Roberts Settlement," has been holding homecomings on July 4th since 1923. About 150 people attend each year, coming from northeastern states, California, and Florida. An important part of the event is preserving the cemetery that has been an African-American burial site since the 1830s. Children from nearby schools come to Roberts Chapel and the cemetery to learn about the community's history. Homecoming is generally observed to commemorate the past, reconnect with the family, and to transmit the rituals and history to the younger generations. According to Yvonne V. Jones in her book *Kinship Affiliation through Time: Black Homecomings and Family Reunions in a North Carolina County*, homecomings also "symbolized obligations and responsibilities towards kin and community and acted to restore a connection between the living and the dead."

Contact and Website

Asbury United Methodist Church
926 11th St., N.W.
Washington, DC 20001
202-628-0009; fax: 202-783-0519
http://www.asburyumcdc.org

Further Reading

Butler, Anne. "Historic African-American Church in West Feliciana Still Making a Joyful Noise Unto the Lord." Town of Francisville, LA, 2005. http://www.where2guide.com/Articles/afton2005.html

Dodson, John. "Religion and Dry Fork." Bland County (Virginia) History Archives, 2000. http://www.blandcountyhistoryarchives.org/dryfork/dfreligion.html

Church Revivals

Date Observed: Varies
Location: Churches nationwide

C hurch revivals are religious gatherings that became popular during the early 19th century. Traditionally, revivals are Methodist, Protestant, or Evangelical Christian events intended to help church members renew their faith and also to welcome new members into the church.

Historical Background

In the late 1700s and throughout the 1800s, traveling preachers often visited rural areas for several days at a time. During these visits, people would gather to listen to the preachers speak. These gatherings served to create a sense of community for isolated people who lived demanding lives on farms, plantations, or the western frontier. These early revivals were called "camp meetings" or "tent revivals" because people sometimes traveled a great distance to attend, and then camped in wagons or tents for the duration of the revival. Camp meetings were especially popular in the South, and usually occurred once a year in late summer or fall, after the crops were harvested but before winter set in.

Many early traveling preachers did not discriminate and would preach to everyone in the area. As a result, camp meetings often included men and women, whites and African Americans, free people and slaves, and people of all Christian denominations. Although African Americans were not usually allowed in white churches, and women were expected to be silent and reserved during worship, at these early revivals anyone could participate in any way. At camp meetings, it was not uncommon for African Americans and whites to join together for singing or praying, although this did not generally occur outside of the revival tent. Women were also allowed to sing or speak in response to the preacher. In these ways, revivals changed the way people prayed by allowing attendees to express themselves in ways that were normally frowned upon during a church service.

Creation of the Observance

It is difficult to say exactly when and where camp meetings first took place, although historians believe that these gatherings were occurring as early as the 1700s. One of the first documented camp meetings was in 1803, on Shoulderbone Creek in Hancock County, Georgia. Revivals grew in popularity through the 1800s and were considered to be one of the most effective methods of preaching.

Revivals have taken many forms over their long history, depending on factors such as the time of year, the number of preachers in attendance, and geographical location. The earliest revivals held in the East were planned as structured and organized events. By contrast, the camp meetings of the South and West tended to be more spontaneous events that depended upon the availability of traveling preachers. No matter where they were held, revivals could go on for days, sometimes with continuous preaching throughout the day and night. Camp meetings could be unruly, with people jumping up and shouting or singing during the preaching, often at the invitation of the preacher. One early camp meeting tradition involved the use of the "anxious bench," where those who wanted to repent for their sins would sit, under the attention of the entire revival, until they were converted. Revivals often concluded when everyone in attendance was physically exhausted by the energetic, continuous preaching.

Observance

Revivals are now held all over the country by both rural and urban churches. Individual churches determine their own schedule for revivals, and most still follow the basic model of the earliest camp meetings. There is always at least one preacher in attendance, and people gather to reaffirm their faith, sing hymns, and listen to sermons. These gatherings are held throughout the year, indoors or outside, for varying lengths of time. Hundreds of camp meeting sites exist throughout the country, and old-fashioned camp meetings are still held for extended revivals. Tent revivals are popular in southern churches, particularly among Southern Baptists, Methodists, and Pentecostals.

Many churches find ways to organize a revival while still allowing for spontaneous creative expression. The revival event is usually well planned, with arrangements for preachers and other speakers made far in advance. Some revivals focus on a specific theme, such as faith renewal, community building, involvement of young people, or attracting new members to the church. Other revivals cover many different themes in one event, by choosing topics for preachers to focus on during specific days or sessions. Revivals are seen as time set apart from daily life and normal worship activities, and are intended to give people the opportunity to focus on spiritual matters and recommit to their faith.

Further Reading

"'The Meeting Continued All Night, Both by the White and Black People': Georgia Camp Meeting, 1807." History Matters: The U.S. Survey Course on the Web, undated. http://historymatters.gmu.edu/d/6518/.

Ostwalt, Conrad. "Camp Meetings." The Tennessee Encyclopedia of History and Culture, 2017. https://tennesseeencyclopedia.net/entries/camp-meetings/

Shakelton, Paula G. "Revivals and Camp Meetings." The New Georgia Encyclopedia, updated 2017. https://www.georgiaencyclopedia.org/articles/arts-culture/revivals-and-camp-meetings

Colorado Black Arts Festival

Date Observed: Five days in mid-July
Location: Denver, Colorado

The Colorado Black Arts Festival, earlier known as Denver Black Arts Festival (DBAF), is held for five days in July each year, and is designed to raise public awareness of and appreciation for black arts and their beneficial impact on the Denver community. The festival provides opportunities for African Americans in the visual and performing arts to showcase their talents.

Historical Background

In the past, Denver, like many other cities and communities across the United States, offered limited resources and opportunities for African Americans to exhibit their art and present music, dance, and other performances. But with the combined efforts of volunteers, local businesses, cultural institutions, and the media, plus grants from foundations, the city's first African-American arts festival took place in 1987. In 2009, DBAF was renamed as "Colorado Black Arts Festival." The festival has received the Mayor's Award for Excellence in the Arts and in 2019, will celebrate 33 years of operation.

Creation of the Festival

In 1986 Perry Ayers, his brother Oye Oginga, and a group of artists and art lovers formed a committee to launch an arts festival the following year. The first festival took place during two days of rain, so the committee decided to plan subsequent festivals in July to avoid what are called in Colorado the "August monsoons." Attendance has grown with each festival, from more than 30,000 in 1989 to double that number the following year. Today the festival attracts more than 100,000 attendees.

Observance

The festival occurs over a long weekend in mid-July, and its venues have included a comedy showcase; exhibits of artwork and crafts by local artists and vendors; American and African dance companies; marching bands; drill, step, and drum teams; historical exhibits at various institutions; a people's marketplace offering African-American, African, and Caribbean merchandise; performance stages that feature dance troupes, poetry readings, and gospel singers; a children's pavilion with such activities as dance and storytelling; community mural painting; a sculpture garden; and living exhibit of an African compound, called "Joda Village."

The festival also celebrates top African-American achievements in performing and visual arts by presenting an annual award for excellence. On Saturday of the weekend event, there is a Boogaloo Celebration Parade that includes floats, bands, step and drill teams, and school and church groups.

Along with all the celebratory events, there are health and civic pavilions. Businesses or organizations may offer health screenings, volunteer opportunities, and distribute promotional materials.

The Colorado Black Arts Festival conducts its annual celebration of African-American art and culture at the historic Denver City Park West.

Contact and Website

Colorado Black Arts Festival
1700 City Park Esp.
Denver, CO 80205
303-306-8672
https://www.denver.org/listing/city-park/6822

Corn-Shucking Festival

*Date Observed: Between early November
and mid-December
Location: Southern plantations*

Corn shucking was a harvest festival held between early November and mid-December on plantations in areas around the Chesapeake Bay, in the Carolinas, Georgia, Kentucky, Tennessee, Alabama, and east Texas. Plantation owners encouraged slaves to compete (usually in teams) to see who could shuck the most corn. Afterward, slaves shared a feast and held a dance.

Historical Background

The harvest period in the pre-Civil War South meant extensive labor for slaves. They harvested crops such as cotton and tobacco, and then had to cut the field corn and remove the husks—time-consuming and tedious tasks when no modern machinery was available. Following the harvests, they had to prepare the fields for the next year's plantings.

Creation of the Festival

Corn-shucking festivals emerged during the late 18th century. Plantation owners wanted to speed up the corn-husking process so their slaves could go back to their field work. Owners created incentives for their slaves to work quickly by promising such rewards as feasts, whiskey, and socializing. A planter would invite slaves from nearby plantations to gather at his barn, usually at night after the day's labor was done.

Observance

Neighboring plantation owners allowed their slaves to attend corn-husking festivals, because they expected to be compensated in the same way. Slaves

Shucking the Corn

Shuckers were usually men, and they worked swiftly and efficiently. As Roger D. Abrahams, a professor of folklore, explained:

The men would stand or sit around the edges of the pile, in a ring. The shuckers picked up an ear with their left hand with the silk top facing upward, and tore downward with their rights, often with the aid of a hardwood pin strapped onto and emerging from the palm of the right hand. Their left hand then fastened on the back half of the shuck and tore it off to the shank, or butt. The ear was then broken off, the shuck thrown behind the shucker, and the ear thrown back into the pile. A good shucker could do the sequence in a matter of seconds.

came from miles around, looking forward to the shucking because they could take part in a community gathering in which work and recreation were combined. At some corn shuckings, whites and blacks worked together, but that was the extent of their socialization.

Before the event itself, slaves pulled corn (still in husks) from stalks in the field and hauled the crop to the plantation yard. There they would pile bushel upon bushel of corn in a high mound. When slaves had gathered, the mound was divided into two sections with a fence rail or pole, and two teams were chosen to compete in husking the corn. Or, huskers simply competed among themselves, and the person who shucked the most corn won an award, sometimes cash or a suit of clothes. Anyone who found a red ear of corn also received a reward—perhaps a kiss from a young woman or a jug of whiskey.

As the corn husking continued, a captain led the singing, making the job easier as the workers kept up with the rhythmic songs: "Come to shuck that corn to-night/Come to shuck with all your might...." Much of the singing was call and response, a verse and chorus, verse and chorus, many times over. Singing might stop for a time, and jokes and stories flew back and forth.

While the shucking was going on, plantation owners provided the workers with jugs of whiskey, and slave women prepared a huge supper which everyone could enjoy, slaves and planters alike. Late at night after the work was done, the frolic began. Fiddlers and banjo players created the music, and dancing went on for hours, sometimes until dawn.

Because of the festive nature of corn shuckings, some historians concluded that slaves were "happy" captives on the plantation. But others point out that slaves viewed this event as a rare opportunity to socialize and to have some relief from debilitating field work. Still, corn-shucking festivals continued even after emancipation into the 20th century, including among freedmen farmers who assisted each other with the huge task (*see also* **Emancipation Day**).

Contact and Website
Montgomery County Historical Society
111 W. Montgomery Ave.
Rockville, MD 20850
301-340-2825; fax: 301-340-2871
E-mail: info@montgomeryhistory.org
https://montgomeryhistory.org

Further Reading
Abrahams, Roger D. *Singing the Master.* 1992. Reprint. New York: Penguin Books, 1993.

Berlin, Ira, Mark Favreau, and Steven Miller, eds. *Remembering Slavery: African Americans Talk about Their Personal Experiences of Slavery and Freedom.* 1998. Reprint. New York: The New Press, 2011.

Federal Writers' Project of the Works Progress Administration for the State of Maryland. *Slave Narratives: A Folk History of Slavery in the United States From Interviews with Former Slaves. Vol. VIII. Maryland Narratives.* Washington, DC, 1941. https://www.loc.gov/item/41021619/.

White, Shane, and Graham White. *The Sounds of Slavery.* Boston: Beacon Press, 2005.

Crispus Attucks Day

Date Observed: March 5
Location: Boston, Massachusetts, and New Jersey

Crispus Attucks was the first American to die during the Boston Massacre on March 5, 1770, a key event leading up to the Revolutionary War. For this reason, he is considered the first American fatality of the war. Crispus Attucks Day, or Boston Massacre Day has been observed since 1771, mainly in Boston, Massachusetts. Since 1949, Crispus Attucks Day has also been a legal day of observance in the state of New Jersey.

Historical Background

Since the 1760s Britain had been imposing more and more taxes on American colonists. The colonists protested the taxation as illegal, since they could not elect their own representatives to the British Parliament by decree of the British constitution. Thus, a clamoring cry helped to rally leading patriots behind the cause of America's coming Revolutionary War: "No taxation without representation!" When King George III sent British troops across the Atlantic Ocean to keep the colonists in line, the colonists responded with boycotts of British goods. Middle-class merchants and businessmen suffered the harshest losses, as did their employees and laborers.

Additionally, the advent of British troops on American shores meant that soldiers were literally headquartered among the populace, walking the same streets, frequenting the same drinking establishments, and vying for the same young ladies. There was economic competition as well, since off-duty troops looked to supplement their earnings by working part-time hours, at lower wages than locals required for full-time employment. Another cause of tension, particularly between Americans of African descent and the British, was the constant concern that the latter might conscript the former into service in the Royal Army or Navy.

In 1996 President Bill Clinton directed the U.S. Mint to create this commemorative coin in honor of Crispus Attucks. The front shows a portrait of Attucks, and the reverse illustrates the design of a planned Black Patriots Memorial to be placed on the National Mall in Washington, D.C.

On Friday, March 2, 1770, tensions came to a head outside the Old State House in Boston, Massachusetts, where a skirmish took place between some locals and British soldiers. One of those involved was Crispus Attucks. Born into slavery in nearby Framingham, he had escaped and spent nearly two decades of his adult life in and out of the Boston seaport, working on whaling ships and as a ropemaker. Reputed to have a fiery temperament, Attucks also is commonly reported to have been the ringleader of the tensions that built up over the course of the next few days.

On the evening of Monday, March 5, the prior week's scuffle escalated into a full battle. Firsthand accounts vary on how it all began. Some contend that church bells rang out—which at the time was a common fire alarm—and someone yelled "Fire!," which could have signaled a command to shoot. When the shooting stopped, five colonists were dead, among them Attucks. All were immediately elevated to martyrdom status, and their burial rites at Faneuil Hall days later involved 10,000 of the town's 16,000 citizens. Although customs of the time precluded it, Attucks was accorded an honored burial alongside his fallen white comrades.

This event became known as the "Boston Massacre" and, for those anxious to break ties with the British Crown, became a propitious propaganda tool in their arsenal of arguments. Prior to this event, agitators for independence had carefully distanced themselves from the mobs and their street violence. Now they embraced them, sensing a chance to unite the colonists by portraying the "massacred of Boston" as heroes. Attucks's death that day in 1770 helped to turn the tide in the nation's quest for independence. Just a few years later, on April 19, 1775, at Lexington and Concord and Bunker Hill, the Revolutionary War began. The colonists' fight for independence from Britain was now being fought in earnest, with American blood being shed on the battlefield christened by Attucks.

In addition to the role that Attucks played in America's road to independence, he can also be credited with inspiring others of African heritage to seek personal freedom and liberty. Authors Sydney and Emma Kaplan wrote in their book *The Black Presence in the Era of the American Revolution*, "His spirit doubtless spurred New England Blacks to openly question the anomaly of human bondage in a nation about to be born and fighting for its independence under the slogan 'Liberty or Death!'" They add that, in succeeding years, slaves commonly wrote to government officials using the argument that, in one slave's words, "We expect great things from men who have made such a noble stand against the designs of their fellow-men to enslave them."

In 1888, a Crispus Attucks Monument was erected in Boston Commons to commemorate the man, over the objections of both the Massachusetts Historical Society and the New England Historic Genealogical Society.

Creation of the Observance

The Boston Massacre and Crispus Attucks's death have been commemorated in Boston since 1771, the year following the event.

In 1858, black abolitionists in Boston set aside March 5 as Crispus Attucks Day. They believed that Crispus Attucks's contributions to America's independence from Britain had been grossly unrecognized. Not only did they feel that it was unjust for Attucks not to receive acclaim as a great American hero, but also felt that such recognition would bolster their cause (that is, to help others come to the belief that blacks should not be enslaved). For an unknown number of years thereafter, abolitionists paid tribute to the man who was the first to die in the fight for his own and his fellow man's liberty.

On April 25, 1949, the state of New Jersey entered Crispus Attucks Day as a designated day of observance into its state statutes.

From 1966 to 1976 there was an annual Crispus Attucks Parade in Newark, New Jersey. During the 1990s organizers revived the event, but renamed it the "African American Heritage Parade."

Observance

Each year the Boston Massacre is reenacted outside the Old State House, where a circle of cobblestones marks the historic event. The reenactors are members of two groups: the Massachusetts Council of Minutemen and Militia, representing the Americans, and His Majesty's 5th Regiment of Foot, representing the British soldiers. Attendees can also view exhibits and listen to talks at the Old State House museum.

In 1996 President Bill Clinton signed a law that directed the U.S. Mint to design and strike a commemorative Black Patriots Coin. Today Crispus Attucks's likeness adorns one side of a coin available only to collectors, while the other side depicts the still-to-be constructed Black Patriots Memorial that will be symbolically situated on the capitol's National Mall. At the same time, a four-postage stamp set was approved, consisting of Attucks, Frederick Douglass, Salem Poor, and Harriet Tubman (*see also* **Frederick Douglass Day and Harriet Tubman Day**). The United States minted a coin in the year 1998 to honor Attucks on his 275th birth anniversary.

Contacts and Websites

Crispus Attucks online museum
http://www.crispusattucksmuseum.org

The Crispus Attucks Association
605 South Duke St.
York, PA 17401
717-848-3610; fax: 717-843-3914
http://crispusattucks.org

DanceAfrica

Date Observed: Varies according to location
Location: Brooklyn, New York; Washington, D.C.; and
Chicago, Illinois

DanceAfrica is a festival of African and African-American dance founded in 1977 in Brooklyn, New York, by dancer and choreographer Chuck Davis. Since 2015, the program has been handled by Abdel R. Salaam. The event seeks to educate diverse people about the rich heritage of African-influenced music, dance, and culture. This weekend-long festival also includes master classes, film screenings, art exhibitions, an outdoor bazaar, community events, and a marketplace consisting of African, African-American, and Caribbean arts, crafts, and food featuring over 200 vendors. The festival attracts up to 30,000 visitors per year.

Historical Background

Enslaved Africans brought their dancing traditions to the Americas and the Caribbean islands. On the slave ships, Africans frequently were brought up from the hold to the deck to dance, and sometimes forced to do so with a whip.

For slaves, dance became a way to mock slave owners and communicate with each other. The "cakewalk," for example, derives from a competitive couples dance that parodied European pattern dances, such as quadrilles and cotillions.

Some plantation owners forbade slave dances, and even the mere act of raising a foot could be interpreted as dancing. Thus, many slaves took to gliding and limiting their arm and torso movements as much as possible.

As time passed, however, and as slaves were allowed and even encouraged to worship as Christians, they began to integrate traditional African dance rituals into ceremonies. Plantation owners were swayed, in time, to encourage dance events and make them competitive.

For whites, slave dances were a form of entertainment. Whites in blackface traveling in minstrel shows in the late 1700s through the late 1800s helped to popularize the cakewalk, waltz, shuffle, and other dances. The minstrel show, however, perpetuated a distorted view of blacks within white society, especially when the white performer Thomas "Jim Crow" Rice imitated an elderly lame slave, a caricature of African Americans kept alive for decades.

The stereotypical white view of black entertainers did not change until after World War I. By that time many African Americans had migrated from the South to the North and West. In the 1920s the Harlem Renaissance generated an explosion of literary, artistic, and musical creativity (*see also* **African American Day Parade** *and* **Harlem Week**). All aspects of the arts were impacted and dance no less notably. During this period, the old plantation standard of tap dancing was revived, combined with elements of shuffling and acrobatics, and was featured on stages from Broadway to Chicago.

Development of the juke joints and speakeasies of the era offered venues for African Americans to experiment and create their own forms of dance art. Thus, the Charleston, Ballin' the Jack, and the Jitterbug were born.

Several African Americans founded important dance companies during the 20th century. Modern dancer and choreographer Martha Graham, whose influence on American dance has been compared to the influence of Picasso on the visual arts, opened her first dance company in 1925 and went on to reshape modern dance. In 1937 dancer, choreographer, and anthropologist Katherine Dunham established the Negro Dance Group in Chicago, Illinois. Dunham's travels to the Caribbean inspired her to create a dance company that helped establish the credibility of African ritual dances as an art form. Anthropologist Pearl Primus, born in Trinidad, made a similar impact. In 1946 she founded a dance company in New York City. In 1958, dancer and choreographer Alvin Ailey started his renowned company. And, in 1967, Chuck Davis, founder of DanceAfrica, formed his dance company at Bronx Community College in New York.

Creation of the Festival

In 1977, dancer and choreographer Chuck Davis conceived the idea for the festival after watching an old Tarzan movie, in which the "natives" are depicted

Praise for Davis

In *Dance Magazine* K. C. Patrick summarizes what artistic director Chuck Davis has done with DanceAfrica performances: building and "crossing a bridge—a bridge constructed through the years by Davis to connect the roots and branches of Africa and African American dance. He shows the whole spectrum, from traditionalists to the avant-garde. It wasn't always so; what now seems self-apparent exists because Davis started building the bridge twenty-five years ago."

as primitive stereotypes. He decided to show that people of African descent were "not about 'ooga-booga,'" and that was the origin of DanceAfrica.

Davis produced the first DanceAfrica festival at the Brooklyn Academy of Music with just his own company. By year two, the roster had notably expanded to include Charles Moore and Dances and Drums of Africa; International African-American Ballet; Nana Dinizulz and His Dancers, Drummers and Singers; and the Arthur Hall Afro-American Dance Ensemble.

The festival was so successful that it spread to other cities over the years. In 1988 the first DanceAfrica was held in Washington, D.C. And in 1991 DanceAfrica was inaugurated in Chicago, Illinois.

Observance

The original DanceAfrica in New York takes place over Memorial Day weekend, at the end of May, each year. It is hosted by the Brooklyn Academy of Music. DanceAfrica in Washington, D.C., is hosted at the Dance Place each year during the second week in June. The Dance Center of Columbia College is headquarters for DanceAfrica Chicago, where the annual festival occurs in late October.

Each DanceAfrica festival showcases African and African-American dance in all its varieties. Performances draw upon authentic African components—from the use of traditional percussion instruments and rhythmic beats to the exquisitely designed and colored costumes. The desire is to create a cultural bridge, uniting people of all ages, genders and races.

Contacts and Websites

Brooklyn Academy of Music, Inc.
Bldg. 30, Lafayette Ave.
Brooklyn, NY 11217
http://www.bam.org

DanceAfrica in Washington, DC
3225 8th St., N.E
Washington, DC 20017
202-269-1600
http://www.danceplace.org

Further Reading

Farley Emery, Lynn. *Black Dance: From 1619 to Today.* 2nd rev ed. Hightstown, NJ: Princeton Book Company, 1988.
Patrick, K. C. "Chuck Davis and Dance Africa." *Dance Magazine,* April 2004.
Welsh-Ashante, Kariamu, ed. *African Dance: An Artistic, Historical and Philosophical Inquiry.* Trenton, NJ: Africa World Press, 1994.

DC Black Pride

Date Observed: Last weekend in May
Location: Washington, D.C.

DC Black Pride is held in Washington, D.C., in May over Memorial Day weekend each year. The District festival starts off a summer of Black Pride events that take place annually in cities across the United States. DC Black Pride is one of the nation's first and largest African-American LGBTQA+ Pride events and attracts more than 35,000 participants.

Historical Background

In 1991, Ernest Hopkins, Theodore Kirkland, and Welmore Cook recognized a need to rally the Washington, D.C., community around the HIV/AIDS epidemic. t Members of the LGBTQA+ community of all ethnicities have long suffered discrimination, harassment, and brutal—and sometimes deadly—assaults. The first DC Black Pride drew 800 people to Banneker Field for a Pride celebration featuring the theme "Let's All Come Together." More than 300,000 blacks identify as LGBTQA+ and many historically have been ostracized from their African-American communities as well. Thus, black LGBTQA+ celebrations, which originated in Washington, D.C., have become a way to demonstrate pride as well as to educate and raise funds for programs that address health concerns such as HIV/AIDS.

Creation of the Festival

The source of DC Black Pride Has been attributed to a and annua; Memorial Day party that began in 1975 at the Clubhouse, a popular Washington, D.C. Although everyone was welcome at the Clubhouse, patrons were primarily black gay men and lesbians. The annual party was originally called the "Childrens Hour" and was attended by hundreds of African-American gay men and lesbians.

In 1990, the Clubhouse closed because of financial problems and because many of the club's staff had died of AIDS. Soon, another group formed to concentrate on raising funds for the growing number of HIV-positive black men. In 1991, the group sponsored a Sunday Black Pride festival that brought in about $3,000 for organizations helping AIDS patients. After that event, the festival grew and became an annual Memorial Day Weekend celebration organized by the DC Black Lesbian and Gay Pride Day, Inc.

Observance

In 1991, the DC Black Pride celebration was held on the grounds of Banneker Field. Each year rain disrupted the festivities, so in 2000, the festival moved indoors to the Washington Convention Center. About 15,000 people attended, and, according to organizers, it was the largest such event in the world.

Subsequent festivals have featured African-American recording artists, authors, and other notables. The four-day event includes workshops on health issues, Black Pride films, arts and crafts, and food vendors.

The Washington, D.C., festival has encouraged the development of similar Black Pride events in numerous other U.S. cities. The Philadelphia Black Gay Pride happens on the last weekend in April; the Windy City Pride is held in Chicago, Illinois, around July 4; the Central Florida Black Pride in Tampa takes place during the first weekend in August; and in Atlanta, Georgia, the group Life Atlanta organizes an annual Labor Day Black Gay Pride celebration. Other Black Pride events take place from Baltimore, Maryland, to Miami, Florida, and from Detroit, Michigan, to Dallas, Texas.

More than 50,000 women and men from all over the globe attend DCBP each year and experience Washington's excellent culture and history. Since its foundation, DCBP has inspired countless annual Black LGBT pride activities in the USA, Canada, the United Kingdom, Brazil, Africa, and the Caribbean. Every year, over 250,000 people participate in Black LGBTQAI+ Pride events.

Contacts and Websites

DC Black Pride Black Lesbian and Gay Pride Day, Inc.
http://www.dcblackpride.org

In The Life Atlanta, Inc.
1530 Dekalb Ave.
Atlanta, GA 30307
http://www.inthelifeatl.com

Philadelphia Black Gay Pride, Inc.
http://phillyblackpride.org

Further Reading

Norton, Eleanor Holmes. "Honoring the 13th Annual DC Black Pride
   Celebration and Earl D. Fowlkes." *Congressional Record*, May 14, 2003.

DC Caribbean Carnival

Date Observed: Second week of July
Location: Washington, D.C.

The DC Caribbean Carnival is an annual colorful, educational, and cultural event held in the nation's capital. Since 1993, it has showcased the diverse cultures of Caribbean immigrants who make their homes in the Washington metropolitan area. Since 2012, the organizers of the festival, DC Caribbean Carnival, Inc. have joined forces with the Caribbean American Carnival Association of Baltimore, who previously organized the Baltimore carnival and festival to form the single Baltimore Washington One carnival.

Historical Background

2017 U.S. Census Bureau data reported that the Black or African American population in Washington, D.C., to comprises 47.1 percent of the entire population of the city. At least 7,000 islands, islets, reefs, and cays make up the geographical area known as" the Caribbean," or the "West Indies." Thirty-three territories make up the West Indies, and include sovereign states, overseas departments, and dependencies. (Puerto Rico, and the U.S. Virgin Islands are two of three U.S. dependencies; the third is Navassa Island.) The countries and islands of the Caribbean are located south and east of Mexico and north and west of Venezuela in South America.

Most of the Caribbean came under European rule in the 15th to 19th centuries. The Spanish, French, Dutch, and English each carved out portions of the islands for themselves, and some transported enslaved Africans to work on plantations there. In 1804, Haiti was the first Caribbean nation to gain independence, making Haiti the world's oldest black republic and the second oldest republic in the Western Hemisphere. The country's path to freedoms began as a slave rebellion, the Haitian Revolution, that was led by Toussaint

Costumed children at the 1998 DC Caribbean Carnival.

Louverture (*see also* **Haitian Flag Day**). Many other Caribbean nations gained their freedom from European nations during the 19th century. However, some are still governed by them today.

Creation of the Festival

The first DC Caribbean Carnival was held in 1993 and was celebrated until 2011. The not-for-profit organization that organized the event, DC Caribbean Carnival, Inc., sought to bring an authentic Caribbean-style parade to Washington, D.C. Additionally, organizers hoped to encourage cross cultural awareness of the Caribbean to the Washington metro area in an entertaining way and to educate both adults and youth about the arts, crafts, and culture of the Caribbean. In that first year, nine local bands participated in the parade during an event that drew about 150,000 spectators.

Observance

The DC Caribbean Carnival is held over the second week of July. The highlight of the festival takes place on the opening day: a five-hour-long Carnival Parade. Participation has increased to more than two dozen bands—steel bands, calypso, and soca, all culled locally—and about 5,000 masqueraders, whose colorful costumes are mostly homemade. The route begins on the corner of Georgia and Missouri Avenues in the N.W quadrant of the city, and proceeds to Banneker Field, which is located directly across the street from famed HBCU Howard University.

Banneker Field is the site where "De Savannah," or the International Marketplace, hosts local and international artisans, live entertainers, food vendors, and others. The carnival drew in excess of 300,000 people during its last year.

Contacts and Websites

DC Caribbean Carnival, Inc.
4809-A Georgia Ave., N.W., Ste. 112
Washington, DC 20011
202-726-2204
https://dccarnival.com

Destination DC
901 7th St., N.W., 4th Fl.
Washington, DC 20001-3719
202-789-7000; fax: 202-789-7037
http://www.washington.org

Further Reading

Carr, Robert T. *Black Nationals in the New World: Reading the African-American and West Indian Experience.* Durham, NC: Duke University Press, 2002.

Haviser, Jay B., ed. *African Sites: Archeology in the Caribbean.* Princeton, NJ: Marcus Wiener Publishers, 1999.

Denver Pan African Film Festival

Date Observed: Last week in April
Location: Denver, Colorado

The Denver Film Society and the Starz Entertainment Group co-sponsor the week-long Denver Pan African Film Festival each April. Held in Colorado's state capital, the festival hosts local, national, and international visitors who gather at this award-winning competitive showcase and educational exchange about black filmmaking.

Historical Background

Long before there were Pan African film festivals or motion pictures of any kind, the term "Pan Africanism" has signified the idea that Africans and Africans of the diaspora, wherever they are located, share a common history and culture and should unify in efforts to gain equality through social, political, and economic power. These concepts were expressed at the First Pan African Congress in London in 1900, and also at similar congresses in other countries later in the century.

Since the early 1900s in the United States, Pan Africanism has found a voice through nationalists, such as Marcus Garvey, and through such art forms as literature, music, dance, and films. (*See also* **African Film Festival; African World Festival in Detroit; African World Festival in Milwaukee; DanceAfrica; Ghanafest; Marcus Garvey's Birthday; Odunde Festival;** *and* **Pan African Film & Arts Festival**).

Creation of the Denver Festival

The first Denver Pan African Film Festival was held in 2000 and was organized under the auspices of the Pan African Arts Society, a Denver metro area non-profit organization that focuses on cultural arts as a means to bring about social change. Founder Ashara Saran Ekundayo calls herself an "activist artist," and she established the festival in order to showcase feature films, shorts, documentaries, videos, and other art forms from the African diaspora to prompt dialogue on social issues.

Observance

The Denver Pan African Film Festival extends a full week in April each year. Dozens of films from around the globe—North and South America, Europe, the Caribbean—are screened throughout the week. Juries present awards such as the SoulSpirit Award, given to a film director, producer, or actor whose work raises the social consciousness of audiences and prompts people to be socially responsible or to become activists.

The Denver festival also includes workshops, panel discussions, and an educational youth fest. In 2006, an African marketplace was added to garner exposure of black fine-art craftsmanship.

Contact and Website

Denver Film Society
1510 York St.
Denver, CO 80206
303-595-3456
http://www.denverfilm.org

Further Reading

Dernerstein, Robert. "Award, Family Await Cheadle in Denver." *Rocky Mountain News* (Denver, CO), April 29, 2005. http://www.infernofilm.com/comoviepress.html

Kennedy, Lisa. "A Festival Filled with Powerful Moments." DenverPost.com, November 23, 2005. https://www.denverpost.com/2005/11/23/a-festival-filled-with-powerful-moments/.

Down Home Family Reunion

Date Observed: Third weekend in August
Location: Richmond, Virginia

The Down Home Family Reunion in Richmond, Virginia, is an annual festival of African-American folklife held during the third weekend in August. The Reunion's events demonstrate and celebrate the connections between West African and African-American cultures.

Historical Background

The Down Home Family Reunion is presented by the Elegba Folklore Society, which was formed in 1990 to provide a forum for the diversity of African culture through the arts and to link West African and African-American cultural traditions. The society is named for the orisha, or deity, Esu Elegbara (eh-shew eh-leg-bah-rah), a spirit or force of nature in the tradition of the Yoruba people, a West African cultural group that speaks its own language.

According to Yoruba beliefs, Esu Elegbara (also known as "Ellegua") is a gate-keeper who opens the way to, and also guards the paths of, communication between the divine and humanity. *Elegba* in Yoruba means "messenger of the gods," a mythical messenger of destiny who keeps people connected. He also is known as a trickster who can open or close doors that lead to a happy or sorrowful life and said to know the fate of each person.

Creation of the Observance

The Elegba Folklore Society began the annual Down Home Family Reunion in 1991 with the support of the City of Richmond and various businesses. It also presents **Juneteenth** and **Kwanzaa** celebrations.

Observance

During the Down Home Family Reunion, more than 13,000 people take part in dance, oral traditions, music, children's events, down-home food, and crafts. Activities have included an oral historian with expertise in the late 1800s, who tells stories in rhyme about love and life; blues and reggae performances; African dance music; songs about life in Africa; gospel singers; and demonstrations of the chants and rhythms of railroad workers, who laid rail long before machinery was available to do the hard labor. Children can take part in making crafts, and a Heritage Market offers an assortment of unique items.

Contacts and Websites

Elegba Folklore Society's Cultural Center
101 E. Broad St.
Richmond, VA 23219
804-644-3900
http://efsinc.org

Richmond Region Tourism
401 N. Third St.
Richmond, VA 23219
800-370-9004
https://www.visitrichmondva.com

DuSable Museum Arts & Crafts Festival

Date Observed: Second weekend in July
Location: Chicago, Illinois

T he DuSable Museum of African American History in Chicago has presented the annual Arts & Crafts Festival since 1974. Each year, over
the second weekend in July, local artists and craftspeople exhibit works
that relate to African-American history and culture.

Historical Background

The DuSable Museum of African American History is the first and oldest
museum in the nation devoted to African-American cultures. In 1961, a group
of Chicago artists, among them artist and educator Margaret Goss Burroughs
and her husband Charles Burroughs, founded the museum. The museum site
was the Burroughs's home, a mansion that had once been a boardinghouse
for black railroad workers. First called the "Ebony Museum" and later named
the "Museum of Negro History and Art," it was designed to present black
history and culture, which were only slightly but mostly never included in
most museums and educational institutions of the time. The museum was
renamed again in 1968, after a black Haitian fur trader, Jean Baptiste Pointe
DuSable (1745–1818). Historical accounts indicate that DuSable was the first
non-native person to settle in Chicago.

After the Chicago Park District granted the museum use of a former administration building in Washington Park, the DuSable Museum of History and Art
moved to that location in 1973. It became a memorial to DuSable and a home
for permanent collections of such items as African and African-American
artifacts, rare books, slave documents, civil rights memorabilia, paintings, photographs, films, wood and ivory carvings, sculptures, and African masks and

statues that are collected on loan from individuals or institutions. Currently, the DuSable Museum has about 15,000 various memorials, including paintings, sculpture, print works, and historical memorabilia.

Creation of the Festival

In 1974, one year after the DuSable Museum moved to Washington Park in Chicago, the museum held its first festival, with eight artists participating. Margaret Burroughs and Sophie Wessell were among them, and the two decided to organize an annual event that would allow artists to exhibit their work without juries or critics. In addition, young artists from Chicago schools would be included.

In 1984, the curator, the late Ramon Price, established a Purchase Award Program in which a panel of judges recommended purchase of outstanding works for inclusion in the museum's collection of contemporary African-American art. The collection is loaned for exhibitions at such institutions as the University of Wisconsin at Milwaukee, Eastern Illinois University in Charleston, and Columbia College in Chicago. The festival serves as a homeplace for the local, national, and international artists to exhibit their fine art and unique handcrafted work. It features artists working in traditional, ethnic, and experimental fine arts and crafts related to African American themes, history, and culture.

Observance

The annual DuSable Museum Arts & Crafts Festival is held on the second weekend in July and continues to showcase local artistic talent. The festival is enhanced by some added features such as music, and food and market vendors, and offers traditional, ethnic, and experimental works. In recent years, almost 200 artists and craftspeople have taken part in the festival.

Besides the Arts & Crafts Festival, the DuSable Museum also conducts celebrations of **Juneteenth** and **Black Music Month** in June.

Contact and Website

DuSable Museum of African American History
740 E. 56th Pl.
Chicago, IL 60637
773-947-0600
http://www.dusablemuseum.org

Further Reading

Dickerson, Amina J. "DuSable Museum." Encyclopedia of Chicago, an online cooperative effort of the Chicago Historical Society, the Newberry Library and Northwestern University. http://www.encyclopedia.chicagohistory. org/pages/398.html.

Feldman, Eugene Pieter Romayn. *The Birth and the Building of the DuSable Museum.* Chicago: DuSable Museum Press, 1981.

Lindberg, Richard C. "DuSable, Jean Baptiste Pointe." In *African American Lives*, edited by Henry Louis Gates Jr. and Evelyn Brooks Higginbotham. New York: Oxford University Press, 2004.

Eastern Shore AFRAM Festival

Date Observed: Second weekend in August
Location: Seaford, Delaware

The annual Eastern Shore AFRAM Festival in Seaford, Delaware, takes place on the second weekend of August. "AFRAM" stands for "African American. Developing Cultural Awareness" and displaying African-American heritage and pride are two of the underlying reasons for the festival.

Historical Background

African-American festivals have been taking place on a widespread scale in the United States since the 1980s. Many of these festivals have been initiated to connect the past with the present in black communities and to foster understanding of the African diaspora and the contributions people of African descent have made worldwide. These festivals also provide opportunities for local black communities to display their talents and highlight their accomplishments.

Creation of the Festival

The Eastern Shore AFRAM Festival originated as "a big vision for a small county," according to its founder Councilwoman Pat Jones, the first African American to serve on the city council. It was designed to promote a positive outlook in the African-American community, and it has turned into one of the largest cultural events in Sussex County, Delaware.

The first Eastern Shore AFRAM festivals were held in the 1990s, but after 1999, there was a hiatus for four years. In 2003, Jones chaired a committee that resumed the event.

Sankofa

The term *sankofa* has been applied not only to performance companies (such as the Dover group and the Williams College Step Team) but also to newsletters about Africana and titles of films and books. According to Eric Kofi Acree of the Cornell University Library, *sankofa* stems from words in the pictorial writing system of the Akan people in Ghana, and means "one must return to the past in order to move forward." The Sankofa symbol is also associated with a proverb meaning "go back and fetch it" or "return to the source and fetch (learn)." A flying bird turning its head completely around to face backward is often used to symbolize Sankofa. The reason for using the symbol and/or term is to focus on the rediscovery of traditions that may be lost or forgotten and to give them meaning and significance in present-day life.

Observance

The festival has grown since its inception. The number of floats in the parade also increased, and the festival reflects a greater diversity of people—a goal the committee had hoped to accomplish. Activities include a 5k walk/ run, car show, cultural displays, a pageant with entrants competing for Little Miss and Mr. AFRAM titles, musical entertainment, games, and, of course, food.

A traditional West African ritual to honor elders is also part of the festival. The cultural hour for the year 2019 is handled by the Trinidad-n-Tobago Steel Drum Band, which is a performance company that focuses on African dance and percussion instruments. Other performances at the festival have included a Christian rapper and a rhythm and blues group. In 2019, the festival is celebrated with the theme of UJIMA, which is recognized as the ADINKRA symbol, taken from the seven principles of Kwanzaa. The term "UJIMA" stands for "Cooperative Work and Responsibility." The festival on the Eastern Shore celebrates and shares the history and the rich culture of the African-American African Diaspora community.

Contacts and Websites

Eastern Shore AFRAM Festival
P.O. Box 687
Seaford, DE 19973
302-628-1908
E-mail: pj@easternshoreafram.org
https://www.easternshoreafram.org

City of Seaford
414 High St.
P.O. Box 1100
Seaford, DE 19973
302-629-9173; fax: 302-629-9307
http://www.seafordde.com

Emancipation Day

Date Observed: January 1, September 22, and Other Dates
Location: Communities nationwide

On September 22, 1862, during the U.S. Civil War, then President Abraham Lincoln issued a preliminary proclamation to free slaves in states and parts of states "in rebellion against the United States." The famous Emancipation Proclamation became effective on January 1, 1863, and African Americans across the nation gathered together on the evening of that New Year (*see also* **Watch Night**) and on New Year's Day. Since the signing of the proclamation, Emancipation Day, sometimes called "Jubilee Day," has been observed on January 1 in many areas of the United States. Some communities celebrate September 22 as the anniversary of the preliminary proclamation. Others commemorate local anniversaries of emancipation, such as April 16 in Washington, D.C. (*see* **Emancipation Day in Washington, D.C.**), and May 29 in Upson County, Georgia.

Historical Background

Long before the Civil War began in 1861, abolitionists and pro-slavery advocates were embroiled in political, economic, moral, and religious conflicts over the institution of slavery. Anti-slavery groups such as the Society of Friends (Quakers) and Mennonites in Great Britain and colonial America were active during the 1700s. The first American abolitionist society was founded a year before the 1776 Continental Congress declared the colonies independent and free of British rule.

After the American Revolutionary War, political efforts to abolish slavery included an attempt by the U.S. Congress to ban slavery in the Northwest Territory, from which states would be formed to become part of the union. The proposal was defeated, but in the years during and following the Revolutionary War, whites and blacks in northern states noted the hypocrisy of fighting for

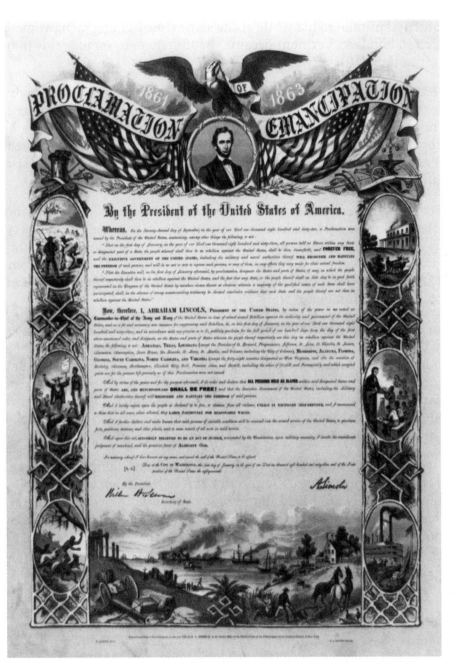

Artist W. Roberts produced this engraving around 1864 to celebrate President Lincoln's Emancipation Proclamation.

fundamental human rights while at the same time holding men, women, and children in bondage. Vermont became the first state to remedy this injustice when it outlawed slavery in 1777.

In 1787, the Free African Society (FAS) formed in Philadelphia, Pennsylvania, under the leadership of Absalom Jones, who became the first black pastor of the Episcopal Church, and Richard Allen, who founded the African Methodist Episcopal (AME) Church (*see also* **Founder's Day/Richard Allen's Birthday**). The FAS promoted abolition and provided financial and medical assistance for African Americans.

By 1804, all northern states had passed laws prohibiting slavery, but most of these laws allowed only gradual emancipation, which meant that slavery was slowly abolished over a set time period. With gradual emancipation, children born into slavery remained in bondage until a certain age, ranging from ages 21 to 28. In some cases, gradual emancipation meant being enslaved until the end of a specific number of work years.

Following the 1807 British example of banning the importation of slaves, the United States legally prohibited the slave trade on January 1, 1808. For some free-born African Americans this was a time to celebrate. Certainly that was the view of Reverend Absalom Jones, who urged that January 1 be an annual day of thanksgiving. During a worship service on January 1, 1808, his congregation at St. Thomas AME Church in Philadelphia, Pennsylvania, joined in a song of praise written especially for the celebration.

However, the 1808 ban did not stop smugglers from bringing tens of thousands more enslaved Africans into the country and selling them to southern cotton planters, especially after Eli Whitney's invention of the cotton gin, a device that removed seeds from cotton, made it possible to boost production. Slaves had previously performed this task by hand—a time-consuming job. As the demand for cotton grew, planters could increase their wealth by purchasing more slaves to plant and raise even more cotton.

Abolitionist Societies

Opponents of slavery continued to speak out and form abolitionist societies in most states, including some in the South, where an abolitionist movement flourished between 1816 and 1817. Some African Americans belonged to white organizations; others established many of their own abolitionist groups. In addition, dozens of African-American orators, preachers, and writers advanced the abolition cause.

By the 1830s, a widespread abolitionist movement was under way in the U.S. During the decade, an evangelistic fervor swept through the land, and Christians—black and white—began to denounce slavery as sinful and morally indefensible.

The American Anti-Slavery Society, established in 1833, was a major force in campaigns to eradicate human bondage. It was responsible for getting thousands of anti-slavery petitions signed and sent to the U.S. House of Representatives in 1836. But because of gag rules (procedures that limit or prevent debate on particular issues that were in effect at the time, Congress

---

A Speech Before the Ladies' Anti-Slavery Society

Anti-slavery societies of the 1830s and 1840s included numerous women's groups, such as the Ladies' Anti-Slavery Society of Philadelphia. In 1836, the group invited James Forten Jr., son of an outspoken black abolitionist, to present a speech. In a forceful and dramatic style, Forten urged the women to continue their anti-slavery efforts. He noted in part:

> It is not by force of arms that Abolitionists expect to remove one of the greatest curses that ever afflicted or disgraced humanity; but by the majesty of moral power. Oh! How callous, how completely destitute of feeling, must that person be, who thinks of the wrongs done to the innocent and unoffending captive, and not drop one tear of pity—who can look upon slavery and not shudder at its inhuman barbarities? It is a withering blight to the country in which it exists—a deadly poison to the soil on which it feeds, like a vulture, upon the vitals of its victims. But it is in vain that I attempt to draw a proper likeness of its horrors; it is far beyond the reach of my abilities to describe to you the endless atrocities which characterize the system. Well was it said by Thomas Jefferson, that "God has no attribute which can take sides with such oppression."

did not discuss proposals to end slavery. Free debate returned, however, when the gag rules were repealed in 1844.

Throughout the 1830s and 1840s, abolitionists published a great variety of materials to present the case against slavery. Newspapers, magazines, children's books, autobiographies of former slaves, advertisements and handbills announcing anti-slavery rallies, sheet music, and printed sermons were all part of the effort.

Whatever the abolitionist materials, they did little to persuade most southerners that the slave system should be outlawed. Instead, southerners argued that they needed slave labor to maintain the South's economy. Some also viewed slavery as a way to convert Africans to Christianity and to control bondspeople, whom they considered inferior.

As abolitionists increased their accusations that owning slaves was wrong, southerners resisted by attempting to ban anything and anyone from the North—books, mail, and people opposing slavery. Hostility also flared in the North. Pro-slavery gangs frequently attacked homes of people suspected of harboring runaway slaves, broke up anti-slavery meetings, and tried to destroy abolitionist newspapers. In 1837, for example, a mob in Illinois set fire to a warehouse for an abolitionist newspaper, killing editor Elijah Lovejoy, who was trying to guard his new printing press.

The Compromise of 1850

In 1850, the nation had become increasingly divided over the slavery issue, and tensions between the North and South mounted as western territories sought to enter the United States. California, for instance, wanted to join as a free state. The union then consisted of 30 states, and admitting California as a free state would tip the balance of 15 slave and 15 free states. The U.S. Senate had to decide not only California's fate, but also the status of other western lands.

After months of debate on the slavery issue, the Senate passed the Compromise of 1850, which was actually a series of laws that supposedly would settle North-South conflicts. The act provided that California would be admitted as a free state; western territories that included New Mexico, Nevada, Arizona, and Utah would be allowed to decide for themselves whether to apply for statehood as free or slave states; and the slave trade would be banned in

Washington, D.C. As a concession to the slave states, the Compromise also revised the 1793 Fugitive Slave Act to provide for more stringent enforcement.

The Fugitive Slave Act proved to be the most contentious of the statutes and the most devastating for African Americans—free or enslaved. The act mandated that citizens help capture runaway slaves and return them to the State or Territory from which such persons may have escaped or fled." Law officers were required to use all means necessary to carry out provisions of the act or face a fine of $1,000.

Along with escaped slaves, free African Americans in the North were captured and, without a trial or any legal recourse whatsoever, sent to slaveholders in the South. After passage of the law, hundreds of African Americans immediately fled to Canada. Between 1850 and 1860, an estimated 20,000 fugitives and free blacks escaped across the U.S.–Canada border. It was during this time that escaped slave Harriet Tubman returned to the South and led her family and others to freedom via the Underground Railroad (*see also* **Harriet Tubman Day** *and* **Sugar Grove Underground Railroad Convention**).

The Fugitive Slave Law prompted many abolitionists to become more active in the Underground Railroad. Abolitionists also became more vocal and took part in direct action to prevent the return of fugitives. In 1851, for example, abolitionists rescued an escaped slave named Shadrach from a Boston, Massachusetts, courtroom, and in Syracuse, New York, a crowd from an anti-slavery convention forced law officials to surrender captured runaway slave William Henry Jerry (*see* **Jerry Rescue Day**).

However, Anthony Burns, who fled from Virginia to Boston, met another fate in 1854. His owner hunted him down and had him arrested. While he was imprisoned inside the courthouse, about 2,000 anti-slavery citizens gathered and a small group managed to break down the door in an attempt to free Burns. The state militia and federal troops were called in to stand guard and await the decision to return Burns to his owner. Charlotte Forten, the sixteen-year-old granddaughter of black abolitionist James Forten, expressed disgust with a government that "cowardly assembles thousands of soldiers to satisfy the demands of slaveholders."

Escalating Conflicts

White sympathy toward fugitive slaves in the North could not counter the growing hostility in the South. Many southern planters believed that the activities of abolitionists were encouraging slaves to run away. They feared

149

as well that escaped slaves and free blacks were plotting attacks against white planters and industrialists.

Between 1850 and 1860, conflicts over the institution of slavery escalated. As the decade progressed, many abolitionists began to lose hope that slaves could be emancipated by peaceful or political means. Some of the events of the decade indicate not only the deep divisions within the nation but also the violence that was a prelude to the outbreak of the Civil War.

Consider reactions to the Kansas-Nebraska Act of 1854, which provided for the doctrine of "popular sovereignty." That meant people living in the Kansas-Nebraska Territory could decide for themselves whether they should be admitted to the Union as a slave or free state. Armed pro-slavery and anti-slavery forces rushed to Kansas to gain control and to determine the outcome. Bloody confrontations raged until 1861, when Kansas was admitted as a free state.

Another event that created great discord was the highly controversial decision of the U.S. Supreme Court in the Dred Scott case (*Dred Scott v. Sanford*, 1857). The case concerned Dred Scott, a slave whose owner years before had taken him from the slave state of Missouri to Illinois and the Wisconsin territory, where slavery was banned. Scott tried several times to gain his freedom. After returning to Missouri, he filed a lawsuit in 1847, claiming that since he had lived on free land, he should be free. In 1857 the Court declared that no matter where Scott had traveled, he was still a slave, and he did not have the right to sue because he was not a Missouri citizen. In the majority decision, the Court also determined that the U.S. Constitution did not give African Americans the right to citizenship, and territories had no power to abolish slavery until the people applied for statehood.

The decision delighted southerners who were convinced that slavery could now expand into the territories. Northerners promised a fight to overturn the ruling. In short, the rift between North and South widened further.

Slave rebellions and uprisings added to the debate. Armed slave revolts had already taken place during the early part of the 1800s, and rumors that blacks were plotting to kill whites were constantly circulating. In 1859, one of those plots became a reality, but it was initiated by a white man, John Brown. A Kansas abolitionist, Brown, along with a small group of followers, carried out a plan to seize the federal arsenal at Harpers Ferry, Virginia. Brown hoped to arm slaves for a rebellion. But slaves did not rise up, and Brown was captured a day after his attack. He was arrested, convicted of treason, and executed by hanging.

Some abolitionists declared that Brown was a martyr to the anti-slavery cause and called for slave revolts. This further alarmed people in the South, who began to talk about seceding—pulling out of the Union—as their only means to protect themselves.

During the presidential campaign of 1860, four major parties ran candidates for the presidency. Only the Republican Party was anti-slavery, albeit in a token

Uncle Tom's Cabin

According to some historians, anti-slavery opinions were bolstered in the North by the novel *Uncle Tom's Cabin*. The novel, which was first published in magazine serial format and then as a book in 1852, sold 300,000 copies worldwide within a year.

Written by Harriet Beecher Stowe, the novel tells the story of Uncle Tom, a pious slave who faithfully serves his owner. After his owner's death, Tom is sold to Simon Legree, a barbaric Yankee plantation owner who whips Tom to death. The story also revolves around other characters who are slaves, slaveholders, and traders, and depicts the evils of the American slavery system and the strength of slaves who have faith in God and Christianity.

Stowe, who lived in the free state of Ohio, was motivated to write the novel as a response to the Fugitive Slave Law and the repression of free blacks wherever they were located. She based her work on her contacts with Underground Railroad workers and slaveholding relatives in Kentucky.

The sentimental and emotional story of slave suffering and courage in the face of death had an enormous impact on readers and garnered sympathy for the abolitionist movement, which infuriated its opponents. In recent years, the book has been criticized for its racist stereotypes, many of which have carried over to this day. The term "Uncle Tom" is one example. This term has been used to negatively label a black person who is subservient to a white person. Critics also have denounced the book for its depiction of African Americans as childish, ignorant, and nonresistant. Still, in its time, the novel played a significant role in bringing about emancipation.

way. Republicans did not advocate abolition, but instead wanted to prevent the extension of slavery into the territories.

When Republican Abraham Lincoln was elected president, Southerners believed that the "Black Republicans," as the party sometimes was called, would violate states' rights and ban slavery. For many Southerners, the only recourse was secession. Even before Lincoln took office, South Carolina seceded in December 1860. Seven other southern states followed in February 1861, and formed the Confederate States of America, with its own military.

Lincoln took office in March 1861, and he still hoped to hold the Union together by political means. He moved cautiously, offering to reimburse slave-holders if they voluntarily freed their slaves over a gradual time period. This

This photo depicts a May 20 Emancipation Day celebration at Horseshoe Plantation, near Tallahassee, Florida, during the 1930s. On May 20, 1865, Union General Edward McCook announced and read the Emancipation Proclamation in Tallahassee—an anniversary that continues to be observed into the 21st century.

was an attempt to keep some slaveholding border states from seceding, but Lincoln's plan was soundly rejected.

In the meantime, Confederate forces began to take over federal arsenals and forts. When Confederates attacked Fort Sumter in South Carolina on April 13, 1861, civil war could no longer be avoided. The Union and Confederate soldiers would fight each other for four long years.

Many fugitive slaves fled to Union forces. The escaped slaves, abolitionists, and some members of Lincoln's administration began to pressure for emancipation, and in 1862 the U.S. Congress abolished slavery in the District of Columbia (see **Emancipation Day in Washington, D.C.**). Congress also outlawed slavery in western territories, setting the stage for Lincoln's Emancipation Proclamation. Although slaves in Confederate states were freed, the proclamation did not apply to slaves in Union areas or border states loyal to the Union. Slavery was not completely abolished until ratification of the 13th Amendment to the U.S. Constitution on February 1, 1865 (see **National Freedom Day**).

Creation of the Observance

Whether in slave quarters, fields, or towns and cities, wherever slaves received the news that they were free, celebrations occurred. Free African Americans gathered in the North on New Year's Eve to hold vigil. In Washington, D.C., where slaves were freed in 1862, African Americans gathered to celebrate. At one church, the pastor read the Emancipation Proclamation that was printed in the *Washington Evening Star*. "This was the signal for unrestrained celebration characterized by men squealing, women fainting, dogs barking, and whites and blacks shaking hands," according to historian John Hope Franklin, writing in *Prologue* magazine. He also noted that "the Washington celebrations continued far into the night. In the Navy Yard, cannons began to roar and continued for some time."

Some slave owners refused to tell their slaves about the proclamation immediately. In addition, news traveled so slowly that, in some locales, days or weeks went by before slaves knew they were free. Slaves in Upson County, Georgia, did not learn about the declaration of their freedom until May 29, 1863. In Texas, that news did not arrive until June 19, 1865, and the 19th eventually became a state holiday celebrating freedom (see **Juneteenth**).

The Emancipation Proclamation

January 1, 1863
By the President of the United States of America:

A Proclamation.

Whereas, on the twenty-second day of September, in the year of our Lord one thousand eight hundred and sixty-two, a proclamation was issued by the President of the United States, containing, among other things, the following, to wit:

"That on the first day of January, in the year of our Lord one thousand eight hundred and sixty-three, all persons held as slaves within any State or designated part of a State, the people whereof shall then be in rebellion against the United States, shall be then, thenceforward, and forever free; and the Executive Government of the United States, including the military and naval authority thereof, will recognize and maintain the freedom of such persons, and will do no act or acts to repress such persons, or any of them, in any efforts they may make for their actual freedom.

"That the Executive will, on the first day of January aforesaid, by proclamation, designate the States and parts of States, if any, in which the people thereof, respectively, shall then be in rebellion against the United States; and the fact that any State, or the people thereof, shall on that day be, in good faith, represented in the Congress of the United States by members chosen thereto at elections wherein a majority of the qualified voters of such State shall have participated, shall, in the absence of strong countervailing testimony, be deemed conclusive evidence that such State, and the people thereof, are not then in rebellion against the United States."

Now, therefore I, Abraham Lincoln, President of the United States, by virtue of the power in me vested as Commander-in-Chief, of the Army and Navy of the United States in time of actual armed rebellion against the authority and government of the United States, and as a fit and necessary war measure for suppressing said rebellion, do, on this first day of January, in the year of our Lord one thousand eight hundred and sixty-three, and in accordance with my purpose so to do publicly proclaimed for the full period of one hundred days, from the day first above mentioned, order and designate as the States and parts of States wherein the people thereof respectively, are this day in rebellion against the United States, the following, to wit: Arkansas, Texas, Louisiana, (except the Parishes of St. Bernard, Plaquemines, Jefferson, St. John, St. Charles, St. James Ascension, Assumption, Terrebonne, Lafourche, St. Mary, St. Martin, and Orleans, including the City of New Orleans) Mississippi, Alabama, Florida, Georgia, South Carolina, North Carolina, and Virginia, (except the forty-eight counties designated as West Virginia, and also the counties of Berkley, Accomac, Northampton, Elizabeth City, York, Princess Ann, and Norfolk, including the cities of Norfolk and Portsmouth[)], and which excepted parts, are for the present, left precisely as if this proclamation were not issued.

And by virtue of the power, and for the purpose aforesaid, I do order and declare that all persons held as slaves within said designated States, and parts of States, are, and henceforward shall be free; and that the Executive government of the United States, including the military and naval authorities thereof, will recognize and maintain the freedom of said persons.

And I hereby enjoin upon the people so declared to be free to abstain from all violence, except in necessary self-defence; and I recommend to them that, in all cases when allowed, they labor faithfully for reasonable wages.

And I further declare and make known that such persons of suitable condition will be received into the armed service of the United States to garrison forts, positions, stations, and other places, and to man vessels of all sorts in said service.

And upon this act, sincerely believed to be an act of justice, warranted by the Constitution, upon military necessity, I invoke the considerate judgment of mankind, and the gracious favor of Almighty God.

In witness whereof, I have hereunto set my hand and caused the seal of the United States to be affixed.

Done at the City of Washington, this first day of January, in the year of our Lord one thousand eight hundred and sixty-three, and of the Independence of the United States of America the eighty-seventh.

By the President: ABRAHAM LINCOLN

WILLIAM H. SEWARD, Secretary of State.

Observance

Following the first Emancipation Day celebration, the anniversary was widely commemorated in the 20th century. In 1916, for example, a Columbus, Ohio, newspaper announced a "monstrous" celebration of the Emancipation Proclamation.

Over the years, musicians composed Emancipation Day songs that were performed at celebrations. One composition was titled "On Emancipation Day," with words by poet Paul Laurence Dunbar and music by Will Marion Cook. For the 50th anniversary of emancipation, James Weldon Johnson wrote a poem titled "Fifty Years" that the *New York Times* published on January 1, 1913.

Celebrations of emancipation have not always been held on January 1, however. In Washington, D.C., April 16 commemorates the day slaves were freed in the nation's capital. African Americans in Maryland celebrate November 1, the anniversary of the day the state constitution abolished slavery in 1864. Since 1863, an annual Emancipation Day celebration in Upson County, Georgia, has taken place on May 29, the day slaves there learned of their freedom.

Further Reading

Blight, David W. "Emancipation." In *The African-American Experience: Selections from the Five-Volume Macmillan Encyclopedia of African-American Culture and History*, edited by Jack Salzman. New York: Macmillan, 1998.

Fishel, Leslie H., Jr., and Benjamin Quarles, eds. *The Negro American: A Documentary History.* Glenview, IL: Scott, Foresman and Company, 1968.

Franklin, John Hope. *The Emancipation Proclamation.* 1963. Reprint. Garden City, NY: Doubleday & Company, 1994.

———. "The Emancipation Proclamation: An Act of Justice." *Prologue*, a quarterly publication of the National Archives and Records Administration, Summer 1993. http://www.archives.gov/publications/prologue/1993/summer/emancipation-proclamation.html.

Kachun, Mitch. *Festivals of Freedom: Memory and Meaning in African American Emancipation Celebrations, 1808–1915.* Amherst: University of Massachusetts Press, 2003.

McKissack, Patricia C., and Fredrick L. McKissack. *Days of Jubilee: The End of Slavery in the United States.* New York: Scholastic, 2003. (young adult)

Wiggins, William H., Jr. *O Freedom! Afro-American Emancipation Celebrations.* Knoxville: University of Tennessee Press, 2000.

Emancipation Day in Hutchinson, Kansas

Date Observed: Early August
Location: Hutchinson, Kansas

The Emancipation Day celebration in Hutchinson, Kansas, commemorates the abolition of slavery. Originally celebrated in Atchison, Kansas, on September 22—the anniversary of President Abraham Lincoln's preliminary proclamation of 1862—the event eventually moved to Hutchinson, and organizers rescheduled the festival to be held in August.

Historical Background

During and after the Reconstruction period (1867–1877), when the federal government and local Republicans governed former Confederate states, the majority of freed African Americans did not have equality or protection from discrimination. Former slaves worked on plantation lands as tenant farmers (renters), often paying their rent with a portion of their crops. These arrangements left black farmers and their families poor, since white owners continued to own the land and tools, and demanded payments that left many barely able to subsist.

In general, black males were able to vote and some were elected to government offices. But the majority faced white racist attitudes and groups intent on destroying black voting rights, educational opportunities, and economic advances. During a period known as "redemption," southern supremacists—those who believed whites were superior to blacks—fought to overthrow Reconstruction policies. Organizations such as the Ku Klux Klan terrorized African Americans with arsons, whippings, and murders.

Freed blacks in the South feared they would once again be in the same situation that had existed during slavery, and in 1879 thousands migrated to

Kansas, where they could find refuge. During what was called the "Kansas Fever Exodus," an estimated 15,000 to 20,000 African Americans left the South for Kansas, where they hoped to claim free land as provided in the Homestead Act of 1862. The Act allowed people to select a plot owned by the federal government, live on and cultivate the land, and after five years, receive a deed for the property.

Some "Exodusters," as these African Americans were called, established their colonies in Kansas (*see also* **Homecoming Emancipation Celebration**). Others settled in towns like Topeka, Atchison, and Hutchinson.

Creation of the Observance

During the late 1800s, African Americans from across Kansas and nearby states attended an Emancipation celebration in Atchison, Kansas. The event was called the "Lincoln Day Celebration," and it was celebrated on September 22, the anniversary of the day President Abraham Lincoln issued his preliminary Emancipation Proclamation in 1862. But in 1889, organizers decided to hold the Emancipation Day festival in Hutchinson, Kansas, because of its central location in the state. By the 1930s, the observance was held in early August. It is possible that the August date was chosen in remembrance of the **West Indies Emancipation** of August 1, 1838, but this is not verified by available records.

In 1931, Hutchinson Mayor I. E. Lewis Oswald proclaimed August 4 "a legal holiday for all members of the Negro race in the city of Hutchinson" and expressed "admiration for their efforts toward their won advancement and their unselfish contribution to the welfare and happiness of all people." The Emancipation Proclamation Day Celebration Committee started in 1936 to celebrate the abolition of slavery under a proclamation by former President Abraham Lincoln that took effect in 1863 according to a proclamation created by the City of Hutchinson.

Observances

Throughout the 1900s and into the 21st century, the Hutchinson Emancipation Day celebrations have been launched with a parade. Festivities have included a barbecue picnic, baseball game, basketball tournament, and other sporting events (such as boxing and wrestling matches), bathing beauty and diving contests at the municipal pool, and an evening dance. Well-known musicians, such as the famed Lionel Hampton Orchestra, have played for the dances. The event has grown over the years with an increased number of activities and wider community involvement for the three-day celebration. Some of the highlights of the event are a jazz concert, art show, gospel music fest, and a golf tournament.

Contacts and Websites

City of Hutchinson
125 E Ave. B
P.O. Box 1567
Hutchinson, KS 67501
620-694-2611; fax: 620-694-2673
http://www.hutchgov.com

Hutchinson Emancipation Day Committee, Inc.
P.O. Box 701
Hutchinson, KS 67504-0701
620-663-6673 (or) 620-669-3931
http://www.shopkansas.net/eday/misc.html

Hutchinson/Reno County Chamber of Commerce
P.O. Box 519
117 N. Walnut
Hutchinson, KS 67504
620-662-3391; fax: 620-662-2168
www.hutchchamber.com

Further Reading

Blight, David W. "Emancipation." In *The African-American Experience: Selections from the Five-Volume Macmillan Encyclopedia of African-American Culture and History*, edited by Jack Salzman. New York: Macmillan, 1998.
Leonnig, Carol D. "Celebrating the Day Freedom Arrived." *Washington Post*, April 17, 2005.

Emancipation Day in Washington, D.C.

Date Observed: April 16
Location: Washington, D.C.

Emancipation Day celebrates the freedom of more than 3,000 slaves in the District of Columbia on April 16. On that date in 1862, President Abraham Lincoln signed the Compensated Emancipation Act, which freed enslaved persons in the District eight months before the president issued the Emancipation Proclamation. The day became an official holiday in Washington, D.C., in 2005.

Historical Background

The District of Columbia Emancipation Act of 1862 freed all slaves in the District and granted compensation of up to $300 for each slave to loyal Unionist slaveholders. The law also provided $100 to each former slave who voluntarily left the United States for colonies in Africa.

The proposal that African Americans emigrate to Africa had been argued since the 1700s by both blacks and whites. The American Colonization Society (ACS) was founded in 1816. Made up primarily of prominent white men, the ACS persuaded some black leaders to promote the cause. They contended that blacks could succeed in Africa but could not in America.

A small number of African Americans did emigrate to West Africa and settle in a colony named "Liberia" on land that the ACS purchased. However, most African Americans were opposed to colonization plans. They believed that America was their country, a nation they had helped build and for which they had fought and died. This attitude prevailed when the 1862 Emancipation Act passed, and the majority of former slaves did not emigrate. Yet colonization

CELEBRATION OF THE ABOLITION OF SLAVERY IN THE DISTRICT OF COLUMBIA BY THE COLORED PEOPLE, IN WASHINGTON, April 19, 1866.—[SKETCHED BY F. DIELMAN.]

This 1866 sketch by Frederick Dielman illustrates the first Emancipation Day celebration in Washington, D.C., on April 19, 1866. It was published in Harper's Weekly, May 12, 1866.

proposals continued, and evolved into the Back-to-Africa movement of the 1900s (*see also* **Marcus Garvey's Birthday**).

Creation of the Holiday

The first Emancipation Day celebration in Washington, D.C., was held in 1866. Thousands of marchers wound their way through downtown and stopped at Franklin Square for speeches. Over 10,000 spectators were part of the event. A parade was held thereafter each year until 1901.

In 2002, then D.C. Councilman Vincent B. Orange Sr. introduced a bill to make Emancipation Day a legal public holiday in the District. He and others believed the day should be memorialized, and it became an official public holiday in 2005.

Observance

The first observance as a public holiday took place over the weekend of April 14 through April 17, 2005. A parade and festival commemorated this event, which also included step shows, poetry, choir performances, and a variety of activities for children. One of the celebrities in attendance was Frederick Douglass IV, the great-great-grandson of Frederick Douglass, the famous abolitionist who was partly responsible for persuading President Lincoln to abolish slavery in the nation's capital (*see also* **Frederick Douglass Day**).

Contacts and Websites

"Emancipation Day"
District of Columbia Mayor's Office
John A. Wilson Bldg.
1350 Pennsylvania Ave., N.W.
Washington, DC 20004
202-727-2643
E-mail: eom@dc.gov
https://mayor.dc.gov/release/
mayor-bowser-announces-2019-dc-emancipation-day-festivities

Franklin Square/Emancipation Day Parade
"Treasures of Congress," an online exhibit at the National Archives and Records Administration
8601 Adelphi Rd.
College Park, MD 20740
866-272-6272 (or) 301-837-2000
E-mail: inquire@nara.gov
https://www.archives.gov/college-park

Further Reading

Blight, David W. "Emancipation." In *The African-American Experience: Selections from the Five-Volume Macmillan Encyclopedia of African-American Culture and History*, edited by Jack Salzman. New York: Macmillan, 1998.
Leonnig, Carol D. "Celebrating the Day Freedom Arrived." *Washington Post,* April 17, 2005.

Festival Sundiata

Date Observed: Mid-June
Location: Seattle, Washington

Festival Sundiata (Soon-jah-tah) is an African and African-American cultural arts festival held since 1981 in Seattle, Washington. Presented in mid-June, the event brings together the people of African descent in the Pacific Northwest as well as those of other cultural backgrounds.

Historical Background

The festival was named after a 13th-century king of the Mali Empire in West Africa, Sundiata Keita (1210–1260). He was known for reigning over a flourishing economic and cultural period of the kingdom.

Legends about the king have been passed on for centuries. According to the stories, Sundiata was the son of the Mandingo king Nare Fa Maghan and his second wife. The prophecy said that the second wife would produce a child who would become the greatest king of Mali. However, Sundiata's childhood did not bode well for someone who would be king. He was sickly and developed slowly; he still could not walk at the age of seven. Yet Maghan declared Sundiata heir to the throne, a decision that angered Maghan's first wife, mother of the king's first son. After Maghan died, the first son, a teenager, was placed on the throne.

The first wife berated Sundiata's mother for having a handicapped child. Then, in a miraculous effort, Sundiata was able to stand and walk. By the time he was 10 years old, Sundiata appeared to be a threat to the teenage king, and the first wife hatched a plot to kill him. But Sundiata's mother fled with her son and two other children to another kingdom hundreds of miles away.

In exile, Sundiata developed in physical and mental strength and became a powerful fighter. He eventually assembled an army and marched on Mali,

163

This book by D. T. Niane tells the story of Sundiata and the rise of the Mali Empire. Originally published in English in 1965, Niane wrote that he heard this version of the epic from a griot (an African oral historian) named Djeli Mamadou Kouyate.

which was no longer controlled by his half-brother but had been conquered by another king. Sundiata and his army took back the territory and set up the foundation for an empire.

Creation of the Festival

In 1981, Terry Morgan, CEO and founder of Modern Enterprises, a Seattle promotion company, and the Seattle Center created Festival Sundiata to gather African Americans in the Pacific Northwest for a celebration of African heritage. Unlike some other cities in the United States, Seattle's black population is scattered throughout the city and surrounding areas and makes up only seven percent of the population. Thus, the festival provides an opportunity for African Americans and Africans to meet and participate in a shared cultural event.

Observance

Traditional African drumming and dance open Festival Sundiata. During the weekend, attendees can visit a black art exhibition with paintings, sculptures, quilts, photographs, and multi-media works. They can hear tributes to black professionals and black pioneers; enjoy gospel, hip hop, jazz, rap, rhythm, and blues music; and watch cooking demonstrations by top barbecuers Smokin' Black Chefs of the Northwest. Children's activities, such as mask-making and storytelling, are part of the festival as well.

On February 11 1990, the first day of the festival that year, anti-Apartheid leader Nelson Mandela was freed after 27 years of imprisonment in South Africa. Mandela went on to negotiate the end of Apartheid in South Africa and to become the country's first black president. Attendees were ecstatic at the news, which occasioned a joyful beginning to the festival that year, according to the founder Terry Morgan.

The festival showcases art, education, and entertainment depicting the perspectives, culture, and history of African descent people of African descent. The Sundiata African American Cultural Association (SAACA) offers a platform to showcase the mix of creative skills for seasoned and new artists. The organization aims for year-round promotion, encouragement, and support of public interest in traditional and contemporary African America Heritage, culture, arts, and history. Through the support of over 150 volunteers, Sundiata showcases native and regional entertainment such as art and photography exhibits, retail and food merchants, and a dynamic children's place.

Contact and Website
Sundiata African American Cultural Association
P.O. Box 24723
Seattle, WA 98124-0723
866-505-6006; fax: 206-420-6184
E-mail: info@festivalSundiata.org
http://www.festivalsundiata.org

Further Reading
Banner, Ellen M. "Festival Sundiata Brings African-American Community Together." *Seattle Times*, February 20, 2006. http://seattletimes.nwsource.com/html/home/.
Holdcroft, Leslie. "Festival Sundiata: It's a Fun Time of African and African American Culture Appreciation." *Seattle Post-Intelligencer*, February 17, 2006. http://seattlepi.nwsource.com/lifestyle/259786_fam17.html.

Fillmore Jazz Festival

Date Observed: First weekend of July
Location: San Francisco, California

The Fillmore Jazz Festival is a free outdoor event held on the Saturday and Sunday of the first week of July. This is the largest free jazz festival on the West Coast, drawing over 100,000 visitors over the Independence Day (July 4) weekend and blending art and soul in one of the country's most unique neighborhoods.

Historical Background

San Francisco's ethnically diverse Fillmore neighborhood has a long and colorful history. Known as "the Fillmore," the neighborhood has been the scene of important moments in jazz and rock music history. After San Francisco was devastated by a major fire and earthquake in 1906, rebuilding efforts transformed Fillmore Street into an entertainment district. Many theaters were built for public performances, and young artists such as Al Jolson began their careers there in the 1920s and 1930s.

Jazz reigned on Fillmore Street throughout the World War II years. Dozens of jazz nightclubs opened on Fillmore Street. These clubs featured performances by well-known artists such as Ella Fitzgerald, Count Basie, Duke Ellington, John Coltrane, Charlie Parker, Louis Armstrong, and Billie Holiday (*see also* **Charlie Parker Jazz Festival** *and* **Satchmo SummerFest**). During the 1960s, the neighborhood became a haven for artists representing all forms of entertainment, including writers, actors, and musicians of all types.

The Fillmore has developed into one of the most culturally diverse neighborhoods in the United States, and become home to communities of Filipino, Mexican, African-American, Japanese, Russian, and Jewish residents. The

166

neighborhood, which has always included a mix of homes and businesses, was revitalized by an infusion of new development in the 1980s. In 1999 the Fillmore Jazz Preservation District was dedicated in recognition of the street's history as a cultural landmark. The neighborhood now hosts a wide variety of gourmet restaurants, boutiques, and specialty shops, including Marcus Books, the nation's largest African-American bookstore. Today, Fillmore Street continues its long tradition of celebrating art and culture by hosting numerous festivals and street fairs throughout the year.

African Americans and Jazz

Jazz began as a distinctly African-American musical genre, developing from two older styles of African-American music—the blues and ragtime. The roots of the jazz sound can be traced even farther back to African rhythms, drums, call-and-response singing, foot-stomping, and hand clapping. These musical elements became part of the essential foundation of jazz music. They were layered with more complex sounds to create the modern variations of jazz heard today.

The first African-American jazz bands were formed in New Orleans, Louisiana, in the early 1900s. By the 1920s, jazz clubs were opening in many larger cities such as Chicago, New York, and Los Angeles. Once jazz spread geographically, rather than remaining concentrated mostly in one city, different forms of jazz music began to emerge. African-American musicians created new styles of jazz as the genre evolved. Louis Armstrong pioneered the jazz solo in the 1920s, and in the 1930s, musicians like Duke Ellington and Count Basie popularized the big band swing jazz sound. By the mid-1940s, Dizzy Gillespie, Charlie Parker, and Thelonius Monk were focusing on smaller bands and an innovative performance style that became known as bebop. The 1960s saw the emergence of fusion, free jazz, and cool jazz that was played by such artists as Miles Davis and Ornette Coleman. More recently, jazz musicians like Wynton Marsalis are reviving the more traditional styles heard in the early days of jazz.

Creation of the Festival

The Fillmore Merchants Association helped to launch the first Fillmore Jazz Festival in 1985. The festival was intended to celebrate the roots of jazz and the importance of the Fillmore Street nightclubs during the early days of jazz music. In its first year, the festival was held on three blocks of Fillmore Street and showcased all forms of jazz from fusion to Latin, as well as jazz standards.

Observance

Performers representing the entire spectrum of jazz music are showcased during the two-day event. A wide variety of musicians perform on several different stages and admission to the event is free. The music performance is interspersed with fine-art displays, craft vendors, and gourmet food. The music festival takes place on Fillmore Street in San Francisco and covers an entire 12-block area between Eddy Street and Jackson Street. The 34th annual festival started on Saturday, June 29, and continued to Sunday, June 30, 2019, from 10 A.M. to 6 P.M. daily.

Contacts and Websites

Hartmann Studios
1150 Brickyard Cove Rd., Ste. 202
Point Richmond, CA 94801
www.hartmannstudios.com

Steven Restivo Event Services, Inc
P.O. Box 151017
San Rafael, CA 94915
800-310-6563; fax: 415-456-6436
https://www.sresproductions.com/contact

Further Reading

"A Fair to Remember: Throngs Shop, Eat, Bounce Along to Jazz at the Fifteenth Annual Festival Despite Cold." *San Francisco Examiner*, July 2, 2000.
Goines, Leonard. "Jazz." In *The African-American Experience: Selections from the Five-Volume Macmillan Encyclopedia of African-American Culture and History*, edited by Jack Salzman. New York: Macmillan, 1998.
"Music: Major African American Musical Forms." *New York Public Library African American Desk Reference*. New York: John Wiley & Sons, 1999.

Football Classics

Date Observed: Varies
Location: Varies

Annualy, historically black colleges and universities (HBCU) football games, known as "Classics," are held at various locations throughout the country. Most Classics take place as part of a weekend full of social activities including reunions, parades, and marching-band competitions.

Historical Background

Football rivalry is a tradition as old as the game itself, and many Classics were formed around a longstanding competition between the two schools. In these Classics, the same two schools play each other every year. The Turkey Day Classic, held on Thanksgiving, has played out the traditional rivalry between Alabama State University and Tuskegee University for more than 94 years. The Orange Blossom Classic began as a contest between Florida A&M and Howard University in 1933. Other examples of this type of Classic include the Morehouse–Tuskegee Classic, the Southern Heritage Classic played by Jackson State University and Tennessee State University, the Atlanta Football Classic played by Florida A&M and Tennessee State University, the Bayou Classic played by Grambling State University and Southern University, and many more.

Other Classics are hosted by the same team every year, but the match is against a different opponent each time. These games are normally always played in the same location. Still other Classics feature two different teams each year, but again, usually in the same location. These Classics are similar in concept to the various postseason bowl games played around the country, but include all the extra activities normally associated with football Classics. The Circle City Classic in Indianapolis, Indiana, is one of the largest Classics of this type (*see* **Indiana Black Expo's Summer Celebration**).

Creation of the Observance

It is unclear when the first football Classic game was played between African-American collegiate teams, although Classics were being played as early as 1924. In that year, Alabama State played Tuskegee in the first Turkey Day Classic held in Montgomery, Alabama. Since then, numerous Classics have been created and many traditions have formed around these events. Far more than just another college football game, the Classics give participating schools a chance to showcase the African-American college experience.

African Americans in the Early Days of Football

Football became a popular sport in the United States in the late 1800s, and African-American players immediately excelled at the game. The first African Americans to play football held positions on the teams of white universities, which were generally the only organizations with enough money to have teams at that time. The first football game between HBCUs took place in North Carolina in 1892 (Biddle defeated Livingstone, 4-0). However, it would be nearly 20 years later before most HBCUs would be able to establish football teams.

During the early years of the sport, African-American players endured racial discrimination on and off the field. African-American students who attended white colleges and universities were not allowed to live in dormitories, and the cost of living off campus added to the financial burden of going to school. Some players enrolled in white colleges anyway, specifically because they wanted to play football, only to be told that they would not be allowed to join the team. Some schools limited the number of African Americans allowed on the team to only one or two. If they were accepted on the team, African-American players would have to sit out a game if the opposing team was segregated and refused to play against them. African Americans also often suffered brutal treatment in the course of the violent game, as white players sometimes took the opportunity to act on racial hatred. Rough tackles resulting in broken bones or even more serious injuries were quite common. In spite of all this, African Americans continued to play and to distinguish themselves as football athletes mainly because, at that time, there were no other real opportunities for African-American participation in major competitive team sports.

African Americans won more places on collegiate teams during the 1920s. In the 1930s, dozens of African Americans playing for white colleges earned reputations as football stars. By this time, African-American colleges had created their own southern football conference, featuring many outstanding and talented players. Teams at Morgan College (now Morgan State University) and Tuskegee Institute (now Tuskegee University) dominated black college football through the 1930s and early 1940s. Interest in football at HBCUs continued to grow and eventually developed into a tradition of annual matches known as Classics.

The Florida A&M University "Marching 100" marching band.

Observances

Numerous Classics are held all over the country each year, with many occurring over Labor Day weekend or on Thanksgiving Day. Dates, locations, and schedules for the games and related events are determined by the participating schools and vary from year to year. Football Classics are attended by thousands of people, with most games selling out far in advance.

The football game is the focal point of a weekend full of social, cultural, and educational activities. There is usually a large parade with floats, marching bands, and appearances by various dignitaries and celebrities. At half-time or immediately after the game, there is often a battle of the bands, which pits the rival schools' marching bands against each other in competition. Most Classics include tailgate parties, step shows, pep rallies, and concerts given by popular artists. Educational activities often include college preparation workshops, college recruiting fairs, and job or career fairs. Charitable activities include fundraisers and scholarship award ceremonies. Some Classics also include a beauty pageant, golf tournament, football and cheerleading clinics, prayer and worship services, awards and recognition programs, reunions, and special luncheons or dinners.

Contact and Website

Bayou Classic
1433 N. Claiborne Ave.
New Orleans, LA 70112
504-827-1892; fax: 504-455-7103
E-mail: info@mybayouclassic.com
http://www.mybayouclassic.com

Founder's Day/Richard Allen's Birthday

Date Observed: Mid-February
Location: AME churches worldwide

F ounder's Day in African Methodist Episcopal (AME) churches marks the birthday of Richard Allen on February 14. He founded the Bethel AME Church in Philadelphia, Pennsylvania, which was dedicated in 1794. AME churches across the United States and around the globe commemorate Founder's Day, usually on or around Allen's birth date.

Historical Background

Born a slave in Philadelphia on February 14, 1760, Richard Allen and his family became the property of Stokley Sturgis, a resident of Dover, Delaware, in 1768. Sturgis allowed Allen to attend Methodist meetings held by itinerant preachers. This exposure led Allen to convert to Methodism, a religion founded by John Wesley who was steadfastly opposed to slavery. After listening to a Methodist preacher, Sturgis also converted and became convinced that slavery was morally wrong. Because Sturgis was in debt, he offered to let Allen buy his freedom for $2,000.

Richard Allen worked at various jobs over several years to pay Sturgis. After he gained his freedom in the 1780s, Allen became a Methodist circuit rider, preaching without pay to blacks and whites in several states. He was asked to preach to African-American church members at St. George's Methodist Church in Philadelphia, and he eventually settled in the city. He worked as a shoemaker to support himself and his wife, Flora (who died in 1791), and later his second wife, Sarah, and the couple's six children.

In 1787, Allen helped form the Free African Society of Philadelphia, a mutual aid organization. When he learned two years later that the nondenominational

This lithograph, produced around 1876, presents a portrait of Richard Allen (center), circled by other bishops of the AME Church. Their portraits are framed by places and scenes associated with the AME Church, such as Wilberforce University (top left) and the Payne Institute (top right).

society planned to become an affiliate of the Episcopal Church, Allen's dedication to Methodism prompted him to leave the organization.

Allen continued to preach at St. George's, increasing the membership of black parishioners. Because of the growing number of black members, the white congregation became uneasy. In response, Allen requested a separate church for African Americans so they could worship in their own spontaneous and traditional ways. Instead, the white leaders decided to increase the seating in the church by constructing a new balcony over an existing one. African Americans helped build the new gallery and then were forced to sit there rather than in the older gallery over the main part of the church. This segregation angered Allen, but he stayed with St. George's until one Sunday in November 1787.

On that day, black members, including Reverend Absalom Jones (who later became the first black Episcopal priest in the United States), were on their knees praying in the gallery when a church official pulled Jones by the arm and ordered him and the others to get up and leave. Allen, Jones, and other African Americans not only left the area, they left the church and founded their own place of worship.

"Let Us Pray"

Years after being forcefully removed from St. George's Methodist Church, Richard Allen wrote about the incident:

> When the colored people began to get numerous in attending the church, they moved us from the seats we usually sat on and placed us around the wall, and on Sabbath morning we went to church, and the sexton stood at the door, and told us to go in the gallery . . . we would see where to sit. We expected to take the seats over the ones we formerly occupied below . . . just as we got to the seats, the elder said, "Let us pray." We had not been long upon our knees before I heard considerable scuffling and low talking. I raised my head and saw one of the trustees H— M— having hold of the Rev. Absalom Jones, pulling him up off of his knees, and saying, "You must get up—you must not kneel here." Mr. Jones replied, "Wait until prayer is over." Mr. H— M— said, "No, you must get up now, or I will call for aid and force you away." . . . With that, he beckoned to one of the other trustees, Mr. L— S— to come to his assistance. He came and went to William White [another prominent black member] to pull him up. By this time prayer was over, and we all went out of the church in a body, and they were no more plagued with us in the church.

Allen and others who left St. George's rented a vacant store to use for worship services for a time. While Jones went on to lead an Episcopalian congregation, Allen remained a Methodist and established his church on a plot of land that he had purchased years earlier. The church was dedicated in 1794 as Bethel African Methodist Episcopal Church, frequently called Mother Bethel Church.

Yet, the church was not completely free of conflicts with St. George's. Pastors and trustees at St. George's wanted to force Allen to bow to their authority and tried to control financial affairs of Allen's church; in one instance, they attempted to take over church property. But Allen was determined to maintain

Adding Insult to Injury

In 1793, a yellow fever epidemic hit Philadelphia, killing thousands. Because of the erroneous belief that African Americans were less likely to get the disease, the mayor of Philadelphia and prominent physician Dr. Benjamin Rush asked Richard Allen and Absalom Jones to help victims. In spite of their fears, Allen and Jones enlisted the help of other blacks to visit homes and to aid the suffering. They also helped remove the dead. Yet their efforts were attacked by a Philadelphia publisher Mathew Carey. He accused African Americans of making a profit on the sick and stealing from victims' homes.

The mayor placed ads in newspapers defending the African Americans and criticizing Carey. Besides, Allen and Jones published a pamphlet titled *A Narrative of the Proceedings of the Black People, during the Late Awful Calamity in Philadelphia, in the Year 1793: And a Refutation of some Censures, Thrown upon them in some late Publications*. In the pamphlet the authors refuted Carey's arguments and pointed out that they had saved the lives of hundreds of people, adding:

> We feel ourselves sensibly aggrieved by the censorious epithets of many, who did not render the least assistance in the time of necessity, yet are liberal of their censure of us, for the prices paid for our services, when no one knew how to make a proposal to anyone they wanted to assist them. At first, we made no charge, but let it to those we served in removing their dead, to give what they thought fit—we set no price until the reward was fixed by those we had served. After paying the people we had to assist us, our compensation is much less than many will believe.

The pamphlet also included detailed listings of cash the men and their workers received for burying the dead and their contaminated beds. For coffins they "received nothing."

a church that allowed African Americans to handle their affairs while subscribing to Methodism. A lawsuit that reached the Pennsylvania Supreme Court eventually decided the outcome. The court ruled on January 1, 1816, that Allen's church was legally independent.

Blacks in other states followed Allen's example and established independent African Methodist churches. Allen oversaw the rapid growth of the AME's Mother Church in Philadelphia, which grew to 7,500 members in the 1820s.

Several months later, at Allen's request, ministers of African-American churches from Maryland, New Jersey, and Pennsylvania met in Philadelphia to form the African Methodist Episcopal Church. The representatives elected Allen as the first bishop of the denomination, which quickly expanded across the United States and to other countries, such as Canada and Haiti. The denomination became, by all accounts, the most significant black institution in the 19th century. By the 21st century, the AME had more than 6,000 churches and over 2 million members.

Legacy

During his lifetime, Richard Allen's achievements went beyond establishing the AME church. He was a leader in the community and helped form numerous organizations established to improve the lives of African Americans, among them schools for black children. During the War of 1812 (1812–1814)—a nearly forgotten war waged against Great Britain to control the seas—the British threatened to attack Philadelphia. Allen, Jones, and others recruited black soldiers to serve, primarily with the U.S. Navy. Allen also wrote pamphlets and preached sermons against slavery.

In 1830, Allen presided over the first National Negro Convention in the Bethel Church, which was convened to encourage improvement in African-American lives through education, the pursuit of professional occupations, and resistance to oppression. From the convention, the American Society of Free Persons of Color was formed. The society published a document, signed by Richard Allen, that included an "address to the free persons of color," criticizing the American Colonization Society that advocated relocating free blacks to Africa. At first, Allen had not opposed society but later concluded that African Americans who left the United States would be forsaking their brothers and sisters in slavery.

Allen died in Philadelphia in 1831. Since then, he has been honored by religious, educational, and cultural institutions that bear his name. These include the Greater Allen Cathedral of New York; the Allen Temple in Cincinnati, Ohio; the Richard Allen Cultural Center in Leavenworth, Kansas; the Richard Allen Center for Culture and Art in New York City; and the Richard Allen Museum that is part of Bethel Church in Philadelphia.

Creation of the Observance

AME churches individually organize their own Founder's Day celebrations, which are often held on a Sunday closest to or on February 14, Richard Allen's birthday. Even though this date falls within **African-American History Month** and may be part of that celebration, Founder's Day is frequently a separate observance in many churches.

Observance

Before AME Founder's Day worship services, some churches may hold a parade. In Savannah, Georgia, for example, the Sixth Episcopal District's parade has included horse drawn carriages, a high-school marching band, and floats.

Service usually begins with a procession of bishops, other church leaders, and a choir. In some churches, choir members dress in handmade African garments. Some services include liturgical dancers. Some present dramatic renderings of Richard Allen and Absalom Jones being thrown out of St. George's Church.

One common element for Founder's Day observances is a focus on the life of Bishop Richard Allen and the founding of Mother Bethel Church. Along with honoring Allen and his wife Sarah, churches frequently recognize other AME church pioneers. Besides, several churches in an area may join together for services. Part of the message delivered may be a reminder that Richard Allen believed the church could perform four basic functions: spiritual support, evangelism, education, and building black pride.

Contacts and Websites

African Methodist Episcopal Church
500 8th Ave., S.
Nashville, TN 37203

615-254-0911; fax: 615-254-0912
E-mail: cio@ame-church.com
http://www.ame-church.com

Mother Bethel A.M.E. Church and Richard Allen Museum
419 Richard Allen Ave.
South 6th St.
Philadelphia, PA 19147
215-925-0616; fax: 215-925-1402
E-mail: info@motherbethel.com
https://www.motherbethel.org/content.php?cid=13

Further Reading

Allen, Richard. *The Life, Experience, and Gospel Labours of the Rt. Rev. Richard Allen. To Which is Annexed the Rise and Progress of the African Methodist Episcopal Church in the United States of America. Containing a Narrative of the Yellow Fever in the Year of Our Lord 1793: With an Address to the People of Colour in the United States. Written by Himself.* Philadelphia: Martin & Boden, 1800.

Jones, Absalom, and Richard Allen. *A Narrative of the Proceedings of the Black People, during the Late Awful Calamity in Philadelphia, in the Year 1793: And a Refutation of some Censures, Thrown upon them in some late Publications.* Philadelphia: Printed for the authors, by William W. Woodward, 1794.

Mills, Frederick V. "Allen, Richard." In African American Lives, edited by Henry Louis Gates Jr. and Evelyn Brooks Higginbotham. New York: Oxford University Press, 2004.

Nash, Gary B. "Allen, Richard." In *The African-American Experience: Selections from the Five-Volume Macmillan Encyclopedia of African-American Culture and History*, edited by Jack Salzman. New York: Macmillan, 1998.

Frederick Douglass Day

Date Observed: On or around February 14
Location: Communities nationwide

The birthday of famed abolitionist, orator, writer, and escaped slave Frederick Douglass is celebrated during the second week of February in many locations across the United States. February 14 is generally the date on which Douglass's birthday is observed (though there are no historical records that confirm the date).

Historical Background

Born into slavery in February 1818, Frederick Augustus Washington Bailey was the son of Harriet Bailey, a slave. He never knew his father, a white man, and he seldom saw his mother, who worked in the cornfields on a plantation near Easton, Maryland. His maternal grandmother, who lived in a nearby cabin, cared for him until he was six years old when she took him to the Lloyd Plantation where he was to join his brother and two sisters—siblings he did not know. It was on this plantation that he learned of the terrible brutality of slavery and "the bloody scenes that often occurred" there.

Frederick himself became a victim of brutal beatings and the depravity of various slave masters. But, while in bondage to Hugh and Sophia Auld in Baltimore, he learned to read and write, even though this was forbidden or illegal in much of the South. In Baltimore, Frederick heard and read about the work of abolitionists and as a teenager began to dream about emancipation. However, freedom seemed an impossible dream when he was sent to the plantation, owned by Hugh's brother Thomas, to work in the fields. Still, he managed to organize a secret school for slaves, which Thomas Auld and other whites quickly broke up.

Frederick was sent once more to Hugh Auld in Baltimore, where he began to make plans to escape. He also met a group of educated free blacks, among

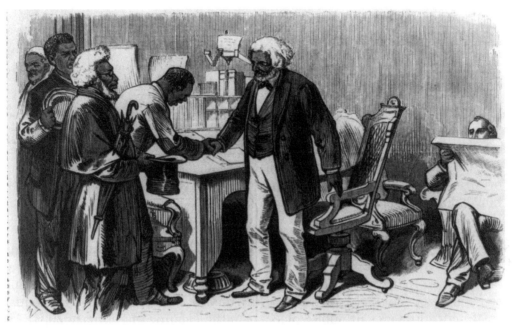

This sketch depicts Frederick Douglass in his office while he served as U.S. marshal for the District of Columbia. It was published in Frank Leslie's Illustrated Newspaper *on April 7, 1877.*

them a free black woman, Anna Murray. The two fell in love and were engaged in 1838, which added to Frederick's frustration and bitterness over his slave status.

In September 1838 he dressed as a sailor and with a friend's certificate documenting that he was a free black man, Frederick made his way to free soil in Pennsylvania and then to New York City. There he met David Ruggler, a leader in the Underground Railroad network, with whom he stayed until Anna Murray could join him. The couple were married and traveled to New Bedford, Massachusetts, where Frederick found work as a day laborer. He also began using Douglass as his last name to shield his fugitive status.

In New Bedford, Douglass became involved in the abolitionist movement and soon was making speeches before anti-slavery groups. Abolitionist William Lloyd Garrison hired Douglass to be an agent for the Massachusetts branch of the American Anti-Slavery Society, and within a short time, Douglass became well known among abolitionists in the United States and also in England and Ireland, where he spent two years speaking out against slavery and for women's rights. In his speech, Douglass often described his years as a slave and also documented those years in his *Narrative of the Life of Frederick Douglass, An American Slave.* His speeches and writings countered the propaganda by southern writers who declared that slaves had an easy, contented life and were treated kindly.

During the Civil War, Douglass met with President Abraham Lincoln and helped in the formation of the Massachusetts 54th and 55th black regiments who fought on the Union side (*see also* **Battle of Olustee Reenactment**). After the war and throughout the rest of his life, Douglass worked for the civil rights of African Americans and served in a variety of government positions—U.S. marshal of the District of Columbia (D.C.), recorder of deeds, and minister to the Republic of Haiti.

Meantime, Douglass continued to speak and write, producing numerous documents, letters, and books. He tirelessly campaigned for anti-lynching laws, voting rights for African Americans, and social and economic reforms to counteract the widespread discriminatory practices that prevented equal treatment for blacks in public places. On the evening of February 20, 1895, after spending the day at a women's rights meeting, Douglass died of a heart attack in his Washington, D.C., home.

Creation of the Observance

Harvard scholar Carter G. Woodson was responsible for designating a week in February that would include the birthday commemoration of Frederick Douglass. In 1926 Woodson initiated the first Negro History Week to take place during the second week of February. He chose this date to correspond with the birthday observances of Frederick Douglass and President Abraham Lincoln, both of whom had a great impact on African Americans. Eventually, the week became **African-American History Month**, during which numerous African-American contributions are highlighted.

Observances

A Frederick Douglass birthday tribute takes place each year around February 14 at the Frederick Douglass National Historic Site in Washington, D.C. The site is the home where Douglass lived during the years he was in the nation's capital. Events include speakers, musical performances, and a speech contest.

Excerpt from *Narrative of the Life of Frederick Douglass*

Frederick Douglass wrote about the first bloody scene that he witnessed as a young child when slave master Aaron Anthony whipped his aunt. This excerpt is from Chapter 1 of *Narrative of the Life of Frederick Douglass* (1845):

> Before he commenced whipping Aunt Hester, he took her into the kitchen, and stripped her from neck to waist, leaving her neck, shoulders, and back, entirely naked. He then told her to cross her hands, calling her at the same time a d——d b——h. After crossing her hands, he tied them with a strong rope, and led her to a stool under a large hook in the joist, put in for the purpose. He made her get up on the stool and tied her hands to the hook. She now stood fair for his infernal purpose. Her arms were stretched up at their full length so that she stood upon the ends of her toes. He then said to her, "Now, you d——d b——h, I'll learn you how to disobey my orders!" and after rolling up his sleeves, he commenced to lay on the heavy cowskin, and soon the warm, red blood (amid heart-rending shrieks from her, and horrid oaths from him) came dripping to the floor. I was so terrified and horror-stricken at the sight, that I hid in a closet, and dared not venture out till long after the bloody transaction was over.

The New Bedford Historical Society hosts a Frederick Douglass Read-a-thon each February. Participants read aloud from the *Life and Times of Frederick Douglass*. Besides, locals observe September 17, the anniversary of the day in 1838 when Douglass and his wife arrived in the city via the Underground Railroad.

Frederick Douglass is also remembered with churches, museums, bridges, memorial halls on college campuses, and other places bearing his name. In Rochester, New York, where Douglass lived and did much of his work, his home is preserved. The city also has a statue of Douglass, and Mt. Hope Cemetery marks his burial place.

Contacts and Websites

Frederick Douglass National Historic Site
1411 W. St., S.E.
Washington, DC 20020
202-426-5961
http://www.nps.gov/frdo

Frederick Douglass Papers
Library of Congress
101 Independence Ave., S.E.
Washington, DC 20540
202-707-5000
https://www.loc.gov/collections/frederick-douglass-papers/
about-this-collection

Frederick Douglass Papers
Indiana University-Purdue University at Indianapolis
902 W. New York St.
Indianapolis, IN 46202-5157
317-274-5834
E-mail: douglass@iupui.edu
https://frederickdouglass.infoset.io/make-contact

Further Reading

McCurdy, Michael, ed. *Escape from Slavery: The Boyhood of Frederick Douglass in His Own Words.* New York: Alfred A. Knopf, 1994. (young adult)

McFeely, William S. *Frederick Douglass.* 1991. Reprint. New York: W. W. Norton & Company, 1995.

Preston, Dickson J. *Young Frederick Douglass: The Maryland Years.* Baltimore: Johns Hopkins University Press, 1980. Reprint. Johns Hopkins University Press, 2018.

Writings by Frederick Douglass

Life and Times of Frederick Douglass. Hartford, CT: Park Publishing Company, 1881.

Narrative of the Life of Frederick Douglass, An American Slave, Written by Himself. Boston: Anti-Slavery Office, 1845.

George Washington Carver Day

Date Observed: January 5
Location: Various U.S. Communities

George Washington Carver Day is observed on January 5, the day on which the pioneering botanist and educator died in 1943, in remembrance of his outstanding contributions to the nation and the world of science.

Historical Background

George Washington Carver was born into slavery around 1864 or 1865, just before the end of the Civil War. He and his mother were stolen by Confederate raiders; Carver was returned, as an orphan, to his owners Moses and Susan Carver, with whom he remained even after emancipation.

The majority of slaves in the United States did not have educational opportunities. Legislation banning the education of slaves was not uncommon. Literate slaves were not only frowned upon but also often feared. For years after the Civil War, blacks' access to education remained limited, which also restricted occupational choices. It took many efforts to begin breaking down such barriers of racial discrimination. The biggest early strides were made by a small number of determined and talented individuals who proved that skin color did not impede achieving greatness. Carver was one of the first African Americans to do so.

Frail and sickly from birth, Carver was drawn to nature and earned the nickname "plant doctor." He was one of the fortunate few to receive a formal education. After graduating from high school, Carver applied and was accepted at Highland College in Kansas—even meriting a scholarship. Upon his arrival at Highland, however, the school president turned him away with the words, "Why didn't you tell me you were a Negro?"

George Washington Carver in 1906.

Undefeated, Carver went on to Iowa's Simpson College, initially indulging his love of art. One of his instructors, Etta Budd, recognized Carver's horticultural skills and advised him to study at Iowa State College of Agriculture and Mechanic Arts (now Iowa State University). After graduating from the institution, he joined the faculty and soon thereafter earned his master's degree. Before long, Carver's research was drawing wide notice. In 1896 Booker T. Washington, one of the most prominent African-American leaders of the time, asked Carver to join the faculty of Tuskegee Institute, now Tuskegee University (*see also* **Tuskegee Airmen Convention**). There Carver taught students the value of understanding and applying the forces of nature to agriculture.

Carver turned his attention to the plight of the southern farmer, hit hard by the boll weevil. He educated farmers in the art of crop rotation, knowing that the peanut plant had powers to restore nitrogen to depleted soil, which in turn would increase both the quantity and quality of staple cotton and tobacco crops, as well as increase the value of the peanut crops. Carver earned his "Mr. Peanut" title by finding ways for farmers to make use of the vast amounts they were able to produce. He was similarly inventive with sweet potatoes and other crops.

Due to his overwhelming contributions, Carver was showered with recognition and attention during his lifetime. He was a consultant to the U.S. Congress as well as to titans of business and industry and was considered both peer and friend of Henry Ford and Thomas Edison. He gave nutritional advice to Mahatma Gandhi, acted as a consultant to the Russian government, and provided massage therapy to the Iowa State football team.

186

Yet Carver remained a modest and simple man. He was convinced that science held the answers to all of life's questions and that one just needed to have a "receptive ear." Carver chose to secure a mere three patents and was highly respected for his non-profiteering nature. He was noted as repeatedly saying about his ideas and discoveries, "God gave them to me. How can I sell them to someone else?" He helped pave the way for other African-American scientists and inventors to make their contributions with greater facility.

George Washington Carver believed strongly that nature was God's laboratory. In his words, "We get closer to God as we get intimately and understandingly acquainted with the things he has created." In a brief essay on this topic, he wrote in part:

> The study of nature is not only entertaining, but instructive and the only true method that leads up to the development of a creative mind and a clear understanding of the great natural principles which surround every branch of business in which we may engage. Aside from this it encourages investigation, stimulates and develops originality in a way that helps the student to find himself more quickly and accurately than any plan yet worked out.
>
> The singing birds, the buzzing bees, the opening flower, and the budding trees, along with other forms of animate and inanimate matter, all have their marvelous creation story to tell each searcher for truth. . . .
>
> More and more as we come closer and closer in touch with nature and its teachings are we able to see the Divine and are therefore fitted to interpret correctly the various languages spoken by all forms of nature about us.[1]

Upon Carver's death in 1943, his birth site and surrounding area were designated historic sites and a monument was erected in his honor.

Creation of the Observance

Public Law 290 was passed during the 79th Congress to designate the George Washington Carver Recognition Day on January 5 of each year. The President

---

[1] Reprinted from *George Washington Carver: In His Own Words* by Gary R. Kremer, by permission of the University of Missouri Press. Copyright © 1987 by the Curators of the University of Missouri.

Carver Peanut Products

The Tuskegee University compiled a list of more than 300 peanut products and by-products attributed to George Washington Carver, including foods, beverages, cosmetics, dyes, medicines, and many other items.

of the United States is authorized to issue a proclamation calling on government officials to display the national flag at half staff on all government buildings on that day.

Observance

Tuskegee University, where Carver taught and conducted so much of his research, honors him in several ways. Since 1984, the George Washington Carver Public Service Award has been given annually to individuals whose work mirrors the philosophy of the world-recognized scholars. In 1999 Tuskegee began holding a yearly George Washington Carver Convocation. The ceremonies are held in late January or early February in the school's chapel, near Carver's burial site. The event celebrates Carver's life and legacy, recognizing his contributions to science, agriculture, and the humanities. Besides, the school selects a recipient for a George Washington Carver Distinguished Achievement Award. The award recipient is chosen based upon merits that mirror the standards set by Carver, and he or she offers remarks at the Convocation.

Carver's memory and contributions have been and continue to be honored in ways other than acknowledgment on one particular annual date. On July 14, 1953, for example, the George Washington Carver National Monument, located near his birthplace in Diamond, Missouri, was officially dedicated. Also, many elementary and high schools across the country are named after him. Science fairs and science project events frequently evoke Carver's name. Two U.S. stamps and a commemorative coin bear his likeness, and two U.S. submarines, now decommissioned, were named in his honor. Carver received honorary doctorates and memberships in professional organizations, both while living and posthumously. In 2005, the entire body of Carver's work was designated a National Historic Chemical Landmark.

Perhaps least surprising of all, Carver is well remembered by the National Peanut Board. This not-for-profit organization established its own Dr. George Washington Carver Award in 2001 with prize monies awarded to undergraduate and graduate students; matching funds are donated to their academic institutions. In 2008, Biotechnology Innovation Organization (BIO) created the George Washington Carver Award that is given during the annual World Congress on Industrial Biotechnology and Bioprocessing convention to innovators in the field of biotechnology.

Contact and Website

George Washington Carver National Monument
5646 Carver Rd.
Diamond, MO 64840
417-325-4151
http://www.nps.gov/gwca

Further Reading

Gibbs, C. R., and Dayo Akinsheye, ed. *Black Inventors: From Africa to America, Two Million Years of Invention and Innovation.* Silver Spring, MD: Three Dimensional Publishing, 1995.

Kremer, Gary B., ed. *George Washington Carver: In His Own Words.* 1987. Reprint. Columbia: University of Missouri Press, 1991.

MacKintosh, Barry. "George Washington Carver: The Making of a Myth." The Journal of Southern History, November 1976.

Potter, Joan. *African American Firsts: Famous Little-Known and Unsung Triumphs of Blacks in America.* New York: Kensington Publishing, 2002. Reprint. Kensington Publishing, 2009 (young adult)

Reed, Christopher Robert. *"All the World Is Here!": The Black Presence at White City.* Bloomington: Indiana University Press, 2000.

Georgia Sea Island Festival

Date Observed: *Last week of May and First week of June*
Location: *St. Simons Island, Georgia*

The annual Georgia Sea Island Festival at St. Simons Island, Georgia, celebrates African and African-American history and the heritage of Gullah, or Geechee, people. The terms "Gullah" and "Geechee" describe the people, their language, and the unique culture they have maintained since slavery and all are on display during the summer weekend festival.

Historical Background

St. Simons Island is one of the Sea Islands, a cluster of islands along the coasts of South Carolina and Georgia. It is the historic site in 1803 a group of Igbo slaves were brought from the region of West Africa that is now southern Nigeria. In Savannah, Georgia, they had been auctioned off to two plantation families on the island and transported on a small ship. While below decks, the Igbo, known to be fiercely independent, rebelled against their agents and forced the white men to jump overboard.

When the group of chained Igbo came on to the dock at the Dunbar Creek landing, they refused to go ashore and instead followed Chief Obo, chanting along with him, "The Sea brought me and the Sea will bring me home." They drowned themselves in Dunbar Creek rather than accept a life of slavery. The site is now known as Ebo Landing and was consecrated in 2002 as holy ground, although there is no historical marker to commemorate the site.

Numerous versions of the Ebo Landing story have been passed on in the oral tradition of African slaves. Many of these oral histories were collected in the late 1930s by the Federal Writers Project and have been published in *Drums and Shadows: Survival Studies among the Georgia Coastal Negroes.*

From the early 1800s to the present day, people of West African descent on St. Simons Island have preserved their language and culture. Through the generations they have passed on their traditions and celebrate them during the Georgia Sea Island Festival.

Creation of the Festival

The festival originated in 1977 with the assistance of the Georgia Sea Island Singers, who perform nationwide. It was an annual celebration until 1998 and was revived in August 2002, when the St. Simons African-American Heritage Coalition hosted the event. The coalition formed in 2000 because of the loss of black-owned property on the island. Although African Americans once owned the entire island, only a few hundred remain among the 20,000 or more residents. Historical buildings have been torn down and replaced with expensive resort homes. Thus, to preserve the St. Simons heritage, the coalition implemented a "Don't Ask, Won't Sell" campaign to educate the community about the value of their property. As part of the preservation campaign, the coalition brought back the Georgia Sea Island Festival.

Observance

Traditional Gullah arts and crafts, food, and musical performances are part of the annual festival. The Georgia Sea Island Singers often perform as well. Highlighted are drums, rhythms, dance performances, basket weaving, carpentry, and fish-netting demonstrations. There are also exhibits of carvings and wood sculptures, pottery, and quilting. A Children's Corner offers storytelling along with music and dance.

The festival provides a way to educate the public about the history and language of African and African-American people who not only survived, but also created a life beyond the horrors of slavery. For Africans of the diaspora who participate, the festival is also a way to maintain bonds.

See also **Hilton Head Island Gullah Celebration** *and* **Penn Center Heritage Days.**

Contact and Website

St. Simons African American Heritage Coalition
P.O. Box 20145
291 S. Harrington Rd.
St. Simons Island, GA 31522
912-634-0330
http://ssiheritagecoalition.org

Further Reading

Georgia Writers Project, Work Projects Administration. *Drums and Shadows: Survival Studies Among the Georgia Coastal Negroes*. Athens: University of Georgia Press, 1986.

Goodwine, Marquetta L., ed. *The Legacy of Ibo Landing: Gullah Roots of African American Culture*. Atlanta, GA: Clarity Press, 1998. Reprint. Clarity Press, 2011.

Pollitzer, William S. *The Gullah People and Their African Heritage*. Athens: University of Georgia Press, 1999.

Tanenbaum, Barry. "Living History." Shutterbug, October 2003. https://www.shutterbug.com/content/living-historybrtony-arruzas-offshore-interests.

Ghanafest

Date Observed: Last Saturday of July
Location: Chicago, Illinois

Ghanafest is a festival of thanksgiving that celebrates the heritage of Ghanaians in the metropolitan Chicago area. It has been held in various incarnations since 1987. Each year, the festival revolves around a theme and the theme for the year 2019 was "Akwaaba," which means "welcome back" in the Ghanaian-Akan language Twi.

Historical Background

The Ghana Club of Chicago (GCC) is a socioeconomic organization that has, over the years, come to be an umbrella group for the various peoples from Ghana who live in the Chicago area. In 1987 the GCC joined with the Ga-Dangme community (an expatriate ethnic group from Ghana) to co-celebrate the Ga-Dangme Homowo Festival of Thanksgiving. This communal celebration was successful and had a broad-based appeal across the Ghanaian community. The decision was made to repeat the event and seek funding and support from the city of Chicago. A grant was received, and in 1988, monies, tents, toilets, parking space, and other forms of sponsorship were provided. In addition, Chicago's then-mayor Richard Daley himself made an appearance at that year's Homowo celebration (*see also* **Homowo Festival** *in Portland, Oregon*).

In 1989 GCC negotiated with the Okupaman Association (which represented another Ghanaian ethnic group) to merge the Homowo celebration with the Odwira festival. In doing so, they sought to create a "Ghanaian Durbar"—a gathering that is similar to a rulers' court with music and dance, ceremonies to honor ancestors, and opportunities to unify the people. This merger increased recognition of the festival, which began to draw more attention at the local, national, and international levels.

Creation of the Festival

In 1990, the Ghanaian organizations met and agreed to expand the festival to represent all Ghanaian ethnic groups. Former GCC Vice-Chairman A. C. Eddie-Quarterly coined "Ghanafest" as the all-inclusive title that would be used from that time forward. The festival was created to celebrate the history and culture of Ghana, the West African nation that was formerly a British colony known as the "Gold Coast." The festival maintains a special bond of unity between Ghana and the United States while educating the community about Ghana's rich traditions.

Words from the Ghana National Council of Chicago

During the 2002 Ghanafest, Clement Timpo, ex-president of the Ghana National Council of Metropolitan Chicago, noted:

> Whatever way one may look at it, as Ghanaians in this Diaspora, our faith, progress, and basic economic and socio-economic survivals are intricately linked to the progress and stability in Ghana. We, therefore, share in the dilemma, and the economic and socioeconomic frustrations and survival of Ghana.
>
> Even though we have been away for far too long, we are still an integral part of Ghana; we have loved ones and relatives at home; we send money to our loved ones and relatives regularly; we help in the local community developments; at our council and affiliate organization meetings, we are always thinking and concerned with, and deliberating on the developmental progress of local councils and local communities in Ghana.
>
> We are continuously organizing fundraisers for the hospitals, clinics and other local economic infrastructures in Ghana . . . even though we are now part of North America, we! are also an integral part of Ghana.

Observance

Beginning mid-morning and lasting until nearly day's end, Ghanafest is rife with the sights, sounds, and smells of the native western coast of Africa from which its traditions hail. Local chieftains, queen mothers, princes, princesses, and other court members parade majestically in opulent regalia. Drums beat out rhythmic melodies. Regional cuisine is dished out as liberally as the hospitality. Both the national anthems of the United States and Ghana are played, reminding attendees of the bonds that cement these two countries. Native-born Americans intermingle with citizens of Ethiopia, Liberia, and Nigeria—some distant, or possibly not too distant, kin. There is dancing and merriment, art and excitement, and, most important of all, thanksgiving for the abundance of the camaraderie of spirit inherent in this annual festival.

Contacts and Websites

Ghana National Council of Metropolitan Chicago
E-mail: gncmetrochi@gmail.com
http://www.ghananationalcouncil.org

Further Reading

Gocking, Rogers. *History of Ghana.* Westport, CT: Greenwood Publishing Group, 2005.
Salm, Steven J., and Toyin Falola. *Culture and Customs of Ghana.* Westport, CT: Green-wood Publishing Group, 2002.

Goombay!

Date Observed: September
Location: Asheville, North Carolina

Goombay! is an outdoor festival held every September in Asheville, North Carolina (*see also* **Miami Bahamas Junakoo Festival**). It stresses appreciation of African and West Indian traditional music and dance in commemoration of the emancipation of Caribbean slaves (*see also* **West Indies Emancipation Day**).

Historical Background

Goombay! is a celebration that dates back hundreds of years among slaves in the Caribbean. *Goombay* is a Bantu word for a goatskin drum that is beaten with the hands; it also refers to music associated with the drum.

On August 1, 1834, Great Britain abolished slavery throughout its Caribbean territories. Ever since that date and event have been heartily commemorated in the Caribbean as well as in the United States before emancipation (*see also* **Emancipation Day**).

Creation of the Festival

The Young Men's Institute Cultural Center, Inc. (YMICC) organized the first Goombay! celebration in 1982. The mission of YMICC is to celebrate African-American culture and diversity in the community. YMICC's desire to preserve the past and create a bridge to the present and future laid the groundwork for the creation of Goombay! The festival continues to grow in popularity and is now put on through the cooperative efforts and assistance of Asheville's Parks and Recreation Department, the North Carolina Arts Council, the Community Arts Council of Western North Carolina, and the Friends of YMI Cultural Center.

The YMICC is housed in a landmark building that was commissioned by George Vanderbilt in 1892 and is on the National Register of Historic Places. It was built by and for the same black workmen who constructed Mr. Vanderbilt's own famed Biltmore House in Asheville.

At 18,000 square feet, the YMICC building housed everything from the corner drugstore to the public library to bathing facilities. For Asheville's black population, it was the hub of almost every facet of their lives for decades.

In 1980 a major renovation program was undertaken and YMICC took on the role it holds today: offering direction and leadership to the African-American constituents whom it serves.

Observance

Goombay! is held each September over a three-day weekend. Events begin about midday. The first two days of the festival run until late evening; on the final day, closing ceremonies conclude around 6 P.M.

Goombay! is family oriented, so activities are planned for all ages, with both a main and a children's stage providing entertainment. In any given year, attendees can expect to see drum circles, steel drums, stilt-walkers, traditional African-American dancers replete with feathered headdresses and elaborate costumes, contemporary rhythm bands, and much more. Vendors display African and Caribbean arts and crafts. Commercial vendors, food, handicapped access, music, and public transportation are additional features of the festival.

Contacts and Websites

Asheville Convention & Visitors Bureau
36 Montford Ave.
Asheville, NC 28801
828-258-6129
http://www.exploreasheville.com

YMI Cultural Center
39 S. Market St.
Asheville, NC 28801
828-257-4540
https://ymiculturalcenter.org

Further Reading

Hull, Arthur. *Drum Circle Spirit: Games, Exercises and Facilitation.* Northampton, MA: White Cliffs Media, Inc., 1998.

Olatunji, Babatunde, with Robert Atkinson. *Beat of My Drum: An Autobiography.* Foreword by Joan Baez. Philadelphia: Temple University Press, 2005.

Greek Organizations' Conventions

Date Observed: Varies
Location: Varies

The national conventions of African-American fraternities and sororities are held in various locations throughout the year. These gatherings serve as annual reunions and provide opportunities for socializing, networking, business-related meetings and workshops, and celebration of brotherhood and sisterhood.

Historical Background

Greek letter fraternal organizations have existed in the U.S. since 1776. The first fraternities were founded at colleges and universities on the East Coast, and they were intended primarily as social clubs for white men. As the idea of college fraternities began to gain widespread popularity, some organizations broadened their focus to include scholarship, spirituality, and brotherhood in addition to purely social objectives. Sororities, Greek letter organizations for women, did not begin to form until around the 1850s. For the most part, these fraternities and sororities were not integrated and very few African Americans were accepted as members.

African-American Greek letter organizations began to form in the early 1900s. Most of the African-American fraternal clubs that are active today were founded at Howard University, a historically black university in Washington, D.C. These fraternities and sororities were founded in part to create stronger bonds among African Americans, who faced racial discrimination on and off campus. Some groups welcomed all African-American students while others were created for specific professions or areas of study, such as education or

Sigma Pi Phi

Sigma Pi Phi is generally recognized as the oldest black fraternity in the U.S. It was founded in Philadelphia, Pennsylvania, in 1904 by six African-American men. The founders were all educated professionals and included a pharmacist, a dentist, and four physicians. Sometimes called the Boulé, Sigma Pi Phi differed from other fraternities by placing its emphasis on life after college instead of on the undergraduate years. Traditionally, Sigma Pi Phi members are college graduates who have achieved a level of status in their communities. It is considered to be a very elite fraternity for only the most successful black men. For this reason, Sigma Pi Phi membership numbers remained lower than other African-American fraternities. By 1954, there were only 500 members. Membership grew to about 3,000 by 1992; by 2004, it exceeded 4,000. The Sigma Pi Phi annual convention is known as the Grand Boulé and is usually attended by several thousand members and their spouses.

Alpha Kappa Alpha

The first black sorority was formed in 1908 by nine women at Howard University in Washington, D.C. Alpha Kappa Alpha was the first African-American fraternal organization to be founded at a historically black college or university (HBCU). The sorority had strict standards from the beginning, requiring that prospective members complete the first half of their second year of studies while maintaining high grades. Alpha Kappa Alpha has become the largest African-American sorority with more than 120,000 student and alumni members in more than 800 chapters worldwide.

Over the years, Alpha Kappa Alpha has made many important contributions on international, national, and local levels. In 1938 the sorority founded a full-time lobbying organization to work for passage of civil rights legislation. In the late 1940s, Alpha Kappa Alpha became an accredited observer organization at the United Nations. In 1948, Alpha Kappa Alpha created the American Council for Human Rights, inviting the other major African-American Greek societies to work together to end racial discrimination. Their "Black Faces in Public Places" project supported the establishment of public monuments to important African Americans in the 1980s. The annual Alpha Kappa Alpha convention draws tens of thousands of members for a weeklong celebration and reunion.

On November 3, 2005, Jessica Lawrence, vice president of Alpha Kappa Alpha at Clemson University in South Carolina, lit candles during a vigil for Rosa Parks, who had passed away on October 24 of that year.

business. Major African-American fraternities include Alpha Phi Alpha, Kappa Alpha Psi, Omega Psi Phi, Phi Beta Sigma, and Sigma Pi Phi. Major African-American sororities are Alpha Kappa Alpha, Delta Sigma Theta, Sigma Gamma Rho, and Zeta Phi Beta.

These organizations soon became a powerful influence on college campuses as well as on the African-American community as a whole. Throughout their history, African-American fraternal clubs have focused on serving the needs of the larger community in addition to sponsoring social activities. Many chapters maintain ongoing local community service projects, while others have established charitable foundations to provide scholarships and other opportunities for young people. African-American fraternal groups have also emphasized involvement in politics, and have been instrumental in the civil rights movement. Alumni members generally take on leadership positions at the national level and set goals for the fraternal clubs as a whole, often conducting this business at the national convention.

Creation of the Observance

The national conventions were established by individual fraternities and sororities as a means of gathering together all members for a program of activities based on shared interests and experiences. Over the years, these annual gatherings came to be known as boulés (pronounced "boo-lays").

Observance

Each national convention is different, but there are general similarities among the gatherings. The conventions function as reunions where members can reconnect with each other and renew old friendships. Programs and symposia are offered on such topics as African-American health concerns, African-American social issues, current events and politics affecting African Americans, and African-American community service. Educational workshops and training sessions are often held, along with general meetings of organization leadership and committees. The achievements of individual members and chapters are usually celebrated in an awards ceremony, and special recognition is given to those who have been members for a certain amount of time (for example, 50 or 75 years). Some conventions include a memorial service for deceased members. Conventions usually also include at least one black-tie formal event for socializing or fundraising for a particular project.

Contacts and Websites

Alpha Kappa Alpha
5656 S. Stony Island Ave.
Chicago, IL 60637
773-684-1282
http://www.aka1908.com

Alpha Phi Alpha Fraternity, Inc.
2313 St. Paul St.
Baltimore, MD 21218-5211
410-554-0040; fax: 410-554-0054
E-mail: membersupport@apa1906.net
https://apa1906.net

Delta Sigma Theta Sorority, Inc.
1707 New Hampshire Ave., N.W.
Washington, DC 20009
202-986-2400; fax: 202-986-2513
E-mail: dstemail@deltasigmatheta.org
http://www.deltasigmatheta.org

Kappa Alpha Psi Fraternity, Inc.
2322-24 N. Broad St.
Philadelphia, PA 19132-4590
215-228-7184; fax: 215-228-7181
E-mail: info@kappaalphapsi1911.com
http://www.kappaalphapsi1911.com

Omega Psi Phi Fraternity, Inc.
3951 Snapfinger Pkwy.
Decatur, GA 30035
404-284-5533; fax: 404-284-0333
E-mail: info@oppf.org
http://www.oppf.org

Phi Beta Sigma
145 Kennedy St., N.W.
Washington, DC 20011
202-726-5434; fax: 202-882-1681
http://www.pbs1914.org

Sigma Gamma Rho Sorority, Inc.
1000 Southhill Dr., Ste. 200
Cary, NC 27513
888-747-1922 (or) 919-678-9720; fax: 919-678-9721
http://www.sgrho1922.org

Sigma Pi Phi Fraternity
260 Peachtree St., N.W., Ste. 1604
Atlanta, GA 30303
404-529-9919
E-mail: info@sigmapiphi.org
https://www.sigmapiphi.org

Zeta Phi Beta Sorority, Inc.
1734 New Hampshire Ave., N.W.
Washington, DC 20009
202-387-3103
E-mail: info@zetaphibetasororityhq.org
http://www.zphib1920.org

Further Reading

"1904–2004: The Boulé at 100: Sigma Pi Phi Fraternity Holds Centennial Celebration." *Ebony*, September 2004.

Cooper, Desiree. *Detroit Free Press*, July 11, 2006.

Lehman, Jeffrey, ed. *The African American Almanac*. 9th ed. Detroit: Gale, 2003.

Soyer, Daniel. "Fraternities and Sororities." In *The African-American Experience: Selections from the Five-Volume Macmillan Encyclopedia of African-American Culture and History*, edited by Jack Salzman. New York: Macmillan, 1998.

Haile Selassie's Birthday

Date Observed: July 23
Location: Rastafarian communities

To African Americans and Africans of the diaspora who practice the Rastafarian religion, Ethiopian Emperor Haile Selassie I was and is considered to be *Jah*, "God incarnate." Also known by the honorific "Ras Tafari," his birth date, July 23, is deemed one of the holiest days of the year for Rastafarians and a cause for great celebration.

Historical Background

Selassie was named Tafari Makonnen at his birth on August 23, 1892, in Ejarsagoro, Harar, Ethiopia. According to legend, his lineage is traceable to King Solomon and the Queen of Sheba. Selassie was raised as a Christian in the royal court of Addis Ababa. At a young age, he was said to have demonstrated an excellent memory, a capacity for hard work, and a mastery of detail. By age 14, he had been appointed governor of Gara Maleta, a province of Harar; by age 20, he was *dejazmatch* (commander) of Sidamo province. In 1916, he was regent (acting ruler in the absence of the Empress) and heir to the throne of Ethiopia, going by his birth name "Tafari," with the honorific "Ras."

Selassie's interests in modernizing the nation were often contrary to the conservative philosophies of Empress Zawditu during the time that they shared power. In 1923 Selassie negotiated Ethiopia's admittance to the League of Nations. In 1930, the Empress died, and he was named Haile Selassie I of Ethiopia, *Negusa Negast* (King of Kings). In addition, he assigned himself the title "His Imperial Majesty, Emperor Haile Selassie I, King of Kings and Lord of Lords, Conquering Lion the Tribe of Judah, Elect of God."

Selassie was viewed as an autocratic leader, with an eye toward moving his nation into the modern world. He introduced a written constitution in 1931,

Haile Selassie at his palace in Addis Ababa, Ethiopia, in the early 1940s.

which allowed non-noble participation in official government politics for the first time. However, he also reaffirmed royal succession to his direct bloodline and maintained much actual control.

In 1936 Italy invaded Ethiopia and Selassie went into exile. He sought aid, unsuccessfully, from the League of Nations. He was able to return in 1941, thanks to the resistance of his countrymen and the Allied troops. During his time away, Selassie had gained some international stature and was named *Time* magazine's "Man of the Year" for 1935. Selassie enjoyed the spotlight, and eager to have his nation recognized by the western world, supported Ethiopia's becoming a charter member of the United Nations.

In the years that followed his homecoming, Selassie's critics say he was more focused on his world presence than with happenings in Ethiopia; they contend that, while he spoke of change, he did little to effect it beyond revising

Rastafari

Rastafari is a religion, a culture, and a social movement. According to Randal L. Hepner, in the *Encyclopedia of African and African-American Religions*, "Rastafari prefer the term *livity*, contending that Rastafari is a way of life informed by theocratic [divine governance] principles." Two main tenets guide Rastafari: (1) Haile Selassie I is the true and living God (Jah), and (2) for black people, salvation is only possible by freeing oneself from the white domination of the Western world (Babylon) and returning to Africa (the black Zion). Rastafarians base their way of life on biblical references, which, in their interpretation, confirm that God is black, and God—Jah—is a transcendent being who is present in all beings.

There are no fixed rules or practices to the religion, although most are vegetarians and take care to respect the laws of nature (for example, eating and using natural and organic products and avoiding environmental pollution). Most avoid drinking alcohol and follow biblical injunctions against eating pork.

While there are no formal marriage rites, fidelity between couples is considered an important principle, and children are sometimes blessed by their elders in rites of passage. There are several Rastafarian organizations, such as the Ethiopian World Federation, Inc., and the Twelve Tribes of Israel, but very few Rastafarians formally affiliate with these groups. Worship ceremonies vary widely and are commonly held in people's homes. Singing and dancing, often to the accompaniment of reggae music, are part of the event. There are usually long sessions of debate or discussion (called "reasoning") and the cannabis herb *ganja* is often used to facilitate this. Contrary to common belief, Rastafarians do not smoke marijuana recreationally, only sacramentally; there are some who do not use it in their religious practices at all.

Another myth is that all Rastafarians wear dreadlocks; only the one group that abides by the biblical injunction that men should not cut their hair follow this fashion. Rastafarians are noted for often wearing African garb and for wearing the distinctive color combination of red, gold, green, and black. These colors respectively symbolize bloodshed/historic Rastafarian struggles, faith/prosperity/sunshine, the land and its produce, and the color of the Rastafarian people. Many wear lion medallions, the symbol of Ras Tafari's imperial Ethiopian throne, or crosses, which symbolize the burden of life.

Ethiopia's constitution in time for the celebration of his coronation's Silver Jubilee in 1955. As Emperor, he retained significant powers under the constitution, which nevertheless extended popular political participation by making the lower house of parliament an elected body. A 1960 coup attempt caused Selassie to respond with more conservative policies, which were not viewed favorably.

On May 25, 1963, Selassie welcomed 32 African heads of state and government to Addis Ababa and presided over the establishment of the Organization of African Unity (OAU). Selassie's welcoming address helped to set the tone that would lead to the adoption of a charter:

> We seek, at this meeting, to determine whether we are going and to chart the course of our destiny. An awareness of our past is essential to the establishment of our personality and our identity as Africans. . . . Today, We name as our first great task the final liberating of those Africans still dominated by foreign exploitation and control. . . . We look to the vision of an Africa not merely free but united. . . . History teaches us that unity is strength and cautions us to submerge and overcome our differences in the quest for common goals, to strive, with all our combined strength, for the path to true African brotherhood and unity.

Selassie's overall popularity among his own people came to an abrupt end. Dissatisfaction grew rapidly across the land, and even abroad, as the news came to light about mass famine and other tragedies that had, up until then, been unreported. Selassie was placed under house arrest in September 1974. On August 27 of the following year, it was announced that he had died.

Ethiopianism and other movements that emphasized an idealized Africa began to take hold among black slaves in the Americas in the 18th century, from which the roots of Rastafarianism can be traced. The Bible offered hope through such passages as Psalm 68:31, foretelling of how "Princes shall come out of Egypt and Ethiopia shall soon stretch out her hands unto God" for those who had been converted to Christianity. The ethos was strengthened through the late-19th-century rise of the modern Pan-African movement and in particular, the teachings of Jamaican-born Marcus Garvey, who reportedly told his followers to "Look to Africa where a black king shall be crowned, he shall be the Redeemer." In addition to this, influential proto-Rastafarian texts such as *The Holy Piby* and *The Royal Parchment Scroll of Black Supremacy to Jamaica* gained audiences in the 1920s.

Creation of the Observance

Upon Selassie's coronation in 1930, Marcus Garvey and his followers established the Rastafarian religion in Jamaica (*see also* **Marcus Garvey's Birthday**). Garvey espoused a pan-African philosophy and had prophesied in 1927 that an African ruler would arise and champion the cause of people of African descent around the world. In his view, Selassie was that champion, and many others agreed.

By the 1940s, Rastafarians were celebrating Haile Selassie's birth—as well as his coronation and Marcus Garvey's birth.

Observance

Some Rastafarians observe Haile Selassie's birthday by holding a *binghi*, a celebration that can include prayers, reggae music, and dancing. Rastafarians regard Haile Selassie I's birthday as the holiest of celebrations, closely followed by the anniversary of his coronation and the birth of Marcus Garvey. Two other dates many Rastafarians mark are Grounation Day, April 21—the date in 1966 that Haile Selassie I arrived for his one and only visit to the island of Jamaica—and February 6, the birth date of Jamaican reggae singer Bob Marley in 1945. Ethiopia allowed Marley to be commemorated with an annual festival in the country beginning in 2004. Remembering important people, African culture, and equality of the people are themes observed at this festival.

Contact and Website

Lion of Judah Society
305A Halsey Street
Brooklyn, NY 11216
646-600-5352; fax: 614-573-0724
E-mail: rastafariground@gmail.com

Further reading

Barret, Leonard E. *The Rastafarians*. Boston: Beacon Press, 1997.
Henze, Paul B. *Layers of Time: A History of Ethiopia*. New York: Macmillan/ Palgrave, 2000.
Hepner, Randal L. In *Encyclopedia of African and African-American Religions*, edited by Stephen D. Glazier. New York: Routledge, 2001.

Ras, Nathaniel. *50th Anniversary of His Imperial Majesty Emperor Haile Selassie I First Visit to the United States (1954–2004)*. Oxford: Trafford Publishing, 2004.

"Rastafarians." In *Africana: The Encyclopedia of the African and African American Experience: The Concise Desk Reference*, edited by Kwame Anthony Appiah and Henry Louis Gates Jr. Philadelphia: Running Press, 2003.

Writing by Haile Selassie

The Autobiography of Emperor Haile Selassie I: King of Kings and Lord of All Lords; My Life and Ethiopia's Progress 1892–1937 (Vol. 1). Translated by Edward Ullendorff. New York: Frontline Books, 1999.

Haitian Flag Day

Date Observed: May 18
Location: Haiti and some U.S. cities

Haitian Flag Day is observed on May 18 in Haiti and several U.S. cities with large populations of Haitian Americans. Many Africans of the diaspora, regardless of their ancestry, also join in the holiday celebration, because it commemorates the slave revolt in Haiti that led to the country's independence from France and also prompted slave uprisings in America.

Historical Background

During the 1700s in the French West Indies colony of St. Domingue (later renamed Haiti), a few French families owned huge sugar plantations and brought in more than one half million enslaved people from Africa to work the fields. As in some other parts of the Western Hemisphere, many plantation owners treated slaves brutally, often working them to death.

In 1789 a revolution broke out in France, and the ideals of liberty and equality expressed by the revolutionaries quickly spread to the colonial plantation owners and merchants, who demanded freedom from French rule. Free blacks and people of mixed races wanted social justice. And slaves were ready to fight for their freedom.

The most successful slave uprising in history began in August 1791. A former Creole slave, Toussaint Louverture, was a leading figure in the revolution. He trained an army of slaves who fought against tens of thousands of French, Spanish, and British soldiers. An estimated 350,000 people died, most of them slaves, in the Haitian Revolution before independence was won in 1804.

The French captured Toussaint in 1802 and sent him to France, where he died in prison in 1803. Two other Haitian leaders took up the fight: Jean Jacques Dessalines and Henri Christophe.

Creation of the Holiday

When Dessalines and other leaders decided to march on what is now Port-au-Prince, they wanted to carry a flag that would represent their troops. On May 18, 1803, they pieced together a design for the official flag. Since then, May 18 has been known as Haitian Flag Day.

The design of the new flag began with the French flag made up of blue, white, and red bands. The white band was removed to indicate that the French no longer controlled the colony. A woman named Catherine Flon sewed the new flag together, using vertical bands of blue and red cloth. Blue represented blacks and mixed-race people, and red symbolized their blood.

Over the years the nation's flag has been modified several times, but Flag Day itself has remained the same as the day the nation's flag was first sewn together. May 18 is a major national holiday in Haiti.

The Haitian Flag

The current Haitian flag is made up of two horizontal bands: a blue one on top and a red one below. Red symbolizes the blood and sacrifices made during the Haitian Revolution, and blue stands for hope and unity. The slogan on the flag reads *L'union fait la force*, "In unity we find strength."

Observance

Haitians celebrate Flag Day on the grounds of the national palace, and Haitians in the diaspora also honor the Haitian flag. In the United States, for example, Haitian Flag Day is celebrated in cities with Haitian-American populations. Students are likely to carry the Haitian flag with them during a week of commemoration, and school events emphasize Haitian history and culture.

Each year on the last Sunday in May, New York City's Haitian Day Parade processes down Toussaint Louverture Boulevard (also known as Nostrand Avenue) in Brooklyn. Organized by the Haitian-American Carnival Association since 2002, the parade is followed by a festival featuring Haitian music and food.

Boston observes May as Haitian Heritage Month. Events include a Flag-Raising Day as well as a parade. In Florida, Haitian Flag Day is celebrated in cities such as Tampa, Delray Beach, Miami, Fort Lauderdale, Fort Myers, and others, and events include Haitian food, music, and art exhibits.

In 2004 special festivities in such cities as Brooklyn, New York, and Miami, Florida, marked the 200th anniversary of Haiti's independence.

Contact

Haitian Americans United
10 Fairway St., Ste. 218
Mattapan, MA 02126
617-298-2976

Further Reading

Aptheker, Herbert. *American Negro Slave Revolts.* 5th ed. New York: International Publishers, 1987.
Charles, Jacqueline. "Parties, Protests Mark Haiti Flag." *Miami Herald,* May 18, 2005. Lush, Tamara. "Haitian Roots Deepening." *St. Petersburg Times,* May 6, 2002.
Simon, Darran. "Haitians to Raise Flags for Unity." *Miami Herald,* May 17, 2004.

Harambee Festival

Date Observed: Last Saturday in February
Location: Benedict College, Columbia, South Carolina

The Harambee Festival is part of Benedict College's annual **African-American/ Black History Month** celebration. The one-day event aims to draw in the larger community for African-American art, music, workshops, and health screenings.

Historical Background

Harambee is a Bantu word from Kenya that translates literally as "let us all pull together." According to Susan Njeri Chieni of Moi University in Kenya, Harambee "embodies the idea of mutual assistance, joint effort, mutual social responsibility, and community self-reliance." From her vantage point, Harambee is a principle that has more or less always existed in traditional Kenyan societies: the security and prosperity of the individual and the group have always been intertwined; for the group to benefit and survive, each person has always had to be cognizant of the needs of others; one cannot succeed when another fails.

The modern Harambee movement emerged during the 1960s, the early years of Kenya's independence, and Harambee was cultivated through widespread communal activities that addressed sorely needed projects, such as building schools. These projects were intended to benefit the majority rather than reap individual gain or profit.

Creation of the Festival

The first Harambee Festival at Benedict College was held in 1989. The festival was the vision of George Devlin, the associate vice president of student affairs, who has directed the event since its inception. Organizers hope to start

214

a scholarship fund from festival proceeds. Following the spirit of "Harambee," the event also aims to unify the college community and the general public in a day of inspirational and enjoyable activities.

Observance

The Harambee Festival takes place at the college's Benjamin E. Mays Resource Center arena. The College's gospel choir, dance company, and jazz ensemble perform, as do rap artists and student poets. The festival features all-day stage performances with nationally known gospel and R and B performers, contemporary music, empowerment workshops, an art exhibit, health screenings, the African Village (which offers hard-to-find merchandise items), and a children's village. Vendors also offer food, clothing, jewelry, and other items.

Contact

Benedict College
1600 Harden St.
Columbia, SC 29204
803-705-4519; fax: 803-705-6654

Harlem Week

Date Observed: July through August
Location: Harlem, New York

Harlem Week takes place in Harlem in New York City's borough of Manhattan. In past years, festivities took place over a week, and the celebration was called "Harlem Week." The name has stuck even though, in recent years, a wide range of events have been scheduled beginning in July and stretching through August. Harlem Week celebrates the past, present, and future glories of Harlem, as well as the people who comprise the community.

Historical Background

During the 1600s, the Dutch settled in a rural area of New York that they called "New Haarlem," named for a Dutch city. The settlers imported African slaves to work the farms, and the area was primarily farmland and country estates until the late 19th century (*see also* **Pinkster**). It became rapidly urbanized with the construction of housing and elevated railroads.

During the first decade of the 20th century, blacks began to move into Harlem in large numbers, and the neighborhood became an African-American cultural hub. The area earned worldwide fame with the advent of the Harlem Renaissance—a literary and artistic flowering that occurred from the late 1910s through the mid-1930s. Luminaries of the movement included poets Langston Hughes (1902–1967) and Countee Cullen (1903–1946), and writer and anthropologist Zora Neale Hurston (1891–1960). Other notable residents were labor leader A. Philip Randolph (1889–1979), singer and actor Paul Robeson (1898–1976), and businesswoman Madame C. J. Walker (1867–1919) (*see also* **Paul Robeson's Birthday** *and* **Zora Neale Hurston Festival of the Arts and Humanities**; *for more on Harlem, see also* **African American Day Parade**).

A bookseller on Harlem's 125th Street in 1943.

Creation of the Festival

In 1974 a group of residents organized Harlem Day to celebrate and preserve Harlem's cultural history. The festival proved to be so successful that, over the years, organizers added new activities. The festival's growth prompted "Harlem Day" to become "Harlem Week."

Observance

Harlem Week's schedule of events offers a great variety of activities. There are musical and dance performances, a film festival, a food festival, special children and family events, a health fair and sports clinic, a fashion show, an auto show, basketball and tennis classics, the National Historic Black College Fair and Exposition, and more. Near the end of the month, the National Black Sports and Entertainment Hall of Fame holds its annual induction and awards ceremony.

Contacts and Websites

Greater Harlem Chamber of Commerce
200A W. 136th St.
New York, NY 10030-7200
212-862-7200
https://www.greaterharlemchamber.com

Schomburg Center for Research in Black Culture
New York Public Library
515 Malcolm X Boulevard (135th St. and Malcolm X Blvd.)
New York, NY 10037
917-275-6975

Further Reading

Banks, William H., Jr. *Beloved Harlem: A Literary Tribute to Black America's Most Famous Neighborhood, From the Classics to the Contemporary.* New York: Doubleday-Broadway/Harlem Moon, 2005.

Cunningham, Michael, and Craig Marbarry. *Spirit of Harlem: A Portrait of America's Most Exciting Neighborhood.* New York: Doubleday, 2003.

Harris, Leslie M. *In the Shadow of Slavery: African Americans in New York City, 16261863.* Chicago: University of Chicago Press, 2004.

Osofsky, Gilbert. *Harlem: The Making of a Ghetto.* 2nd ed.Chicago: Ivan R. Dee, Publisher, 1996.

Harriet Tubman Day

Date Observed: March 10
Location: Communities nationwide

Harriet Tubman, one of the most courageous conductors of the Underground Railroad, is honored on March 10, the date of her death in 1913. In 1990, the U.S. Congress designated March 10 as Harriet Tubman Day "to be observed by the people of the United States with appropriate ceremonies and activities."

Historical Background

Born around 1820 in Dorchester County, Maryland, Harriet Tubman was named Araminta Ross by her slave parents. Years later she adopted her mother's first name, Harriet. She grew up among both enslaved and free African Americans who worked in plantation fields. Her father, Ben Ross, gained his freedom according to the provisions of his owner's will. But the rest of the family, which included nine children, remained enslaved and in 1824 became the property of Edward Brodess.

To pay the costs of operating his land holdings, Brodess "rented out" the people he enslaved or sold them to slaveholders in other states. Brodess sold some of Harriet's siblings and rented her to various planters, most of whom were cruel and given to beating slaves. Under harsh conditions, she was forced to work at tasks ranging from long hours of housekeeping to heavy fieldwork and felling timber. On one occasion, Harriet refused to help an overseer tie up a slave so he could be punished with a beating. The overseer threw a two-pound lead weight at her, hitting her in the head. She suffered an injury that caused periodic seizures for the rest of her life.

About the mid-1840s, she married John Tubman, a free African American. Harriet Tubman soon planned to escape slavery, hoping to take some

The photo of Harriet Tubman on the left is believed to have been taken sometime between 1860 and 1875. The one on the right was taken about two years before her death.

of her family with her. But John Tubman refused to leave, and during her first effort to run away, her brothers turned back. In 1849, Tubman escaped alone, making her way on foot at night. During the day, she hid and slept.

Tubman found work in Philadelphia, saved money, and returned to Maryland to guide family members and friends through the Underground Railroad, a secret network of former slaves, free blacks, and whites who helped escaped slaves to freedom in Canada (*see also* **Sugar Grove Underground Railroad Convention**). With the aid of then-Senator and later U.S. Secretary of State William H. Seward, she bought a home in Auburn, New York. In one of her most daring escape plans, she arranged for a wagon driver to bring her elderly parents to Auburn to live with her.

Between 1849 and 1860, Tubman, known as the "Moses of Her People," may have freed up to 300 slaves, although accounts vary on the actual number of escapees. Regardless, none of the slaves were lost, primarily due to the many

> "I looked at my hands to see if I was the same person," Harriet Tubman recalled after she safely reached Pennsylvania and freedom. "There was such glory over everything; the sun came like gold through the trees, and over the fields, and I felt like I was in heaven."
>
> —Harriet Tubman, in Sarah H. Bradford's *Harriet Tubman: The Moses of Her People*

techniques Tubman used to prevent detection, including threatening to kill anyone who wanted to retreat, tranquilizing babies so they would not cry, and constantly urging and prodding her charges to persevere.

During the Civil War, Tubman nursed many of the wounded and also served as a spy for the Union. After the war, she married a former Union soldier, Nelson Davis, but kept the surname Tubman. Her work during the late 1800s included support for women's rights and numerous fund-raising efforts to establish schools for newly freed black children and to support elderly and poor African Americans. She spent her last two years in the Harriet Tubman Home for the Elderly, which she established. She died there in 1913.

Creation of the Observance

In 1990, the 101st Congress passed Public Law 252 that designated March 10 as the day to commemorate Harriet Tubman's life and deeds. In 2001, the state of Maryland marked March 10 to honor Tubman, and in 2003, the state legislature in New York passed a law making the Harriet Tubman Day of Commemoration official statewide. Other states and local communities also have established the day in tribute to Tubman.

Over the years, Harriet Tubman has been highly praised and widely honored for her heroism. Some other tributes include a World War II ship named for her, the designation of her home as a historic landmark in 1974, and a commemorative postage stamp with her image issued in 1978. On February 7, 2019, the Federal Government reintroduced The Harriet Tubman Tribute Act, a legislation that directed the Secretary of the Treasury to print Harriet Tubman on $20 Federal Reserve notes that are to be printed after December 31, 2020.

Observance

Harriet Tubman Day is marked in a variety of ways across the United States. In Auburn, New York, a commemoration may include a tour through the historic Harriet Tubman Home and a reenactment of her life. Also, the Home hosts an annual Tubman Pilgrimage over Memorial Day weekend.

The Harriet Tubman Organization, formed in 1990, conducts tours in Dorchester County, Maryland, where Tubman was born. On her commemorative day, as at other times of the year, a tour may include a visit to the Harriet Tubman Memorial Garden in Cambridge and a stop at a roadside marker near the farm where she was raised. Walking tours guide visitors through the fields where Tubman worked while enslaved.

In Houston, Texas, a re-enactor performed "The Resurrection of Harriet Tubman" on Harriet Tubman Day in 2005. The performance took place at the Buffalo Soldiers National Museum (*see also* **Buffalo Soldiers Commemorations**).

Contacts and Websites

Dorchester County Office of Tourism
2 Rose Hill Pl.
Cambridge, MD 21613
410-228-1000 or 800-522-8687
https://visitdorchester.org

Harriet Tubman National Holiday
P.O. Box 832127
Stone Mountain, GA 30083
302-762-8010
http://www.harriettubman.com/index.html

The Harriet Tubman Home
180 South St.
Auburn, NY 13201
315-252-2081
E-mail: Hthome@localnet.com
https://www.harriettubmanhome.com

The Harriet Tubman Organization, Inc.
424 Race St.
Cambridge, MD 21613
410-228-0401
http://htorganization.blogspot.com

Further Reading

Bennett, Lerone, Jr. "Harriet Tubman's Private War: Iconic Freedom Fighter Waged Unremitting Struggle Against the Slave System." *Ebony*, March 2005.

Bentley, Judith. *Harriet Tubman*. New York: Franklin Watts, 1990. (young adult)

Bradford, Sarah H. *Harriet Tubman: The Moses of Her People*. Hansebooks, 2017.

Cannon, Angie. "Secret Paths to Freedom." *Philadelphia Inquirer*, February 24, 2002.

Clinton, Catherine. *Harriet Tubman: The Road to Freedom*. New York: Little, Brown and Company, 2004.

———. "On the Road to Harriet Tubman: She Has Become One of the Most Famous of All American Women, But to the Biographer She Is a Tantalizingly Elusive Quarry." *American Heritage*, June–July 2004.

Hilton Head Island Gullah Celebration

Date Observed: Month of February
Location: Hilton Head Island, South Carolina

The Hilton Head Island Gullah Celebration, earlier known as the Native Islander Gullah Celebration, is a series of events that are held on Hilton Head Island throughout the month of February each year. Developed to create economic opportunities for minority residents, the cultural festivities also add to area tourism and spotlight the uniqueness of the Gullah people living in the region, which includes a chain of isles known as the Sea Islands (*see also* **Georgia Sea Island Festival** *and* **Penn Center Heritage Days**).

Historical Background

In 1663, an English sea captain named William Hilton found an island off the coast of South Carolina. At the time, although both English and Spanish explorers had come around and settled on nearby isles, only native Indian people inhabited what would come to be named Hilton Head Island. After Hilton's "discovery," the British took control of the island and established a plantation system to grow indigo, and later, cotton.

During the Civil War, the Confederates first occupied the island, but their position was eventually usurped by Union forces. When the War ended, many of the island's prior residents left, and the majority who remained were newly freed slaves.

The isolation of Hilton Head Island allowed residents to preserve much of their culture, primarily because they were cut off from the mainland and were able to maintain a close community, passing on their beliefs, folktales, crafts, language, and food over the generations. The Gullah people are direct descendents of the first West Africans brought to the area as slaves. "Gullah" refers to the language, culture, and the peoples along the southern Carolina, Georgia, and northern Florida coasts. The language is a mixture of Creole, English, and African, heard and only truly understood by someone born and bred in the "Lowcountry."

The word *Gullah* may be a derivative of the name of the southwestern African country of Angola; many Gullahs trace their lineage to this region. Another school of thought attributes the word's origin to the Gola tribe that inhabits the border between Liberia and Sierra Leone. Various sources put forth both theories. Although there seems to be no complete resolution on the issue, there is basic agreement about the West African root of the word.

Because Hilton Head was, in effect, cut off from much of the modern world from the end of the Civil War through the mid-20th century, the Gullah people maintained a lifestyle unique in almost every aspect: how they farmed and fished, sewed and cooked, sang and praised during worship, and educated their children.

The Island seemed to escape the notice of the outside world until it caught the eye of hunters and developers in the 1950s. Three years into that decade, the first car ferry was operational; three years after that, a toll bridge connected Hilton Head Island to the mainland, and its days of seclusion were at an end.

Not surprisingly, however, development of the Island did not automatically bring prosperity to the native islanders. Regardless, the Gullah remain a proud people who are determined to cherish and retain their cultural heritage. In efforts to reach out to their extended West African family members, Gullah groups have traveled to Sierra Leone to participate in homecomings in 1989, 1997, and 2005.

Creation of the Festival

Established in 1996, the Hilton Head Island Gullah Celebration festival is an initiative of the NIBCAA, which is in partnership with the Native Islanders Property Owners Association, Beaufort County and South Carolina Parks, the Town of Hilton Head Island, Recreation and Tourism. The event's initial aims were: (1) to create economic opportunities for Hilton Head Island's minority business owners; (2) to develop a cultural tourism market for the region; and (3) to significantly increase visitor traffic during the island's slowest tourist month, which, at the time, was February.

Observance

Every day in February can be viewed, unofficially, as part of the annual Hilton Head Island Gullah Celebration. Officially, there is a published schedule of events each year detailing specific dates and activities. In order to capitalize on the growing number of state, national, and even international tourists who are attracted to the celebration, the major events tend to be scheduled, whenever possible, on Valentine's Day, Presidents' Day, weekends, and around schools' winter breaks.

In addition to a month-long art exhibit, an Arts/Crafts/Food Expo offers demonstrations of such crafts as the age-old art of sweetgrass basket sewing and indigo dying. Gospel music may be part of the program, or a speaker, or an African dance group. **National Freedom Day** always draws a crowd, with its varied and inspired agenda. Some of the most noted highlights of the celebration month are the panel discussions in which guest residents share some aspect of Gullah traditions.

Contacts and Websites

Chicora Foundation, Inc.
P.O. Box 8664
861 Arbutus Dr.
Columbia, SC 29202
803-787-6910
http://www.sciway.net/hist/chicora/mitchelville-6.html

Coastal Discovery Museum
P.O. Box 23497
Hilton Head Island, SC 29925
843-689-6767
E-mail: info@coastaldiscovery.org
http://www.coastaldiscovery.org

Hilton Head Island-Bluffton Chamber of Commerce and Visitor & Convention Bureau
1 Chamber of Commerce Dr.
P.O. Box 5647
Hilton Head Island, SC 29938
843-785-3673 (or) 800-523-3373

Further Reading

Branch, Muriel Miller. *The Water Brought Us: Story of the Gullah Speaking People*. Orangeburg, SC: Sandlapper Publishing Company, 2006. (young adult)

Coakley, Joyce. *Sweetgrass Baskets and the Gullah Tradition*. Mount Pleasant, SC: Arcadia Publishing, 2006.

Goodwine, Marquetta L., ed. *The Legacy of Ibo Landing: Gullah Roots of African American Culture*. 1998. Reprint. Atlanta, GA: Clarity Press, 2011.

Miller, Edward A. *Gullah Statesman: Robert Smalls from Slavery to Congress, 1839- 1915*. 1995. Reprint. Columbia: University of South Carolina Press, 2008.

Pollitzer, William S. *The Gullah People and Their African Heritage*. 1999. Reprint. Athens: University of Georgia Press, 2005.

Hollywood Black Film Festival

Date Observed: One week in June
Location: Hollywood, California

The Hollywood Black Film Festival has fast become an industry-recognized cinematic event since its inception in 1999. The June festival highlights the talents of both up-and-coming and established African-American men and women in the filmmaking profession.

Historical Background

African-American filmmakers have been producing movies since the early 1900s, particularly after the release of D. W. Griffith's 1915 film *The Birth of a Nation*. That silent film depicted the post-Civil War South being overtaken by blacks, glorified the racist and violent actions of the Ku Klux Klan, and generally characterized African Americans (usually played by whites in blackface) as disreputable, stupid, and devious. To counter the stereotypes, which were widely accepted by white America at that time, black filmmakers produced motion pictures that presented African Americans in positive, real-life portrayals. But African-American producers did not work within the Hollywood environment. Instead, they were independent and sought their own financing, distribution, and audiences.

One of the independent filmmakers was the famed Oscar Micheaux (1884–1951), the son of former slaves, who began his own film company and released his first film in 1919. From that date until 1948, he produced dozens of silent and "talking" (sound) films. He was the first African American to produce a feature movie in sound. His work was part of a genre called "race films," because they were directed to primarily black audiences.

Over the years, black filmmakers have continued to make movies aimed at African-American viewers, but they have also made films that are considered "crossovers"—appealing to a wide range of audiences. In order to get their movies noticed, independent black filmmakers depend on festivals and similar events, such as the African Diaspora Film Festival, New York, New York; Colored Pictures, Durham, North Carolina; Pan African Film & Art Festival, Beverly Hills, California; Houston Black Film Festival, Houston, Texas; and Reel Black Men, Los Angeles, California, for showings (*see also* **African American Women in Cinema Film Festival**; **American Black Film Festival**; **Denver Pan African Film Festival**; *and* **Pan African Film & Arts Festival**).

Creation of the Festival

The Hollywood Black Film Festival (HBFF) was founded in 1998 by its executive director, Tanya Kersey, with an objective to foster and develop the vision of independent filmmakers by bringing their films to the attention of the industry, media and public through a public exhibition and competition program. The festival has screened over 1,000 films from the U.S., Canada, and 25 countries around the world.

In 1999 the HBFF screened its first films in an effort to unite black filmmakers, television and film actors, writers, directors, industry executives, up-and-coming talent, and new audiences. By bringing these varied groups together, organizers aimed to help launch careers and movies that might otherwise languish from want of exposure.

Observance

The main thrust of the HBFF, dubbed "The Black Sundance," is to screen a wide variety of independent films submitted from all parts of the globe. Entries include features, shorts, documentaries, student films, and music videos. Screenings are held at the Harmony Gold Preview House located on Sunset Boulevard. Juried prizes are a highlight of the week's closing events.

An Infotainment Conference is also scheduled in concert with the festival. Talk-show style forums comprised of top stars, directors, producers, agents, business managers, and the like are a popular draw. Conference classes run the gamut from film distribution and production to writing for film and TV to pitching a script; even actor-specific workshops are offered.

Contact and Website

Harmony Gold USA, Inc.
7655 W. Sunset Blvd.
Los Angeles, CA 90046
323-851-4900
http://harmonygold.com

Homecoming Emancipation Celebration

Date Observed: Last weekend of July
Location: Nicodemus, Kansas

The Homecoming Emancipation Celebration in Nicodemus, Kansas, usually takes place during the last weekend of July to commemorate the only remaining all-black western town established after the Civil War. The event also marks the August 1, 1834, anniversary of the emancipation of slaves in the West Indies, which created hope for American blacks in bondage (*see also* **West Indies Emancipation Day**).

Historical Background

After the Civil War and the Reconstruction period in the United States, newly freed blacks in the South faced harassment by southern politicians and a reign of violence by groups such as the Ku Klux Klan, who opposed black civil rights and economic justice. Fearing for their safety and lives, many African Americans began to move north and west during the late 1870s. Tens of thousands migrated to Kansas, where several African-American towns were established, but only one has survived to this day—Nicodemus. Located along the Solomon River, Nicodemus was settled by about 300 former slaves from Kentucky and Tennessee.

A white land developer, W. R. Hill, and a black minister, William H. Smith, planned the town of Nicodemus, naming it for a slave who, according to legend, was able to buy his freedom. Hill and Smith urged southern black families to relocate to this "promised land" in Kansas, where people could homestead and own property. However, when African Americans arrived in Nicodemus during the winter, the cold weather prevented people from building homes, so

"Exodusters"

The Exoduster Movement of 1879, or the "Colored Exodus," as it is sometimes called, was prompted by the oppressive conditions that African Americans endured in the South after Reconstruction. Many blacks who hoped to own land could not find Southerners willing to sell or lease farmland to them. So they sought land in the West, available under the Homestead Act of 1862. All a person had to do was pick a 160-acre plot on federally owned land, pay a registration fee, live on the plot, cultivate part of it, and at the end of five years the land belonged to the homesteaders.

One enterprising pioneer was Benjamin "Pap" Singleton (1809–1892), who became known as the Father of the Exodus and Moses of the Colored Exodus. A former slave born in Nashville, Tennessee, Singleton began looking for land in Kansas in the early 1870s. In 1877 he helped form the Edgefield Real Estate and Homestead Association that encouraged blacks to move from Tennessee to Kansas to set up black colonies.

It was no simple matter for African Americans to migrate and take up farming in Kansas. The exodusters needed at least $1,000—a huge sum for former slaves—to pay for transportation, a team of mules, plows, lumber, and other necessities. Yet, between 1877 and 1879, more than 20,000 African Americans made the journey. Between 1870 and 1880, the black population in Kansas increased from 17,108 to 43,107.

Not all of the migrants came from Tennessee. Others from areas along the lower Mississippi River also headed for Kansas in what has been called a "spontaneous mass migration." White southerners were so upset by the loss of their workforce that they tried to prevent riverboats from carrying blacks north. Yet, African Americans pushed on, determined to reach the promised land.

In Kansas, many blacks remained poor and endured great hardships, but the majority believed they were better off than they were living under the repressive conditions in the South. They at least owned their land, had the right to vote and run for political office, and the opportunity to educate their children.

Festivalgoers at the 1998 celebration assemble in Township Park to await the National Park Service ceremony that will officially dedicate the town as Nicodemus National Historic Site. The U.S. Congress had designated it as such in 1996.

they, like other pioneers to the West, were forced to find shelter in dugouts, literally holes dug into mounds of earth.

In the spring, families planted crops, but there was little to harvest because of the harsh growing conditions and stormy weather that often blew seeds and plants away. Some became so discouraged that they returned to the southeast.

Yet, Nicodemus did begin to develop as a bonafide town, and by the 1880s, a bank, several stores, three churches, two hotels, a newspaper, and a school had been established. Townspeople hoped for continued growth and tried to convince the Union Pacific Railroad to extend track to Nicodemus. But town leaders and the railroad could not reach an agreement about financing, which left Nicodemus without rail service. As a result, some businesses began to leave and the town began to decline, although a reported 600 residents were living in this farming community during the first decade of the 1900s. Some Nicodemus farmers who stayed to work their land prospered, but farm prices fell during the Great Depression and a three-year drought in the 1930s. The Kansas dust bowl of 1935 further devastated the town, whose population dropped to 76. In 1996 Nicodemus was designated a national historic site, which includes five original buildings: the First Baptist Church, the African Methodist Episcopal Church, the township hall, the St. Francis Hotel, and the school. As of the early 21st century, about two dozen people lived in Nicodemus.

Creation of the Festival

Since 1878, settlers in Nicodemus have held an Emancipation Day celebration on August 1, the day in 1834 when Britain ended slavery in all its Caribbean colonies. The West Indies Emancipation Celebration of August 1 was highly symbolic for U.S. slaves, who saw hope for their own freedom. Now held on the last weekend in July, the Homecoming Emancipation Celebration draws former residents and descendants from many parts of the United States.

Observance

The original Emancipation celebration has become a Homecoming with about 600 people attending to reunite with family and friends. They share stories about the past and visit with the director of the Nicodemus Historical Society, Angela Bates-Tompkins, who once lived and worked in Washington, D.C., but returned to Nicodemus to make her home and boost the historical significance of the town. In addition, participants enjoy a variety of activities, such as a parade, wagon rides, and tours, horse rides for children, a **Buffalo Soldiers** exhibition, a fashion show, food and craft vendors, dances, church services, and gospel music. Some events celebrated during the 141st celebration in the year 2019 include the Historic Ellis Trail Tour, children activities such as face painting, a Gospel Extravaganza, and games for adults such as cards, UNO, dominoes, bid whist, and spades.

Contacts and Websites

Nicodemus Historical Society & Museum
611 S. 5th St.
Nicodemus, KS 67625
785-839-4280
https://www.nicodemushistoricalsociety.org/
nicodemus-kansas-historical-society-contact-us

Nicodemus National Historic Site
304 Washington Ave.
Nicodemus, KS 67625-3015
785-839-4233; fax: 785-839-4323
https://www.nps.gov/nico/contacts.htm

Further Reading

Attoun, Marti. "The Spirit of Nicodemus." *American Profile*, January 26–
    February 1, 2003. https://www.nps.gov/nico/learn/management/upload/
    Nicodemus_Final_singlesided.pdf.
Chu, Daniel, and Bill Shaw. *Going Home to Nicodemus: The Story of an African
    American Frontier Town and the Pioneers Who Settled It*. Parsippany, NJ:
    J. Messner, 1994. (young adult)
Horton, James Oliver, and Lois E. Horton, eds. *A History of the African
    American People: The History, Traditions & Culture of African Americans*.
    Detroit: Wayne State University Press, 1997.
Painter, Nell Irvin. *Exodusters: Black Migration to Kansas after the
    Reconstruction*. 1977. Reprint. New York: W. W. Norton, 1992.
Wiggins, William H., Jr. "The Emancipation of Nicodemus." *Natural History*,
    July–August, 1998.

Homowo Festival

Date Observed: August
Location: Portland, Oregon

T he Homowo Festival held each summer in Portland, Oregon, is named for a traditional harvest festival that takes place in Ghana. In Portland, the event had been celebrated with drumming, dancing, and singing over a weekend in August since 1989. In 2005 the festival became a one-day event focusing on one of Africa's ancient traditions: storytelling.

Historical Background

Every year, the Ga people in the West African nation of Ghana observe a thanksgiving festival for the harvest. Centuries ago, the Ga migrated across Africa to the west coast, and during their years of travel they were faced with famine. But they helped one another survive and reached what is now the Accra region. There they settled to grow crops, particularly millet, which they believe the gods ordained because the harvest was so plentiful. The solution to famine allowed the people to laugh at hunger, which is the meaning of the word *homowo* (hoh-moh-woh)—"hooting at hunger."

Each year, between four and six weeks before the harvest, the Ga people in Accra ban music, and everyone becomes quiet as they pray that their crops will be bountiful. They believe that noise will hurt those who are hungry and may be dying of starvation. When the crop grows, however, the drumming and festivities begin for Homowo.

Creation of the Festival

In order to share the African traditions and to pass this heritage to new generations, the festival was founded in 1989 by the Homowo Arts and Cultures organization. People of all ethnic and cultural backgrounds assemble together in a setting of celebration and harmony for this festival.

Homowo in Ghana

In 1993, an essay on Homowo by Marion Kilson, former dean of the Graduate School at Salem State College in Oregon, appeared in *Sextant*, an academic journal. The following excerpt describes what happens on Homowo feast day in Ghana and the following day:

> Early on Homowo morning, women begin to prepare the festal meal of kpekpei (kpokpoi), a palm oil fish stew consisting of steamed corn dough, bream, and okra. In Accra, chiefs offer the first libations to their ancestors and sprinkle kpekpe. The heads of Ga families then sprinkle kpekpe and offer libations to their ancestors. Finally, living Ga enjoy their meal. All the family members within a house gather around a bowl of kpekpe simultaneously dipping into the stew. The eating of kpekpe further illuminates the timeless nature of the Homowo period, for ordinarily the serving of food expresses sharp distinctions of rank, with senior members eating before junior members and men eating before women.
>
> Following the festal meal, the Homowo dance is performed. In Accra, Homowo dances begin formally. . . [but] quickly develop into joyful boisterous jostling dances in which anyone may participate, anyone may touch anyone else, people may dress in tattered rags, people may don the clothing of the opposite sex, and people may sing songs ridiculing prominent personages. . . . In short, while the Homowo dance is performed, all customary social statuses and constraints are in abeyance.
>
> Reprinted with permission from Marion Kilson, "Homowo: Celebrating Community in Ga Culture," *Sextant: The Journal of Salem State College*, Volume IV, Number 1, 1993.

In 1990 Obo Addy, a master drummer from Ghana, brought the Homowo tradition to Portland, Oregon, where he works as a teacher and performer. Called an American "king" of African music, Addy has performed in numerous shows across the nation and has appeared frequently at the Kennedy Center in Washington, D.C. He was the artistic director of Homowo African Arts and Culture, a non-profit group that tours the country to share the traditional music and dance of Ghana and create awareness of African culture through its festival.

Observance

The annual Homowo Festival in Portland takes place in early August. In past years, it included dancing, drumming, and singing by performers from the Homowo African Arts and Culture organization. Food and craft vendors, children's activities, and workshops also have been part of the event. In 2005, however, the festival organizers decided to scale back the festival to a one-day celebration of traditional African storytelling (*see also* **National Black Storytelling Festival and Conference**).

Contact

Homowo African Arts & Cultures
7725 N. Fowler Ave.
Portland, OR 97217
503-288-3025

Honoring Santería Orishas

Date Observed: Varies
Location: Santería homes and communities nationwide

F ollowers of the Santería faith honor several orishas (aw-REE-SHAWS), intermediary deities or spirits, on days that correspond to certain Roman Catholic saints' days.

Historical Background

The Santería religion emerged in Cuba, where, from the 1500s to the late 1800s, many thousands of enslaved Africans were shipped to labor on plantations. Cuba was ruled by Spain, a Roman Catholic country, until 1902. Under Spanish law, slaves were forced to follow the Roman Catholic faith. Yoruba slaves, mainly from Nigeria, noted similarities between their traditional faith and the new religion. Like the Christian god, the Yoruba have a supreme god, Olodumare (oh-low-DOO-may-ray), who created the universe. And like Roman Catholic saints, Yoruba orishas are considered to be spiritual beings who can serve as intermediaries to the supreme god on behalf of humans. By honoring orishas as Roman Catholic saints, slaves found ways to continue their own faith while outwardly appearing to adhere to Roman Catholicism. Thus, the religion became known as Santería, meaning "the way of the saints."

After slavery was abolished, Santería practices continued in Cuba, although they were often suppressed. Devotees carried their belief system with them when they fled Cuba after the revolution of 1959. Thousands of exiled Cubans, many of whom were Santería believers, found refuge in the United States, settling in south Florida, New Jersey, and New York. And some went to Puerto Rico. In the early 1990s, there were an estimated one million adherents of Santería in the United States.

A worshipper (left) prays to Shango at his altar in a church in Hialeah, Florida, in the company of the church's head priest.

Because Catholic clerics imposed the Santería name on practitioners, some current devotees and scholars prefer to call their religion Lukumí (loo-koo-ME), a word from the Yoruba language and culture. Or they use the term *la regla de ocha*, meaning "the rule of the orishas."

Creation of the Observance

The honoring of Santería orishas harkens back to ancient Yoruba religious practices of worshipping orishas. Various ceremonies and rituals, including prayers, offerings, and divination, are used in honoring orishas.

Santería and its practices frequently have been presented as "idolatrous, dangerous, or a product of a backward people," according to religious scholar Miguel A. De La Torre, who grew up in a Santería household and is a former believer. But in his book on Santería, De La Torre disputes these stereotypes and points out the spirituality and rituals that are part of this faith tradition.

People of West African heritage in the United States also observe Santería rituals. Some of these believers reject the Catholic influence, considering it a vestige of slavery; instead, they follow the religious rituals as practiced in West Africa. Black nationalists in New York City, for example, accepted some aspects of Santería but developed their own form of the religion. The Oyotunji African Village, established in the 1970s in South Carolina, is an attempt to connect to the original Yoruba religious practices (*see also* **Ifa Festival and Yoruba National Convention** *and* **Olokun Festival**).

Observance

Ceremonies to honor Santería orishas take place wherever there are large communities with African-Cuban roots, as well as in places where people of the Yoruba diaspora have settled, such as in the Americas and Caribbean Islands. People may worship in their own homes or gather at the home of a local priest or priestess. Although tributes vary depending on the community and individual adherents, devotees usually set up a shrine or altar for each orisha, who is assigned certain colors, numbers, and objects (*see* Table with heading Items Associated with Selected Orishas). There are many *ebbos* (offerings) of food also. Praise songs and drummers are part of community ceremonies, as are dancers, who perform movements characteristic of the orisha being honored.

During honoring ceremonies, Santería followers often recall the *patakis*, or legends, about the orisha being honored. There is no standard text or holy book in the tradition, but legends, poetry, history, and proverbs concerning orishas are now contained in a text known as the "Corpus of Ifa." However, the text is never completed; priests and priestesses transcribe their varied experiences in notebooks and these are passed on to followers.

Some major orishas, their patakis, and associated Roman Catholic saints are outlined below.

Babalú-Ayé (bah-bah-LOO-eye-ay) is considered equivalent to St. Lazarus, and both are honored on the saint's day, December 17. Devotees believe that people with broken limbs and many of the poor could be personifications of Babalú-Ayé, and that the orisha will punish those who do not help and respect the unfortunate. One legend about Babalú-Ayé claims he was a promiscuous deity and was punished by contracting a venereal disease. Sometimes this story is told to educate people about AIDS and HIV. Another version says that because Babalú-Ayé did not show respect for elder orishas, he was infected with smallpox.

Cuban entertainer Desi Arnaz, who played Ricky Ricardo in the 1950s sitcom "I Love Lucy," frequently sang to Babalú-Ayé while keeping the beat on a drum. Very few viewers were aware that "Ricky Ricardo was singing to Babalú-Ayé," according to author Miguel De La Torre. Ricky "was engaged in a sophisticated choreography that descended from the African civilization of the Yoruba, long before Europe was ever deemed civilized."

Obatala (aw-bah-tah-LAH) is honored at the same time as the Roman Catholic saint Our Lady of Mercy, also known as Our Lady of Ransom, who is commemorated on September 24. According to legend, Obatala is the chief spirit who descended from heaven on a golden chain to spread soil over a watery earth. Obatala eventually landed on earth at a place that became what is the Nigerian city of Ile-Ife (ee-LAY-ee-FAY), where tradition says creation began. It is said that Obatala created the world and humankind and encompasses both genders. Obatala's creative powers can bring forth a great variety of humans with diverse physical abilities and challenges. This deity also enforces justice and can bring peace, compassion, and intelligence to the world.

Ogun (aw-GOON) is another better-known orisha. Ogun's Catholic counterpart is St. Peter the Apostle, whose feast day is June 30. The guiding spirit of iron and metals, Ogun also is characterized as a fierce, fully armed warrior. However, because he oversees all mechanical things, he is responsible for

---

Oriki Ogun—Praising the Spirit of Iron

This is a traditional prayer offered by devotees to praise Ogun.

Ogun awo, Olumaki, alase a juba.

Spirit of the mystery of Iron, Chief of Strength, the owner of power, I salute you.

Ogun ni jo ti ma lana lati ode.

Spirit of Iron dances outside to open the road.

Ogun onire, onile kangun-dangun ode Orun, egbe l'ehin,

Spirit of Iron, owner of good fortune, owner of many houses in Heaven, Help those who journey,

Pa san bo pon ao lana to.

Remove the obstructions from our path.

Imo kimo 'bora, egbe lehin a nle a benge ologbe.

Wisdom of the Warrior Spirit, guide us through our spiritual journey with strength.

Ase. So be it.

---

farming tools, surgical instruments, and medicine. In other words, he can destroy as well as rebuild or restore all things.

Oshun is honored along with Our Lady of Charity on September 12, or September 8 in some locations. She is a compassionate goddess of fertility and sexuality and is associated with the arts and creativity. According to centuries-old legends, Oshun is the owner of all rivers and fresh waters. Devotees may toss offerings to her into a river or lake, a practice also followed during a festival that takes place each year in Philadelphia, Pennsylvania (*see also* **Odunde Festival**).

Oya has power over fire, and is recognized on February 2, which is the feast day of Our Lady of the Presentation of Our Lord (Santa Virgen de la Candelaria; *Candelaria* means "conflagration," or a huge fire). Oya has power over the

Items Associated with Selected Orishas

Orisha	Colors	Foods	Objects & Number
Babalú-Ayé	purple	popcorn, sesame seed candy, grains	icon in sack cloth, crutches, dog figurines No. 17
Obatala	white with accent colors such as red, purple, green	bread, rice, meringue, white wine	silver coins, white beads & flowers No. 8
Ogun	green and black	honey, palm oil, fruits, rum	knife, any iron or steel item No. 7 or 3
Oshun	amber, yellow, coral	pumpkins, honey	copper pennies No. 5
Oya	brown, red, burgundy, copper	palm oil, corn meal, grapes, plantains, okra, fish, beans with rice	buffalo horn, jars of water, flowers or flowerly materials No. 9
Shango	combination red & white	bananas, corn meal, okra	mortar to mix spells, warrior image holding a hatchet in one hand and a sword in the other Nos. 4 & 6

winds, storms, tornadoes, and hurricanes. She also guards the gates of ceme-
teries. She represents death and rebirth into a new life. The mythical Oya is
a warrior queen and god Shango's favorite wife, fighting alongside him and
using thunderbolts to aid him in battle.

Shango (or Chango) is on the feast day of St. Barbara, December 4. Some
accounts say that Shango personifies the king of ancient Oyo, Nigeria, and that
he experimented with magic, which caused a violent storm. Lightning struck
his palace and killed many of his wives and children. As a result, Shango hung
himself, and people in Oyo held him in contempt. That brought more storms,
which Shango devotees believe was the orisha's revenge.

Contacts and Websites

HistoryMiami
101 W. Flagler St.
Miami, FL 33130
305-375-1492
E-mail: info@historymiami.org
https://www.historymiami.org

Church of the Lukumi Babalu Aye
436 Palm Ave.
Hialeah, FL 33012
E-mail: olukumi@hotmail.com
http://www.churchofthelukumi.com

Further Reading

Barnes, Sandra T. *Africa's Ogun: Old World and New.* 2nd ed. Bloomington:
Indiana University Press, 1997.
Bellenir, Karen, ed. *Religious Holidays and Calendars: An Encyclopedic
Handbook.* 3rd ed. Detroit: Omnigraphics, 2004.
Brandon, George. *Santería from Africa to the New World: The Dead Sell
Memories.* Bloomington: Indiana University Press, 1997.
Clarke, Kamari Maxine. *Mapping Yoruba Networks: Power and Agency in the
Making of Transnational Communities.* Durham, NC: Duke University
Press, 2004.
Curry, Mary Cuthrell. *Making the Gods in New York: The Yoruba Religion in
the African American Community.* New York: Garland, 1997.

De La Torre, Miguel A. *Santería: The Beliefs and Rituals of a Growing Religion in America*. Grand Rapids, MI: William B. Eerdmans Publishing Company, 2004.

Degiglio-Bellemare, Mario. "Cuba: Santería, Scarcity, and Survival." February 13, 2005.

Occasional Paper Series, Institute for Cuban and Cuban-American Studies, University of Miami, November 2001.

González-Wippler, Migene. *Santería: The Religion.* St. Paul, MN: Llewellyn Publications, 2004.

Murphy, Joseph M. *Santería: African Spirits in America.* 1993. Reprint. Boston: Beacon Press, 2011.

Núñez, Luis Manuel. *Santería: A Practical Guide to Afro-Caribbean Magic.* Dallas, TX: Spring Publications, 1992.

O'Brien, David M. *Animal Sacrifice and Religious Freedom: Church of the Lukumi Babalu Aye v. City of Hialeah.* Lawrence: University Press of Kansas, 2004.

Sanchez, Sara M. "Afro-Cuban Diasporan Religions: A Comparative Analysis of the Literature and Selected Annotated Bibliography." Occasional Paper Series, Institute for Cuban and Cuban-American Studies, University of Miami, August 2000.

Idlewild Music Festival

Date Observed: Second weekend of July
Location: Idlewild, Michigan

The Idlewild Music Festival, earlier known as Idlewild Music Festival, is an annual July event in historic Idlewild, Michigan, known as the "Black Eden." The festival features outdoor entertainment, jazz movies, local documentaries, and workshops for high-school students.

Historical Background

Idlewild is one of the oldest African-American resorts in the United States. Founded in 1912, the community is on an island with footbridges connecting it to the mainland. Idlewild was established as a place where black urban professionals, most of them affluent, could relax and enjoy recreational activities— hunting, fishing, swimming, boating—far from the racism and discrimination so prevalent elsewhere during the early part of the 20th century.

In 1912 white developers formed the Idlewild Resort Company (IRC) and bought 3,000 acres of land and the island. The developers organized train and bus tours to bring African Americans from midwestern cities such as Chicago, Illinois; Detroit, Michigan; and St. Louis, Missouri, to the resort.

In the mid-1920s, the IRC turned the island over to prominent African Americans who formed the Idlewild Improvement Association (IIA). The IIA then sold property to such well-known African Americans as W. E. B. Du Bois, millionaire businesswoman Madame C. J. Walker, and novelist Charles Waddell Chesnutt.

As an increasing number of African Americans visited or bought property in and around Idlewild, the area became known as "Black Eden." A dozen jazz clubs, such as the Flamingo and the Paradise Club, and other businesses developed. By the 1950s, numerous black entertainers were appearing at the night spots. Among the nationally known performers were Della Reese, Count Basie, Sarah Vaughn, Duke Ellington, Louis Armstrong, and many more (*see also* **Satchmo SummerFest**). Idlewild historians say it is likely that every major African-American entertainer visited the resort at one time or another. In addition, a variety of political activists visited, including members of Marcus Garvey's organization (*see also* **Marcus Garvey's Birthday**).

During the late 1960s and through the 1970s, the resort area began to decline. With the passage of the Civil Rights Act of 1964, African Americans began to find more choices in where and how they could vacation. The Idlewild resort seemed to be of little interest to a younger generation.

By the 1990s, however, the resort began to revive. Businessman John O. Meeks formed the Idlewild African-American Chamber of Commerce in 2000. The Idlewild Music Festival is also part of the effort to carry on revitalization and to attract new businesses and tourists.

Creation of the Festival

The festival was launched in 2002 by Idlewild history buffs who hoped that they could help connect the present with the past. They wanted a celebration that would replicate the resort's heyday. One of the events linked to times past was an amateur hour on the first night, and top blues and jazz performers on Saturday. Gospel music took center stage on Sunday.

Observance

The annual Idlewild Music Festival, held the second weekend of July, includes jazz, blues, and soul performances. It has featured such artists as Eric Alexander, Rod Hicks, and harpist Onita Sanders. At the 2005 festival Eric Alexander arrived by boat on Lake Idlewild, and trumpeter Jim Rotondi left the stage to walk aboard a boat, playing while sailing away. High-school musicians, food vendors, jazz movies, a marketplace, writers' workshops, and a book tent are also part of the festivities. Ten years later, the organizers brought national attention to the festival and, by the following years, they hosted a sold-out venue and therefore moved the sessions to the Auditorium and University Center of the Ferris State University campus.

Festivalgoers may visit the Idlewild Museum, where they can learn about the founders of the resort. Exhibits also show how famous African Americans from many walks of life built summer homes or permanent residences in Idlewild.

Contacts and Websites

Idlewild African American Chamber of Commerce
P.O. Box 435
Idlewild, MI 49642
678-492-6814
http://www.iaacc.com

Idlewild Historic & Cultural Center
7025 Broadway Ave.
Idlewild, MI 49642
http://www.historicidlewild.org

Further Reading

Stevens, Ronald. *Idlewild: Black Eden of Michigan.* Charleston, SC: Arcadia Publishers, 2001.

Walker, Lewis, and Benjamin C. Wilson. *Black Eden: The Idlewild Community.* East Lansing: Michigan State University Press, 2002. Reprint. Michigan State University Press, 2007.

Ifa Festival and Yoruba National Convention

Date Observed: Annually in July
Location: Oyotunji African Village, South Carolina

T he Ifa Festival and Yoruba National Convention is held each year in July, in the Oyotunji African Village in Beaufort County, outside Sheldon, South Carolina. Yoruba religious devotees from across the United States and other countries gather to honor Ifa (ee-FAH), considered the wisest of all orishas (or deities) and the chief counselor of the supreme being Olodumare (oh-low-DOO-may-ray).

Historical Background

Oyotunji means "rises again" in the Yoruba language, and Oyotunji Village is a kingdom patterned after kingdoms in West Africa's Yorubaland. At one time, there were about 20 such kingdoms, and each one was ruled by its own king.

The founder of Oyotunji was Walter King, who was initiated into the Yoruban religious society of Ifa. He changed his name and became Oba (King) Oseijeman Adefunmi I, who has been called the "father of the African cultural restoration movement." His Royal Highness Oba Oseijeman was crowned in 1981 in Ife, Nigeria. He reigned until his death in February 2005. A new king, Oseijeman Adefunmi II, was crowned in July 2005.

During the 1960s, when African Americans were seeking to assert their own cultural and spiritual identities, Oseijeman Adefunmi I established several Yoruba temples in Harlem. In the mid-1960s he sought a rural area to continue to develop the religious movement. In 1970 he bought land where the village exists today. It is the only traditional African village in the United States, and a sign greets visitors: "Welcome to Oyotunji. You are now leaving the

United States of America and about to enter the Yoruba kingdom of Oyotunji African Village."

The number of Oyotunji villagers fluctuates, but since the 1990s, eight or nine families have been residents under the rule of the king and a council of chiefs. Village children attend a private school called the" Royal Academy." Students learn not only subjects required by the state of South Carolina, but also Yoruba language, culture, and history.

Residents in this small village hold festivals for specific orishas each month except November (*see also* **Olokun Festival**). The festivals are part of a Yoruba way of life dating back centuries.

Creation of the Festival

The Ifa Festival in Oyotunji began with the founding of the village, which is similar to a small village in what is now Nigeria. Following the Yoruba tradition, the festival focuses on Ifa, who is said to know the destiny of each person and which orisha she or he is destined to worship (*see also* **Honoring Santería Orishas**).

Observance

The July festival in the Oyotunji Village brings together those who follow traditional Yoruba religious practices. There are dances, drum performances, and recitations to Ifa, the deity of destiny. Participants may also seek guidance from psychic readers and listen to lectures by the king and chiefs.

Because Ifa is also a form of divination, a high priest referred to as *babalawo* (bah-bahLAH-woe), meaning "father of secrets," calls upon Ifa, the oracle of divination, to mediate between the orishas, ancestors, and participants. The priest scatters cowry shells or palm nuts and then reads the patterns into which they fall to determine how supernatural forces may affect a particular person. As a result, the babalawo can suggest actions a person can take to better her or his life.

Contact and Website

Kingdom of Oyotunji African Village
56 Bryant Ln.
Seabrook, SC 29941
843-846-8900
E-mail: info@oyotunji.org
https://www.oyotunji.org

Further Reading

"An Interview with Oba Osijeman Adefunmi I of Oyotunji, South Carolina."
   Isokan Yoruba Magazine, Fall 1996-Winter 1997.
https://yeyeolade.wordpress.com/2008/03/15/a-yoruba-village-in-south-
   carolina-amerikkka/
Tyehimba, Cheo. "African Gods in South Carolina." *Essence*, December 1995.

IFE-ILE's Afro-Cuban Dance Festival

Date Observed: February
Location: Miami

The IFE-ILE Afro-Cuban festival preserves, nurtures, and promotes Afro-Cuban culture through music, dance, and other art forms.

Historical Background

The arrival of Cuban refugees to the United States can be traced to the historic "Mariel boatlift," a reference to the mass immigration of Cubans from Cuba's Mariel Harbor to the United States between April and October 1980. This mass exodus was in response to a sharp downturn in the Cuban economy and is regarded as one of the most impactful events of the Cuban revolution. Immigration from Cuba had its beginnings much earlier. Early immigrants from Cuba were wealthy sugar-mill owners and successful professionals whose property had been confiscated by the Communist regime. These pioneers had to start anew, often working in low-paying jobs and struggling to set up small businesses.

The steady influx of Cuban immigrants coupled with their strong entrepreneurial skills led to the emergence of a thriving community of Cuban Americans in Miami. Over the course of time, this community emerged as a strong political and economic force in the U.S. During the dramatic Mariel boatlift of 1980, this community of Cuban Americans hired boats from Key West and Miami to lift Cubans seeking to flee Cuba in search of economic opportunities and political freedom. Although an agreement had been reached by the administration of then-U.S. President Jimmy Carter and then-president of Cuba Fidel Castro on the migration of Cubans to the United States, the mass exodus of Cuban refugees to the United States posed problems for the Carter administration. This made it necessary to halt Cuban immigration by mutual agreement. But, as many as 125,000 Cubans had already reached Florida by the time the embargo was put in place. Settling mostly in Miami, these refugees built their lives in their new homeland, but this chaotic exodus had changed the lives of the Cuban immigrants forever and also transformed the demography and culture of Miami.

Little Havana, the famous Cuban stronghold and home to many exiles in Miami, stands as a testimony to the mass exodus of Cubans across the Florida Straits following the communist takeover of Cuba. From cigars and mojitos to Cuban food and street dancers, everything there is distinctly Cuban. Besides being home to Cuban exiles, Miami is also home to Central Americans, African Americans, and Mexicans. The complex racial dynamics of the region have led to more and more communities (like the Afro-Cubans) seeking to establish their cultural identity and be recognized for their contributions toward the history of Miami.

Creation of the Festival

The IFE-ILE festival of dance was founded by IFE-ILE, a non-profit organization whose mission is to promote and preserve the Afro-Cuban culture through the medium of traditional and contemporary art performances, education, and community service. The annual dance festival debuted in 1998, and the nationally acclaimed Afro-Cuban choreographer and dancer Neri Torres curated the inaugural festival. Since then, the festival has provided a platform to celebrate the cultural traditions of the Cuban African diaspora in the U.S. and Latin America. Torres named the festival IFE-ILE, a phrase which roughly translates as the "house of love" in Yoruba, the language of her ancestors. The IFE is an ancient Nigerian kingdom believed by the Yorubas (an African ethnic group inhabiting West Africa) to be the place where God created humanity.

Observance

Since its debut, the music and dance festival founded by Torres has expanded its horizons to become a symbol of the multiethnic culture of South Florida. Celebrations extend over a week, and the festival agenda includes dance performances and drumming workshops; film shows; and food and dance parties. Some of the content showcased at the festival focuses on the "occult" elements of the culture, which has hitherto been shrouded in mystery and not revealed in public forums.

The week-long festival offers children and adults an opportunity to learn tumbadoras (congas), claves, guiros (shekeres), and bells. Festivalgoers get to participate in cleansing ceremonies and join the procession, which dances the congo along the street in downtown Miami. Traditional food is cooked and served to the festival-goers, and panelists discuss the deep significance of food in worship and religion. The finale is a dance gala featuring guest artists and dancers from the IFE-ILE Afro-Cuban Dance Company.

The festival stages popular Afro-Cuban dance forms, including Rumba, Chancleta, Son, Salsa, and many others that share African roots. The repertoire also includes the ritual Orishas dances—Afro-Cuban folklore dances which are strongly intertwined with the culture and religion of the Afro Cubans. This dance form is a kind of apotheosis wherein the dancer becomes a shrine and the orishas (gods) mount the body of the dancer when they come to visit the physical world. Trance is a prominent element of this dance form and features complex and highly syncopated musical incantations. The music is polyrhythmic and accompanied by drum beats and ritualistic body movements, the details of which vary greatly according to the deity represented.

Contacts and Websites

Koubek Center
2705 SW 3rd St.
Miami, FL 33135
305-284-6001 or 786-704-8609
E-mail: ifeiledancecompany@yahoo.com
https://www.koubekcenter.org

Afro Cuban Forum Inc.
269 NW 7th St., Ste. 117
Miami, FL 33136
E-mail: contact@afrocubanforum.org
www.afrocubanforum.org

Further Reading

https://www.nber.org/papers/w3069.pdf
http://bruegel.org/2017/06/the-mariel-boatlift-controversy/
Garcia, Jose Manuel. *Voices from Mariel: Oral Histories of the 1980 Cuban Boatlift.* Florida: University Press of Florida, 2018.

Indiana Black Expo's Summer Celebration

Date Observed: Mid-July
Location: Indianapolis, Indiana

The Summer Celebration in Indianapolis, Indiana, is the Indiana Black Expo's largest annual fundraising event. This 10-day festival highlights the importance of African-American artistic, cultural, and historic contributions and draws more than 300,000 visitors annually.

Historical Background

In the midst of the ongoing racial discrimination and inequality that characterized the early 1970s, the Indiana Black Expo worked to encourage African Americans to achieve their highest potential. Early organizers sought advice from prominent African Americans, such as Rev. Andrew J. Brown of the Southern Christian Leadership Conference and local businessman James C. Cummings Jr. Cummings became the organization's first chairman, and formed a plan for the first Summer Celebration. This major event was intended to honor African-American culture, while raising financial support for the development of additional programs that would benefit the African-American community. By presenting positive images of successful African Americans, the Indiana Black Expo hoped to inspire young people to greatness.

Creation of the Festival

The first Summer Celebration was held in 1971 at the Indiana State Fairgrounds. More than 50,000 people attended the two-day event. This overwhelming success prompted organizers to move the event to the Indianapolis Convention Center in 1972. Several major new events were introduced to

Summer Celebration that year, including the Muhammad Ali Amateur Boxing Tournament and the Star Quest talent competition. Since then, Summer Celebration has grown substantially, attracting more than 300,000 people to Indianapolis for the 10-day festival each year. The focus of Summer Celebration has also grown to include the entire African-American community across the U.S.

Indiana Black Expo

The Indiana Black Expo was created in 1970 with the goal of becoming an effective voice and vehicle for the advancement of African Americans. Founded by a small group of community leaders in Indianapolis, Indiana Black Expo has grown to include twelve chapters throughout Indiana. The organization has had a profound impact on African Americans in Indiana and surrounding areas.

Many events are sponsored throughout the year, with Summer Celebration being the largest. The group also produces an **African-American History Month** Celebration, Back-to-School Rallies, a television newsmagazine show, numerous programs to address poverty, and many special programs for youth. The Circle City Classic weekend in October includes a football game played by teams from historically black colleges and universities, or HBCUs (*see also* **Football Classics**). The events held on this weekend typically raise many thousands of dollars that benefit students at HBCUs.

Observance

Summer Celebration, also known simply as the Expo, is a massive event featuring African-American art, culture, entertainment, and educational programming. More than 25 large-scale programs are run during Summer Celebration, covering topics including health education, political activism, business development, personal development, entertainment, a film festival, and activities for children and young people.

Business networking among African Americans is promoted at the Black Business Conference, which includes the Black Enterprise Wealth Building Seminar, employment-opportunity job fairs, and a Youth Entrepreneur Seminar. The largest Black and Minority Health Fair in the U.S. is held in conjunction with Summer Celebration, where the Indiana Black Expo recently introduced the Rev. Charles Williams Prostate Cancer Mobile Unit to raise awareness and provide onsite diagnostic screenings. Various religious services are held, a celebrity basketball game is played, and notable African Americans are honored each year with the Founder's Award and the Freedom Award.

Special guest speakers are invited each year to present the keynote address at the Summer Celebration Corporate Luncheon. In 2005 the Indiana Black Expo made national news headlines when President George W. Bush spoke at the luncheon. This marked the first time a sitting U.S. president attended Summer Celebration.

Contact and Website

Indiana Black Expo, Inc.
3145 N. Meridian St.
Indianapolis, IN 46208
317-925-2702; fax: 317-925-6624
http://www.indianablackexpo.com

J'Ouvert Celebration and West Indian-American Day Carnival

Date Observed: First Monday in September
Location: Brooklyn, New York

The J'Ouvert Celebration and West Indian-American Day Carnival draw upon island traditions that involve art, craftsmanship, cuisine, dance, and music. The Carnival has been held in September since the 1940s, while J'Ouvert began in the 1980s. The celebration has become one of the most prominent multiethnic festivals in the city.

Historical Background

Carnival originated in medieval Roman Catholic Europe as feasting parties held before the beginning of Lent in late February or early March. During Lent, Roman Catholics were obligated to abstain from certain foods, so many participated in Carnival as a last indulgence before the 40 days of Lent. As countries such as Spain and France colonized the Americas beginning in the 16th century, their Carnival celebrations came with them. After the abolition of slavery in the West Indies in 1834, free blacks began to have a strong influence on the celebrations of Carnival, adding street theater and their own musical and dance traditions (*see also* **West Indies Emancipation Day**).

The term "J'Ouvert" (joo-VAY) combines the French words *jour* and *ouvert* and means the "beginning of the day." The J'Ouvert procession has been the traditional opening of Carnival in the West Indies nation of Trinidad and Tobago for more than 100 years and kicks off at the break of dawn. J'Ouvert is said to have derived from a much earlier festival that was held at night by slaves gathered to celebrate their emancipation. It included masquerading, singing, and dancing, and eventually got swept up into the Trinidadian Carnival festivities.

Trinidadian dancers at the 2002 West Indian-American Carnival parade.

Creation of the Festival

Brooklyn is home to the largest West Indian population outside of the Caribbean. Therefore, it comes as no surprise that the prevalent custom of celebrating Carnival traveled with those who emigrated to New York. In the 1920s and 1930s, Carnival was mostly observed in the form of indoor balls, due to the colder temperatures found in the North during the traditional time for the pre-Lenten festival. Jessie Wattle (or Waddle), a Trinidadian woman, and others from the West Indies are reported to have organized such events in Harlem ballrooms.

In the 1940s Wattle sought and obtained a street permit for an outdoor Carnival parade in Harlem, replete with bands and costumed masqueraders; this event was held in September because the weather was more pleasant.

Various racial tensions and unrest during the mid-1960s led to the revocation of the Harlem event permit, so others—led by Rufus Goring, a costume designer from Trinidad—organized a Carnival parade in Brooklyn, where it has remained ever since. A few years later, Goring passed the leadership baton off to Carlos Lezama, who formed the group that now coordinates the annual parade: the West Indian-American Day Carnival Association (WIADCA).

The J'Ouvert part of the celebration began during the 1980s, when members of the Pan Rebels Steel Orchestra ventured out in the wee hours and began performing for some all-night partiers. This led to a spontaneous parade—with some masqueraders reputed to be costumed only in their pajamas—heading down the street, picking up others until they numbered 100. In 1994 the nonprofit J'Ouvert City International, Inc. was formed to coordinate the pre-dawn event.

Observance

Approximately two million people participate in the Labor Day festivities in New York each year. About 10 percent of that number, a hardy 200,000 revelers, take part in J'Ouvert, which commences at 2 A.M. on the first Monday of September. This is characterized by a gathering of steel bands, playing traditional pan music without any influence from or bowing to modern culture. The musical groups are joined by hordes of costumed masqueraders who dance along. Some are dressed elaborately, others in tatters and rags. They paint their faces and their bodies, some with mud, others with talcum. Some dress as devils, witches, and all manner of evil spirits; others choose to satirize politicians of the day through their dress and via the placards they carry. Innocent bystanders must beware of having mud, paint, or powder flung on them from the barrels of such substances wheeled along the route for "refreshing" the masqueraders throughout their revelry.

The West Indian-American Day Carnival begins with its parade at 11 A.M. and lasts until 6 P.M. Similar to J'Ouvert, there are costumed and masqueraded participants at this event. The music, however, is more varied; much of it is blared from sound trucks and ranges from calypso to soca to reggae to the latest pop music offerings from any of the Caribbean isles. Those who come to line the two-mile parade route are urged to "Bring your flag! Represent your country with your national flag or rag," further underscoring the broadening of the event from its Trinidadian roots.

Food is a central part of the day and has gravitated from pure Trinidadian-based dishes to those that will provide attendees with the opportunity to experience

Steel Band Music

The steel band, which is an integral part of Carnival, is said to have originated in Trinidad around the 1930s, although historians debate both the location and date. Today, the bands are popular throughout the Caribbean, as well as in the United States, during West-Indian celebrations.

Steel bands are comprised of pan players who make music on instruments fashioned from the heads of used oil drums, pounded into a concave shape, and tuned by creating flattened areas that produce a variety of tones when struck. Pan players also have created percussion instruments from other kinds of metal containers such as biscuit tins, trash barrels, and paint cans.

The forerunners of steel bands were bamboo tamboo stick bands, which came about when British rulers in Trinidad banned drumming among blacks because whites viewed it as rebellious activity. To replace the drum, Africans created a different kind of music, using bamboo to beat on boxes and metal pieces. Eventually a rhythmic music called "bamboo tamboo" evolved, and an ensemble of players used thick bamboo from four to six feet long as instruments by pounding them on the ground and beating them with sticks. The open end of the sticks hitting the earth created a deep sound, with variations in tone depending on the size of the bamboo.

Bamboo tamboo bands marched in Carnivals and other festive events. About the mid-1930s these bands became a mixture of bamboo instruments and metal pans, although accounts about how that fusion began vary considerably. Basically, so the story goes, a bamboo band was parading in Trinidad and one of the members broke the bamboo he was using, and supposedly picked up a pan or can and began beating on it.

Whatever the makeup of a band, none paraded during World War II when Carnival was banned. Following the war, parades again took place, especially during celebrations of victories in Europe and Japan in 1945. By that time, steel bands were the rage and ever since have continued to evolve. Some have become professional companies that perform internationally.

a broad culinary spectrum: jerk chicken, chicken stew, fried chicken, beef stew, oxtail, rice and peas, salad, macaroni pie, fried flying fish, curry goat, roti, callaloo, souse, salt fish, fried bake, coconut bread, and more. Non-food vendors are on hand, as well, displaying arts and crafts and other African-American and Caribbean-related wares.

Contacts and Websites

Brooklyn Tourism and Visitors Center
Brooklyn Borough Hall
209 Joralemon St.
Brooklyn, NY 11201
718-802-3700; fax: 718-802-3778
https://www.brooklyn-usa.org

West Indian-American Day Carnival Association
323-325 Rogers Ave.
Brooklyn, NY 11225
718-467-1797
wiadcainc@gmail.com
http://wiadcacarnival.org

Further Reading

Allen, Ray, and Lois Wilcken, eds. *Island Sounds in the Global City: Caribbean Popular Music and Identity in New York.* Urbana: University of Illinois Press, 2001.

Arching, Gerard. *Masking and Power: Carnival and Popular Culture in the Caribbean.* Minneapolis: University of Minnesota Press, 2002.

Kasinitz, Philip. *Caribbean New York: Black Immigrants and the Politics of Race.* Ithaca, NY: Cornell University Press, 1992.

Jackie Robinson Day

Date Observed: On or around April 15
Location: Major-league ballparks in the U.S.

Jackie Robinson Day pays tribute to the first African-American man to break the color barrier in America's national pastime, the game of professional baseball. In recognition of the date on which Jackie Robinson played his first major-league game, on or around April 15 each year, commemorative celebrations are held at professional baseball stadiums across the country.

Historical Background

Born in Cairo, Georgia, in 1919, Jack Roosevelt Robinson, called "Jackie," was the son of Jerry Robinson, a plantation farm worker, and Mallie McGriff, a domestic worker. Jackie was one of five children in the family. Robinson's father left his family not long after Jackie's birth, and his mother sought a better life and income in California. Urged by his mother to "turn the other cheek" to incidents of racial intolerance, Jackie experienced the rampant racial discrimination characteristic of the 1920s and 1930s firsthand and sometimes failed to heed her words of restraint when rocks were thrown his way or crosses were burned nearby by racists.

Robinson began his sports career at the University of California at Los Angeles, where he demonstrated broad athletic abilities by lettering in baseball, basketball, football, and track and field. He left school in his senior year to join the Army and served in World War II. Robinson successfully pushed for admittance to Officer Training School and was a first lieutenant when honorably discharged in 1944. He had risked court-martial for refusing to move to the back of a military bus and later was cleared of insubordination.

Upon his return to civilian life, Robinson tried out for the Kansas City Monarchs, a black baseball club. Scouts working for Brooklyn Dodgers

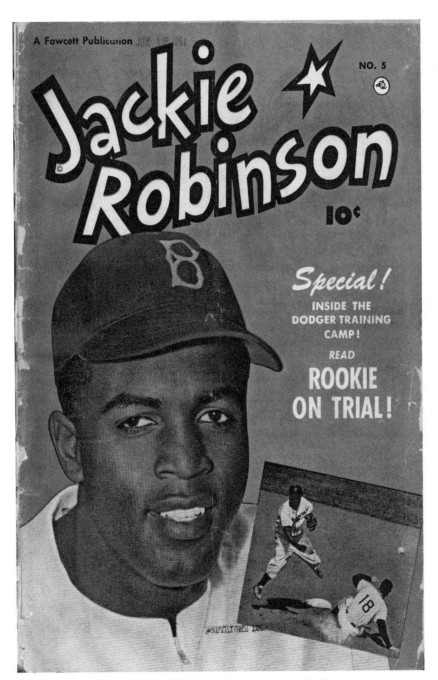

Cover of a 1951 Jackie Robinson comic book.

Early Baseball Segregation

The Weeksville of New York beat the Colored Union Club 11-0 on September 28, 1860, at the first black-versus-black baseball game held at Elysian Fields in Brooklyn, New York. After the Civil War, the first professional baseball team, the Cincinnati Red Stockings, was organized in 1869. In 1871 the National Association of Professional Baseball Players was chartered (this would one day evolve into today's National League). Throughout the decade additional leagues formed, one being the Western League, which became the American League.

Up until the mid-to-late 1870s, around the end of the Reconstruction period and the institution of Jim Crow laws, some blacks did play baseball with minor league clubs and even a rare few with major league teams. But they were commonly subjected to verbal and physical abuse from teammates, competitors, and spectators. In 1868, white-run baseball took the official stance of prohibiting the hiring of blacks. That same year, the National Association of Baseball Players voted unanimously to bar "any club which may be composed of one or more colored people." In 1887 the Chicago White Stockings threatened to boycott a game against the integrated Newark Giants.

With such segregationist attitudes working against them, blacks began decades of struggle to develop and maintain various leagues that would allow them to take part in America's national pastime. Today, these endeavors are collectively referred to as "The Negro Leagues."

The first professional black baseball team was formed in 1885 by a white businessman of Trenton, New Jersey, Walter Cook, who came across a group of Argyle Hotel waiters and porters playing for fun in Babylon, New York. Cook was successful in attracting more white fans to games by naming his team the Cuban Giants.

In 1920 Andrew "Rube" Foster, known as the Father of Black Baseball, founded the first Negro professional league—the National Negro Baseball League. In the following years other black leagues were formed. All the while, a parallel all-white baseball system was in operation. These two segregated sporting systems continued through the early 20th century.

President Branch Rickey spotted Robinson and soon he was on Rickey's short list of African Americans slated to be the first to transition to the big leagues. Although Major League Baseball Commissioner "Happy" Chandler had set up a Committee on Baseball Integration, many of Rickey's fellow managers were not supportive. So, initially, Rickey allowed everyone to believe that, up until the last possible moment, he was scouting black players to field his own Negro League. But, when he met with Robinson on August 28, 1945, he made certain that Jackie knew otherwise. Reports of that meeting are legendary, having Rickey hurling vile racial invectives at Robinson to see if the athlete had the fortitude to weather the verbal abuse to which he would be subjected as a black man in the world of white baseball. As recounted in historian Jules Tygiel's book, Robinson eventually responded, "Do you want a ballplayer who's afraid to fight back?" Rickey replied, "I want a player with guts enough not to fight back."

By 1947, Robinson had made it to the big leagues and his name had been added to the Brooklyn Dodgers roster. The announcement prompted death threats against Robinson and his family. At odds with the naysayers, however, was Robinson's sheer ability to play ball. In his first year in the majors, he was named Rookie of the Year, and his contributions undeniably helped lead the Dodgers to win the pennant.

Although Robinson never did completely shy away from speaking up for himself when he believed the occasion warranted it, he also became a great role model in the school of "letting talent speaks for itself." Not long after Robinson was signed to the Dodgers, other teams began to look to the Negro Leagues to supplement their traditional talent pools. Before long, Major League Baseball was designating those it had previously denied admittance as some of its "greats."

Robinson accomplished much on the field of baseball. Highlights during his 1947–1956 career with the Dodgers include stealing home base 19 times; being named National League All Star six times; earning the 1949 National League batting title with a .342 average and being awarded the League's Most Valuable Player title that same year. Robinson chose to retire in 1957 upon learning that he was to be traded to the Dodgers' archrival, the New York Giants.

But as much as Robinson racked up impressive statistics, his actions and presence—both on and off the playing field—contributed just as much to his legacy. During his playing career and after, Robinson advocated for integration and cooperation between the races. He was a strong proponent of greater minority hiring in baseball, additionally pressing for representation in management and ownership.

Robinson had many detractors during his day, but he also had supporters. In 1962 Robinson became the first African American admitted into Cooperstown, New York, Baseball Hall of Fame. He died of a heart attack in 1972.

In 1997, to honor the 50th anniversary of Robinson's first game with the Dodgers (the team has since moved to Los Angeles) Major League Baseball permanently retired his "42" uniform number—it would never be given to another player on any team. In March of 2005, Robinson was awarded a Congressional Gold Medal. The Jackie Robinson Day in 2019 is special since it is the 100th birthday of Jackie Robinson.

Creation of the Observance

In 2004, organized baseball took steps to honor Robinson's memory and achievements in an annual fashion by designating every April 15 Jackie Robinson Day. In a Major League Baseball press release, Commissioner Alan H. "Bud" Selig noted:

> "By establishing April 15 as 'Jackie Robinson Day' throughout Major League Baseball, we are further ensuring that the incredible contributions and sacrifices he made—for baseball and society—will not be forgotten."

April 15, 2004, marked the first of what continues to be seen as a celebration of a truly remarkable man, "Jackie" Roosevelt Robinson, honored as much for his baseball prowess as for his betterment of the human condition in his quest for the equal treatment of minorities.

Observance

Each year, on or about April 15 (depending upon scheduled game days), Major League Baseball teams across the nation collectively celebrate the memory and accomplishments—both on and off the field—of Jackie Robinson.

There are some commonalities in the ways that the 14 American and 16 National League teams honor Robinson each year. The ceremonies are

Early into his rookie year with the Dodgers, Jackie Robinson's talents attracted attention. Such feats as those documented on this front page of the Pittsburgh Courier from April 19, 1947, led to Robinson being named Rookie of the Year.

coordinated by whichever team is at home on Jackie Robinson Day. The majority of ceremonies are typically conducted pre-game, although some events may run concurrently with the actual game (for example, trivia quizzes run on electronic scoreboards).

Often, Jackie Robinson Foundation scholarship recipients are invited to participate in some manner, for example, throwing out the ceremonial first pitch. Major League Baseball provides the home teams with commemorative bases to use at the games, as well as ceremonial first pitch home plates. Special line-up cards are typically issued, and memorabilia, such as photos of Robinson, old team photos, and Negro League-related items, may be offered as special crowd giveaways.

Prominent people associated with Major League Baseball, the Jackie Robinson Foundation, other charitable youth organizations, and many accomplished, inspirational African Americans have taken part in the event. Throughout the American and National Leagues, teams have become quite creative in the ways that they recognize Robinson's legacy. Most employ a significant amount of community outreach in their planning for the annual event, involving numerous facets of the community, often on both the local and state levels. Similarly, many teams use the opportunity to draw attention not only to the athletic component of Robinson's achievements, but also to focus on a broad spectrum of African-American culture and accomplishments in their communities.

Contacts and Websites

The Jackie Robinson Foundation
One Hudson Sq.
75 Varick St., 2nd Flr.
New York, NY 10013-1917

Major League Baseball Advanced Media
75 Ninth Ave.
New York, NY 10011
212-485-8959; fax: 212-485-3456
http://mlb.mlb.com/mlb/official_info/about_mlb_com

Negro Leagues Baseball Museum
1616 E. 18th St.
Kansas City, MO 64108

816-221-1920; fax: 816-221-8424
E-mail: info@nlbm.com
http://www.nlbm.com

Official Website of Jackie Robinson, presented by CMG Worldwide
10500 Crosspoint Blvd.
Indianapolis, IN 46256
317-570-5000
http://www.jackierobinson.com

Further Reading

Denenberg, Barry. *Stealing Home: The Story of Jackie Robinson.* 1990. Reprint. New York: Scholastic,1997. (young adult)

Frommer, Harvey. *Rickey and Robinson: The Men Who Broke Baseball's Color Barrier.* 2003. Reprint. Boulder, CO: Taylor Trade Publishing Company, 2015.

Lamb, Chris. *Blackout: The Untold Story of Jackie Robinson's First Spring Training.* Lincoln: University of Nebraska Press, 2004.

Major League Baseball. "Major League Baseball Declares April 15 Jackie Robinson Day," March 3, 2004.

Peterson, Robert W. *Only the Ball Was White: A History of Legendary Black Players and All-Black Professional Teams.* New York: Oxford University Press, 1992.

Robinson, Sharon. *Promises to Keep: How Jackie Robinson Changed America.* New York: Scholastic, 2004.

Rutkoff, Peter M., ed. *Cooperstown Symposium on Baseball and American Culture 1997: Jackie Robinson.* Jefferson, NC: McFarland & Company Publishers, 2000.

Tygiel, Jules. *Baseball's Great Experiment: Jackie Robinson and His Legacy.* New York: Oxford University Press, 1997.

Writing by Jackie Robinson

With Alfred Duckett. *I Never Had It Made: An Autobiography of Jackie Robinson.* New York: Harper Collins Publishers, 2003.

Jerry Rescue Day

Date Observed: October 1
Location: Syracuse, New York

This observance celebrates the rescue of William Jerry Henry. Known as "Jerry," Henry was a fugitive slave who was captured in Syracuse, New York, but freed from jail on October 1, 1851, with the help of abolitionists. Originally a protest against the Fugitive Slave Law of 1850, the "Jerry Rescue" was commemorated on that day each year from 1852 to 1858, and on occasion after that time.

Historical Background

William Jerry Henry was a runaway slave working as a barrel maker in Syracuse, New York, when a harsher version of the 1793 Fugitive Slave Law passed as part of the Compromise of 1850 (*see also* **Emancipation Day**). Black and white abolitionists operated a station on the Underground Railroad in Syracuse. Among them was Jermain W. Loguen, an escaped slave from Tennessee who became a bishop of the African Methodist Episcopal Zion Church. They were adamantly opposed to the Fugitive Slave Law and vowed to thwart it, in spite of criticisms from then U.S. Secretary of State Daniel Webster, who insisted the law would be carried out.

On October 1, 1851, U.S. marshals arrested Jerry at his workplace, charging him with theft. Once he was in shackles, marshals told Jerry the real reason for his arrest: the Fugitive Slave Law that required federal officials and citizens to capture runaways and return them to their owners or face steep fines. Jerry fought his captors but was restrained with chains and forced to face a U.S. commissioner in his office. Abolitionists managed to get into the office and free Jerry, but he was quickly recaptured.

While Jerry was being held, news of his arrest circulated quickly at the Liberty Party's Anti-Slavery Convention taking place in a nearby church. Following a pre-arranged signal, the church bells began to ring and about 2,500 people gathered in the street. With a battering ram, men broke down the door to the commissioner's office. Confronted with such a huge crowd, marshals surrendered Jerry to his rescuers. For several days, Jerry, who had been injured, hid in an abolitionist home until a wagon driver was able to take him to Lake Ontario, where he crossed by ship into Canada. Jerry died there a few years later.

Creation of the Observance

Gerrit Smith, a strong abolitionist who was elected to the U.S. House of Representatives in 1852, supported members of a Jerry Rescue Committee in initiating an annual event that became known as the "Jerry Rescue" in Syracuse. Each year between 1852 and 1858, Smith delivered speeches on October 1, or a day near that date, addressing abolitionist issues and praising those who had freed William Jerry Henry. The 1858 commemoration included a speech by famed abolitionist Frederick Douglass. In an earlier letter to Smith, Douglass had called the Jerry Rescue "one of the most important and honorable events in the history of American liberty" (*see also* **Frederick Douglass Day**).

In 1859, Smith declined an invitation to give a speech at the annual commemoration. He wrote to John Thomas, chairman of the Committee, that he was frustrated and disappointed with efforts to abolish slavery. He believed that there would be no end to it, because abolitionists had been unable to change the views of the majority of the public.

Observance

A reenactment of the "Jerry Rescue" took place in Syracuse on the 150th anniversary of the event in 2001. Since then, commemorations of the Jerry Rescue have included ceremonies at a permanent monument in Clinton Square in downtown Syracuse. In addition, the Onondaga County Historical Association Museum offers an audiovisual show that relives the Jerry Rescue and a permanent exhibit called "Freedom Bound: The Story of Syracuse and the Underground Railroad."

Contact and Website

Onondaga Historical Association Museum & Research Center
321 Montgomery St.
Syracuse, NY 13202
315-428-1864; fax: 315-471-2133
http://www.cnyhistory.org

Further Reading

Loguen, Jermain Wesley. *The Rev. J. W. Loguen, as a Slave and as a Freeman. A Narrative of Real Life.* Syracuse, NY: J. G. K. Truair & Co.: Stereotypers and Printers, 1859.
Documenting the American South. University Library, University of North Carolina at Chapel Hill, 1999. http://docsouth.unc.edu/neh/loguen/loguen.html.

Jubilee: Festival of Black History & Culture

Date Observed: Last weekend in September
Location: Columbia, South Carolina

The annual Jubilee: Festival of Black History & Culture in Columbia, South Carolina, celebrates African-American heritage and culture as well as the life of Celia Mann, a freed slave who was a midwife in Columbia before the Civil War. Many of the festivities take place over the last weekend in September at or near the Mann-Simons, named for Celia Mann, her second husband Bill Simons, and their descendants.

Historical Background

Celia Mann first lived in a one-room Columbia home about 1844. She was born a slave in 1799 in Charleston, South Carolina, and gained her freedom sometime during the 1840s. No record of how she was freed has been located. According to legend, she traveled from Charleston to Columbia on foot.

Along with earning her living as a midwife, Celia Mann helped establish the First Calvary Baptist Church in Columbia. The congregation originally met in the basement of the cottage.

Creation of the Festival

The Historic Columbia Foundation has managed the annual Jubilee Festival since 1978. Organized in 1961, the Foundation preserves and restores homes of historic significance in Columbia, South Carolina, the state's capital. Among these restored homes is the Mann-Simons home, where Celia Mann lived from about 1844 until 1867. The home remained in her family until the 1960s, when it was sold to the Columbia Housing Authority. A grassroots effort to preserve the home followed. The Historic Columbia Foundation gained supervision of the Mann-Simons home in 1978, continues to conduct tours of the home and other historic house-museums, and is responsible for maintaining artifacts connected with Celia Mann and her descendents.

Observance

Each year the Jubilee Festival at the Mann-Simons demonstrates the heritage of African Americans as represented by the Mann-Simons family, who lived in the home for more than 100 years. Artifacts in the cottage show that members of the Mann-Simons family earned their livelihoods as bakers, tailors, seamstresses, and musicians. In the 1900s, some became educators. Exhibits also provide information on how the cottage was restored.

The festival has grown over the years, and now includes additional venues with trolley tours called "Homeplaces, Workplaces, Resting Places" to African-American sites. Buffalo Soldiers reenactments, musical performances, African-American storytelling, African drumming, and craft demonstrations from basket-weaving to carving wooden walking sticks have been featured (*see also* **Buffalo Soldiers Commemorations**). Local African-American authors have appeared as well for book signings. Food vendors and craft activities for children are also part of the festival.

Contact and Website

Historic Columbia Foundation
1601 Richland St.
Columbia, SC 29201
803-252-7742; fax: 803-929-7695
http://www.historiccolumbia.org

Further reading

Edgar, Walter. *South Carolina: A History*. Columbia: University of South Carolina Press, 1998.
"Jubilee: Festival of Heritage in Columbia, SC, Promotes Diversity and Cultural Awareness." *Carolina Arts*, August 2003. http://www.carolinaarts.com/803jubilee.html.

"Jubilee! Historic Columbia Celebrates African-American Heritage This Weekend with Singing, Art, Dance, Drama." *Leisure Magazine, The Times and Democrat* (Columbia, SC), August 25, 2004. http://www.timesanddemocrat.com/articles/2004/08/25/pm/pm1.txt.

Juneteenth

Date Observed: June 19
Location: Worldwide Celebration

Juneteenth marks the anniversary of June 19, 1865, the day that Texas slaves learned they were free. It is commemorated across the United States and is an official state holiday in Texas.

Historical Background

The Juneteenth celebration was a time for reassuring each other, praying, and gathering remaining family members together. Juneteenth continued to be celebrated in Texas decades later. On this date, many former slaves and descendants make an annual pilgrimage back to Galveston.

The Emancipation Proclamation, issued by President Abraham Lincoln on January 1, 1863, freed slaves in the Confederate states and areas not under Union control, but the slaves in Texas were not told they were legally free for more than two years. They had no idea that emancipated slaves, as well as free blacks and white abolitionists, were celebrating freedom on New Year's Eve and New Year's Day in 1863 (*see also* **Emancipation Day** *and* **Watch Night**). The Proclamation was not enforced in Texas because of the lack of Union soldiers. But on June 19, 1865, two months after the Civil War had ended, a regiment of Union soldiers arrived in Galveston, Texas, and Major General Gordon Granger, representing the U.S. government, read from the President's General Order No. 3, which began:

> The people of Texas are informed that in accordance with a Proclamation from the Executive of the United States, all slaves are free. This involves an absolute equality of rights and rights of property between former masters and slaves, and the connection heretofore existing between

them becomes that between employer and free laborers. The freedmen are advised to remain quietly at their present homes and work for wages. They are informed that they will not be allowed to collect at military posts and that they will not be supported in idleness either there or elsewhere.

This order freed the remaining slaves in the United States—250,000 of them—and thousands immediately began to celebrate. Many crowded courthouses to get licenses to legally marry. According to historical accounts, some newly freed slaves threw away their tattered clothing and dressed in clothes taken from their former owners. Many left the plantations and went to neighboring states to reunite with family members in Louisiana, Arkansas, and Oklahoma.

Juneteenth celebrants in 1900 at "East Woods" in Austin, Texas

Creation of the Holiday

The first major Texas commemoration of June 19 was held in 1866 on the first anniversary of the state's emancipation day, which soon became known as Juneteenth. It also has been called "African-American Independence Day" or "Freedom Day" (not to be confused with **National Freedom Day**, the anniversary of the 13th Amendment). At the state capital, the first Juneteenth celebration was held in 1867. The celebration spread to other states via African Americans who moved out of Texas and took their commemorative activities with them.

During the 1960s, the emphasis on civil rights overshadowed Juneteenth celebrations. In fact, many African Americans did not want to be reminded of slavery and instead were actively involved in efforts to gain social and economic equality. As author Charles Taylor put it in the *Madison* (Wisconsin)

At the annual Juneteenth celebration in Galveston, reenactors listen during the ceremony in which the Emancipation Proclamation is read.

Times, "while the painful side of slavery makes it difficult for many blacks to celebrate Juneteenth, it is the positive legacy of perseverance and cooperation that makes it impossible for others to ignore."

By the 1970s, African Americans in Texas were renewing interest in their cultural heritage and ties with ancestors who were freed on June 19. People began campaigning for a state holiday and a bill was introduced in the Texas House of Representatives. The legislature passed an act in 1979 making Juneteenth a paid holiday, and the first official celebration was held in 1980.

Observance

During early observances of Juneteenth, some Texas officials forced African Americans to celebrate outside their city limits. But black organizations formed and raised funds to buy acres of land where celebrations could be held. These sites were commonly called "Emancipation Parks."

Over the years, people have traveled for miles to attend Juneteenth celebrations. For example, more than 5,000 African Americans from across Texas congregate in Denton for its annual celebration, which includes a Ms. Juneteenth Pageant and a gospel extravaganza. Festivalgoers from other states also make the pilgrimage to observe Juneteenth with family and friends in Texas.

Usually there is a thanks-giving service, which includes a group rendition of "Swing Low, Sweet Chariot" and "Lift Every Voice and Sing." Readings of the Emancipation Proclamation, the 13th Amendment, and General Order No. 3 are common during observances. Celebrations consist of barbecues—centerpieces of most commemorations—in public parks, along with recalling family histories, playing or watching baseball games (a favorite activity), listening to political speeches, and taking part in numerous other activities.

In general, a committee of local business and community leaders plans a host of events for this festival. Over tens of thousands turn out to participate in many cities. Parades, rodeos, races, Miss Juneteenth contests, and barbecues are common for an outdoor celebration. To get the youth involved, school essay and poster contests are conducted. To keep costs low (or free) for attendees, local businesses and city governments come on board as sponsors.

Nationwide Observances

The celebration of Juneteenth spread across the United States over the years. By 2006, Juneteenth was recognized as an unpaid state holiday observance in Oklahoma, Florida, Delaware, Idaho, Alaska, Iowa, California, Wyoming, Missouri, Connecticut, Illinois, Louisiana, New Jersey, New York, Arkansas, Kentucky, Michigan, New Mexico, and the District of Columbia. In Washington, D.C., the National Juneteenth Observance Commission sponsors an annual event in the capital. The commission, along with advocates across the country, have campaigned for a National Juneteenth Independence Day. Some members of the U.S. Congress have urged the president to issue a special proclamation for a national observance, but, as of 2006, the White House had not acknowledged such requests. In 2013, the U.S. Senate passed the Senate Resolution 175 to acknowledge Lula Briggs Galloway (late president of the National Association of Juneteenth Lineage) who tirelessly worked to bring a national recognition to the Juneteenth Independence Day. As of May 2014, when the Maryland legislature approved official recognition of the holiday, a total of 43 of the 50 U.S. states and the District of Columbia have recognized Juneteenth as either a state holiday or ceremonial holiday, meaning that Juneteenth was still not recognized as a national holiday.

Even where there is no official recognition of Juneteenth, however, observances take place in diverse towns and cities. In Mississippi, for example, Natchez observes a Juneteenth celebration that draws hundreds of thousands of participants from the Mississippi-Louisiana area as well as from Texas, Alabama, and Tennessee. A libation ceremony to give thanks for African-American heritage is part of the observance. Other Mississippi celebrations occur in Tupelo, Jackson, Brookhaven, Meridian, and Hattiesburg.

In 1991 Florida legislation recognized Juneteenth as a statewide observance, and cities such as Miami, Lakeland, and St. Petersburg hold Juneteenth festivals. In 1987 Jeanie Blue, a resident who had recently moved back to Florida from Texas, organized the first Juneteenth celebration in St. Petersburg. She had been inspired by the commemorations she observed in Texas. The St. Petersburg Juneteenth celebration includes live entertainment, storytelling, and health booths.

In Kansas, Kansas City and Witchita hold celebrations, but the largest and oldest Juneteenth observance in the state is in Topeka. The Stardusters

The Negro National Anthem

In 1900 poet James Weldon Johnson wrote the lyrics and his brother John Rosamond composed the music for "Lift Every Voice and Sing," the song that would become known as the "Negro National Anthem."

Lift every voice and sing
Till earth and heaven ring.
Ring with the harmonies of Liberty;
Let our rejoicing rise
High as the listening skies,
Let it resound loud as the rolling sea.
Sing a song full of the faith that the dark past has taught us,
Sing a song full of the hope that the present has brought us;
Facing the rising sun of our new day begun,
Let us march on till victory is won.
Stony the road we trod,
Bitter the chastening rod,
Felt in the days when hope unborn had died;
Yet with a steady beat,
Have not our weary feet
Come to the place for which our fathers sighed?
We have come over a way that with tears has been watered

We have come, treading our path through the blood of the slaughtered
Out from the gloomy past
Till now we stand at last
Where the white gleam of our bright star is cast.
God of our weary years,
God of our silent tears,
Thou who has brought us thus far on the way:
Thou who has by Thy might,
Led us into the light.
Keep us forever in the path, we pray.
Lest our feet stray from the places,
Our God, where we met Thee,
Lest our hearts, drunk with the wine of the world, we forget Thee,
Shadowed beneath Thy hand,
May we forever stand.
True to our God,
True to our native land.

At Virginia Key Beach in Miami, Florida, a 2005 Juneteenth observance at sunrise included gathering offerings for ancestors, placing them on a raft, and sending them out to sea.

Juneteenth Planning Committee has been hosting events since 1976, with activities conducted over a three-day period. Because attendance has grown over the years, the 2019 celebration in took place in the 18th & Vine Historic District.

Juneteenth is also observed annually on numerous college campuses. For example, Indiana University's Neal-Marshall Black Culture Center features a parade, musical performances, and a drama about the Underground Railroad.

Contacts and Websites

Denton Juneteenth Committee
P.O. Box 51291
Denton, TX 76206
940-349-8575
E-mail: dentonjuneteenth40@yahoo.com
http://www.juneteenthdentontx.org

Juneteenth.com provides a database of celebrations in the U.S. and around the world
P.O. Box 871750
New Orleans, LA 70187
504-245-7800
http://www.juneteenth.com/general_order_no_3.htm

Neal-Marshall Black Culture Center Indiana University
275 N. Jordan Ave.
Bloomington, IN 47405
812-855-9271; fax: 812-855-9148
nmgrad@indiana.edu
https://blackculture.indiana.edu

St. Petersburg/Clearwater Area Convention and Visitors Bureau
13805 58th St. N., Ste. 2-200
Clearwater, FL 33760
877-352-3224 (or) 727-464-7200
https://www.visitstpeteclearwater.com

Further Reading

Abernethy, Francis Edward, ed. *Juneteenth Texas: Essays in African American Folklore.* 1996. Reprint. Denton: University of North Texas Press, 2010.

Pemberton, Doris Hollis. *Juneteenth at Comanche Crossing.* Austin, TX: Eakin Press, 1983.

Taylor, Charles A. *Juneteenth: A Celebration of Freedom.* Greensboro, NC: Open Hand Publishing, 2002. (young adult)

Wiggins, William H., Jr. *O Freedom! Afro-American Emancipation Celebrations.* Knoxville: University of Tennessee Press, 2000.

Junkanoo

Date Observed: December 26 to January 1
Location: West Indies and formerly in the
southeastern United States

Junkanoo is a Christmas-time celebration that originated among slaves in the British West Indies and spread to the southern United States as early as the 18th century. While Junkanoo is no longer held in the United States, it continues to be a major national cultural event in the Caribbean, particularly in the Bahamas, and also in Jamaica, Guyana, Bermuda, and other former British colonies. Depending on where it is celebrated, Junkanoo is known by a variety of names, such as Jonkanoo, Johnkankus, John Canoe, John Kuner, John Kooner, and Kunering.

Historical Background

There are numerous word-of-mouth accounts on the origins of Junkanoo—both the festival and the etymology of the word itself. For example, some attribute the name to Scottish settlers in the Bahamas. The attire of Junkanoo paraders was composed of at-hand materials, such as shrubs, leaves, stones, bottles, and paper. It is said that Scots referred to the costumes as *junk enoo*, which translates as "junk enough." Another suggests French lineage; the definition of *gens l'inconnu*, meaning "unknown people," speaks to the secret identities of the masked Junkanoo participants. Further French attribution has been given to the festival's short prominence in the eastern United States, where sugarcane field hands were referred to as *jeunes caneurs*. Another theory is that the name might have referred to a type of small household canoe that parade participants carried.

Most Bahamians and scholars who have researched various possibilities have found common ground in the person of John Canoe (also known as John Connu,

Jony, Jonny, John Kooner, and Junkanoo). This African chief was born around 1720 in Ghana along the Ivory Coast. Reputed to be influential in the West Indian slave trade, John Canoe reportedly outwitted the Dutch and English, gaining control of Fort Brandenbury on the coast of Ghana, which furthered his herolike status among his people.

Another traditional tale also links Junkanoo's roots to Africa. The name of Yokonomo, or Jankomo, was recorded nearly two and one-half centuries before slaves were transported to the Bahamas. He is said to have created the hypnotic one-step-forward/two-steps-backward dance that is one of the central components of the modern Junkanoo.

Creation of the Festival

Junkanoo celebrations stem from West Africa, dating back to at least the 18th century, when slaves were brought to the West Indies and the southeastern coast of America. In the West Indies, slaves were given three days off per year—January 1, December 25, and December 26—with permission granted to perform cultural observances on the first and last of these dates. The most popular legend states that the name originated from John Canoe, an African tribal chief who demanded the right to celebrate with his people even after being brought to the West Indies in slavery, During pre- and post-slavery days, Christmas was the greatest time for celebration in the Bahamas, and Junkanoo was the highlight (*see also* **West Indies Emancipation Day**).

West Indian practices spread with slaves taken to the port cities of North Carolina, where they carried on the tradition at Christmas, calling it Johnkankus, John Kooner, or a similar name (*see also* **Slaves' Christmas**).

Observance

To prepare for the festival, participants made drums out of animal skins stretched over frames and other musical instruments from animal bones, sticks, and triangles. Costumes were fashioned from a variety of found materials. On Christmas morning, the masqueraders would parade through town, entertaining onlookers. They would also stop at wealthy homes to dance and sing in return for gifts. African-American observances of Junkanoo diminished after the Civil War. Freed slaves were not interested in maintaining connections with their former lives of bondage, and Junkanoo died out around 1865.

However, at about the same time, young whites revived the ritual and called it "coonering." During the Christmas holidays, they would parade around in old clothes, looking bedraggled. By the early 1900s, though, the custom was no longer practiced.

In the Bahamas, however, Junkanoo remains a major event. About 50,000 people attend the Junkanoo events in Nassau. Locals—and the more adventurous tourists—become active participants, starting out as "standees" and then turning into "revelers," who rush along designated city blocks as the spirit moves them. Each day's parade (as the celebration is commonly called) begins at 1 A.M. and lasts until 9 A.M.

There are three main components to Junkanoo: music, dance, and costume. Each intertwines into a kaleidoscope of color and sound that has become an intrinsic part of the Bahamian culture, so much so that the Ministry of Youth Sports and Culture has jurisdiction over the official competitions which judge Junkanoo participants and award coveted prizes. Entrants begin preparations as much as six months in advance and are subsidized by corporate sponsors; costs can run as high as $100,000.

Entrants known as "Groups" are drawn from almost all of the 14 islands and commonly consist of 500-1,000 people. Four major groups, the Valley Boys, the Saxon Superstars, Roots, and One Family, compete today, with dozens of others also participating at lesser competitive levels. Until the 1960s, paraders were male only. Now, competition is coed, and there is even a Junior Junkanoo Parade in an effort to apprentice cultural craftsmanship and foster Bahamanian heritage.

Elaborate costumes are designed around each group's particular and highly guarded theme. Materials have evolved from at-hand, "junk enough" to six simple items: corrugated cardboard, crepe paper, aluminum rods, tie wire, contact cement, and glue. The Junkanoo beat is created by a mélange of goatskin-covered drums, cowbells, horns, whistles, and brass instruments. The centuries-old one-step-forward/two-steps-backward dance remains central. However, variations such as the "Vola Shuffle" have appeared upon the scene and even professional choreographers have been introduced into the mix.

Contact and Website

Government of the Bahamas Ministry of Youth Sports and Culture
Thompson Blvd.
P.O. Box 4891
Nassau, N.P.
The Bahamas
242-502-0600; fax: 242-322-6546
E-mail: mysc@bahamas.gov.bs
http://www.bahamas.gov.bs

Further Reading

Barlas, Robert. *Cultures of the World: Bahamas*. New York: Marshall Cavendish, 2000.

Eklof, Barbara. *For Every Season: The Complete Guide to African American Celebrations, Traditional to Contemporary*. New York: HarperCollins, 1997.

Gulevich, Tanya. "Jonkonnu." In *Encyclopedia of Christmas and New Year's Celebrations*. 2nd ed. Detroit: Omnigraphics, 2003.

Smalls, Irene. "Roots of an African-American Christmas." http://www. melanet.com/johnkankus/roots.html.

Williams, Colleen Madonna Flood, and James Henderson, eds. *The Bahamas* (Discover the Caribbean Series). Broomall, PA: Mason Crest Publishers, 2002. (young adult)

Kunta Kinte Heritage Festival

Date Observed: September
Location: Annapolis, Maryland

The annual Kunta Kinte Heritage Festival is a two-day event that marks the arrival of Kunta Kinte, an African ancestor of acclaimed novelist Alex Haley, on the Annapolis, Maryland, docks on September 29, 1767. Since 1987 the festival has educated, entertained, and energized participants about black experience and culture.

Historical Background

During the 1960s and 1970s, Alex Haley researched his genealogy. In 1976 the story of his family's origins in Africa was published as the novel *Roots*, which quickly became a bestseller. Haley had traced his great, great, great, great-grandfather Kunta Kinte back to his ancestral roots in The Gambia. It was here that Kinte was born and lived prior to being captured, then transported across the Atlantic Ocean and ultimately sold into slavery on the shores of North America.

Over the course of its history, The Gambia witnessed many stories similar to that of Kunta Kinte. The region was once part of the Ghana and Songhai empires. Several European countries struggled for control of the area from the 15th through the 18th centuries. It was a valuable trade base for gold, ivory, and human slaves. Of the latter, most were initially sent to Europe, but as the need for labor expanded with growing colonization of new lands, Gambian slaves soon found themselves on ships bound for the West Indies and North America.

Slave trading was abolished by the British Empire in 1807, which, at that time, had a substantial yet shared interest in The Gambia. However, various efforts by the British to put an end to the region's slave trade were subsequently unsuccessful. It was not until passage of a 1906 ordinance, sometime after The Gambia had become a self-governing British Crown colony, that slavery was officially abolished.

Alexander Murray Palmer Haley

Alex Haley was born in Ithaca, New York, and, during his first career in service with the U.S. Coast Guard, spent 30 years on the high seas and in various locales. Regardless, Haley considered himself to be a native son of the state of Tennessee.

Both of Haley's parents were teachers: Simon Haley, his father, was a college professor and his mother, Bertha George Haley, taught grade school. The eldest of three sons, Alex spent a good deal of his youth with his mother's mother in Henning, Tennessee. At her side, young Haley first heard the family tales of his ancestors.

After completing high school at age 15, Haley attended college for two years, then enlisted in the U.S. Coast Guard. Writing was his passion, and he practiced his craft while onboard ships, submitting manuscripts and receiving rejection letters for eight years before his work gained some acceptance. Thirteen years after his enlistment, the Coast Guard created a new rating for Haley, that of Chief Journalist. Haley remained in the service for seven more years, until he decided to pursue writing full time.

Haley's first published book was *The Autobiography of Malcolm X* (1965). He spent hours talking with Malcolm X to put the black leader's life story into prose (*see also* **Malcolm X's Birthday**). The book became a classic. From there, Haley researched and then wrote the epic novel *Roots* that would change his life—and those of many others, particularly African Americans. Based upon his extensive genealogical investigation, Haley discovered that his maternal great, great, great, great-grandfather was a man named Kunta Kinte born in The Gambia, a region of west Africa, and sold into slavery. Haley's compelling storytelling, which traced his family lineage from Kunta Kinte to his own family's arrival in Henning, Tennessee, vaulted *Roots* to the #1 best-selling hardback book in U.S. publishing history. The tale was made into a television mini-series in 1977, attracting a record-breaking viewing audience.

Many would make a strong case that, with *Roots*, Haley did as much to strengthen black pride and to increase awareness of the many indignities and injustices wrought upon people of color over the past centuries as did almost any African-American leader of the 20th century.

Kunta Kinte's and Alex Haley's Roots

One day, while out in the West African jungle making a drum near his native town of Jufferee in The Gambia, 17-year-old Kunta Kinte was accosted by four men. Before long, he and 139 others were aboard the *Lord Ligonier,* a slave ship that set sail on July 5, 1767, bound for Annapolis, Maryland. When the ship docked on September 29 that year, 42 of its human cargo had perished.

On October 7, Kunta Kinte became the property of John Waller of Spotsylvania County, Virginia. Despite being renamed "Tobey," Kunta Kinte demanded that his fellow slaves call him by his birth name. He made repeated escape attempts, the fourth of which resulted in a choice of punishments: castration or amputation of his foot. Kinte chose the latter and ended up being taken in by Waller's brother, a doctor, who was horrified by John's cruel retribution. Kinte remained with Dr. Waller for the rest of his life, working as a gardener and buggy driver. At Dr. Waller's home he met Bell, the woman with whom he would father Kizzy, ensuring the future of his lineage. From the time she was born, Kizzy was regaled with Kunta Kinte's stories of his African youth; she learned the words of his native tongue and of the value he placed on human freedom.

At age 16, Kizzy was sold to a North Carolina plantation owner, to whom she bore a son, to be one day known as Chicken George due to his skills as a gamecock trainer. He went on to marry Matilda; they and their family of eight children were eventually sold to a man named Murray. The fourth of these eight children was named Tom. He married a slave girl (also of half-Indian blood) named Irene. They, too, raised a family of eight.

Once emancipation was declared in the United States, Chicken George and his numerous offspring banded together with Tom and his large family (*see also* **Emancipation Day**). They headed west and ended up in Henning, Tennessee. There, one of Tom's daughters, Cynthia, met and married William Parker. Their daughter, Bertha, gave birth to Alex Haley in 1921.

Haley's literary saga, *Roots,* first appeared in print in 1976 and received the National Book Award and Pulitzer Prize. It has since been translated into more than three dozen languages.

Creation of the Festival

In 1987 Kunta Kinte Celebrations, Inc., coordinated the first Kunta Kinte Heritage Festival. Nearly 10 years after the publication of Alex Haley's *Roots,*

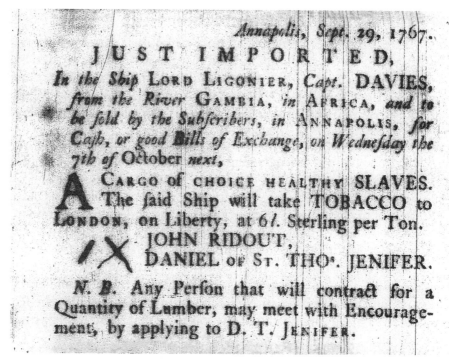

Alex Haley's research led him to believe that Kunta Kinte was one of the Africans advertised for sale in this notice that appeared in the October 1, 1767, issue of the Maryland Gazette.

there was a desire to celebrate the author and his book, as well as to commemorate the arrival of Haley's now world-famous ancestor, Kunta Kinte. Organizers selected the site of Kunta Kinte's disembarkment in America as the ideal location for the event.

However, the festival was created not only as a means of commemorating two men. Organizers also aimed to educate people about the broader cultural contributions of African Americans. The festival was designed to provide a prominent showcase for individuals and groups from a vast array of literary, performing and visual arts.

Observance

The 30th Annual Kunta Kinte Heritage Festival will be held on September 28, 2019 at Annapolis City Dock. The date was selected to closely coincide with the timing of Kunta Kinte's arrival in America at the Maryland docks, recorded as September 29, 1767.

The festival is family oriented, and all age groups are encouraged to attend and participate. There is a Family Education Tent with booths operated by a variety of organizations and businesses with displays on social issues, health, and history. Black authors, storytellers, and oral historians are also popular annual draws at this venue.

More specifically for young people, the Chesapeake Children's Museum offers such activities as mask making and traditional storytelling. Staff members share Kunta Kinte's tale and life lessons.

Two stages, main and performing arts, ensure that the entertainment bill holds something for everyone. In addition to nearly nonstop live musical entertainment that spans such styles as Caribbean, gospel, hip hop, jazz, rap, and rhythm and blues, African dancers, marching bands, magicians, steel drum bands, storytellers, and others perform.

In addition, Kunta Kinte Celebrations, Inc., assists with numerous genealogical efforts each year, as individuals and families—anticipating or inspired by the festival—seek to reconnect and/or discover their own personal "roots."

Contact and Website

Kunta Kinte-Alex Haley Foundation, Inc.
Asbury United Methodist Church
87 W. St., Second Fl.
Annapolis, MD 21401
410-295-9395; fax: 410-295-9396
E-mail: info@kintehaley.org
http://www.kintehaley.org

Kuumba Festival

Date Observed: June
Location: Knoxville, Tennessee

T he annual Kuumba Festival is a three-day festival in June designed to convey the beauty and diversity of African-American culture by showcasing a wide variety of music, dance, art, and food.

Historical Background

"Kuumba" (koo-OOM-bah) is a Swahili word meaning "creativity," as well as the term designating the sixth day of **Kwanzaa,** when participants pledge to make their communities and homes better than they found them. They also promise to use their talents and energies to improve young minds and hearts.

Creation of the Festival

The Kuumba Festival is hosted by the non-profit 501(c)3 arts organization African American Appalachian Arts, Inc. (AAAA) and focuses on positive social and community development by utilizing creative education methods through cultural-artistic programming and development.

The Kuumba Festival began in 1989 as a modest two-day celebration in a local park. Its organizers were mostly neighborhood artists and activists looking for a venue from which to increase community awareness of African-American cultural heritage in Appalachia. In the early 1990s, they established African American Appalachian Arts, Inc., and hired an executive director to oversee the annual event.

Each year, Kuumba has grown in attendance numbers, ambition, scope, and recognition. The festival has been honored with the City of Knoxville's "Mayor's Art Award for Special Programs." In addition to its original Market

Square/Downtown, its venues now include the Haley Heritage Square and Morningside Park.

Observance

Some artists and vendors who participate in Knoxville's Kuumba Festival are drawn from diverse areas across the United States. Others come from the African continent. However, most people participate live in the area. Each year, the Kuumba Festival organizers aim to draw in a more ethnically diverse attendance. Through broader community-wide participation, Knoxville's Kuumba celebrants share their rich heritage.

Contacts and Websites

Visit Knoxville
301 S. Gay St.
Knoxville, TN 37902
800-727-8045 or 865-523-7263
https://www.visitknoxville.com

Kumba Kamp
2725 Wimpole Ave.
Knoxville, TN 37914
865-221-1576
E-mail: kuumbakamp@yahoo.com

Kwanzaa

Date Observed: December 26–January 1
Location: Communities and homes nationwide

The seven-day Kwanzaa holiday is observed by millions of African Americans as well as by people of African descent worldwide. The holiday was created for black Americans to honor and celebrate their African heritage and to serve as an alternative to Christmas. Celebrations take place in homes and communities from December 26 through January 1.

Historical Background

Although Kwanzaa is a relatively recent African-American holiday that has spread worldwide, its customs and symbols are said to be rooted in ancient Africa. The name itself—Kwanzaa—comes from the Swahili phrase *matunda ya kwanza*, or "first fruits." The extra "a" at the end of Kwanzaa was added to indicate that the term stood for an African-American celebration. "First fruits" refers to the ancient tradition of harvest festivals in Africa that celebrate the first crops of the season.

The Kwanzaa holiday has gone far beyond the founder's creation. It began as a way to reject white culture and focus on African traditions and black power, but has become a holiday that emphasizes bringing people together and appreciating African culture and heritage. In the United States Kwanzaa is embraced by a broad range of African Americans, educational and religious institutions, museums, corporations, the media, and federal and state governments.

Creation of the Holiday

Kwanzaa's reason for existence, its length of seven days, its core focus, and its foundation are all based on values adopted from the African philosophical framework called "Kawaida." Kawaida is a communitarian African philosophy

A table set for Kwanzaa

and is considered to be an ongoing synthesis of the best of African thought and practice in constant exchange with the world.

Maulana Karenga, a professor of Black Studies at California State University at Long Beach, created Kwanzaa in 1966 in order to establish a holiday controlled by blacks and created especially for people of African descent. He hoped to bolster the bonds between African Americans and Africa.

Karenga's given name Ronald McKinley Everett when he was born in 1941 in Maryland. After moving to California to go to college, he earned a degree at Los Angeles City College and began work on his doctorate degree at the University of California, but dropped out to take part in the Black Power

Movement in the 1960s, a time of racial unrest and upheaval. He eventually earned a doctorate in political science at the U.S. International University and a doctorate in social ethics from the University of Southern California.

As a 1960s radical black nationalist, he took the name Maulana Karenga and supported Malcolm X and the concepts of black power (*see also* **Malcolm X's Birthday**). He also created an organization known as "US" or "Us," whose mission was and is to liberate blacks from white oppression. He and members of the US were involved in violent activities that resulted in Karenga's imprisonment in 1971. Several years after his release in 1974, he was hired to the faculty of the Black Studies Department at California State University at Long Beach. Karenga has continued his involvement with US, which promotes Kwanzaa through its website, and with a publishing arm in Los Angeles called "University of Sankore Press."

To symbolize Kwanzaa, Karenga chose the colors black, red, and green, which were used decades earlier by Marcus Garvey to represent black nationalism (*see also* **Marcus Garvey's Birthday**). According to Karenga in a 1998 interview with *Ebony*magazine, "Black is for Black people, first . . . red is for struggle, and green is for the future and the promise that comes from struggle."

Observance

Candles in black, red, and green are an important part of any observance of Kwanzaa. They are usually displayed in a seven-tiered candelabra called a *kinara*, with one black candle in the middle, three red candles on the right, and three green ones on the left. Together, these candles are known as the *mishumaa saba* (seven candles). Each night of the weeklong celebration is dedicated to one of principles. Umojo (ooMO-jah), or Unity, is represented by the black candle. Three principles are represented by red candles: Kujichagulia (koo-gee-cha-goo-LEE-yah), or Self-determination; Ujima (oo-GEE-mah), or Collective Work and Responsibility; and Ujamaa (oo-JAH-mah), or Cooperative Economics. The remaining principles represented by green candles are Nia (nee-YAH), or Purpose; Kuumba (koo-OOM-bah), or Creativity; and Imani (ee-MAH-nee), or Faith.

Each African-American household may celebrate Kwanzaa in its own way, but there is usually a display of symbolic objects on a table covered with a colorful cloth in African designs. The seven basic symbols which represent values and concepts reflective of African culture, A *mkeke*, or straw place mat, as the

Foods for Kwanzaa

Foods prepared for a Kwanzaa feast frequently are linked to traditional dishes of the African diaspora, from African-American soul foods to those from the Caribbean, South America, and Africa. In recent years, recipes for dishes and desserts to serve at a Kwanzaa feast have been published in newspapers, magazines, and books, or posted on the Internet. Some of the items served include (but certainly are not limited to):

Roast turkey	Southern-style green beans	Red beans and rice
Fried chicken	Black-eyed peas	Benne cakes
Sweet potato dishes/pies	Potato salad	Pecan pie
Cornbread	Southern-fried okra	Peanut soup
Collard greens	African vegetarian stew	Biscuits
		Lemonade

foundation (to represent African heritage) for the kinara and other meaningful items: *muhindi*, ears of corn that represent all children of the community, rather than just the immediate family; and *kikombe cha umoja*, a unity cup which holds a libation, or liquid, to recall and welcome ancestral spirits. (All present may sip from the cup.) *Mazao*—fruits and vegetables in a bowl made of natural materials—is likely to be on the table to represent the harvest. And *zawadi* (gifts) of books and other educational materials about African culture also may be displayed.

When a Kwanzaa family celebration takes place, it begins on the first night— December 26—by placing the seven candles in the holder and lighting the black candle for unity. Author Antoinette Broussard explains her family's tradition after the first night in her book *African-American Celebrations and Holiday Traditions* (2004):

> On the second night of Kwanzaa, the family gathers and the black candle for unity is lit along with the red candle for self-determination. . . . On the third evening . . . the black candle and the red candle and the green candle for collective work and responsibility [are lit]. This

sequence of lighting the candles and discussing the principle of the day extends through the seven days of Kwanzaa. . . . The discussion each evening centers around what that day's particular principle means to each individual, and how each has applied it in his or her life. All the participants commit to practice that particular principle throughout the coming year.

Some families observe at least one evening of Kwanzaa with relatives—perhaps several generations of a family—or with friends. Educational or handmade gifts may be presented to the children and, on December 31st especially, Kwanzaa observers enjoy an African feast named "Karamu."

City and Community Celebrations

Across the United States, as well as in other countries, cities and communities may set aside the week, or a day or two, to observe Kwanzaa and include people of diverse ethnic backgrounds in these celebrations although the celebration remains Afrocentric.

In Chicago, Illinois, one of the largest celebrations in the nation takes place at Malcolm X College. In 1995, then-president of the college, Zerrie D. Campbell, spearheaded the first Kwanzaa celebration. It is a joint endeavor with Chicago's Afrocentric school "Shule Ya Watoto." During the week the Kwanzaa celebration includes African-inspired ceremonies, music and dance, a fashion show, an African marketplace, and traditional African foods.

The Kwanzaa Capital City Festival is a one-day celebration in Richmond, Virginia. It is presented by the Elegba Folklore Society, a nonprofit organization that promotes activities focusing on African-American culture. The name of the organization comes from Esu Elegbara (AY-shew eh-lehg-bah-rah), a deity or saint in the West African Yoruba tradition who is the guardian of the crossroads and keeps people connected. Since 1990, the festival has been a celebration of the holiday—not the holiday itself. It draws three to four thousand people and has featured an African market, children's craft making, dance performances, and poetry.

In New York, the American Museum of Natural History holds a Kwanzaa celebration over three days. It includes activities for the entire family, such as African folklore performances, workshops, a marketplace, and Kwanzaa foods in the various food courts.

A libation ceremony was part of the 2003 Kwanzaa observance at the African Burial Ground in New York City. Reverend Stephen Marsh (right) poured water to honor the ancestors. Attendees included New York City councilman Charles Barron (left) and Reverend Herbert Daughtry (center).

The Kwanzaa Heritage Festival in Los Angeles, California, begins with a colorful parade. The two-day festival features African dance groups, drumming, poetry and folk tale performances, a children's village, and an international food court.

Wherever Kwanzaa celebrations are held, it is common for many participants to wear kente cloth, a traditional African garment. Kente cloth originated in Ghana during the 12th century and was once worn only by kings and queens for special ceremonies. Weavers made the cloth out of four-inch wide strips in complex designs and bright colors; the strips were woven together to make garments of various sizes.

African Americans now wear kente cloth, sometimes as a shawl or as a full-length wrap, to show pride in their African heritage. Head ties, which also are part of traditional African attire, may be worn by African-American women during Kwanzaa as well.

Kwanzaa Products

As Kwanzaa celebrations have spread across the United States, many merchants have reported that sales of items for the holiday, such as candles, candle holders, mats, fabric with African designs, and books and games about Kwanzaa, have been in great demand. Although such items are part of family celebrations, they are also used in schools, libraries, museums, religious institutions, and other public places during educational programs about the holiday. In addition, a variety of videos, coloring books, e-cards, printed greeting cards, clip art, crafts, and software related to Kwanzaa are advertised and

The Restoration Dance Company performed at the 2002 Kwanzaa celebration at New York City's Museum of Natural History.

sold on the Internet. With all of these varied products being marketed, some Kwanzaa participants worry that commercialization will diminish the values of the holiday. Others contend that the proliferation of Kwanzaa items can help create public awareness of African culture, heritage, and pride.

In 1999 the U.S. Postal Service issued the first Kwanzaa stamp. In 2004, a new first-class postage stamp featuring Kwanzaa was issued by the Postal Service at the DuSable Museum of African American History in Chicago, Illinois. Artists who created the design endeavored to balance formality with a celebratory, festive mood. The seven figures in colorful robes listed below represent the seven days of Kwanzaa, and the seven principles they signify.

Seven figures

Mazao (The Crops) symbolizes African harvest celebrations and the rewards of productive and collective labor.

Mkeka (The Mat) symbolizes tradition and history, and therefore, the foundation on which celebrants build.

Kinara (The Candle Holder) symbolizes roots, ancestors—continental Africans.

Muhindi (The Corn) symbolizes children and the future they embody.

Mishumaa Saba (The Seven Candles) symbolizes the Nguzo Saba, the matrix and minimum set of values that African people are obliged to live by in order to rescue and reconstruct their lives in their own image and in accordance with their own needs.

Kikombe cha Umoja (The Unity Cup) symbolizes the foundational principle and practice of unity, which makes all else possible.

Zawadi (The Gifts) symbolizes the labor and love of parents and the commitments made and kept by the children.

Bendera (The Flag) and Nguzo Saba Poster (Poster of the Seven Principles) are the two supplemental symbols.

Contacts and Websites

Malcolm X College
American Museum of Natural History
Central Park W. at 79th St.
New York, NY 10024
212-769-5000; fax: 212-496-3605
http://www.amnh.org

Capital City Kwanzaa Festival
101 E. Broad St.
Richmond, VA 23219
804-644-3900; fax: 804-644-3919
http://www.elegbafolkloresociety.org

Kwanzaa Heritage Foundation
One Kwanzaa Circle
GMF: 60205
Los Angeles, CA 90060
E-mail: kwanzala7@yahoo.com
https://www.kwanzaaheritage.org

Malcolm X College
1900 W. Jackson Blvd.
Chicago, IL 60612
312-850-7000
http://malcolmx.ccc.edu

African American Cultural Center
3018 W. 48th St.
Los Angeles, CA 90043-1335
323-299-6124; fax: 323-299-0261
http://www.officialkwanzaawebsite.org/index.shtml

Further Reading

Anyike, James C. *African American Holidays: A Historical Research and Resource Guide to Cultural Celebrations.* Chicago: Popular Truth, 1991.
Barashango, Ishakamusa. *African People and European Holidays: A Mental Genocide, Book 1.* Washington, DC: IVth Afrikan World Books, 1979.

Barashango, Ishakamusa. *African People and European Holidays: A Mental Genocide, Book 2.* Lushena Books, 2001.

Broussard, Antoinette. *African-American Celebrations and Holiday Traditions: Celebrating with Passion, Style, and Grace.* New York: Citadel Press, 2004.

Brown, Scot. *Fighting for US: Maulana Karenga, the U.S. Organization, and Black Cultural Nationalism.* New York: New York University Press, 2003.

Collier, Adore. "The Man Who Invented Kwanzaa." *Ebony,* January 1998.

Eklof, Barbara. *For Every Season: The Complete Guide to African American Celebrations, Traditional to Contemporary.* New York: HarperCollins, 1997.

Karenga, Maulana. *Kwanzaa: A Celebration of Family, Community and Culture.* Los Angeles: University of Sankore Press, 1998.

Riley, Dorothy Winbush. *The Complete Kwanzaa: Celebrating Our Cultural Harvest.* New York: Perennial, 1996.

Maafa Commemoration

Date Observed: 2nd and 3rd week of September
Location: Brooklyn, New York

During the Maafa Commemoration in Brooklyn, New York, members of the African-American community come together to memorialize and honor the millions of Africans who suffered the horrors of the TransAtlantic Slave Trade and Middle Passage of the 1700s. It is held each year during the second and third week of September.

Historical Background

Maafa (mah-AH-fah) is a Kiswahili term meaning "great disaster" or "terrible occurrence." It has come to refer to what some call the "African Holocaust"—the transporting of millions of Africans in the holds of ships across the Atlantic Ocean to lives of slavery. Those who survived the indignities and peril of this passage arrived in foreign lands, no longer in control of their own destinies, subject in most cases to decades of oppression, emotional and physical injury, and even death.

Dr. Marimba Ani is credited with appropriating the word "maafa" to collectively commemorate this historical occurrence. In a 2000 *Essence* magazine article, Ani noted:

> We needed a term that would let us claim this experience for ourselves. So I contacted friends who knew various African languages and asked for a term for disaster. The Middle Passage and slavery had their own horror, which brought on a new kind of horror. We have been duped into believing that we are free and healthy, but we are still living in Maafa. Only by going through the pain and the grief can we find our way to Sankofa, an acceptance of our being, our spirit.

Creation of the Observance

In 1995 New Orleans-born preacher Johnny Youngblood, pastor of New York City's St. Paul Community Baptist Church, organized the first Maafa Commemoration to help African Americans heal from the psychic and spiritual damage they collectively bore that he felt had gone undetected and untreated for centuries.

Since that time, the annual Maafa observance at St. Paul's Community Baptist Church has grown considerably. Through word-of-mouth and outreach efforts, other religious communities have been receptive to the idea, and the practice of commemorating Maafa has spread to other locations in the U.S.

Observance

Various activities occur throughout the Maafa Commemoration. There are repeated performances of the moving theatrical production "Maafa Suite—A Healing Journey," which aims to educate, reconcile, and heal collective memories. In addition, there are worship services, lectures, tours of the Maafa Museum, opportunities to participate in the Garden of Gethsemane Sweat Lodge Journey, workshops on resisting institutional racism, special programs for seniors and youth, and a ceremony on the shores of the Atlantic.

Contact and Website

St. Paul Community Baptist Church
859 Hendrix St.
Brooklyn, NY 11207
718-257-1300; fax: 718-257-2988
https://www.spcbc.com/commemoration-of-the-maafa

Further Reading

Anderson, S. E. *The Black Holocaust for Beginners.* New York: Writers and Readers Publishing, 1995. Reprint. For Beginners LLC, 2007.
Black, Albert W. *The Other Holocaust: The Sociology and History of African Americans, Vol. I.* Boston: Pearson Custom Publishing, 2002.
Cose, Ellis. *Bone to Pick: Of Forgiveness, Reconciliation, Reparation, and Revenge.* New York: Simon & Schuster, 2005.

McKinney, Lora-Ellen. *Christian Education in the African American Church: A Guide for Teaching Truth.* Foreword by Johnny Ray Youngblood. Valley Forge, PA: Judson Press, 2003.

Thomas, Laurence Mordekhai. *Vessels of Evil: American Slavery and the Holocaust.* Philadelphia: Temple University Press, 1994. Reprint. Temple University Press, 2010.

Malcolm X's Birthday

Date Observed: May 19
Location: Communities nationwide

May 19 marks the birth of Malcolm X, whose given name was Malcolm Little at the time of his birth on May 19, 1925. Malcolm X is remembered on his birthday in cities across the United States and in other countries for his leadership and activism for civil rights on behalf of African Americans and people of African descent everywhere. Hundreds of public forums pay tribute to Malcolm X on his birthday, but only in Berkeley, California, is the date an official holiday with city offices and schools are closed.

Historical Background

During the 1950s and early 1960s and after his death in 1965, Malcolm X was a highly controversial figure among the predominantly white American public but an icon to many African Americans, especially on college campuses. He advocated black nationalism, which promotes cultural pride among African Americans, rebuffs racial integration, works to advance black economic power, and develops African-American political organizations. Black nationalism also promotes interaction between people of African descent wherever they happen to live. Malcolm X's ideas, however, developed over his short and sometimes volatile lifetime.

Born on May 19, 1925, in Omaha, Nebraska, Malcolm was one of eight children of Earl and Louise Little. Malcolm's father was a Baptist minister who spoke out for civil rights. He supported Marcus Garvey's Universal Negro Improvement Association, whose purposes included unifying people of African descent whatever their nationality, improving their living conditions, founding black businesses, and establishing independent black states in Africa (*see also* **Marcus Garvey's Birthday**).

Earl Little's advocacy for racial justice brought death threats from a white supremacist group known as the Black Legion. In an attempt to escape these threats, the family moved to Lansing, Michigan, but in 1929 their home was burned down. Another tragedy struck in 1931, when Malcolm's father was found dead on the trolley tracks. The Little family was convinced that the Black Legion was responsible, but according to police both the arson of the Little home and death of Earl Little were accidental.

Malcolm X in 1962.

Following his father's death, Malcolm's mother had an emotional breakdown and had to be institutionalized. As a result, the children were separated and sent to different foster homes and juvenile facilities. Malcolm was an excellent student and hoped to become a lawyer, but he became disillusioned when a teacher told him that a black man in the 1940s could not realistically achieve that goal. He left school and drifted into a life of crime in Harlem and Boston.

In 1946 Malcolm was arrested for burglary in Boston. He received a sentence of 10 years in prison and served seven years. There, he was exposed to the teachings of the Nation of Islam—Black Muslims. He was determined to turn his life around and became a follower of the religion and the teachings of Minister Elijah Muhammad. It was then that he took the surname X, in keeping with the Nation of Islam's practice to symbolize that a person was an ex-Christian, ex-Negro, and ex-slave. In other words, the X meant that Malcolm would no longer be known by a name that came from a white slave owner.

Nation of Islam Leader

After he was paroled in 1952, Malcolm X became a preeminent spokesperson for the Nation of Islam, helping to increase membership by the thousands. He

313

often bitterly denounced white domination of African Americans and was a fervent supporter of black nationalism.

The concept of black nationalism did not begin with the Nation of Islam. During the 1800s and early 1900s, black leaders such as Paul Cuffe (1759–1815), Martin Delaney (1812–1885), and Marcus Garvey (1887–1940) urged African Americans to find true equality by creating a separate black nation rather than being assimilated into the white-dominated United States. With the rise of the Nation of Islam, racial separatism became a religious doctrine, and Elijah Muhammad publicly rebuked whites as being an "evil race" that misleads black people with its emphasis on wealth and power. In a July 1970 issue of the *Muhammad Speaks Newspaper,* he wrote: "Black Man, these are your days. The white man's days are gone."

At the same time, however, Muhammad stressed that African Americans should seek their own individuality and not accept the "Negro" and "colored" identity as defined by the dominant white society. He also emphasized economic independence. His sermons and writings often focused on "Knowledge of Self" and "Do for Self."

Echoing these themes, Malcolm X continued to proselytize for the Nation of Islam, and by 1954, Muhammad had appointed him minister of New York Temple No. 7 in Harlem. In 1957, he became the Nation's national representative, second in rank to Muhammad himself. The following year, Malcolm X married Betty Sanders, who became Betty Shabazz, and the couple had six daughters. While raising their family, Betty Shabazz earned a master's degree in public-health administration and a doctorate in education from the University of Massachusetts at Amherst.

During the 1960s, Malcolm X was ever more militant in his fiery speeches. After President John F. Kennedy was assassinated in 1963, Malcolm X publicly declared that the president's death amounted to "the chickens coming home to roost, that the hate in white men had not stopped with the killing of defenseless black people, but that hate, allowed to spread unchecked, had finally struck down this country's Chief of State."

Because of the public outrage that followed, Elijah Muhammad banned Malcolm X from speaking publicly for three months, which was extended to a longer period of time. The ban was one reason Malcolm X resigned from the Nation of Islam. He also became disillusioned after learning that Elijah

Muhammad had fathered children with two of his former secretaries. This act of adultery would be reason to expel any other Muslim, but Muhammad kept his high position in the Nation of Islam.

In 1964 Malcolm X established his own Organization of Afro-American Unity and the Muslim Mosque, Inc., which held a series of Sunday night public rallies in Harlem. There, Malcolm gave speeches and also appeared in other cities to outline his militant philosophy. He declared that blacks should carry weapons to defend themselves against whites, and argued that blacks were justified in arming themselves because the government would not do its job and protect African Americans. In his view, the only way blacks could truly be free and achieve equality was through revolution. During one talk in 1964 at Palm Gardens in New York, he declared, "Historically, you just don't have a peaceful revolution. Revolutions are bloody, revolutions are violent, revolutions cause bloodshed and death." He noted that revolution could be achieved in the United States "without violence and bloodshed. But America is not morally equipped to do so." On April 3, 1964, Malcolm X gave his famous and controversial "The Ballot or the Bullet" speech in Cleveland, Ohio, which added that African Americans needed to recognize their common oppression and use either votes or guns to stop the racial exploitation.

Malcolm frequently criticized Martin Luther King Jr. for promoting nonviolence and civil disobedience. He believed these were fruitless strategies that appeased whites and made "Uncle Toms" of African Americans. He also argued against integration and for African Americans to separate themselves from dominant white society.

A Life Change

During 1964, Malcolm made the Hajj—the pilgrimage to Mecca, Saudi Arabia—and thus fulfilled one of the pillars of Islam. The trip changed his life. He met people of other cultures and was treated with respect. From Jeddah, Saudi Arabia, Malcolm X wrote a letter to his family and friends about his impressions. This excerpt of his letter appears in his *Autobiography*: "There were tens of thousands of pilgrims from all over the world. They were of all colors, from blue-eyed blondes to black-skinned Africans. But we were all participating in the same ritual, displaying a spirit of unity and brotherhood that my experiences in America had led me to believe never could exist between the white and non-white."

Malcolm X speaking at a rally in Harlem, New York, on June 29, 1963.

After completing the pilgrimage, he took the Muslim name El-Hajj Malik El-Shabazz, and returned to the United States a changed person. He was ready to lead a movement for racial justice and to unify African Americans in the struggle. Although he still did not agree with King's approach, Malcolm offered to help in the nonviolent civil rights movement by sending armed units to defend King and other leaders. But King refused such an approach on moral grounds.

Even as he talked of defending others, Malcolm himself was threatened and several attempts were made on his life, including a firebombing of his home. Tragically, he was assassinated on February 21, 1965, at the Audubon Ballroom in Harlem where he was to deliver a speech. As he stood to speak, three men in front of him fired guns at the same time, killing him. Three Nation of Islam members were convicted of murdering Malcolm X: Talmadge Hayer, Norman 3X Butler, and Thomas 15X Johnson.

On February 27, 1,500 people attended the funeral of Malcolm. Malcolm's friends took the shovels from the gravediggers at Ferncliff Cemetery in Hartsdale, New York, and buried the coffin themselves. After Malcolm's funeral, Martin Luther King Jr. sent a telegram to Betty Shabazz, saying, "While we did not always see eye-to-eye on methods to solve the race problem, I always had a deep affection for Malcolm and felt he had a great ability to put his finger on the existence and the root of the problem. He was an eloquent spokesman for his point of view and no one can honestly doubt that Malcolm had a great concern for the problems we face as a race."

Legacy of Malcolm X

The legacy of Malcolm X is not always easy to see because people generally "don't think about the internal change it produced," according to James H. Cone, professor of religious studies at Union Theological Seminary in New York and author of *Martin and Malcolm and America: A Dream or a Nightmare*. In comparing the legacy of Martin Luther King Jr. and Malcolm X for a *News & Observer* (Raleigh, North Carolina) reporter, Cone noted: "King changed the way white people think about black people; Malcolm changed the way black people think about themselves." Sonia Sanchez agreed, and said during a PBS documentary that he "expelled fear for African Americans. That's why we loved him. He said it out loud, not behind closed doors. He took on America for us."

African Americans who were clearly influenced by Malcolm X included leaders in the black power movement, such as Stokely Carmichael/Kwame Toure, who articulated a political philosophy that demanded liberation and self-determination for African Americans. Many African Americans began to embrace the "Black Is Beautiful" concept. In schools, there were demands for black studies and respect for the African roots of black Americans.

Since his death, Malcolm X has been recognized increasingly by people of many ethnic backgrounds for his efforts to fight racism, poverty, and the repression of African people in America and elsewhere. Films such as Spike Lee's *Malcolm X*, music videos, poetry, political essays, and biographies honor

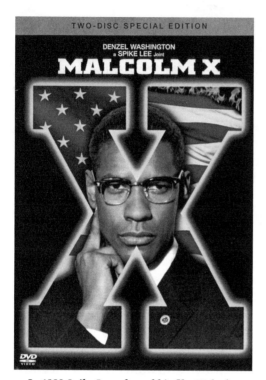

In 1992 Spike Lee released his film Malcolm X. *In February 2005, this DVD was issued as a special edition set to commemorate the 40th anniversary of Malcolm X's death.*

him. So do T-shirts and posters with Malcolm X's words "By whatever means necessary"—doing whatever it takes to empower the oppressed.

In the words of Malcolm X scholar Manning Marable: "Malcolm X was the most remarkable historical figure produced by Black America in the 20th century. That's a heavy statement, but I think that in his 39 short years of life, Malcolm came to symbolize Black urban America, its culture, its politics, its militancy, its outrage against structural racism and at the end of his life, a broad internationalist vision of emancipatory power."

Creation of the Holiday

One of the first Malcolm X birthday celebration was held in Washington, D.C., where Malcolm X Cultural Education Center was established in 1971 to honor his life and legacy. Between 50,000 and 75,000 people attend this event each year.

In 1977 the city of Berkeley, California, designated Malcolm X's birthday, May 19, to be an official city holiday. Citizens had petitioned the city council to do so since the late 1960s. The law became effective in 1979.

Observance

Celebrations of Malcolm X's life occur annually in most major American cities on his birthday May 19, or for several days around that time. Some occur on the third Sunday in May. Malcolm X may also be commemorated during **African-American History Month**.

Celebrations conducted across the United States take varied forms. In Lansing, Michigan, for example, the El-Hajj Malik El-Shabazz Charter School celebrated

Malcolm's life in 2005 with a jazz concert and multimedia presentation on the history of African-American education.

In New York, the Malcolm X Commemoration Committee and the Sons and Daughters of Afrika conduct an annual pilgrimage and caravan to the gravesite of Malcolm X. First conceived by Malcolm's sister Ella Little-Collins, the pilgrimage includes participants who come from as far south as Baltimore and Washington, D.C., and from as far north as Boston.

At the Audubon Ballroom, where Malcolm X was murdered, people gather to honor his life. The Harlem ballroom was reopened on May 19, 2005, as the Malcolm X and Dr. Betty Shabazz Memorial and Education Center.

Other events include the annual photo exhibit of Malcolm X at the Schomburg Center for Research in Black Culture in Harlem; Malcolm X Jazz Festival in Oakland, California; and Malcolm X events on college campuses across the United States.

Contacts and Websites

The Shabazz Center
3940 Broadway
New York, NY 10032
info@theshabazzcenter.org
https://theshabazzcenter.org

Malcolm X Jazz Festival Eastside Arts Alliance & Cultural Center
2277 International Blvd
P.O. Box 17008
Oakland, CA 94601
510-533-6629
eastsideculturalcenter@gmail.com
https://www.eastsideartsalliance.org/contact

Center for Contemporary Black History
760 Schermerhorn Extension–MC 5512
Columbia University
1200 Amsterdam Ave.
New York, NY 10027
212-854-1489; fax: 212-854-7060
http://www.columbia.edu/cu/ccbh/mxp/index.html

"Malcolm X: A Search for Truth," online exhibit Schomburg Center for
Research in Black Culture
515 Malcolm X Blvd.
New York, NY 10037
212-491-2207
http://www.nypl.org/research/sc/malcolmx

Official Website of Malcolm X, presented by CMG Worldwide, agent for the
Estate of Malcolm X
429 N. Pennsylvania St., Ste. 204
Indianapolis, IN 46204
317-570-5000
https://www.cmgworldwide.com/malcolm-x

Further Reading

Breitman, George, ed. *Malcolm X Speaks*. New York: Grove Press, 1966.
Cone, James H. *Martin and Malcolm and America: A Dream or a Nightmare.* Maryknoll, NY: Orbis Books, 1992.
Marable, Manning *Souls: A Critical Journal of Black Politics, Culture and Society.* Westview Press, 1999.
Myers, Walter Dean. *Malcolm X: By Any Means Necessary*. New York: Scholastic, 1994. Reprint. Scholastic, 1999. (young adult).
Rickford, Russel John. *Betty Shabazz: Her Life with Malcolm X and Fight to Preserve His Legacy.* Naperville, IL: Sourcebooks, 2003.
Rummel, Jack. *Malcolm X*. New York: Chelsea House Publications, 2005. (young adult)
Sagan, Miriam. *Malcolm X*. San Diego: Lucent Books, 1996. (young adult)
Terrill, Robert E. *Malcolm X: Inventing Radical Judgment*. East Lansing: Michigan State University Press, 2004. Reprint, Michigan State University Press, 2007.

Marcus Garvey's Birthday

Date Observed: August 17
Location: Varies

T he birthday of Marcus Garvey is celebrated on or around August 17 each year by members of the organization he founded, the Universal Negro International Association (UNIA), as well as by the members of the Rastafarian faith.

Historical Background

Marcus Mosiah Garvey was born in St. Ann's Bay, Jamaica, on August 17, 1887. At the age of 14, he left school and took a job as an apprentice printer to help support his family. During his teens and early adult years, Garvey was exposed to significant economic and political unrest in his native land and this exposure would act as a foundation for his developing philosophies. He committed himself to social reform, participating in the first Printers' Union strike in Jamaica in 1907 and setting up the newspaper *The Watchman*.

Garvey traveled, first throughout Latin America and then to England, broadening his outlook. It was in London where his thinking was most greatly influenced. There, he learned about the developing Pan-African movement and read Booker T. Washington's book *Up from Slavery* (*see also* **Pan African Bookfest and Cultural Conference**). After returning to Jamaica in 1914, Garvey's exposure to new concepts about his African heritage inspired him to found the UNIA. Its motto: "One God! One Aim! One Destiny!"

Initially, Garvey's approach to uplifting the Negro condition was to focus on hard work and demonstrating good moral character. He felt that politics would only interfere with and cloud advancement of the cause. His view changed, however, when he began traveling throughout the United States. Disillusioned about the prospects of racial equality, especially upon seeing

Marcus Garvey in 1924.

how blacks were being treated when they returned home from service in World War I, Garvey became convinced that racial integration would never occur until blacks achieved economic, political, and cultural success by means of their own efforts.

Garvey went to Harlem and established what would become the U.S. headquarters of the UNIA. From there, Garvey began to spread a message of black nationalism, calling for unity, pride in one's African cultural heritage, and complete autonomy from any other race or entity. Central to Garvey's message was a call for blacks to return to the African homeland, a goal that became known as the "back-to Africa movement." In 1920 the organization held its first convention in New York, which opened with a parade down Harlem's Lenox Avenue and was attended by 25,000 people. In the same year, Garvey developed what he called the "Liberia Plan," and even negotiated a deal with the Liberian government for land on which to settle displaced black people from the U.S., the Caribbean, Central and South America, and elsewhere.

Garvey had both supporters and detractors among African Americans. He came under particularly heavy criticism from fellow blacks after a 1922 meeting with the Klu Klux Klan to discuss miscegenation (marriage between races) and social equality. By Garvey's account, UNIA's membership numbered in the millions, and indeed, it had branches throughout the United States, the Caribbean, Canada, and Africa.

Even allowing for inflated statistics, Garvey inarguably led the largest mass movement known to date in African-American history. UNIA's endeavors were varied: the organization owned grocery stores, published newspapers, and operated a factory and shipping line. In 1922 the U.S. government brought charges of mail fraud against Garvey in connection with the shipping business, the Black Star Line. He was convicted on June 21, 1923. Following bail and deportation hearings, Garvey was incarcerated on February 8, 1925. In December 1927, he was released and deported to Jamaica, where he launched the People's Political Party (PPP) and the Jamaica Workers and Labourers Association, but most of his efforts stalled. In 1934, Garvey relocated to London, where he resided until his death in 1940.

In its online biography of Garvey, the University of Northern Colorado's Marcus Garvey Center for Black Cultural Education concludes its assessment of his life in this way:

> Marcus A. Garvey captured the interest of the ordinary Negro as no other leader before or since, but his dream was based on a fatal flaw: his failure to understand that the overwhelming mass of Negroes considered America their rightful home and had no real desire to leave it. His weakness lay in thinking that the Negro, after helping to build America, would abandon it. His greatness lies in this daring to dream of a better future for Negroes somewhere on earth.[1]

Creation of the Observance

Celebrations of Marcus Garvey's birthday originated in various years, depending on the location. In Jamaica, for example, on the centennial anniversary of Garvey's birth in 1987, the government declared August 17 a public holiday in St. Ann. Since then, annual celebrations have been held at 32 Market Street, St. Ann's Bay, where Garvey was born.

Observance

Marcus Garvey's birthday is celebrated in his homeland, Jamaica, and also in Trinidad and Tobego, where the Abiadama Centre for Lifelong Learning commemorates Garvey with lectures and displays of African artifacts, music, and food. Barbados and other West Indies isles also celebrate Garvey's birthday.

---

1 Reprinted with permission from the University of Northern Colorado.

Many Rastafarians in the United States commemorate Garvey's birthday as well. Some celebrate just the date, August 17, while others stretch the commemoration throughout an entire week. Still others honor Garvey with events during the whole month of August each year (*see also* **Haile Selassie's Birthday**). So, while celebrations of Garvey's contributions vary, partly dependent upon the geographic locale of the event, observances often include the recitation of inspiration poems and speeches (sometimes those of Garvey himself) and the performance of traditional African dances and drumming. Larger events might also include the display of African arts and crafts and the presence of native food.

Reggae musicians, many of whom are Rastafarians, often hold festivals and concerts around Garvey's birth date as a way to commemorate him.

Contacts and Websites

African Studies Center
10244 Bunche Hall
405 Hilgard Ave.
P.O. Box 951310
Los Angeles, CA 90095
310-825-3686
fax: 310-206-2250
africa@international.ucla.edu
http://www.international.ucla.edu/africa/mgpp

Marcus Garvey Cultural Center University of Northern Colorado
928 20th St.
Campus Box 41
Greeley, CO 80639
970-351-2351
Fax: 970-351-2337
MGCC@unco.edu
https://www.unco.edu/marcus-garvey-cultural-center

Universal Negro Improvement Association and African Communities League
Thomas W. Harvey Memorial Division

1609-11 Cecil B. Moore Ave., Ste. 121
Philadelphia, PA 19121
215-236-0782
http://www.unia-acl.org

Wisconsin Black Historical Society/Museum
2620 W. Center
St. Milwaukee, WI 53206
414-372-7677
info@wbhsm.org
http://www.wbhsm.org

Further Reading

Ershine, Noel Leo. *From Garvey to Marley: Rastafari Theology.* Gainesville: University Press of Florida, 2005. Reprint. University Press of Florida, 2007

Garvey, Marcus, and Bob Blaisdell, ed. *Selected Writings and Speeches of Marcus Garvey.* 2004. Reprint. Mineola, NY: Dover Publications, 2012.

Jenkins, Everett. *Pan-African Chronology III: A Comprehensive Reference to the Black Quest for Freedom in Africa, the Americas, Europe and Asia, 1914-1929.* 2001. Reprint. Jefferson, NC: McFarland & Company Publishers, 2011.

Mugleston, William F. "Garvey, Marcus." In *African American Lives*, edited by Henry Louis Gates Jr. and Evelyn Brooks Higginbotham. New York: Oxford University Press, 2004. http://marcusgarvey.com/

Mardi Gras in African-American Traditions

Date Observed: Carnival period before Lent
(between February 3 and March 9)
Location: New Orleans, Louisiana

People of all races and backgrounds take part in Mardi Gras, which is a French term meaning "Fat Tuesday." The period before Lent is traditionally a time for feasting and merrymaking. The following day is Ash Wednesday, the beginning of the Christian season of Lent—a 40-day period of fasting and spiritual preparation for Easter. The carnival period that begins two weeks before Fat Tuesday also is known generally as "Mardi Gras." During this time, some festivities are based on African-American traditions, such as the Zulu parade and the appearance of Black Indians in handmade, colorful regalia.

Historical Background

Although Mobile, Alabama, claims title to the oldest Mardi Gras celebration in the United States, the New Orleans carnival is the best known, and, in fact, symbolizes the city. Festivities stem from masked balls and processions that French settlers brought with them in the 1700s. Some scholars speculate that these festivals may have roots in the spring rites of ancient Rome.

In 1857, New Orleans held its first Mardi Gras parade, presented by the Mistik Krewe of Comus, the first krewe—a private club or committee—to organize. Dozens of krewes formed later, sponsoring parades during the carnival. The krewe known as Rex (King) organized in 1872 and held a procession led by a "king" in costume followed by hundreds of people dressed as servants, clowns, saints, or devils.

The number of krewes has grown over the years, and among them are African-American groups. These private clubs organize the dinners, balls, processions, marching bands, floats, and pageants that are part of Mardi Gras and which take place at different times during the carnival season.

Creation of the Observance

A black support group in New Orleans, the Zulu Social Aid and Pleasure Club, sponsored the first African-American parade during Mardi Gras in 1901, but the group did not become known as the Zulus, or Zulu krewe, until 1909. Members of the organization based their parade themes on satire, making fun of white parade kings, similar to the slave parodies during **Pinkster** and **Negro Election Day and Coronation Festivals** in New England. The

A drum major participates in a Mardi Gras parade.

Zulu, however, organized in protest of the exclusive all-white krewes and from the beginning mocked the stereotyped portrayal of blacks by putting on exaggerated blackface of minstrel shows and grass skirts.

Black Indians known as Mardi Gras Indians make up krewes, also called gangs or tribes, that have created some of the most colorful parades in New Orleans. Their handmade regalia and music mesh Native-American and African-American customs. Scholars speculate about the origin of this tradition but many believe that African Americans were motivated by the Plains Indians, whom African Americans from New Orleans fought when they joined the **Buffalo Soldiers** during the late 19th century. In addition, the heritage of some Mardi Gras Indians includes both African and Indian ancestry, and they have carried on the ancient rituals and warrior traditions of both peoples.

Observance

More than 80 cities in Louisiana celebrate Mardi Gras, and thousands of people gather in New Orleans for the annual event—even in 2006 when there was concern that the celebration would not occur because of the severe damage

---

Black Indians

Many African-American families understand from oral histories and written records that their heritage may include Native-American ancestors. The two groups share a long history of efforts to escape white domination and discrimination and claim their own identities. But there have been few studies of connections between the two groups, and certainly, Black Indians have not found a place in most textbooks or been identified for their contributions. Nor have they been depicted in movies and TV shows about the western frontier and cowboys on the range (*see also* **Bill Pickett Invitational Rodeo** *and* **Black Cowboy Parade**).

The heritage of Black Indians includes runaway black slaves who found refuge in Native villages and intermarried, producing offspring who helped build a nation. Undeniably, some indigenous people—known as the "Five Civilized Nations" (Choctaw, Chickasaw, Cherokee, Creek, and Seminole) because they had adopted European (white) ways—also were slaveholders, with the exception of the Seminole. For the other tribes, slavery was an important aspect of their lives, although "the chains of slavery were fitted rather loosely on black people owned by Indians," according to William Katz, author of *Black Indians: A Hidden Heritage*. "Only the Chickasaws had a reputation for treating their slaves as badly as white people."

After the Civil War, some former slaves owned by Indians adopted Native-American culture just as escaped slaves had done in earlier times. This is obviously apparent with the pageant of the Mardi Gras Indians. The Creole Wild West krewe was founded in 1885 by Becate Batiste, a man of African, French, and Choctaw ancestry.

---

from Hurricane Katrina the previous year. The 2006 celebration was the 150th anniversary of the city's first formal parades. Following custom, streets were lined with spectators eager to capture "throws"—beads, trinkets, and other items tossed to the crowd by costumed people in parades.

Traditionally, the Zulu parade is held on the Monday before Fat Tuesday, when the Zulu king and queen arrive on a barge for a riverside festival. Before dawn the next day, the Zulus get on their floats and others prepare to march. Along the route, they distribute throws that are highly prized hand-painted coconuts.

The Mardi Gras Indians perform on Fat Tuesday. There are dozens of tribes known by such names as Hard Head Hunters, Red Hawk Hunters, Mohawk Hunters, Creole Wild West, Black Seminoles, and Golden Blades. They parade in highly structured suits (as they are called), decorated with beads, feathers, and sequins or rhinestones and topped with elaborate headdresses. Each suit is assembled annually, created from parts of the costumes that were used the previous year as well as new components. The suits can weigh over 100 pounds and are expensive to create, costing upwards to thousands of dollars.

During the march, the Mardi Gras Indians perform a ritual of song and dance in a call-and-response style closely related to African music. Each tribe has a "big chief" who heads the pageant that includes spy boys and flag boys who march in front of the krewe. The first spy boy looks out for any rival tribes who may be encountered for mock battles. In earlier days, physical clashes were real, but rivalry in modern pageants is primarily competition over the costuming.

Another Mardi Gras custom that originated with the all-white Comus krewe but has been carried on by African Americans, is the flambeaux spectacle. Parades at night are led by African Americans with torches that not only light up the sky but also are part of the black tradition and total pageantry displayed at Mardi Gras.

Contacts and Websites

New Orleans Convention & Visitors Bureau
2020 St. Charles Ave.
New Orleans, LA 70130
800-672-6124
504-566-5011; fax: 504-566-5046
https://www.neworleans.com/contact-us

Zulu Social Aid and Pleasure Club, Inc.
722 North Broad St.
New Orleans, LA 70119
504-827-1661
http://www.kreweofzulu.com/contact-us

Further Reading

Gay, Kathlyn. *I Am Who I Am: Speaking Out about Multiracial Identity.* New York: Franklin Watts, 1995.

Katz, William Loren. *Black Indians: A Hidden Heritage.* New York: Atheneum, 1986. Reprint. Atheneum, 2012.

Root, Maria P. P., ed. *Racially Mixed People in America.* Newbury Park, CA: Sage Publications, 1992.

Smith, Michael P. *Mardi Gras Indians.* Gretna, LA: Pelican Publishing Co., 1994.

Martin Luther King Jr.'s Birthday

Date Observed: Third Monday in January
Location: Communities nationwide

The third Monday in January is a federal holiday that commemorates Martin Luther King Jr.'s life and his contributions to the U.S. Civil Rights Movement of the 1950s and 1960s. The holiday, which is celebrated nationwide by all communities, normally falls on or around January 18. The first official celebration of his birthday took place on January 20, 1986.

Historical Background

Before Martin Luther King Jr. became involved with the civil rights movement of the 1950s and 1960s, African Americans were struggling to overcome segregation and oppression in the United States. For example, an early civil rights organization, the National Association for the Advancement of Colored People (NAACP), formed in 1909 and began crusades to pass anti-lynching laws and overturn legal racial segregation.

One of the NAACP's important members and promoters was W. E. B. Du Bois (1868–1963), a professor, scholar, author, and activist. In 1910, Du Bois became editor of the NAACP's monthly journal *Crisis*, which reached a large readership of African Americans and helped gain support for the organization's civil rights programs.

Another significant African American fighting for civil rights in the early decades of the 1900s was Asa Philip Randolph (1889–1979). He was a tireless activist for the rights of black workers and often risked his safety and life to obtain equal job opportunities for African Americans. He is best known for founding the Brotherhood of Sleeping Car Porters in 1925. By 1937, under Randolph's leadership, the union had won the right to negotiate with the Pullman Company, which made railroad cars and was the largest single

Martin Luther King Jr. preaching at Ebenezer Baptist Church in 1960.

employer of blacks in the United States. The corporation agreed to raise wages and reduce work hours for porters from 400 to 200 hours per month (*see also* **African-American History Month**).

Randolph also led an effort in 1940 to try to convince then-President Franklin D. Roosevelt to integrate the armed forces and defense industries. When Roosevelt refused, Randolph announced that he would organize a protest march on Washington, D.C. That prompted Roosevelt to sign an executive order to prohibit discrimination in defense industries and established the Fair Employment Practices Committee. Randolph called off the march, which some blacks denounced because they thought there should be a demonstration of black power. However, Randolph continued his fight for black civil rights over the years. He later helped organize the 1963 March on Washington that brought more than 200,000 people to the nation's capital, where they listened to Martin Luther King Jr. delivered his famous "I Have a Dream" speech.

Martin Luther—A Preacher's Son

Born on January 15, 1929, Martin Luther King Jr. was originally named Michael. His father later adopted the name Martin, and when Michael was about six years old, his name was also changed to Martin. His family included an older sister and younger brother.

King's maternal grandfather, Rev. Adam Williams, was the pastor of Ebenezer Baptist Church, and following Williams's death, King's father became pastor of the church. King, too, served the church as co-pastor with his father.

From his mother, Alberta Williams King, a former school teacher, King gained a love for books and was reading by the time he entered first grade. He was an excellent student and graduated from high school at the age of 15, passing an entrance examination to enroll in Morehouse College, a prominent African-American school. For a time he considered studying medicine or the law, but majored in sociology and decided to enter the ministry. After graduating from Morehouse in 1948, he attended Crozer Theological Seminary, where a lecture on the life of Mohandas Gandhi and his quest for ahimsa, or nonviolence, sparked King's interest and desire to learn more about the Indian leader.

King earned a bachelor of divinity degree in 1951 and began doctoral studies at Boston University. There he met Coretta Scott, whom he married in 1953. The couple eventually had four children, Yolanda, Martin III, Dexter, and Bernice.

In 1954, King accepted the position of pastor of the Dexter Avenue Baptist Church in Montgomery, Alabama, where he served until 1960. Those years were momentous times in the Civil Rights Movement (*see also* **National Baptist Convention, USA, Annual Session** *and* **Bessie Smith Strut**).

The Struggle for Civil Rights

From the mid-1950s through the 1960s, the struggle against racism and for the civil rights of people of color frequently meant putting one's life on the line. Some historians have called the Civil Rights Movement a revolution in that activists set out to change a way of life, particularly in southern states were segregation laws established separate facilities, such as restrooms and water fountains, for "white" and "colored." Apartments and hotels carried signs to indicate "white only" or "colored only." Restaurants, laundromats, and movie theaters owned or operated by whites either refused to serve people of color at all or confined them to a segregated section, such as the balcony.

Discrimination against people based on their skin color was not confined to the South, however. Across the nation, African Americans were barred from certain jobs and professions, were not allowed to rent or buy homes in certain neighborhoods, and usually attended separate schools with far fewer resources than all-white schools.

One of the first major changes in federal laws that helped propel the Civil Rights Movement was the 1954 U.S. Supreme Court decision in *Brown v. Board of Education of Topeka.* Oliver Brown, an African-American man in Topeka, Kansas, wanted his daughter Linda to attend an all-white school just a few blocks from where the family lived, but the school board refused to let Linda enroll. The state had set up segregated schools, which were allowed years earlier based on the federal court ruling in (*Plessy v. Ferguson*), which ruled that segregation was legal according to a federal law requiring "separate but equal" facilities.

The educational facilities for blacks and whites were not equal, however. Most black schools lacked basic materials such as books, desks, or even a safe, heated building for students. Whites, on the other hand, were able to attend schools that not only had sufficient supplies but also were conducive to learning.

With the help of the NAACP, Oliver Brown sued the Topeka school board and the case went to the U.S. Supreme Court, which in 1954 overturned the earlier federal "separate but equal" law and ordered that public schools be desegregated "with all deliberate speed" (*see also* **Black August Benefit Concert** *and* **Bridge Crossing Jubilee**).

The Montgomery Bus Boycott

A major civil rights effort to overturn laws that segregated public transportation in the South began in late 1955. African Americans were forced to ride in the back of public buses and had to stand even when there were empty seats. When Rosa Parks (1913–2005), a black woman who had been working all day, got on a public bus in Montgomery, Alabama, and refused to move to the rear of the vehicle, she broke one of the state's segregation laws. She was arrested and jailed (*see also* **Rosa Parks Day**).

A trial for Parks, an NAACP official, was scheduled a few days after her arrest, and NAACP leaders quickly formed the Montgomery Improvement Association. They elected one of their members, Martin Luther King Jr., as president. King organized a boycott of the bus system, which lasted for more than a year. The boycott hurt the bus company financially and also hurt businesses that catered to riders, who were primarily African Americans.

We Shall Overcome

The song that became known as the anthem of the Civil Rights Movement was "We Shall Overcome," which was published in 1960.

We shall overcome, we shall over-
come,
We shall overcome some day,
Oh, deep in my heart I do believe
We shall overcome some day.

We'll walk hand in hand, we'll walk
hand in hand,
We'll walk hand in hand some day,
Oh, deep in my heart I do believe
We shall overcome some day.

We are not afraid, we are not afraid,
We are not afraid today,
Oh, deep in my heart I do believe
We shall overcome some day.

We shall stand together, we shall
stand together,
We shall stand together—now,
Oh, deep in my heart I do believe
We shall overcome some day.

The truth will make us free, the truth
will make us free,
The truth will make us free some day,
Oh, deep in my heart I do believe
We shall overcome some day.

The Lord will see us through, the
Lord will see us through,
The Lord will see us through some day,
Oh, deep in my heart I do believe
We shall overcome some day.

We shall be like Him, we shall be like
Him,
We shall be like Him some day,
Oh, deep in my heart I do believe
We shall overcome some day.
We shall live in peace, we shall live in
peace,
We shall live in peace some day,
Oh, deep in my heart I do believe
We shall overcome some day.
The whole wide world around, the
whole wide world around,

The whole wide world around some day,
Oh, deep in my heart I do believe
We shall overcome some day.
We shall overcome, we shall overcome,

We shall overcome some day,
Oh, deep in my heart I do believe
We shall overcome some day.

Following King's lead, blacks refused to ride the public buses, a major form of transportation but instead created carpools, which police tried to break up. Drivers were sometimes arrested on fabricated charges. King himself was arrested and jailed for allegedly exceeding the speed limit. It was just one of many arrests and imprisonments that he endured in the years ahead.

On February 2, 1956, the NAACP filed a lawsuit in a U.S. district court charging that segregation in public transportation facilities was unconstitutional. Less than three weeks later, King and more than 100 other African Americans were indicted on charges of conspiring to prevent the bus company from doing business.

By June of 1956, the federal court ruled that segregation on city bus lines was unconstitutional, and the U.S. Supreme Court upheld that ruling in November. By December 21, 1956, the successful boycott was over (*see also* **Bud Billiken Parade and Picnic** *and* **Malcolm X's Birthday**).

A Force against Segregation

Beyond efforts to integrate public transportation systems, the Civil Rights Movement became a driving force against segregation in all types of public facilities. Throughout the rest of the 1950s, African Americans made additional strides toward equality. The Voting Rights Act, the first civil rights act since the days of Reconstruction following the Civil War, passed in 1957, and authorized the U.S. Justice Department to file lawsuits on behalf of blacks who had been denied their right to vote. More public services, such as city swimming pools, were integrated.

Expanding the civil rights efforts in the South was one of King's priorities in 1957. He brought together (primarily African-American) ministers who were committed to civil rights, and they formed the Southern Christian Leadership Conference (SCLC). Members elected King president of the SCLC, and he led a pilgrimage to Washington, D.C., where he gave his first major speech that received national coverage.

In 1960, King and his family moved to Atlanta, Georgia. He became co-pastor, with his father, of the Ebenezer Baptist Church; he also continued his involvement with the Civil Rights Movement. By the early 1960s, the movement was making some gains. Nonviolent student sit-in protests brought nationwide media attention to segregated restaurants, theaters, hotels, libraries, and other public places, which eventually led to desegregation. Freedom Riders—blacks and whites from the North and South—rode interstate buses to protest segregated bus stations, and in 1961, the Interstate Commerce Commission banned segregation in bus terminals. There also were numerous voter-registration drives to help blacks throughout the South exercise their right to cast ballots.

King supported or took part in numerous nonviolent protests and was frequently jailed on charges such as violating state trespassing laws, obstructing the sidewalk, parading without a permit, failing to obey a police officer sent to stop a prayer vigil at the Albany, Georgia, city hall. In April 1963, King participated in sit-in demonstrations in Birmingham, Alabama, and was again arrested and jailed. While in the Birmingham City Jail, he wrote an open letter to white clergy members who had criticized his actions (*see also* **Penn Center Heritage Days** *and* **Rondo Days Celebration***and* **Rosa Parks Day**).

Letter from Birmingham City Jail

In reaction to King's protests, eight white religious leaders issued "An Appeal for Law and Order and Common Sense," a public statement arguing against civil disobedience. The statement also inferred that King was an "outside agitator." In his letter, King pointed out that he was hardly an "outsider," since he was president of the SCLC that had affiliates across the South. More important, though, was his argument that direct action was needed to counteract Birmingham's "ugly record of police brutality" and "unjust treatment of Negroes in the courts." He also responded to the religious leaders' charges that protests were "untimely." King wrote in part:

> We know through painful experience that freedom is never voluntarily given by the oppressor; it must be demanded by the oppressed. Frankly, I have never yet engaged in a direct action movement that was "well-timed," according to the timetable of those who have not suffered unduly from the disease of segregation. For years now I have heard the word "Wait!" It rings in the ear of every Negro with piercing familiarity. This "wait" has almost always meant "Never." . . . We must come to see with the distinguished jurist of yesterday that "justice too long delayed is justice denied."

> We have waited for more than three hundred and forty years for our constitutional and God-given rights. The nations of Asia and Africa are moving with jetlike speed toward the goal of political independence, and we still creep at horse and buggy pace toward the gaining of a cup of coffee at a lunch counter.

I guess it is easy for those who have never felt the stinging darts of segregation to say, "wait." But when you have seen vicious mobs lynch your mothers and fathers at will and drown your sisters and brothers at whim; when you have seen hate-filled policemen curse, kick, brutalize, and even kill your black brothers and sisters with impunity; when you see the vast majority of your twenty million Negro brothers smothering in an air-tight cage of poverty in the midst of an affluent society; when you suddenly find your tongue twisted and your speech stammering as you seek to explain to your six-year-old daughter why she can't go to the public amusement park that has just been advertised on television, and see tears welling up in her little eyes when she is told that Funtown is closed to colored children, and see the depressing clouds of inferiority begin to form in her little mental sky, and see her begin to distort her little personality by unconsciously developing a bitterness toward white people; when you have to concoct an answer for a five-year-old son asking in agonizing pathos: "Daddy, why do white people treat colored people so mean?"; when you take a cross country drive and find it necessary to sleep night after night in the uncomfortable corners of your automobile because no motel will accept you; when you are humiliated day in and day out by nagging signs reading "white" and "colored"; when your first name becomes "nigger," your middle name becomes "boy" (however old you are) and your last name becomes "John," and when your wife and mother are never given the respected title "Mrs."; when you are harried by day and haunted by night by the fact that you are a Negro, living constantly at tiptoe stance never quite knowing what to expect next, and plagued with inner fears and outer resentments; when you are forever fighting a degenerating sense of "nobodiness"; then you will understand why we find it difficult to wait. There comes a time when the cup of endurance runs over, and men are no longer willing to be plunged into an abyss of injustice where they experience the bleakness of corroding despair. I hope, sir, you can understand our legitimate and unavoidable impatience.[1]

King's letter was published in pamphlet form by the American Friends Service Committee (a Quaker organization) and was widely quoted. Parts of the letter were reprinted in newspapers and magazines. In addition, the letter or portions of it are read aloud during some celebrations of **African-American History Month**.

---

[1] Reprinted by arrangement with the Estate of Martin Luther King Jr., c/o Writers House as agent for the proprietor New York, NY. Copyright 1963 Martin Luther King Jr., copyright renewed 1991 Coretta Scott King.

The March on Washington, August 28, 1963.

March on Washington

In the summer of 1963, a massive March on Washington was planned to support a new civil rights bill that President John F. Kennedy had sent to Congress. Organizers of the march hoped to pressure congressional members to pass the bill. More than 200,000 black and white marchers gathered before the Lincoln Memorial in Washington on August 28, 1963, and listened to Martin Luther King Jr. present an eloquent address that was televised across the nation. King noted that African Americans were ready to collect on the "promissory note" of equality specified in the Declaration of Independence and U.S. Constitution. He ended with the celebrated words that are repeated time and again during the King holiday: "even though we must face the difficulties of today and tomorrow, I still have a dream. It is a dream deeply rooted in the American dream that one day this nation will rise up and live out the true meaning of its creed—we hold these truths to be self-evident, that all men are created equal."[2]

---

[2] Reprinted by arrangement with the Estate of Martin Luther King Jr., c/o Writers House as agent for the proprietor New York, NY. Copyright 1963 Martin Luther King Jr., copyright renewed 1991 Coretta Scott King.

In 1964, King became the youngest person to receive the Nobel Peace Prize. He was 35 years old. When he learned about his selection, he declared that he would donate the prize money to the Civil Rights Movement. In his acceptance speech, he said that the award was "a profound recognition that nonviolence is the answer to the crucial political and moral question of our time—the need for man to overcome oppression and violence without resorting to violence and oppression. . . . Negroes of the United States, following the people of India, have demonstrated that nonviolence is not sterile passivity, but a powerful moral force which makes for social transformation."[3]

Confrontations and Violence

Advances toward full citizenship rights for African Americans were not peaceful, however. Frequently, nonviolence was met with violent backlashes. One such attack in 1963, perpetrated by members of the Ku Klux Klan (KKK), a racist hate group, killed four girls in the Sixteenth Street Baptist Church in Birmingham.

Brutal attacks greeted civil rights activists who planned to march from Selma, Alabama, to the state's capital in Montgomery. In early 1965, King helped organize the march designed to call for African-American voting rights. When the demonstration began on Sunday, March 7, police were on hand with tear gas and clubs, beating marchers as they crossed a bridge leading out of Selma. This "Bloody Sunday," as it was called, is commemorated with a reenactment in the annual **Bridge Crossing Jubilee**. Three weeks later, with the help of federal officials, the march was completed. Such demonstrations helped gain support for a new Voting Rights Act.

After the assassination of President Kennedy in 1963, Vice-President Lyndon B. Johnson took office as President. In 1965, he signed a new Voting Rights Act and invoked the slogan of the Civil Rights Movement and title of its anthem: "We Shall Overcome."

Yet, overcoming racism, prejudice, and discrimination against African Americans was a daunting task, one that had to be tackled in the North as well as the South. In 1966 King went to Chicago where he hoped to campaign against urban poverty. But he had difficulty organizing blacks who came from diverse economic backgrounds and did not necessarily share the same goals. This was also a time when many black militants were denouncing King's

---

[3] © 1964 The Nobel Foundation.

On Martin Luther King Jr.'s Birthday in 2006, Reverend Al Sharpton and hundreds of healthcare workers marched in New York City for economic justice for home health workers, some of the lowest-paid employees in the state.

nonviolent approach and his call for racial integration (*see also* **Malcolm X's Birthday**).

King continued his message of nonviolence, however, applying it to the Vietnam War and taking an antiwar stance. He also persisted in his anti-poverty efforts, forming the Poor People's Campaign in 1967. Less than a year later he was in Memphis, Tennessee, where he addressed a church audience. The next night, April 4, 1968, while standing on the balcony of a Memphis motel, he was shot and killed. James Earl Ray, a white segregationist, was convicted of assassinating the great civil rights leader.

After her husband's death, Coretta Scott King said that she was "more determined than ever that my husband's dream will become a reality." A forceful activist in her own right, she immediately founded the Martin Luther King, Jr. Center for Nonviolent Social Change and began a campaign to establish her husband's birthday as a national holiday. For the rest of her life, she was an advocate for peace and human rights, traveling the globe and speaking out about racial and economic injustice. She died in 2006.

King's Legacy

The legacy of Martin Luther King Jr. persists to this day. He has been remembered over the decades for his nonviolent protests and passive resistance to achieve civil rights.

Also among his most important contributions were his efforts on behalf of legislation to end racial segregation in public facilities through the Civil Rights Act of 1964 and to expand voting rights with the passage of the Voting Rights Act of 1965.

Because of King's example, thousands of people in the United States as well as around the world have committed themselves to community service. His brief life also has inspired others to develop programs that foster mutual respect among diverse groups and to work for world peace.

Creation of the Holiday

Four days after King's assassination, U.S. Representative John Conyers of Michigan introduced a bill to create a national holiday to commemorate Martin Luther King Jr.'s birthday. The bill stalled in Congress, but during each congressional session over a 15-year period the proposal was resubmitted.

Although many African Americans signed petitions and lobbied Congress for the holiday, there was stiff opposition from diverse groups. Some congressional members claimed that the holiday would cost the federal government $18 million in lost services if employees got the day off. State governments and private businesses were equally concerned as estimates of total costs for the holiday reached $8 billion.

Another argument against the holiday came from those who thought that King was being given preferential treatment over other famous individuals. Certainly, some opposition stemmed from racist attitudes.

For Martin Luther King Jr. Day, 2004, volunteers in Washington, D.C., assembled and delivered disaster-preparedness kits to residents of a low-income apartment complex.

Meantime, though, states began to create their King holidays. Finally, in 1983, the U.S. Congress passed legislation to establish the Martin Luther King Jr. federal holiday, which became effective in 1986.

Observance

Across the United States, the King holiday is frequently observed with a solemn reflection on the principles for which the civil rights leader stood. Many churches hold ecumenical memorial services, bringing together people of diverse racial, religious, and socioeconomic backgrounds.

The weekend of the holiday is also a time for families and friends to meet in private homes. Civic gatherings take place as well, with prominent individuals delivering speeches that recount King's deeds and how he inspired people around the world to seek peace and freedom. Some organizations encourage people to volunteer and spend the day in service to those less fortunate.

343

During the holiday (and all through the year as well) individuals, families, and tour groups may visit the Martin Luther King Jr. Historic Site established in 1980 by the National Park Service. The site is east of downtown Atlanta, Georgia, and includes the home where King was born, the church where he worshipped, and his burial place.

Although public schools are closed for the holiday, King is honored in classrooms on the days before the observance with readings from books about his life, artwork depicting King, choral groups singing "We Shall Overcome," and numerous other activities.

From coast to coast, annual marches and parades are held to honor King in such cities as Albany, New York; Raleigh, North Carolina; Washington, D.C.; and St. Petersburg, Florida.

Since 1982 a nonprofit group called MLK365 has organized events in Sacramento, California. The celebration begins with a 2.5-hour march—a visual portrayal of King's dream with people of diverse backgrounds, races, and ages coming together to show their support. The march ends at the Sacramento Convention Center, where there are job and health fairs and workshops, activities for children, and musical performances.

In Oakland, California, a Mormon Temple has an annual Down Home Martin Luther King Potluck Celebration in which participants bring their favorite dish from "back home" to share. They also see films of significant events from King's life and listen to readings from his works.

Contacts and Websites

American Public Transportation Association
1300, I Street N.W.
Ste. 1200 E.
Washington, DC 20005
202–496-4800; fax: 202-496-4324
http://www.apta.com

The Martin Luther King, Jr. Research and Education Institute
Cypress Hall D
466 Via Ortega
Stanford, CA 94305-4146

650-723-2092; fax: 650-723-2093
E-mail: kinginstitute@stanford.edu

Further Reading

Anyike, James C. *African American Holidays: A Historical Research and Resource Guide to Cultural Celebrations*. Chicago: Popular Truth, 1991.

Branch, Taylor. *At Canaan's Edge: America in the King Years, 1965–68*. 2006. Reprint. New York: Simon & Schuster, 2007.

———. *Parting the Waters: America in the King Years, 1954–63*. 1988. Reprint. New York: Simon & Schuster, 1989.

———. *Pillar of Fire: America in the King Years, 1963–65*. New York: Simon & Schuster, 1998.

Clayborne, Carson. "King, Martin Luther, Jr." *In African American Lives*, edited by Henry Louis Gates Jr. and Evelyn Brooks Higginbotham. New York: Oxford University Press, 2004.

Colaiaco, James A. *Martin Luther King, Jr.: Apostle of Militant Nonviolence*. New York: St. Martin's Press, 1988.

Gay, Kathlyn, and Martin K. Gay. *Heroes of Conscience: A Biographical Dictionary. Santa Barbara*, CA: ABC-CLIO, 1996.

King, Coretta Scott. *My Life with Martin Luther King, Jr.* Revised edition. New York: Henry Holt, 1993.

Williams, Juan, with the Eyes on the Prize Production Team. *Eyes on the Prize: America's Civil Rights Years, 1954–1965*. Intoduction by Julian Bond. 1987. Reprint. New York: Penguin Books, 2013.

Writings by Martin Luther King Jr.

Letter from Birmingham City Jail. Philadelphia: American Friends Service Committee, May 1963.

Nobel Prize Acceptance Speech http://www.nobelprizes.com/nobel/peace/MLK-nobel.html

Stride toward Freedom. New York: Harper & Row, 1958.

A Testament of Hope: The Essential Writings and Speeches of Martin Luther King, Jr. Edited by James M. Washington. 1986. Reprint. San Francisco: HarperSanFrancisco, 2003.

Where Do We Go from Here: Chaos or Community? New York: Harper & Row, 1967.

Miami Bahamas Junakoo Festival

Date Observed: Last weekend in June
Location: Coconut Grove neighborhood,
Miami, Florida

T he Miami Bahamas Junakoo Festival is an annual street festival held during the last weekend in June in the Coconut Grove neighborhood of Miami, Florida. This massive event celebrates the community's Caribbean—and particularly Bahamian—roots, and features the arts, music, and food. In June 2015, the festival was rebranded to Miami Bahamas Junkanoo Festival to focus on youth and empower them through education, employment, leadership, and entrepreneurial opportunities.

Historical Background

Since at least the early 19th century, Bahamians sailed to nearby south Florida, especially the Keys, for fishing and, in earlier times, to trade with the native Seminole Indians. During the latter part of the 19th century, Bahamian craftsmen came to the Coconut Grove area in large numbers. Many worked in construction, building the new city of Miami. One can still see many examples of their handiwork in resorts and homes, in the style of landscaping that remains popular, and in street names.

Creation of the Festival

In 1977, William R. Rolle and several other local citizens produced the first Miami/Bahamas Goombay Festival as a way of honoring the contributions of early Bahamian immigrants. The festival is a vehicle for showcasing the contributions of Bahamians to the city of Miami. The name *goombay* is a

Conch Fritters

Conch fritters are a popular treat at the festival. Conch (pronounced "konk") is a seafood found inside a brightly colored spiral shell. The meat can be eaten raw or cooked, and a common cooked dish is conch fritters. There are numerous recipes for this traditional Bahamian food. Generally, they are made with ground conch (sometimes shrimp or crab meat is substituted, or even calamari) mixed with chopped celery, peppers, onion, and parsley; pressed garlic and various spices; eggs, oil, and pancake mix or flour. The mixture is formed into a spoon-sized ball and deep fried or sautéed. Usually, a dipping sauce is served with the fritters.

Bantu word for a goatskin drum that is beaten with the hands; it also refers to music associated with the drum. Goombay has been celebrated by African slaves in the Caribbean for centuries (*see also* **Goombay!**).

Observance

The Miami Bahamas Junakoo Festival features the sounds of Bahamian and African-American music—and an annual favorite is the Royal Bahamas Police Band. Calypso, blues, reggae, and steel bands perform alongside rappers. There's also a **Junkanoo** band with festive, costumed dancers, accompanied by whistles, cow bells, and washboards.

Hundreds of vendors offer such goods as authentic Bahamian craftwork, tie-dyed T-shirts, Bahamian food, and the most popular food fare of all, conch fritters.

Contacts and Websites

African Heritage Cultural Arts Center
6161 NW 22nd Ave.
Miami, FL 33142
305-638-6771

Greater Miami Convention & Visitors Bureau
701 Bricknell Ave., Ste. 2700
Miami, FL 33131
800-933-8448 or 305-539-3000
http://www.gmcvb.com

Miami/Bahamas Goombay Festival in Coconut Grove, Inc.
4716 Brooker Street
Miami, Fl 33133
305-446-0643; fax: 305-446-6265
http://www.goombayfestivalcoconutgrove.com

Further Reading

Mohl, Raymond A. "Black Immigrants: Bahamians in Early Twentieth-Century Miami." *Florida Historical Quarterly*, January 1987.

Millions More
Movement March

Date Observed: Second weekend of October
Location: Washington, D.C.

The Millions More Movement March was held on October 15, 2005, to commemorate the 10th anniversary of the Million Man March. Both rallies called for African Americans' increased individual responsibility and community involvement. To commemorate the twentieth anniversary of the Million Man March, a rally was held at the National Mall in Washington, D.C., on October 10, 2015. Participants rallied in support of police reform and awareness about discrimination against black people was raised in the event.

Historical Background

Many African-American communities have been plagued with social problems, such as poverty, crime, violence, drug use, lack of education, and unemployment. Louis Farrakhan, minister, and leader of the Nation of Islam, believed that a positive step would be to mobilize African-American men to take action against these widespread problems. In 1995 he decided to plan the Million Man March, hoping to gather one million black men in Washington, D.C., for a national day of atonement and reconciliation for African-American men. Benjamin Chavis Jr., former chairman of the NAACP, served as the march organizer. The event drew the support of prominent African-American leaders such as Rosa Parks and the Rev. Jesse Jackson, African-American governmental leaders and ministers across the country, and several black members of Congress.

This historic event called for African-American men to take a public pledge to better themselves and to work for the betterment of all African Americans. This rally was one of the largest gatherings of African-American men ever

349

On May 2, 2005, veterans of the 1995 Million Man March—from left to right in the foreground: former Washington, D.C., Mayor Marion Barry, Reverend Jesse Jackson, and Nation of Islam leader Louis Farrakhan—held a news conference to announce the Millions More March.

organized, and it made news headlines around the country as well as internationally. Women were excluded from participating in the event but were instead asked to observe a "day of absence"—by not going to work and not shopping or spending any money on that day. This was done as a show of support for the men who were participating in the rally, and also as a demonstration of the economic power of African Americans.

It is unclear exactly how many African-American men gathered on the National Mall in Washington, D.C., on October 16, 1995. Estimates range from 400,000 to two million. Men came from all over the country, some arriving the night before to sleep on the ground or stay awake all night in anticipation of the next day's march. The event resembled a rally more than an actual march, with numerous speakers calling for African-American men to take responsibility for themselves, their families, and their lives. Attendees were urged to fight against rampant poverty, violence, substance abuse, and unemployment.

Many march attendees returned home determined to make lasting changes in their lives and to become more involved in their communities. March organizers claim credit for the more than one million African-American men who registered to vote afterward, and also for the thousands of applications that were submitted to adopt African-American children in the weeks following the march.

Creation of the Observance

In the late 20th century and early 21st century, similar marches followed in the wake of the Million Man March. On October 16, 2000, the Million Family March was held

A scene from the Millions More March in Washington, D.C., on October 15, 2005.

to commemorate the fifth anniversary of the Million Man March. This rally focused attention on public-policy issues that impact the quality of life for everyone, not just African Americans. The success of the Million Man March and the Million Family March resulted in Farrakhan's creation of the Millions More Movement in early 2005. This movement encouraged the development of African-American community-based service organizations to continue the work outlined at the two previous marches. Plans also began at that time for the Millions More Movement March.

In addition, other unrelated groups organized their own rallies using Farrakhan's event as a model. The Million Women March was held in Philadelphia, Pennsylvania, on October 26, 1997, bringing together more than 300,000 African-American women to address social issues. In the Harlem neighborhood of New York, the Million Youth March to empower young African Americans was held on September 5, 1998. The first Million Mom March was organized on May 14, 2000, in Washington, D.C., to protest gun violence and call for stricter gun laws. On October 17, 2004, the Million Worker March took place in Washington, D.C., to draw attention to issues faced by workers around the world.

Observance

The 10th anniversary of the Million Man March was observed with the Millions More Movement March. This rally took place in Washington, D.C., during the second weekend of October, 2005. The Millions More Movement March was intended to give African Americans an opportunity to focus once again on pressing social issues. Particular attention was given to unity within the African-American community, spiritual values, education, economic development, political power, reparations for slavery, eradication of improper law enforcement tactics, health concerns, artistic and cultural development, and peace. The Millions More Movement March was a much more inclusive event, welcoming interested men, women, and children of all races and ethnicities.

Contact and Website

Million Man March 1995, Inc.
7351 S. Stony Island Ave.
Chicago, IL 60649
773-324-6000
http://www.millionsmoremovement.com

Mississippi Delta Blues and Heritage Festival

Date Observed: Third Saturday in September
Location: Greenville, Mississippi

The Mississippi Delta Blues and Heritage Festival is held in Greenville, Mississippi, on the third Saturday in September. Sponsored by the Mississippi Action for Community Education, Inc., since 1978, the festival's purpose is to celebrate the birth of the blues in the region and raise funds for civil rights, anti-poverty, and educational programs. Blues enthusiasts from across the United States and around the world attend the festival.

Historical Background

Blues as a distinctive musical form evolved under nebulous circumstances in the latter 19th century. Proto-blues songs may have existed as early as the 1860s, but it is generally believed that blues sounds were codified in the 1890s among New Orleans street musicians. Blues then migrated to the rural deep South, where it took on a history of its own. This genre of music has been described in numerous ways: an emotional expression, poetry, or, technically, as music with "simple, usually three-chord progressions" that allows for improvisation.

Historically, the blues developed from slave music in the South, such as field chants and hollers, spirituals, and dance music. As the blues grew and spread, musicians performed lyrical monologues whose most prominent subjects were romantic complaints, sexual boasts, rambling by foot or rail, ballad-like tales of violent conflict, physical labor, humorous narratives, and more. Singers usually accompanied themselves on guitar or piano.

Early blues songs were passed on orally as folk songs. Educated composers, such as **W. C. Handy**, collected and revised some of this traditional material and published it under their own by-lines. In the 1920s, the commercial music industry learned that the southern black people (and many white people, too) had a taste for what it called "race music." Singers such as **Bessie Smith**, Ma Rainey, Mamie Smith, and others recorded urbanized, jazz-inflected pop versions of blues, while rural folk-blues artists, such as Texas' Blind Lemon Jefferson and Mississippi's Charlie Patten—along with hundreds of their contemporaries in the southern countryside and African-American districts of such cities as Memphis, Tennessee, and Atlanta, Georgia—recorded prolifically.

Creation of the Festival

The Mississippi Action for Community Education, Inc., organized the first Mississippi Delta Blues and Heritage Festival in 1978 as a fundraiser. The first festival was a simple community get-together in a rural village of less than 100 people with a flatbed trailer as a stage. As the festival has grown, it has encouraged the development of other festivals throughout the Delta and beyond.

Observance

Known as the second oldest blues festival in the nation, the Mississippi Delta Blues and Heritage Festival has drawn people from countries around the world as well as top performers. B. B. King, Sam Chatmon, Son Thomas, Willie Foster, Ruby Wilson, Robert Cray, John Lee Hooker, Muddy Waters, Stevie Ray Vaughan, Albert King, Bobby Rush, and Denise LaSalle have all appeared at the festival in various years. Concerts are presented, and food and crafts vendors are also on hand for the festivities.

Contact and Website

Mississippi Action for Community Education, Inc.
119 Theobald St.
Greenville, MS 38701
662-335-3523; fax: 662-334-2939
E-mail: mace03@deltamace.org or info@deltabluesms.org
http://www.deltamace.org

Further Reading

"Blues." In *Encyclopedia of Black America*, edited by W. Augustus Low and Virgil A. Clift. 1981. Reprint. Da Capo Press, 1984.

Titon, Jeff Todd. "Blues, The." In *The African-American Experience: Selections from the Five-Volume Macmillan Encyclopedia of African-American Culture and History*, edited by Jack Salzman. New York: Macmillan, 1998.

MOJA Arts Festival

Date Observed: Late September to early October
Location: Charleston, South Carolina

T he MOJA Arts Festival celebrates African-American and Caribbean Arts and includes visual arts, classical music, dance, gospel, jazz, poetry, R&B music, storytelling, theatre, children's activities, traditional crafts, ethnic food, and much, much more. The festival takes place in Charleston, South Carolina, from the end of September to early October.

Historical Background

African-American heritage and culture abound throughout Charleston, South Carolina, which was a major port for slave traders bringing captured Africans to North America. Slaves were also imported or sent to the nearby Sea Islands where African-American Gullah/Geechee culture maintains its roots in West Africa (*see also* **Georgia Sea Island Festival**; **Hilton Head Island Gullah Celebration**; *and* **Penn Center Heritage Days**).

African slaves helped establish the first colony in South Carolina near what is now Charleston (first called Charles Town). The forced labor of slaves created great wealth for plantation owners growing rice, indigo, and cotton during the 1700s. Yet, slaves resisted by damaging tools, acting sick or dim-witted, or running away. In 1739 about 100 slaves staged a rebellion, hoping to get to Spanish-controlled St. Augustine, Florida, where they would be granted freedom. But the slaves were captured and most were executed.

In 1822 Denmark Vesey led another revolt. It also ended with executions. Later planned uprisings were uncovered before they could take place. When the Civil War began, the Union army gained control of the Sea Islands, where enslaved people found refuge; Union forces considered the runaways free people.

After the Civil War, African-American accomplishments in Charleston included the founding of the Avery Normal Institute, now called the Avery Research Center for African American History and Culture. During the MOJA Festival, the Center is one of more than 90 venues for presentations of African-American art forms.

Creation of the Festival

African-American arts were first celebrated in Charleston in 1979 and again in 1981 and 1983. In 1984, the first annual MOJA Arts Festival began. Although MOJA appears to be an acronym, it is the capitalized version of *moja*, which is Kiswahili for "one." The festival is under the direction of the City of Charleston Office of Cultural Affairs in partnership with community arts groups and civic leaders. The first Black Arts Festival in Charleston began as a whole celebration of Black Artists and performers from the Lowcountry's contemporary art scene. The festival showcased examples from all the arts disciplines with a major representative exhibition of Black artists from the Southeast region as a backdrop and efficiently communicated the significant contributions of the heritage of African Americans to the cultural life of the region and of the nation. Some of the major highlights of this festival include a duo-piano concert by Wilfred Delphin and Edwin Romain and a visual arts exhibition named "Reflections of a Southern Heritage: 20th Century Black Artists of the Southeast" at the Gibbes Museum of Art.

Observance

The MOJA Arts Festival is an assortment of artistic events: visual arts; classical music; gospel, jazz, and rhythm and blues concerts; poetry and storytelling; theatrical productions; crafts and children's activities; and, of course, ethnic food. Many award-winning artists appear. In addition, there is an annual Caribbean parade and reggae block dance with an estimated crowd of 15,000 people.

In 2005 a "Ceremony for the Unknown Africans" commemorated the many enslaved Africans who died after arriving in Charleston and were placed nameless in the morgue of the Old Slave Mart. There was also an exhibit, "Dialogues from the Diaspora: Art in an Age of Authenticity," at the City Gallery.

Visitors to Charleston who attend the MOJA Festival are encouraged to tour the numerous historical sites that are part of African-American history in the area. These include the Old Slave Mart Museum, Denmark Vesey's house; the Emanuel African Methodist Episcopal Church, the second oldest AME Church in the world (and the site of a horrific race-motivated mass shooting) (*see also* **Founder's Day/Richard Allen's Birthday**); Catfish Row, which inspired George Gershwin to use it as a setting for his opera *Porgy and Bess*; slave quarters throughout the city; and the Gullah Sweetgrass Basket Makers in Charleston's historic market.

Contacts and Websites

Avery Research Center
125 Bull St.
Charleston, SC 29424
843-953-7609; fax: 843-953-7607
E-mail: averyadmin@cofc.edu
https://avery.cofc.edu

Charleston Area Convention and Visitors Bureau
423 King St.
Charleston, SC 29403
843-853-8000 or 800-868-8118
E-mail: datamanagement@explorecharleston.com
https://www.charlestoncvb.com

City Of Charleston Office Of Cultural Affairs
75 Calhoun St., Ste. 3800
Charleston, SC 29401
843-724-7305
http://www.mojafestival.com/home

NAACP Image Awards

Date Observed: Last week of March
Location: Los Angeles, California

The NAACP Image Awards is a gala event that recognizes the achievements and contributions of African Americans and other people of color in entertainment and the arts. Honorees, presenters, and performers include celebrities, political and social leaders, and other dignitaries.

Historical Background

In the early days of radio, motion pictures, and television, African Americans had few opportunities to find work in these industries. The few roles that did exist were often stereotypical portrayals of African Americans and did not reflect the true experiences of most people. At the same time, the contributions and talents of African-American entertainers went largely unrecognized by performing arts awards organizations, such as the Academy of Motion Picture Arts and Sciences that presents the Oscars.

The NAACP Image Awards were created to reward positive, non-stereotypical representations of African Americans in entertainment and the media. Believing that social norms and beliefs are heavily influenced by images presented in movies, television shows, and popular music, organizers instituted the awards to draw attention to the achievements, successes, and positive portrayals of African Americans in the entertainment industry.

The NAACP organized a nationwide protest against the negative portrayals of African Americans in the film "Birth of A Nation" as early as 1915. The founding members of the Association understood the power and influence of the then-new film media and continues to be at the forefront of the struggle for the inclusion of all Americans, regardless of race, in the entertainment industry. In 1942, then-NAACP Executive Director Walter White worked with politicians and studio executives to establish an ad-hoc committee with the major studios to monitor the image and portrayal of African Americans on the screen. In 1955, Medgar Evers, who led the Mississippi Branch of the NAACP, filed a complaint with the Federal Communication Commission (FCC) that the local television affiliate, WLBT, presented the local news in a racially biased manner that did not serve the public interest. Finally, in 1969, the FCC revoked the WLBT's broadcast license. After years of litigation, this marked the only time in the history of FCC history that a television station's license was revoked because of racial bias in programming, which sent a powerful reminder to the rest of the television industry.

Creation of the Observance

Originally conceived as a fundraising dinner for the Los Angeles chapter of the NAACP, the awards have become one of the most celebrated events in the African-American community. The first event was produced in 1962 by Sammy Davis Jr. and included a gala dinner and a separate awards ceremony at the Coconut Grove nightclub in Hollywood, California. Many celebrities and political leaders were in attendance, including Sidney Poitier, Berry Gordy Jr., Diana Ross and the Supremes, Frank Sinatra, Dean Martin, the mayor of Los Angeles, and the governor of California. Most of the awards presented the first year were given to white producers and directors who had displayed sensitivity to African-American concerns, and who made efforts to provide more opportunities for African-American entertainers.

The awards soon grew from a local chapter event into one of the largest and most popular national fundraisers for the NAACP. In 1967, the event became officially known as the "NAACP Image Awards." Public interest grew along with the event, and in the late 1980s, the awards ceremony began to be filmed so that it could be televised later. For several years, the Image Awards aired in a late-night time slot on the NBC network. The Los Angeles chapter continued to produce the event until 1991, when the national NAACP organization took over. In 1996, the awards moved to a prime-time slot on the Fox network. The sale of tickets to the awards events, paid advertising on the television broadcast, and donations from corporate sponsors raise more than a million dollars for the NAACP each year. Beyond the importance of the event as a fundraiser, the NAACP Image Awards are valued for their recognition of positive public images of African Americans.

Observance

Several events are now held each year as part of the NAACP Image Awards. An invitation-only luncheon is usually held for nominees a few weeks before the awards ceremony. The awards ceremony weekend includes a celebrity golf game, and pre-show gala, a pre-show brunch, the awards ceremony itself, and a post-show gala.

Awards are given in more than 40 competitive categories covering motion pictures, television, music, and literature. Honorary awards are also given to acknowledge special achievements, public service, and contributions to racial equality. The Chairman's Award recognizes the dignified representation of people of color, and the Corporate Award acknowledges companies that make commitments to diversity. The NAACP Image Awards Hall of Fame celebrates the lifetime career achievements of notable individuals. The President's Award is given to those who work to further the causes of civil rights. Past President's Award recipients include former President Bill Clinton and U.S. Secretary of State Condoleezza Rice.

Contact and Website

NAACP National Headquarters
4805 Mt. Hope Dr.
Baltimore, MD 21215
410-580-5777; Toll-Free: 877-6222-798
https://www.naacp.org/contact-us

National Baptist Convention, USA, Annual Session

Date Observed: First week in September
Location: Varies

The National Baptist Convention, with more than 7.5 million members, is one of the largest African-American religious groups in the United States and holds its Annual Session during the first week in September, including the Labor Day holiday. Various cities across the country have hosted the Convention which draws 20,000 or more delegates every year.

Historical Background

Since before the Revolutionary War period, black preachers—Baptists and Methodists—have organized congregations and churches. Black Baptists were among the first Americans to establish foreign missions. During the 1780s, former slave George Liele of Georgia, for example, founded churches in Jamaica, and David George, a slave, established a Baptist church in Savannah, Georgia. After joining British troops and gaining his freedom during the Revolution, George organized Baptist congregations in Nova Scotia, Canada, and Sierra Leone in West Africa.

Numerous African-American Baptist congregations existed before the Civil War, but these independent churches in the South were not allowed to function without being affiliated with white organizations. In the North, however, Baptists in Ohio and Illinois organized associations during the 1830s. By 1840, the American Baptist Missionary Convention was founded, bringing together African-American Baptists in New York and mid-Atlantic states. Other black Baptist conventions formed in the West and the South during the 1860s, and after the Civil War, African-American Baptists in the South created state organizations.

At the 1996 National Baptist Convention, USA, in Orlando, Florida, Reverend Henry J. Lyons (left), President Bill Clinton, and Reverend Roscoe Cooper (third from left) listened as Angella Christie played the saxophone.

During the 1870s, regional conventions organized in the West and East, but it was not until 1880 that the National Baptist Convention, USA, Annual Session (NBCUSA) was recognized as a national convention. About 150 Baptist ministers met in Montgomery, Alabama, where they formed the Baptist Mission Convention. Rev. W. H. McAlpine of Alabama was elected as the first President of the Convention. The National Baptist Convention, USA, Inc., which began in 1880 with only 151 delegates, faced several major splits but remains the largest black Baptist convention. Fifteen years later, the NBCUSA was born when the Mission Convention joined forces with two other conventions—the Foreign Mission Convention and the National Baptist Educational Convention.

Although the NBCUSA organized operations among the varied African-American Baptist churches, unity did not prevail. Conflicts developed over the location of the Foreign Mission Board, ownership of the Publishing Board of the NBCUSA, and cooperation with white Baptists. Arguably the split that received the most attention was the formation of the Progressive National Baptist Convention in 1961, which left the NBCUSA because of its lukewarm support for the Civil Rights Movement and its leader Dr. Martin Luther King Jr. (*see also* **Martin Luther King Jr.'s Birthday**).

Another rocky time for the NBCUSA occurred in the mid-1990s, when the president of the convention, Henry J. Lyons of St. Petersburg, Florida, became embroiled in legal problems over finances. Lyons eventually served a prison term of nearly five years for grand theft racketeering. New president, Reverend William Shaw took over in 1999 and, after paying off the debt for NBCUSA's headquarters in Nashville, Tennessee, and establishing new financial controls, was reelected in 2004.

In spite of NBCUSA's ups and downs, the convention spearheaded an assembly of delegates from four major African-American Baptist groups—the NBCUSA, the National Baptist Convention of America, the Progressive National Baptist Convention, and the National Missionary Baptist Convention of America. In 2005, delegates representing 15 million believers gathered in Nashville to participate in a dialogue about social and political issues affecting African Americans. Rev. Jesse Jackson, who attended and spoke at the convention, noted in the *Chicago Tribune*: "We can be out of slavery, out of segregation, have the right to vote, but still starve to death unless you get to the fourth stage, access to capital, industry and technology. . . . That's what the four conventions reconnecting is about."

Creation of the Annual Session

The 1880 meeting of Baptist pastors in Montgomery is considered the origin of the Annual Session of the NBCUSA, which is held each year during the first week of September. Since its inception, the Annual Session convenes to address the business of the Convention, provide opportunities for Christian fellowship, and offer instruction for delegates on various economic, health, and civil rights issues.

Observance

Cities such as Washington, D.C.; Cincinnati, Ohio; Denver, Colorado; Miami, Florida; Atlanta, Georgia; and New Orleans, Louisiana, have hosted NBCUSA

Annual Sessions. Each Session begins with messages from officials. As the week progresses there are prayer breakfasts; worship services and sermons; reports on Christian education, prison ministries, housing, and evangelism; addresses by leaders of auxiliaries; and receptions, banquets, and concerts.

Contact and Website

Baptist World Center Headquarters
1700 Baptist World Center Dr.
Nashville, TN 37207
615-228-6292 or 866-531-3054; fax: 615-262-3917
http://www.nationalbaptist.com

Further Reading

"Baptists." In *Encyclopedia of Black America*, edited by W. Augustus Low and Virgil A. Clift. New York: McGraw-Hill Book Company, 1981.

Brachear, Manya A. "Black Baptists Forge Agenda: Focus on Schools, Jobs, Health Care." *Chicago Tribune*, January 28, 2005.

Fitts, Leroy. "National Baptist Convention, U.S.A." In *The African-American Experience: Selections from the Five-Volume Macmillan Encyclopedia of African-American Culture and History*, edited by Jack Salzman. New York: Macmillan, 1998.

National Black Arts Festival

Date Observed: Second weekend of July
Location: Atlanta, Georgia

The National Black Arts Festival has been held since 1988 throughout the Atlanta, Georgia, metropolitan area. It strives to bring diverse communities together through art and culture in order to celebrate the artists of the African diaspora.

Historical Background

Although a majority of Atlanta's population today is African American, a significant black presence was not established in the area until after the Civil War. By the late 19th century, nearly half of the citizenry was balanced between whites and blacks, but there was not a similar harmony between the two races. In the 20th century and to the current day, the Atlanta community has negotiated a challenging course in the evolution of race relations. To many, Atlanta stands as one of the best examples of U.S. cities in its attempts to balance both racial unity and diversity.

In 1981, metropolitan Atlanta boasted a population of two million, 66 percent of whom were black. As Atlanta crossed into the 21st century, its metro area topped four million, with its African-American representation holding strong at approximately 60 percent. Each mayor elected since 1973 has been black—a first for any major metropolitan area in the United States. Atlanta has witnessed not only population growth in past years, but also commercial and economic growth.

Creation of the Festival

In 1987, Michael L. Lomax, ex-chair of the Fulton County Board of Commissioners and president and chief executive officer of the United Negro College

Fund, founded the nonprofit National Black Arts Festival (NBAF). The first festival was held in 1988. In the early 1980s the Fulton County Arts Council had commissioned a study to assess the potential of a festival that would celebrate and advocate works of African artists in Atlanta. The results of the study showed great promise for such an event, and the festival was born.

Initially, NBAF was set up with a limited scope: mainly to host a biennial arts festival. Over time, with the increased popularity and success of the summertime festival, the organization felt the need to broaden its reach. In 2001, the festival became an annual event. That year NBAF also added year-round programming in education and the humanities.

Observance

More than half a million people take part in the more than 100 program offerings of the annual National Black Arts Festival. Venues for these programs are located throughout the Atlanta area. For example, an Artists Market, which features juried exhibits of original works by visual artists and are available for purchase, might be located at a major Atlanta mall; the popular Vendors Marketplace, where wares primarily reflecting the African diaspora are sold, would be at an entirely different site. Screenings are held to the delight of film fans, eager to see the works of known and unknown cinematic artists. Concert halls across the city fill with listeners coming to hear their favorites: rhythm and blues, gospel, jazz, and more. Famous names in literature also draw crowds. All events are aimed at providing audiences with creative experiences from the arts and crafts of the African diaspora. The United States Congress honored NBAF as a "national treasure" in 2008, and in 2018, NBAF received the Governor's Award for the Arts and Humanities in Georgia.

Contacts and Websites

Atlanta Convention & Visitors Bureau
233 Peachtree St. N.E., Ste. 1400
Atlanta, GA 30303
404-521-6600
https://www.atlanta.net

National Black Arts Festival
Peachtree Center, North Tower
235 Peachtree St., Ste. 1725
Atlanta, GA 30303
http://nbaf.org

National Black Family Reunion Celebration

Date Observed: Second weekend in September
Location: Washington, D.C.

The National Black Family Reunion Celebration is a three-day festival held each September on the National Mall in Washington, D.C. Sponsored by the National Council of Negro Women, Inc., the celebration is intended as a reunion for all African-American families and highlights their historic strengths and values.

Historical Background

During the 1980s, media attention increasingly focused on the black family as "disappearing" and "disintegrating." A 1986 CBS documentary by Bill Moyer, for example, was titled *The Vanishing Family: Crisis in Black America*. After viewing that film, Dr. Dorothy I. Height, civil-rights activist and chair of the National Council of Negro Women, decided to organize a cultural festival that would nourish and support African-American families.

The 26th annual BFRC named "One Day Mega Festival" was held on Saturday, September 10th, 2011. The BFRC has accumulated as many as 400,000 participants over the traditional two-day weekend with crowds that include families and guests from the Washington metropolitan area (D.C., Maryland, and Virginia).

Creation of the Observance

Dr. Height met with Washington, D.C., officials to discuss her idea—a complex of pavilions providing information on education, healthcare, and economic empowerment as well as live entertainment. The officials were not

369

enthusiastic at first and told her she could have a tent in a park. But Height accomplished her vision with the first Black Family Reunion Celebration in 1986.

Observance

During the two-day reunion on the Mall, more than 15 booths and tents offer a mix of information and musical performances. Attendees can get free health screenings, listen to local musicians, learn about job opportunities, or shop at an international arts and crafts marketplace. Soul food, Caribbean food, and other types of food are available from vendors.

Throughout the weekend, a variety of celebrities make special appearances. Rhythm and blues and other musicians entertain, and there is a gospel concert.

Other cities such as Atlanta, Chicago, and Los Angeles also have held reunions. Cincinnati, Ohio, holds a regional Midwest reunion each year. The one-day Rockford event takes place in August and is sponsored by the Rockford Section of the National Council of Negro Women, with people attending from northern Illinois and southern Wisconsin. Washington, D.C., remains the center for the National Black Family Reunion Celebration.

Contact and Website

National Council of Negro Women, Inc.
633 Pennsylvania Ave., N.W.
Washington, DC 20004
202-737-0120
http://ncnw.org

Further Reading

Height, Dorothy I. *Open Wide the Freedom Gates: A Memoir*. 2003. Reprint. New York: PublicAffairs, 2005.

National Council of Negro Women. *The Black Family Reunion Cookbook: Recipes and Food Memories from the National Council of Negro Women*. New York: Fireside/ Simon & Schuster, 1993.

National Black Storytelling Festival and Conference

Date Observed: Month of November
Location: Varies

The National Association of Black Storytellers (NABS) sponsors the National Black Storytelling Festival and Conference over a week in the month of November. Master storytellers perform at a selected location on a given year, sharing stories in the tradition of the griot (GREE-oh), a West African storyteller who carries on the oral history of a village or family.

Historical Background

In 1982, two African-American storytellers—Mary Carter Smith of Baltimore, Maryland, and Linda Goss of Philadelphia, Pennsylvania—founded the National Association of Black Storytellers. The purpose of the organization was, and is, to provide opportunities to share and preserve the African oral tradition.

In 1983, Mary Carter Smith was the official griot of Baltimore. She began to perfect her art form during the 1960s, as she witnessed the lack of understanding among varied groups of people. In a statement of purpose posted on the NABS Website, she declared "I am among those who fight misunderstanding. The weapons I use are stories, drama, songs, poetry and laughter. I bring entertainment with a purpose."

Smith has traveled extensively in the United States, Europe, the Caribbean, and Africa to entertain and inform. Her performance materials are based on her years growing up in Birmingham, Alabama, and her experiences in Kentucky, West Virginia, Ohio, and Maryland. She also has been a teacher, librarian, and community activist, has presented programs on numerous television and radio shows, and has written books of poetry.

Linda Goss prepares to tell a story at the 2003 National Black Storytelling Festival and Conference in Providence, Rhode Island.

Philadelphian Linda Goss is an official storyteller for her city, and also has performed in numerous U.S. and Canadian communities. An award-winning recording artist and author, she is considered an expert in contemporary storytelling. During her presentations, Goss shares African-American legends she has collected over the years and retells some of the stories she learned from her grandfather, who grew up under slavery. She also relates tales from other family members and neighbors in Alcoa, Tennessee, where she was born and reared. As part of her performance, Goss uses field hollers and praise singing to augment a story, and encourages her audiences to participate through call-and-response techniques.

As artist-in-residence at the Rosenbach Museum in Philadelphia, Goss has been presenting *Words and Wisdom: African American Literature from Slavery to the Civil Rights Movement* to hundreds of students each year since 2001. With jazz musician Alfie Pollitt, *Words and Wisdom* focuses on the contributions of African-American writers of the last two centuries.

Creation of the Festival

In 1983, Mary Carter Smith and Linda Goss initiated the first National Black Storytelling Festival in Baltimore and held a second in Philadelphia in 1984. That year the NABS was formally organized; it was incorporated in 1990. The organization sponsors the National Black Storytelling Festival and Conference, which is held in a selected city in November each year.

The NABS has more than a dozen affiliates across the United States. These include the African Folk Heritage Circle, Inc. in New York City; North Carolina Association of Black Storytellers in Raleigh; Cleveland (Ohio) Association of Black Storytellers; Detroit (Michigan) Association of Black Storytellers; Griots' Circle of Maryland in Baltimore; Keepers of the Culture in Philadelphia, Pennsylvania; Kuumba Storytellers of Georgia in Atlanta; Black Storytelling League of Rochester, New York; Black Storytellers of San Diego, California; The Chicago (Illinois) Association of Black Storytellers; Rhode Island Black Storytellers in Providence; Black Storytellers Alliance in Minneapolis, Minnesota; Tradition Keepers: Black Storytellers of Western New York; Nubian Storytellers Of Utah Leadership in Taylorsville and Wichita Griots: Keepers of the Stories in Kansas.

Observance

The NABS and their affiliates represent about 400 storytellers who base their performances on African and African-American experience. They present programs for schools, senior centers, corporate and civic gatherings, religious institutions, and varied special events. Dressed in colorful African-inspired attire, they may read their own story books or act out tales that involve audience participation. Some storytellers may include drums or other instruments during their performances.

Festival attendees learn the importance of the storyteller (griot) in Africa and how storytelling conveys the history of African Americans. At the festival, storytellers also conduct workshops for people interested in using the African oral tradition to communicate with an audience—young or old of whatever skin color, socioeconomic background, or cultural heritage.

Contacts and Websites

National Association of Black Storytellers, Inc.
1601-03 E. North Ave.
P.O. Box 67722
Baltimore, MD 21215
410-947-1117
https://www.nabsinc.org

Rhode Island Black Storytellers
393 Broad St.
P.O. Box 14
Providence, RI 02907
401-312-4347
E-mail: info@ribsfest.org
https://www.nabsinc.org/affiliates

Further Reading

Hajdusiewicz, Babs Bell. *Mary Carter Smith: African-American Storyteller.* Berkeley Heights, NJ: Enslow Publishers, 1995. (young adult)

Hale, Thomas A. *Griots and Griottes: Masters of Words and Music.* 1998. Reprint. Bloomington: Indiana University Press, 2007.

Pershing, Linda. "'You can't do that, you're the wrong race': African American Women Storytellers at a Contemporary Festival." *Women and Language,* Spring 1996.

National Black Theatre Festival

***Date Observed: Between the last week of July and first
week of August
Location: Winston-Salem, North Carolina***

The National Black Theatre Festival celebrates stage productions by, for, and about African Americans. More than 100 productions are staged during the biennial week-long festival, which also offers a wide variety of theater-related programs and workshops.

Historical Background

In the late 1700s, the earliest days of American theatrical performances, African Americans had few opportunities to perform on stage. The roles that did exist were minor parts in plays written and produced by whites. These were often stereotypical portrayals of African Americans that disregarded the true experiences of most people. African-American characters were clownish, servile, unintelligent, and usually only present for comic relief. During this time, there was no real chance for an African-American play to be produced.

The first African-American theater company was formed in 1821. Called the African Grove Theater, it was founded by the members of New York City's free African-American community. The first plays staged there were the works by Shakespeare. The first play written and produced by an African American was performed there in 1823. It was a work by William Henry Brown titled *The Drama of King Shotaway*. Performances were fairly well-attended, although the theater was raided several times by police due to disturbances between white and African-American audience members. The theater was nearly destroyed in one of these raids, and it closed later that same year. Many of the African Grove actors went on to perform plays in rented locations throughout New York City.

The era of African-American minstrels began around the 1850s, although minstrels did not become truly established as stage performers until after the Civil War. Minstrels were limited in what they could perform, and minstrel shows portrayed mostly negative stereotypes of African Americans. In the late 1800s, African-American performers wanted to present a more accurate representation of African-American characters, and new productions began to appear. Musicals written, produced, and performed by African Americans gained popularity, and by the 1920s, African Americans were staging many successful productions each year. But in general, African Americans were still not allowed on the stages of white America.

In the vaudeville era of the 1920s, African Americans created a thriving circuit of traveling performers within the African-American community. African-American singers, dancers, and comedians became so popular that some were eventually able to perform on mainstream stages in white vaudeville revues. During this time, many African-American performers achieved great success in Europe, where audiences were generally not as fixated on the race of talented performers.

The 1930s saw a rise in the popularity of African-American musical, with *Porgy and Bess* becoming the biggest all-African-American production of the decade. All theater productions in America declined during the 1940s and 1950s, due first to World War II and then the invention of television. African-American musicals were still being staged during this time, but theater attendance was down and roles were scarce for everyone. Renewed interest in African-American theater began in 1961. Throughout the 1960s and 1970s, African-American musicals, dramas, and comedic plays were produced regularly, many running for hundreds of performances. However, the contributions and talents of African-American theater professionals were still largely unrecognized by the mainstream theater world.

Creation of the Festival

In 1989, Larry Leon Hamlin, founder of the North Carolina Black Repertory Theater, created the National Black Theatre Festival in an attempt to develop a sense of community among African-American theater companies. At that time, many companies were financially challenged, somewhat isolated, and geographically scattered throughout the U.S. The festival was intended to build an environment in which African-American theater professionals and aspiring amateurs could create relationships that would ultimately ensure the survival and continued success of African-American theater. By providing increased visibility and performance opportunities for established theater companies as well as newer groups, the festival gave African-American writers, directors, producers, and actors much-needed exposure.

In creating the first National Black Theatre Festival, organizers sought the involvement of such celebrities as Sidney Poitier, Oprah Winfrey, and Maya Angelou, who was the festival's first chairperson. The involvement of such well-known personalities drew substantial attention to the festival, as well as national and international media coverage.

It is difficult to clearly define what is classified as African-American theater today. The concept includes plays written and produced by African Americans, starring African-American actors, focusing on African-American stories, or staged within the African-American community. Festival organizers use somewhat loosely defined criteria in selecting productions for each festival, and each festival is distinctly unique. For this reason, the festival has been called one of the most historic and culturally significant events in the history of African-American theater and American theater in general. The National Black Theatre Festival has grown larger each time it has been held.

Observance

Productions are staged in theaters, community centers, and university campus facilities all over Winston-Salem, North Carolina. Various non-theatrical events are also held as part of each festival, such as a formal opening night gala and an international vendors market. Readings and recitations are presented along with seminars and workshops for aspiring writers, directors, producers, and actors. In addition to more traditional stage plays, the festival also spotlights spoken word and poetry performances. These are supplemented with nightly poetry jams in which anyone can participate. Theater professionals and amateurs find many opportunities for networking during scheduled programs or at social receptions held each night.

Contact and Website

North Carolina Black Repertory Company
P.O. Box 95
Winston-Salem, NC 27102-0095
336-723-2266; fax: 336-723-2223
E-mail: info@ncblackrep.org
https://ncblackrep.org

Further Reading

Burger, Mark. "Behind the Scenes: Technical Crew Prepares Path for the National Black Theater Festival." *Winston-Salem Journal*, July 31, 2005.
Dewan, Shaila. "A Six-Day Bash Celebrates Black Theater." *New York Times*, August 6, 2005.
Lehman, Jeffrey, ed. *The African American Almanac.* 9th ed. Detroit: Gale, 2003.

National Freedom Day

Date Observed: February 1
Location: Communities nationwide

N ational Freedom Day commemorates the day in 1865 when President
Abraham Lincoln signed the 13th Amendment to the Constitution,
which outlawed slavery in the United States. In 1948, President
Harry S. Truman issued a presidential proclamation calling for the observance of National Freedom Day. Fifty years later, Congress entered February
1, National Freedom Day, into the U.S. Code of law as an official national and
patriotic observance (*see also* **Black Music Month**; **Emancipation Day**; **West
Indies Emancipation Day**; **Juneteenth**; *and* **Watch Night**).

Historical Background

President Lincoln signed the 13th Amendment to the Constitution on February 1,
1865. It reads as follows:

AMENDMENT XIII

Section 1.

Neither slavery nor involuntary servitude, except as a punishment for
crime whereof the party shall have been duly convicted, shall exist
within the United States, or any place subject to their jurisdiction.

Section 2.

The Congress shall have power to enforce this article by appropriate
legislation.

Passed by Congress January 31, 1865. Ratified December 6, 1865.

*Note: A portion of Article IV, section 2, of the Constitution was super-
seded by the 13th amendment.*

Thirty-Eighth   Congress of the United States of America;

At the _second_ Session,

Begun and held at the City of Washington, on Monday, the _fifth_ day of December, one thousand eight hundred and sixty-_four_

A RESOLUTION

Submitting to the legislatures of the several States a proposition to amend the Constitution of the United States.

Resolved by the Senate and House of Representatives of the United States of America in Congress assembled,

(two-thirds of both houses concurring) That the following article be proposed to the legislatures of the several States as an amendment to the Constitution of the United States, which, when ratified by three-fourths of said legislatures shall be valid, to all intents and purposes, as a part of the said Constitution, namely: Article XIII. Section 1. Neither slavery nor involuntary servitude, except as a punishment for crime whereof the party shall have been duly convicted, shall exist within the United States, or any place subject to their jurisdiction. Section 2. Congress shall have power to enforce this article by appropriate legislation.

Schuyler Colfax
Speaker of the House of Representatives.

H. Hamlin
Vice President of the United States and President of the Senate

Approved February 1. 1865.

Abraham Lincoln

The 13th Amendment to the Constitution was passed by Congress on January 31, 1865, and signed by President Lincoln the next day.

Freedom days or **Emancipation Day** celebrations to commemorate the end of slavery in the United States have been held on a variety of dates. In some states, emancipation is celebrated on June 19th or **Juneteenth**, the date when slaves in Texas learned of their freedom. Kentucky also commemorates Juneteenth National Freedom Day each year. Other states hold freedom days on January 1 to mark the date when the Emancipation Proclamation was issued in 1863. Some celebrate September 22, the day in 1862 that Lincoln issued the preliminary proclamation. Washington, D.C. observes Emancipation Day on April 16 because that was the date slaves were freed in the district.

Creation of the Observance

The first Freedom Day celebration took place on February 1, 1942, in Philadelphia, Pennsylvania, where a wreath was placed at the base of the Liberty Bell. But it was not yet an official observance.

Former slave Richard Robert Wright Sr. (1855–1947) spent many years attempting to establish a National Freedom Day on February 1. Wright, along with his mother and two siblings were freed after the Civil War. He became a teacher, principal, college president, publisher, and banker. He also attained the rank of major during service in the 1898 Spanish-American War fought in Cuba, the Philippines, and Puerto Rico.

Wright believed February 1 was the true emancipation day, because it was the date Lincoln signed the proposed 13th Amendment. In 1948, a year after Wright's death, President Harry S, Truman signed a bill stating that "The President may issue each year a proclamation designating February 1 as National Freedom Day to commemorate the signing by Abraham Lincoln on February 1, 1865, of the joint resolution adopted by the Senate and the House of Representatives that proposed the 13th amendment to the Constitution." In subsequent years, various governors and mayors of Philadelphia have issued proclamations designating February 1 as National Freedom Day.

On August 12, 1998, the U.S. Congress designated February 1 as National Freedom Day to be an annual national and patriotic observance.

Observance

A notable National Freedom Day celebration takes place in Philadelphia. Ceremonies are held at Independence Hall, near where the Liberty Bell is housed. There may be speeches, choral groups singing "We Shall Overcome," and other public presentations emphasizing liberty and the role of Richard Robert Wright Sr. in establishing National Freedom Day.

In public schools, it is common to observe National Freedom Day on the first day of **African-American History Month** in February. Students take part in activities focusing on such topics as the Bill of Rights, the 13th Amendment to the U.S. Constitution, and the history of the abolitionist movement.

Information on local celebrations or events centering on National Freedom Day may be announced prior to and on February 1 every year. For certain people, It is time to promote goodwill, equality, and to appreciate freedom. Annual breakfasts, luncheons, musical entertainment, film screenings, and literature meetings are some events that explore the theme of freedom.

Contacts and Websites

Independence Hall Visitor Center
520 Chestnut St.
Philadelphia, PA 19106
https://www.nps.gov/inde/planyourvisit/independencehall.htm

Independence Visitor Center Corporation
599 Market St.
1 N. Independence Mall West
Philadelphia, PA 19106
https://www.phlvisitorcenter.com

Further Reading

Morris, Robert C. "Wright, Richard Robert, Sr." In *African American Lives*, edited by Henry Louis Gates Jr. and Evelyn Brooks Higginbotham. New York: Oxford University Press, 2004.

Patton, June O. "'And the truth shall make you free': Richard Robert Wright, Sr., Black Intellectual and Iconoclast, 1877–1897. (Vindicating the Race: Contributions to African-American Intellectual History)." *The Journal of Negro History*, January 1996.

Wiggins, William H., Jr. *O Freedom! Afro-American Emancipation Celebrations.* Knoxville: University of Tennessee Press, 2000.

Negro Election Day and Coronation Festivals

Date Observed: Third weekend of July
Location: New England

During the 18th century, slaves in New England were allowed to elect their own governors or kings while their owners voted in colonial elections. Slaves held a day-long festival known as Negro Election Day, or in the case of an elected king, a coronation festival. The title of the elected office depended on whether the colony was self-governing or closely tied to Britain.

Historical Background

Some historians contend that slaves in the New England colonies had relatively more freedom than bonds people in the South. Slave owners allowed various holidays for recreation, and one was election or coronation day in May or June, when slaveowners and slaves alike gathered in the towns to vote. Slaves could not vote for the colony's governor, but in separate outdoor activities sanctioned by slaveholders, slaves annually elected a negro (the term used at the time) as their governor or king. The person elected often either belonged to a wealthy slaveowner or came from a family of chiefs or kings in Africa. For example, in Connecticut, the grandson of an African prince was elected governor, and his son, said to be physically well built and a witty speaker, was elected after him.

The elected person was a leader in the local slave community and served as a judge, mediator, and liaison with slaveowners. He was also an intermediary with ancestors, an important role in many African religions. It is not clear how much power the governor had, but he could mete out punishment—sometimes flogging or even execution—and in general attempted to control morals and manners among slaves. Negro Election Day was relocated to Salem Willows Park in 1885. Since the word "negro" was no longer acceptable, the event's name had become the "Colored People's Picnic." By the 1920s, the picnic became more of a "Sunday School picnic" and was sponsored by black churches from Lynn, Malden, Everett, Cambridge, and Boston on the third Sunday of July. The picnic had church choir performances and track and field events in the early 20th century. Dances were also held with wonderful jazz performers, including Duke Ellington and Cab Calloway. During World War II, the picnic was switched to the third Saturday of July because Black Americans were working in factories and defense plants and weekends were the only options. After World War II, churches began to take a less active role. The name was changed again in 1968, in response to the Civil Rights Movement. Since people objected to being called "colored," the picnic was renamed the "Black Picnic."

Creation of the Observance

Negro Election Day festivities began as early as the 1740s and continued in New England for almost a century. The day-long ceremonies varied somewhat among different communities, but they were generally a blend of African and colonial practices. Slaves were able to maintain some of their African traditions, take part in political activities of their own, and also enjoy socializing, recreation, and colorful processions.

Observance

Before the festivities began on election day, slaves held meetings to listen to candidates' speeches. Over several weeks they debated each other to determine who among them should be chosen governor or king. Once the election took place, the winner paraded through town on a horse borrowed from his master, with aides on each side also riding on borrowed horses. The parade included the entire slave community (or at least all who were able to attend), all dressed in their best festive attire. Some played fifes, fiddles, drums, and horns. After the parade, people gathered for a feast, then competed in athletic contests, danced, gambled, and drank.

For many whites, the election festivities were "amusing" and reinforced their stereotypical view that slaves were mere children imitating their masters. But, for slaves, the elections were opportunities to exert some control over public expression and to demonstrate their solidarity as a community. These events also paved the way for the political engagement of emancipated African Americans in later years.

As African Americans took more control over election days and coronation festivals—as they did with other early festivals, such as **Pinkster**—white authorities began to curtail their observance by passing local laws against black gatherings. In addition, the abolition of slavery contributed to the festivals' demise, after which observances such as **Emancipation Day** and **Juneteenth** held more importance.

Contact and Website

Connecticut State Library
231 Capitol Ave.
Hartford, CT 06106
860-757-6500 (or) 866-886-4478
https://libguides.ctstatelibrary.org/hg/africanamerican/blackgovernors

Further Reading

Lawrence, Lee. "Chronicling Black Lives in Colonial New England." *Christian Science Monitor*, October 29, 1997. https://www.csmonitor.com/1997/1029/102997.feat.feat.1.html.

Piersen, William. *Black Legacy: America's Hidden Heritage*. Amherst: University of Massachusetts Press, 1993.

———. *Black Yankees: The Development of an Afro-American Sub-Culture in Eighteenth-Century New England*. Amherst: University of Massachusetts Press, 1988. White, Shane. "It Was a Proud Day': African American Festivals and Parades in the North, 1741–1834." *Journal of American History*, June 1994.

Odunde Festival

Date Observed: Second Sunday in June
Location: Philadelphia, Pennsylvania

The Odunde Festival brings hundreds of followers of Yoruba cultural and religious traditions to Philadelphia, Pennsylvania, on the second Sunday in June each year. *Odunde* (oh-doon-day) means "Happy New Year" in the Yoruba language of West Africa, and celebrates the coming of another year for African Americans and people of African descent worldwide who observe the Yoruba faith. The festival started in 1975 with a $100.00 grant. Since then, the festival has become a national model for cultural street festivals.

Historical Background

Traditional religious practices celebrated at the festival stems from the Yoruba people of Nigeria, Ghana, Togo, and Benin. In accordance with the belief system, Olodumare (ohlow-DOO-may-ray), the supreme being, holds all power in the universe, gives life, and is directly involved in earthly affairs through hundreds of intermediaries known as "orishas" (aw-REE-SHAWS). Devotees venerate the orishas with rituals either individually or in ceremonies conducted by priests or priestesses.

Creation of the Festival

Lois Fernandez visited Africa in the 1970s and observed festivals for various orishas in Nigerian towns and villages. Upon her return to the United States, Fernandez hoped to duplicate such a festival in Philadelphia, her hometown. She was particularly impressed and moved by ceremonies honoring Oshun (aw-SHOON), an orisha associated with rivers. She had seen Oshun festivals at riverbanks in Nigerian as well as in U.S. cities.

The Odunde procession on the South Street Bridge returns to the festival site after participants make offerings to Oshun. In the center are drummers Baba Crowder and John Wilkie from the Kulu Mele African Dance Ensemble. To the right (in a dark-colored dress) is priest and percussionist Nana Korantemaa Ayeboafa.

Fernandez and a group of family and friends were determined to make the festival happen near the Schuylkill River, but there were bureaucratic hurdles and doubters. However, Fernandez and her supporters had a mission: to convince the community that they could stage a cultural event that would bring African Americans together for a rewarding and long-lasting celebration. The group accomplished its goal when the first festival, then known as the Oshun Festival, took place in 1975 by the Schuylkill River. Later, the name was changed to the Odunde Festival.

Over the years, there has been organized opposition to the festival as neighborhoods have struggled with gentrification—affluent or middle-class people buying and upgrading urban property, and often displacing lower-income people. Opponents have presented petitions to city officials in attempts to get the festival moved to a location other than South Street. But Odunde supporters have prevailed, defending their right to keep the festival where it is.

Observance

The Odunde Festival brings together devotees of Ifa (a god who knows each person's destiny), Santería (Yoruba-based traditions from Cuba), Candomblé (African-based religious traditions in Brazil), and other followers of traditional African cultural and religious systems (*see also* **Honoring Santería Orishas**; **Ifa Festival and Yoruba National Convention**; *and* **Olokun Festival**).

Overseen by a Yoruba priest or priestess, the Odunde ceremonies begin with a procession led by Egungun—dancers who wear masks representing ancestral spirits. Sacred batáa drummers chant and drum to the orishas, and followers dance and sing as they proceed toward the Schuylkill River, where offerings of fruit and flowers are made to Oshun, the Yoruba goddess of the river.

After the procession returns to the starting point on South Street, huge crowds gather along 15 city blocks that feature 2 stages for live entertainment. Vendors from many African nations, the Caribbean, and Brazil sell food, crafts, and other merchandise. Performers on several stages and on street corners entertain participants.

Writer Junious Ricardo Stanton offered this description of his festival experience in *Chicken Bones: A Journal*: "Being at Odunde is like a mystical baptism. The festival there immerses you in a vibratory sea of blackness. You get dipped into a positive spirit of being African and come up revived, energized, and feeling good."

To celebrate the festival's 20th anniversary in 1995, the Philadelphia Folklore Project presented an exhibit on the festival, titled "ODUNDE: Preserving Cultural Traditions." Through photographs, paintings, memorabilia, and narratives, the exhibit was designed to highlight the festival's importance to the city. In 2019 the exhibit was updated to mark Odunde's 44th anniversary. More than 500,000 people attended that year.

Contacts and Websites

ODUNDE Inc.
P.O. Box 21748
2308 Grays Ferry Ave.
Philadelphia, PA 19146
215-732-8510

E-mail: odundefestival@gmail.com
https://www.odundefestival.org/contact.html

"ODUNDE Exhibition"
Philadelphia Folklore Project
735 S. 50th St.
Philadelphia, PA 19143
215-726-1106
http://www.folkloreproject.org

Further Reading

Brandon, George. *Santería from Africa to the New World: The Dead Sell Memories* Bloomington: Indiana University Press, 1997.

De La Torre, Miguel A. *Santería: The Beliefs and Rituals of a Growing Religion in America*. Grand Rapids, MI: William B. Eerdmans Publishing Company, 2004.

González-Wippler, Migene. *Santería: The Religion*. St. Paul, MN: Harmony, 1989.

Murphy, Joseph M. *Santería: African Spirits in America*. 1993. Reprint. Boston: Beacon Press, 2011.

Núñez, Luis Manuel. *Santería: A Practical Guide to Afro-Caribbean Magic*. Dallas, TX: Spring Publications, 1992.

Stanton, Junious Ricardo. "Odunde Celebrates 27th Year: One of America's Largest Street Festivals." *Chicken Bones: A Journal,* n.d. http://www.nathanielturner.com/odundefestival2003.htm.

Olokun Festival

Date Observed: Last weekend of February
Location: Oyotunji African Village, South Carolina

T he Olokun Festival in the Oyotunji African Village near Sheldon, South Carolina, honors an orisha (spirit or deity) known as Olokun (or Olocun) in the last weekend of February. In the Yoruba religion that originated in West Africa, *Olokun* means "owner of the oceans," who was believed to empower barren women with childbirth. Honoring Olokun is just one of nine festivals for an orisha held each year in the Oyotunji African Village (*see also* **Ifa Festival and Yoruba National Convention**).

Historical Background

Orisha myths and rituals are basic to the Yoruba religion, which began in Nigeria centuries ago. The orishas represent the forces of nature, and serve as patrons, or "guardian angels," for those who worship them. Their characteristics and *patakis* (stories) are similar to those of ancient Greek and Roman gods and goddesses. However, unlike the inaccessible Greek and Roman deities, the orishas live among their followers in natural and manufactured objects. Specific colors, numbers, natural elements, icons, drum rhythms, and dance steps are associated with each orisha.

Olokun may be represented as male, female, or both. Some icons picture this orisha as a mermaid; others as a deep-sea king rather like the Greek god Neptune. There are two sides of Olokun: one characterizes the dangerous elements of the ocean that can capsize ships, flood land, and drown people; the other personifies the wealth and mysteries at the bottom of the sea.

For followers, Olokun signifies limitless wisdom—more than can ever be learned or understood. The orisha also has power over dreams, psychic abilities, meditation, mental health, and wealth.

Creation of the Festival

The Olokun Festival began in 1970 when the Oyotunji African Village was founded as a kingdom patterned after those in West Africa. The Olokun Festival was established to celebrate the Yoruba orisha of the deep sea and protector of the African soul.

Observance

During the festival, devotees of Olakun visit a shrine that contains Olokun's colors of deep blue and white, and the orisha's number, 7. Batáa drummers perform special rhythms for Olokun (*see also* **Honoring Santería Orishas**).

Further Reading

Edward, Gary, and John Mason. *Black Gods: Orisa Studies in the New World.* Brooklyn, NY: Yoruba Theological Archministry, 1998.

Ellis, A. B. *Yoruba-Speaking Peoples of the Slave Coast of West Africa.* 1894. Internet Sacred Text Archive, 1999. http://www.sacred-texts.com/afr/yor/yor04.htm.

Mason, John. *Olookun: Owner of Rivers and Seas.* Brooklyn, NY: Yoruba Theological Archministry, 1996.

Pan African Bookfest and Cultural Conference

Date Observed: 10 days in April or May
Location: Fort Lauderdale, Florida

The Pan African Bookfest and Cultural Conference is a 10-day spring event held in Fort Lauderdale, Florida. Sponsored by the Broward County Library, the festival provides an opportunity to take part in literary events grounded in African-American and Caribbean cultural ideals and traditions.

Historical Background

According to scholars Kwame Anthony Appiah and Henry Louis Gates Jr., Pan-Africanism "in its most straightforward version . . . is the political project calling for the unification of all Africans into a single African state to which those in the diaspora can return. In its vaguer, more cultural forms Pan-Africanism has pursued literary and artistic projects that bring together people in Africa and her diaspora."

In 1900, the Pan-African Congress was held in London. There delegates began formulating the idea of creating a unity campaign to champion the rights of African peoples everywhere throughout the globe.

Additional conferences followed in the years spanning 1919–1945 under the leadership of writer and activist W. E. B. Du Bois. The fifth and last conference in October 1945 was held in Manchester, England. It brought together 90 conferees from Africa, the United States, and the Caribbean. All agreed that their peoples' destinies must no longer be under the economic or political control of others. A sense of militancy arose at this meeting, boosting morale for the emerging struggles for independence on the African continent. It was a major event in the 20th century, as the decisions made at this conference led to the independence of African countries.

In 1958, the first meeting of the leaders of all independent African states convened at the All-African People's Conference. At that meeting, specific recognition was given to the role that African Americans and West Indian Americans had played, to date, in the achievement of the Pan-African Movement (*see also* **Haile Selassie's Birthday; Marcus Garvey's Birthday; Pan African Festival of Georgia;** *and* **Pan African Film & Arts Festival**).

Creation of the Festival

In 1986 the first Broward County African American Caribbean Cultural Arts Conference was held, leading to formal incorporation of a nonprofit organization two years later. The annual conference began to expand its horizons. Seeking to draw in more segments of the community, its range expanded beyond a literary event to include visual, performing, and other expressions of the arts as well. In 1989, organizers added the Pan African Bookfest that included visual art, music, dance, and drama as well as literary activities.

In 2002, the African American Research Library and Cultural Center of the East Broward County, Florida, Library opened. Since then, the Broward County Library, the ninth largest library system in the United States, has been the main site of the Bookfest.

In 2006, Members of the Jamaica Folk Singers performed at the Cultural Café, which is a highlight of the Pan Africa Bookfest held at the African American Research Library and Cultural Center in Fort Lauderdale. Dr. Olive Lewin, the director of Jamaican Folk Singers, was a notable personality at the event. Other international authors and scholars who attended the event focused on panel discussions and made presentations on the history and culture of the African-American diaspora and emphasized issues impacting countries in Africa, the Caribbean, and the Latin American region.

Observance

The 10 days over which the Pan African Bookfest and Cultural Conference is held—usually in April or May—offer something for everyone. Among the many highlights are the panel presentations that include authors (both known and emerging); representatives from all media markets such as film, magazines, newspapers, radio, and television; and local, national, and international government leaders and officials. Popular events include book signings, sales, and author readings; receptions, and talks and discussions with noted scholars. Writing and cultural workshops are sometimes held, as are mini film festivals. A "Poet in Residence" and "Visiting Scholar" are selected annually and take part in several events.

By far, the most anticipated day of the entire event falls on the final Saturday. "Bookfest Day" is held at nearby Samuel Delevoe Park and is open to the entire community. Offerings include plenty of ethnic food and drink, drumming, and ceremonial rites that recall African roots and heritage. Multiple activities are planned on this day for children, ranging from their own author meet-and-greets to bookmaking workshops to storytelling and oral history events to a **Junkanoo** Parade. Bookfest Day presents an opportunity for arts and crafts developed over the centuries to be shared with new generations, perhaps kindling new interest to carry on old traditions.

Contact and Website

Greater Fort Lauderdale Convention & Visitors Bureau
101 NE Third Ave., Ste. 100
Fort Lauderdale, FL 33301
800-227-8669 or 954-765-4466
E-mail: gflcvb@broward.org
http://www.sunny.org

Further Reading

Appiah, Kwame Anthony, and Henry Louis Gates Jr., eds. *Africana: The Encyclopedia of the African and African American Experience: The Concise Desk Reference.* Philadelphia: Running Press, 2003.

Bell, Bernard W., Emily R. Grosholz, and James B. Stewart, eds. *W. E. B. Du Bois on Race and Culture: Philosophy, Politics, and Poetics.* 1996. Reprint. New York: Routledge, 2014.

Hurley, Anthony E., Renee Larrier, and Joseph McLarren, eds. *Migrating Words and Worlds: Pan-Africanism Updated.* 1998. Reprint. Trenton, NJ: Africa World Press, 1999.

Kanneh, Kadiatu. *African Identities: Race, Nation, and Culture in Ethnography, Pan-Africanism and Black Literatures.* 1998. Reprint. New York: Routledge, 2002.

Prah, Kwesi Kwaa. *Beyond the Color Line: Pan-Africanist Disputations, Selected Sketches, Letters, Papers and Reviews.* Trenton, NJ: Africa World Press, 1998.

Pan African Festival of Georgia

Date Observed: Last week in April
Location: Macon, Georgia

The annual Pan African Festival of Georgia celebrates influences of the African diaspora. Sponsored by the Tubman African American Museum in Macon, its purpose is to promote understanding between people worldwide through a week of events.

Historical Background

Father Richard Keil of Macon founded the Tubman Museum in 1981. Keil had been involved with the Civil Rights Movement years before, and wanted to build a cultural center that would foster understanding and improve race relations in the South by celebrating African-American accomplishments.

With a coalition of others who shared the same goal, Keil found space in an abandoned downtown building, which was refurbished and opened in 1985 as The Harriet Tubman Center for Spiritual and Cultural Awareness. Its name was changed, however, because many people thought the center focused on Harriet Tubman and her accomplishments (*see also* **Harriet Tubman Day**). Although dedicated to Tubman's spirit, the center became The Tubman African American Museum to reflect the fact that it is dedicated to African-American art, culture, and history.

Creation of the Festival

In 1997, with the sponsorship of the Tubman Museum, Chi Ezekwueche, a local artist and community activist, founded the Pan African Festival of Georgia as a one-day event. She and other Macon leaders designed a festival

397

that would draw a diverse audience into events highlighting African and African-American culture.

Observance

The 23rd annual Pan African Festival of Georgia was held in 2019. Activities included an Oral Traditions Day, with storytellers focusing on African and southern U.S. folktales. A Taste of Soul provided food prepared by celebrity chefs. Poetry and spoken-word performances were presented, as well as Pan-African films, a lecture series, and musical entertainment. A Pan African Festival parade featured music and masquerade. The festival concluded with a Day in the Park in downtown Macon, where vendors offer food and crafts, and musicians perform jazz, rhythm and blues, reggae, and gospel.

Contact and Website

Tubman Museum
310 Cherry St.
Macon, GA 31201
478-743-8544; fax: 478-743-9063
https://www.tubmanmuseum.com/contact

Pan African Film & Arts Festival

Date Observed: February
Location: Los Angeles, California

The Pan African Film & Arts Festival (PAFF) is designed to promote cultural and racial tolerance and dialogue through film and other art forms. Held in Los Angeles, California, each February, the festival presents works by people of the African diaspora from the Americas to Europe to the Caribbean.

Historical Background

Film festivals occur every month of the year in the United States, and often these events showcase films that seldom, if ever, appear in mainstream movie theaters. Black film festivals are no exception, and they have been occurring since the 1980s, usually presenting work created, produced, directed, and acted by people of African descent (*see also* **African American Women in Cinema Film Festival**; **African Film Festival**; **American Black Film Festival**; **Denver Pan African Film Festival**; *and* **Hollywood Black Film Festival**).

The driving force behind the PAFF in Los Angeles is Ayuko Babu. He is founder and executive director of PAFF and got involved because of his political interests and cultural activities. He has called himself "a product of the '60s"—a member of the Black Panther Party, Student Nonviolent Coordinating Committee (SNCC), Pan African Movement, and the Black Student Alliance in Los Angeles that helped establish black studies programs.

Some of Babu's cultural activities included a trip accompanying Stevie Wonder to Nigeria for the 1977 Black Festival of Art and Culture. He also worked with African governments to bring African films to the United States as a

Ayuko Babu (right), founder of the Pan African Film & Arts Festival, and South Africa Consul-General Jeanette Ndhlovu (left) at the 2006 festival's opening night gala.

way to inform U.S. blacks about international issues. A major effort was rallying the black community to urge the U.S. government not to lift sanctions on South Africa, thus helping to rid that country of Apartheid.

Creation of the Festival

The first PAFF was held in February 1992, when public funding became available for cultural activities. In 1995 the Magic Johnson Theaters (now known as Cinemark Baldwin Hills 15 and XD) opened at the Baldwin Hills Crenshaw Plaza and the festival moved to that location.

Observance

The Pan African Film & Arts Festival is scheduled in February as an **African-American History Month** event. It is the official black history celebration in Los Angeles, and it is also considered one of the most important cultural festivals in the city. The festival presents more than 150 new films and showcases the fine artists of African descendants from Africa, the Americas, the Caribbean, Europe, and Canada. The films include documentaries, features, and shorts.

During the festival, there is an Artist Market with a fine-art show along with exhibits of crafts and wearable art. Poets, storytellers, and musicians also appear. Workshops and panel discussions for beginning filmmakers are held, and a studentfest and childrensfest offer opportunities for young people from Los Angeles schools to view age-appropriate black films. A highlight of the festival is the Night of Tribute when individuals are honored for their lifetime achievements.

Contact and Website

The Academy of Motion Picture Arts & Sciences
6820 La Tijera Blvd., Ste. 200
Los Angeles, CA 90045
310-337-4737; fax: 310-337-4736
E-mail: info@paff.org
http://www.paff.org

Paul Robeson's Birthday

Date Observed: April 9
Location: Communities nationwide

Paul Robeson, a scholar, singer, actor, civil-rights activist, and athlete, is remembered on his birthday, April 9, in various locations around the world, particularly since his death in 1976.

Historical Background

Born on April 9, 1898, Paul Robeson was the son of William Robeson, an escaped slave who became a Presbyterian minister, and Maria Bustill Robeson, a school teacher. Robeson grew up in Princeton, New Jersey, and received a scholarship to attend Rutgers College (now Rutgers University), where he graduated as valedictorian. While at Rutgers, he also participated in four sports—football, basketball, baseball, and track—and earned 12 varsity letters.

Robeson went on to Columbia University, where he met and married Eslanda (Essie) Cardozo Goode, who eventually became a scientist and journalist. The couple had one child, Paul Robeson Jr.

After earning his law degree in 1923, Robeson joined a New York City law firm, but was discouraged by the racial discrimination he experienced. He quit the legal profession and, with his wife's encouragement, launched a stage career as an actor and singer. Among his many accomplishments were performances of Shakespeare's *Othello* in London, sold-out concerts in Europe and at Carnegie Hall, starring roles in musicals and films, and hundreds of recordings.

Throughout his acting and singing career Robeson also developed controversial political views. During a 1930s concert tour in the Soviet Union, he was influenced by socialist ideas. In the Soviet Union and other parts of Europe,

Robeson and his family were able to live without the racism they experienced in the United States.

He frequently spoke out against racism, protested racist segregation practices in the United States, and refused to criticize the Soviet Union during the anti-Communist period of the late 1940s and the early 1950s. As a result, his political views brought condemnation from many sources, not the least of which was the U.S. government. He was labeled a Communist, and his passport was revoked for eight years, preventing any concert tours abroad. In the United States, theaters, concert halls, and other venues refused to allow him a stage.

In spite of continual harassment and a great loss of income, he continued his efforts for civil rights and the labor and peace movements. He worked diligently to improve the lives of common people everywhere.

In 2004 the U.S. Postal Service issued this commemorative stamp in honor of Paul Robeson.

During the 1970s, the U.S. public once again began to recognize Paul Robeson's talents and achievements. But not until after his death in 1976 were efforts made to accurately portray his life.

Creation of the Observance

No single celebration of Paul Robeson's birthday on April 9 marks the first observance. But there were many memorials held after his death in 1976. Since the late 1970s, Robeson has been commemorated in cities and towns around the world with proclamations and resolutions that declare April 9 Paul Robeson Day.

Basic Beliefs

Paul Robeson summed up some of his basic beliefs in his book *Here I Stand*:

"I learned that the essential character of a nation is determined not by the upper classes, but by the common people, and that the common people of all nations are truly brothers in the great family of mankind. . . . This belief in the oneness of humankind, about which I have often spoken in concerts and elsewhere, has existed within me side by side with my deep attachment to the cause of my own race."

Observance

Although Robeson's birthday commemorations have been observed to this day, special centennial celebrations took place on April 9, 1998. There were more than 400 observances of Robeson's birthday in the United States, Canada, and other countries. Museums, libraries, and schools featured Robeson exhibits. Film festivals and musical presentations paid tribute to Robeson's work. In school classrooms, students observed Paul Robeson's birthday by learning about his life. Choral readings, speeches, and newspaper and magazine articles honored him on that day, as did documentaries and concerts. Each year Rutgers University, Robeson's alma mater, offers a scholarship in his name.

Paul Robeson has also been remembered with musical tributes, induction into the Rutgers University Football Hall of Fame, dedication of buildings and statues, peace movement and labor union commemorations, a U.S. postage stamp, and multimedia exhibits of his life.

Contacts and Websites

King County Courthouse
516 Third Ave.
Seattle, WA 98104
206-296-0100 or 800-325-6165
https://www.kingcounty.gov/courts/superior-court/locations/kcch.aspx

Rutgers University
600 Bartholomew Rd.
Piscataway, NJ 08854
848-445-3545; fax: 732-445-3151
E-mail: prccrutgers@echo.rutgers.edu
http://prcc.rutgers.edu

Further Reading

Duberman, Martin. *Paul Robeson: A Biography.* Open Road Media, 2014.

Foner, Philip S. *Paul Robeson Speaks: Writings, Speeches, and Interviews, a Centennial Celebration 1918–1974.* Secacus, NJ: Lyle Stuart/Citadel Press, 1978.

Gerlach, Larry R. "Robeson, Paul." In *African American Lives,* edited by Henry Louis Gates Jr. and Evelyn Brooks Higginbotham. New York: Oxford University Press, 2004.

Writing by Paul Robeson

Here I Stand. 1958. Reprint. Boston: Beacon Press, 1998.

Penn Center Heritage Days

Date Observed: Second weekend in November
Location: St. Helena Island, South Carolina

Penn Center on St. Helena Island, South Carolina, has sponsored the annual Penn Center Heritage Days since the 1980s. The celebration on the second weekend in November calls attention to the history and culture of the Gullah, also known as "Geechee" and "Gullah-Geechee," people. The terms describe not only the people, but also the language that has been kept intact since slavery.

Historical Background

St. Helena Island is one of the Sea Islands along the coast of South Carolina and Georgia. Enslaved people were brought to this area from West African nations such as Angola, Ivory Coast, Liberia, Sierra Leone, and Senegal. The enslaved people spoke Creole, a blend of English and African languages that became known as "Gullah."

The slaves and, later, freed Africans preserved much of their culture, primarily because they were cut off from the mainland and thus were able to maintain a close community, passing on their beliefs, folktales, crafts, language, and foods over the generations. Gullah people on St. Helena Island are direct descendents of the first West Africans brought to the area as slaves.

The Penn Center on St. Helena Island is the site of one of the nation's first schools for emancipated blacks. Established in 1862, before the Emancipation Proclamation went into effect, the Penn School (now Penn Center) was part of an experiment by a Pennsylvania abolitionist group that wanted to educate freed African Americans (*see also* **Emancipation Day**).

The school began in one room that soon became too crowded. In 1864 a building was constructed on a section of a 50-acre plot that eventually became a campus with 19 buildings, including a cottage where Martin Luther King Jr. stayed during meetings of civil-rights groups (*see also* **Martin Luther King Jr.'s Birthday**). The campus was designated a national historic landmark in 1974.

Creation of the Festival

An annual heritage festival was held at the Penn Center from the early 1900s until 1948, when the independent school closed and the state took over its administration. In 1981 Emory Campbell, former executive director of the Penn Center, and other graduates of the school, revived the celebration. The group hoped to stimulate interest in the history and culture of the South Carolina and Georgia sea islands and to counteract the negative impact of renovation activities, as well as the derision that many Gullah faced because of their language. Younger generations have tended to view Gullah as quaint speech or a backward dialect.

The first heritage event drew about 200 people for a day of festivities. Since its inception, Heritage Days has grown to more than 10,000 people participating in a three-day celebration.

The festival was postponed in 1999 and 2000, because of a South Carolina tourism boycott by the National Association for the Advancement of Colored People (NAACP). The NAACP protested the Confederate flag flying over the statehouse. Although the flag came down, the organization continued its boycott because a Confederate flag was installed at a soldiers memorial on statehouse land. In 2001, however, the Penn Center restored the festival.

Observance

An opening ceremony at Penn Center Heritage Days includes the presentation of "Flags of the Gullah People." These national flags represent African, South American, and Caribbean countries from which people were captured and enslaved.

During the three-day celebration, there are demonstrations of basketmaking, knitting, and net-making—the last representing the fishery occupations of earlier generations. Musical performances feature blues and gospel singers.

Educational seminars encourage Gullah landowners, who still own much of the property on St. Helena Island as heir property, to retain land that has been in their families for generations. As is true in other locations on the Sea Islands, investors have been purchasing and developing this land and introducing expensive homes and resorts.

See also **Georgia Sea Island Festival** *and* **Hilton Head Island Gullah Celebration.**

Contacts and Websites

Beaufort County Black Chamber of Commerce
711 Bladen St.
Beaufort, SC 29902
843-986-1102
E-mail: info@bcbcc.org
https://bcbcc.org

Penn School National Historic Landmark District
P.O. Box 126
16 Penn Center Circle W.
St. Helena Island, SC 29920
Phone: 843-838-2432
http://www.penncenter.com

Further Reading

Maxwell, Louise P. "Gullah." In *The African-American Experience: Selections from the Five-Volume Macmillan Encyclopedia of African-American Culture and History*, edited by Jack Salzman. New York: Macmillan Library Reference USA, 1998.

Pollitzer, William S. *The Gullah People and Their African Heritage*. Athens: University of Georgia Press, 1999. Reprint. University of Georgia Press, 2005.

Pinkster

Date Observed: Mid May or Early June
Location: New York

Pinkster was a spring celebration that came to America with Dutch immigrants in the 1600s (*see also* **Harlem Week** *and* **African American Day Parade**). These immigrants settled in parts of what are now the states of New York and New Jersey and called their adopted home "New Netherland." Dutch slaveowners allowed enslaved Africans to take part in the holiday festivities. By the 1800s, the Dutch no longer dominated the celebration, and Pinkster became primarily an African-American holiday. In 1811, the town council of Albany, New York, passed a law banning the festival.

Historical Background

During the 17th century, Dutch immigrants celebrated renewal of life in the spring, a festival that corresponded with the Christian holy day Whitsunday, or Pentecost. The Pinkster festival name stems from *Pinksteren*, which is Dutch for "Pentecost," a holiday that takes place seven weeks after Easter and commemorates the coming of the Holy Spirit to Jesus's followers after his death and resurrection. The holiday was also a time for visiting family and friends. Dutch owners allowed their slaves to join the festivities, giving them a brief respite from hard, tedious labor.

Although slavery is commonly associated with the South, there were more than 5,000 slaves in the North in 1700. By 1790, there were more than 32,700 slaves in just two states: New York and New Jersey. Slaves labored on New England farms that were far apart, and often their family members were sold to farmers long distances away.

Creation of the Festival

Between 1790 and 1810, when Pinkster celebrations were at their peak in Albany, New York, the three-to-four-day holiday combined Dutch and African slave cultures. But as the Dutch began to focus more on American holidays such as Independence Day, Pinkster increasingly took on an African flavor and became known as an African-American holiday. Enslaved people who gathered were able to experience independence for a short time; reunite with family and friends; make a little money by selling crafts, berries, herbs, sassafras bark, and beverages; and maintain African traditions. Through speeches, storytelling, and song, slaves also mimicked and poked fun at whites in subtle ways (*see also* **Mardi Gras in African-American Traditions**).

Observance

Weeks before the Albany Pinkster festivities, preparations for the event began on Pinkster Hill, which is now the site of the New York State Capitol. People built brush shelters, much like those in Africa, or set up tents. At the top of the hill, arbors formed an arena for King Charles, a well-known slave from Angola (*see also* **Negro Election Days and Coronation Festivals**).

When King Charles arrived, he led a procession through town and up the hill, where he was welcomed in a royal ceremony. From his heightened position, King Charles could look down upon the town below, a symbolic representation of the importance of African kings and leaders as well as an ironic display of a reversal of power. The king directed the holiday activities, which included long drum and dance sessions.

An authentic recreation of Pinkster takes place for one day in May each year at Philipsburg Manor, which was once a Colonial-era milling and trading complex. At the Manor in Sleepy Hollow, New York, there is music, dance, food, and sports activities plus African folktale presentations and demonstrations of traditional African instruments.

A Pinkster carnival is also held annually at the Wyckoff Farmhouse Museum in Brooklyn, New York. The one-day event in mid-May or early June includes African-inspired music and dance and sports competitions.

Contacts and Websites

Philipsburg Manor
381 N. Broadway
Sleepy Hollow, NY 10591
https://hudsonvalley.org/historic-sites/philipsburg-manor

Wyckoff House Museum
5816 Clarendon Rd.
Brooklyn, NY 11203
718-629-5400
E-mail: info@wyckoffmuseum.org
https://wyckoffmuseum.org

Further Reading

Abrahams, Roger D. *Singing the Master.* New York: Penguin Books, 1993.
White, Shane. "Pinkster: Afro-Dutch Syncretization in New York City and the Hudson Valley." *Journal of American Folklore,* January–March 1989.
Williams-Myers, Albert James. *Long Hammering: Essays on the Forging of an African-American Presence in the Hudson River Valley to the Early Twentieth Century.* Trenton, NJ: Africa World Press, 1994.

Rondo Days Celebration

Date Observed: Third weekend in July
Location: St. Paul, Minnesota

The Rondo Days Celebration in St. Paul, Minnesota, is an annual African-American sponsored multicultural event on the third weekend in July. It seeks to promote a sense of community, stability, and neighborhood values. It celebrates the best of Minnesota's African-American stories, achievements, and culture.

Historical Background

Rondo Avenue in St. Paul was created in the 1850s. The area encompassing it quickly became a melting pot for immigrants from Italy, Sweden, and Russia, as well as from other nations. However, by the 1930s and 1940s, more and more incoming residents were transplanted African Americans from the South who came to view this area as their own geographic haven. Described as vibrant and vital, the predominantly black Rondo community was in many ways almost an island refuge, the center of St. Paul's largest black residential neighborhoods.

In the early 1960s, Interstate Highway 94 was built through the area. The freeway disrupted the cultural, economic, and social balance of St. Paul and essentially erased Rondo. Thousands of African Americans were displaced from not only their physical residences but also from their close-knit community, and lost their sense of belonging and place. A large chunk of history was destroyed along with the destruction of this legendary neighborhood. The lives of people were affected in numerous ways as they were thrust into a discriminatory housing market in a racially segregated city.

Creation of the Festival

In 1982, a small group of St. Paul residents under the leadership of Marvin "Roger" Anderson and Floyd Smaller met to discuss ways in which they might try to resurrect the values of the razed Rondo neighborhood and expand its spirit throughout the greater St. Paul community. The following year, Rondo Avenue, Inc., a non-profit association, was created and the first celebration was held that very year.

Rondo Avenue's mission is to provide a forum and foundation for promoting and developing good family ties and entrepreneurship throughout minority communities within Minnesota's Twin Cities of St. Paul and Minneapolis. It attends to the young and old, the impoverished, and, especially, underserved populations.

Observance

Planning for the Rondo Days Celebration begins early; weekly community meetings are held each May through July. The first festival in 1983 drew about 25,000 people, and that number has more than quadrupled in the succeeding years. As the largest African-American- sponsored festival in Minnesota, it is, however, a multicultural event that celebrates all people, art, music, and foods.

Thursday evening begins with a Senior Social to honor the community's elderly population. Friday night's schedule includes a Gala Opening for adults only, complete with music and food. Saturday kicks off with the annual parade, typically with hundreds of entrants. The parade route ends at the festival grounds, which hosts the Car Show and Gospel/Jazz Fest—a misnomer, actually, since music as diverse as Asian and Mexican can be heard until the weekend draws to a close. There are also other types of live entertainment, merchants and vendors of all sorts, the Frank Adams 5K Walk/Run, dance and drill-team competitions and exhibitions, and the other kinds of fun that participants would expect to find at a "neighborhood" festival.

Contacts and Websites

Minnesota Historical Society
345 W. Kellogg Blvd.
St.Paul, MN 55102
651-259-3000 or 800-657-3773
http://www.mnhs.org

Rondo Avenue, Inc.
1360 University Ave.
P.O Box 140
St.Paul, MN 55104
651-315-7676; fax: 651-538-6511
E-mail: rondoavenueinc@gmail.com
http://rondoavenueinc.org

Further Reading

Fairbanks, Evelyn. *The Days of Rondo.* St. Paul: Minnesota Historical Society Press, 1990.

Taylor, David Vassar. *Voices of Rondo: Oral Histories of Saint Paul's Historic Black Community.* 2005. Reprint. Minneapolis: University of Minnesota Press, 2017.

Rosa Parks Day

Date Observed: December 1
Location: Communities nationwide

Rosa Parks Day on December 1 has been observed statewide in Oregon and Ohio and in various communities across the United States. It is a day to commemorate December 1, 1955, when Rosa Parks, an African-American civil rights activist, refused an order to give up her seat on a segregated bus to a white passenger, sparking a bus boycott in Montgomery, Alabama.

Historical Background

Rosa Parks was born in 1913 to James McCauley, a carpenter, and Leona McCauley, a teacher. At the time Rosa was born, the family, which eventually included a younger brother, Sylvester, lived in Tuskegee, Alabama. They moved to Pine Level, Alabama, to live on a farm with her mother's parents so that Leona McCauley could go back to teaching school in Spring Hill, about eight miles away. James McCauley went north to work, and seldom communicated with his family.

Young Rosa was taught to read at home. Her formal education began when she was six years old in a one-room elementary school, all that was available for blacks in Pine Level. When she was 11 years old, her mother enrolled her in the Montgomery (Alabama) Industrial School for Girls, founded by northern white women who believed black girls should be educated. She completed the 8th grade before the school closed because the aging founders and teachers were unable to continue their work. Rosa received two years of high-school education at a laboratory school at Alabama State Teachers' College for Negroes. She dropped out at the beginning of the 11th grade to care for her ill grandmother.

Her grandmother died within a month, and Rosa returned to Montgomery, where she got a job in a shirt factory and went back to school for a short time. She met Raymond Parks when she was in her late teenage years, and the two married in 1932. Both were active members of the local chapter of the National Association for the Advancement of Colored People (NAACP). Rosa Parks was secretary of the local chapter from 1943 to 1956 and was involved in voter-registration drives.

In her autobiography, Rosa Parks describes numerous cases of verbal and physical harassment and discrimination

Rosa Parks in 1984.

against blacks that occurred during the years following World War II. She was especially incensed that when black veterans, her brother Sylvester among them, came back to the South they were not allowed to vote. Her brother left and moved to Detroit, Michigan.

But lack of enfranchisement was not the only problem. Attacks on African Americans also increased. Parks recalls in her autobiography: "I remember 1949 as a very bad year. Things happened that most people never heard about, because they never were reported in the newspapers. At times I felt overwhelmed by all the violence and hatred, but there was nothing to do but keep going."

The Bus Boycott

On December 1, 1955, Rosa Parks had just left her job and was distracted thinking about her efforts to set up an NAACP workshop. When she boarded a bus, she did not realize the driver was the same person who had evicted her

417

from a bus years earlier. "Most of the time if I saw him on the bus I didn't get on it," she wrote.

She sat down on one of the middle seats of the bus, and when numerous white passengers got on at one of the stops, the driver ordered her to get up and let a white man have her seat. She refused to move, and reported, "People always say that I didn't give up my seat because I was tired, but that isn't true. I was not tired physically, or no more tired than I usually was at the end of a working day. . . . No, the only tired I was, was tired of giving in." She had had enough of the denigrating treatment and the daily indignities imposed by white society.

Rosa Parks was forcefully removed from the bus and arrested. She was released on bail. That was the beginning of a series of actions to challenge racial segregation on public transportation. As part of that effort, African-American leaders, including Martin Luther King Jr., organized a boycott of city buses that lasted for more than a year (*see also* **Martin Luther King Jr.'s Birthday**). Parks lost her job because of the boycott, as did many other blacks who supported the cause.

Meantime, lawsuits against segregation were filed, and in 1956 the U.S. Supreme Court ruled that racial segregation on public transportation was unconstitutional in Montgomery and elsewhere in the South. After that decision, Rosa and Raymond Parks received death threats and could not find jobs, so they, and Rosa's mother, moved to Detroit, Michigan.

Later Life and Honors

In 1965 Rosa Parks went to work for U.S. Representative John Conyers Jr. in his Detroit office, where she was a staff member for 20 years. Rosa Parks continued her activism as well. After her husband died in 1977, she and a friend established the Rosa and Raymond Parks Institute for Self Development, which focuses on human rights. She received numerous honors and awards for her efforts toward social justice. In 1999, then-President Bill Clinton awarded her the Congressional Gold Medal of Honor, the highest civilian award in the United States.

After her death on October 24, 2005, at the age of 92, Rosa Parks's body was transported to the rotunda of the U.S. Capitol Building for a public ceremony. She was the first woman whose body lay in honor in the rotunda. Thousands attended her funeral in Detroit, Michigan, and paid tribute to her.

On December 1, 2005, citizens commemorated the anniversary of the day Rosa Parks refused to leave her bus seat by holding a protest against war, racism, and poverty on Wall Street in New York City. The Sankofa Dance and Drum Ensemble performed for the occasion.

On December 1, 2005, then-President George W. Bush signed legislation directing that a statue of Rosa Parks be created and placed in the National Statuary Hall in the U.S. Capitol Building.

Creation of the Observance

Not long after Rosa Parks's death, the states of Michigan and Ohio marked December 1, 2005, as Rosa Parks Day, and began attempts to make the day an annual observance. In New York City, representatives of numerous activist groups declared December 1, 2005, as a Rosa Parks Anniversary Nationwide Day of Absence against Poverty, Racism and War. The Day was supported by more than 1,000 local and national civilrights and anti-war organizations, such as chapters of the NAACP, the Troops Out Now Coalition, the Teamsters National Black Caucus, and many others. However, the U.S. states of California and Missouri celebrate the observance on her birthday, February 4.

Observance

Observing Rosa Parks Day takes many forms. Across the United States, transit agencies honor the civil-rights champion by reserving a front seat in Parks's name on public buses. The American Public Transportation Association and more than 50 transit agencies around the nation take part. Interior bus cards also focus on Parks and her contributions.

Those organizing around the Rosa Parks Nationwide Day of Absence held marches to protest racism and war and to demand action to alleviate poverty. Activists called for students, educators, civic organizations, labor unions, clergy, professionals, and others to take a day off from school, work, and shopping and to participate in teach-ins on civil rights and anti-war movements. They also held peace vigils.

Schools and libraries observe the day with a variety of activities, such as reenactments of Rosa Parks's refusal to leave her seat on the bus, screenings of the film *The Rosa Parks Story* (2002), and readings from her autobiography.

On December 1, 2005, the Rosa & Raymond Parks Institute in Detroit began a 381-day commemoration with various educational programs and activities to recognize the 50th anniversary of Rosa Parks's arrest and the duration of the Montgomery bus boycott.

Contact and Website

American Public Transportation Association
1300 I St., N.W., Ste. 1200 E.
Washington, DC 20005
202-496-4800; fax: 202-496-4324
http://www.apta.com

Further Reading

Brinkley, Douglas G. *Rosa Parks.* New York: Viking Penguin, 2000. Reprint. Penguin Books, 2005.
Hill, Ruth Edmonds. *Black Heroes*, edited by Jessie Carney Smith. Foreword by Nikki Giovanni. Canton, MI: Visible Ink Press, 2001.
Hine, Darlene Clark. *African American Lives*, edited by Henry Louis Gates Jr. and Evelyn Brooks Higginbotham. New York: Oxford University Press, 2004.

Satchmo SummerFest

Date Observed: Three days in early August
Location: New Orleans, Louisiana

S atchmo SummerFest is a three-day extravaganza of food, fun, and, of course, music in New Orleans, Louisiana. The festival commemorates the birth date of native son and jazz icon Louis "Satchmo" Armstrong.

Historical Background

Louis Armstrong was born in 1901 into an impoverished family in an area known as "The Battlefield" in New Orleans, Louisiana. He earned the nickname "satchel mouth," later abbreviated to "Satchmo," because of his big-mouthed grin. For having fired a gun into the air one New Year's Eve, he was confined to the Colored Waif's Home for Boys—a serendipitous occurrence, because it was there that he received training in singing, percussions, the bugle, and coronet. Upon his release in his early teens, he worked various menial jobs during the day and frequented music venues at night, playing coronet when the opportunity presented itself. By 1919, Armstrong was employed as a horn player in the Kid Ory Band, and his professional career began.

To detail Armstrong's individual accomplishments would be daunting. His legacy includes a body of work that consists of numerous recordings—of which countless are considered to be classics—television and film credits, autobiographies, and magazine articles. Armstrong popularized "hot solos" and ushered in both the eras of the sounds of big band and swing. Satchmo's special style inspired youth to believe that a trumpet is cool. It was said that his vocalizations prompted other singers to try to catch colds in order to imitate his special sound. Armstrong was one of the first to sing "scat," improvising somewhat nonsensical musical sounds in harmony with melodies that other singers such as Ella Fitzgerald went on to make famous. With all of his contributions to jazz, there are many who wonder whether the genre

Louis Armstrong

would be anything even remotely close to what it is today had it not been for Louis Armstrong.

Jazz is a musical style created in America, but its roots come from Americans of African heritage. The music has a basis in a host of predecessors: spirituals, field shouts, sorrow songs, blues, and ragtime. It originated in African-American communities near the turn of the 20th century. Initially, it was slow to catch on, in part, because even the term "jazz" had associations implying loose morals.

However, by the early decades of the 20th century, the syncopated rhythms and harmonic tempos prevailed, and jazz became a widespread form of popular music throughout the United States and Europe. Since then, jazz styles and forms have continued to evolve. Among its various metamorphoses have been New Orleans/Dixieland jazz, swing, bop/bebop, progressive/cool jazz, neo-bop/hard-bop, third stream, mainstream modern, Latin-jazz, jazz-rock, avant-garde/free jazz, and more. While the popularity of jazz has waxed and waned over the decades, jazz is still considered to be uniquely American music, and Louis Armstrong was (and in many senses remains) America's representative—or "Ambassador Satchmo," as he was called—to the world for this musical art form.

Creation of the Festival

French Quarters Festivals, Inc., is a non-profit organization that has hosted the Satchmo SummerFest since its inception in 2001. The first event was meant to be just a one-time occurrence, in honor of Louis Armstrong's 100th birthday. Surprised by its success, the organizers decided to build upon the first year's agenda and schedule additional activities. Before long, it became an annual festival, bringing together many facets of Armstrong's life: the music he made famous, the food he loved to eat and advertised (going as far as closing much of his personal correspondence with "Red Beans and Ricely Yours"), his commitment to children, and his devotion to his city, and its unique culture and people.

Observance

A vast majority of Satchmo SummerFest events are held at the Louisiana State Museum's Old U.S. Mint. SummerFest is family oriented, with many events geared specifically for the younger set. There are multiple concerts with performers from all around the world, including entertainers who once shared the stage with Satchmo. Also, seminars are held to ensure that the festival is a balance of education and entertainment.

Food is another major focus. On the menu are such favorites as smoked pork chops on a stick, stuffed peppers with crawfish dressing, red bean ice cream, and Creole cream cheesecake. Local restaurants may feature "Satchmo Specials" named after his recordings. For example, *Sweet Georgia Brown* inspired a chef to offer a shortcake with fresh peaches, raspberries, and whipped crème.

There is also a "Satchmo Club Crawl/Strut" in which several music clubs, eateries, and businesses across the city participate. This ticketed event usually benefits a local music-oriented charity. Since no New Orleans event would be complete without it, the Satchmo SummerFest, after its annual Jazz Mass, has a traditional "second-line parade," replete with umbrellas and sashes, for any and all to join in on and *les bon temps rouler* ("let the good times roll") in a jazzy, New Orleans style.

Contacts and Websites

French Quarter Festivals, Inc.
400 N. Peter, Ste. 205
New Orleans, LA 70130
504-522-5730; fax: 504-522-5711
http://www.fqfi.org

New Orleans Convention & Visitors Bureau
2020 St. Charles Ave.
New Orleans, LA 70130
800-672-6124 or 504-566-5011
fax: 504-566-5046
https://www.neworleans.com

Louis Armstrong Archives
332-338 Rosenthal Library
Queens College
65-30 Kissena Blvd.
Flushing, NY 11367-1597

Louis Armstrong House
34-56 107th St.
Corona, NY 11368
718-478-8274
https://www.louisarmstronghouse.org

Further Reading

Brothers, Thomas. *Louis Armstrong's New Orleans.* New York: W. W. Norton & Company, 2007.
Burns, Ken C., and Geoffery C. Ward. *Jazz: A History of America's Music.* New York: Knopf, 2002.
Gourse, Leslie. *Louis' Children: American Jazz Singers.* Lanham, MD: Rowman & Littlefield Publishers, 2001.
Jasen, David A., and Gene Jones. *Black Bottom Stomp: Eight Masters of Ragtime and Early Jazz.* 2002. Reprint. New York: Routledge, 2013.
Meckna, Michael. *Satchmo: The Louis Armstrong Encyclopedia.* Westport, CT: Greenwood Publishing Group, 2004.
Wonndrich, David. *Stomp and Swerve: American Music Gets Hot, 1843–1924.* Chicago: Chicago Review Press, 2003.

Scott Joplin Ragtime Festival

Date Observed: Last week of May
Location: Sedalia, Missouri

The Scott Joplin Ragtime Festival is an annual musical get-together held in Sedalia, Missouri. Each year, over the last week of May, the event celebrates the life and music of the legendary musician and composer Scott Joplin, whose work is more popular today than it was during his own lifetime.

Historical Background

Born into the musical family of ex-slave Jiles Joplin and free woman Florence Gives in 1868, Scott Joplin was one of six musically inclined progeny. Lore has it that he taught himself to play the piano in the white-owned homes his mother cleaned.

Joplin's early years were spent in Texarkana, Texas. The rest of his youth, through his teen years, brought him finally to Sedalia, Missouri, where he received his first piano instruction from German-born Julian Weiss, whom historians believe planted the seeds for Joplin's career as a composer. Joplin ended up being technically competent on piano, banjo, coronet, and violin, but his talent, ambition, and pride always lay in the realm of musical composition.

Joplin began a professional musical career in the early 1890s, traveling with minstrel shows and playing first cornet with the Queen City Cornet Band. With his brothers, he formed the vocal group Texas Medley Quartette in the mid-1890s. He also took jobs as a pianist in various cities, playing in cafes and saloons.

In 1899 his composition *The Maple Leaf Rag* caught on with the public and led to fame for Joplin. This piano rag, thought by some to be his greatest piece, was named after one of the two Sedalia black gentlemen's clubs at which he performed. His lawyer negotiated a royalty deal on each sale of the piece, guaranteeing him a living—although not a luxurious one—for the remainder of his life. In its first year, only 400 copies sold, but by 1909, the number jumped to a half-million and that rate stayed steady for another two decades.

In all, Joplin wrote about five dozen musical compositions, of which 40 or so were piano rags. But in addition to this impressive body of work, he also wrote marches, a ballet, and two operas. One of the operas was lost because its copyright application was never properly recorded. The other, *Treemonisha*, was a passion that consumed Joplin's life. He only saw it performed once before he died in 1917 at the age of 49. Joplin's death was attributed to mental illness and dementia, but a contributing cause was syphilis.

During his short career, he never received the acclaim he truly was due, as later critics would determine. In 1976 the Pulitzer Committee recognized Joplin for his contributions to American music. The 1973 movie *The Sting* brought his score of "The Entertainer" to instant popularity and regenerated interest in the ragtime genre. In the minds of many, the name Scott Joplin epitomizes ragtime.

Ragtime is a popular musical style of African-American origin that developed towards the end of the 1800s and remained popular through about 1920. It was characterized by a strongly syncopated, or what some called a "ragged," beat—hence the origin of the term "ragtime." The music is also remembered today as a precursor of yet another uniquely American musical style: jazz.

Creation of the Festival

The first Scott Joplin Ragtime Festival was organized in 1974 by a group of Sedalia ragtime enthusiasts for fellow devotees to gather around their love of the genre. The festival became an annual event in 1980. In 1983 the organizers established the Scott Joplin International Ragtime Foundation. Since then, the festival has grown, a store has been established, and a future goal is to build a museum.

Observance

About 6,000 people gather every year in Sedalia for what many—despite the size—consider a "folksy" sort of gathering. Sedalia's pride in it's

Treemonisha

*T*reemonisha is one of two operas written by Scott Joplin, which he self-published in 1911. The tale, thought to be a tribute to his mother, is set in a rural, black community in Arkansas. Joplin was a strong believer in the power of education for blacks, a belief he passed along from his mother.

The storyline tells how Treemonisha, the only educated person in the community, breaks free from the bondage of ignorance and superstition. The opera conveys Joplin's perspective of the challenges that African Americans faced during the early 1900s and his belief that they could hasten their goal of racial equality by seeking out educational opportunities.

At the time of *Treemonisha's* creation, an editor at *American Musician and Art* ran a lengthy review of the score from Joplin's opera in the magazine's June edition, declaring it to be the most American opera ever composed, far more so than Horatio Parker's *Mona*, which had just won a $10,000 Metropolitan Opera "American Opera" prize. Such high praise did little to aid Joplin in getting his work financed and staged.

Biases against black composers probably played some part in the difficulties Joplin faced in having his dreams realized. In fact, he saw *Treemonisha* performed just once, informally without costumes or orchestra, before he passed away. However, racial inequities were not the only or even main factors working against Joplin in this endeavor. In many respects, where *Treemonisha* was concerned, Joplin just may have been too far ahead of his time. *Treemonisha* was not a ragtime opera, although it did include a few ragtime pieces; rather, it was a serious opera that paid homage to a wide variety of African-American musical styles, including the blues. For some—even African Americans—music of the sort commonly found in saloons and brothels did not fit in with their vision of operatic undertakings.

In 1974 *Treemonisha* was finally recognized for the astounding piece of work that it is. Not only was it revived and performed in its entirety, but *Treemonisha* also made it to Broadway. Joplin's ambition to be recognized as a serious composer was finally realized more than a half-century after his death.

not-quite-native-son is evidenced by a 50-foot vibrant mural of Joplin sitting at his piano that is painted on a prominent downtown building.

A host of both free and ticketed activities are scheduled during the annual Scott Joplin Ragtime Festival. One consistent event is the annual parade, led by a horse-drawn surrey and followed by a fleet of vintage automobiles. Parade participants include contestants clothed in period costumes, as well as various government officials. Each year, the route's end is the same: The Maple Leaf Club, the same venue from which Joplin himself entertained nearly a century ago.

A "theme rag" (one of Joplin's pieces) is selected each year, around which the festival is planned. Activities run the gamut. There are concerts given by both amateur and professional performers, dance lessons, dinner shows, other meal events, symposia, and more. Many of the festivalgoers are repeat attendees and have built a close-knit camaraderie that often extends beyond their shared admiration of Joplin's music. The festival is considered by many ragtime aficionados to be the premiere event of its kind.

Contacts and Websites

Scott Joplin International Ragtime Foundation
P.O. Box 1244
Sedalia, MO 65302
660-826-2271
E-mail: sjfsedalia@gmail.com
http://www.scottjoplin.org

Sedalia Convention and Visitors Bureau
600 E. Third St.
Sedalia, MO 65301
660-826-2932 or 800-827-5295
E-mail: cvb@sedaliamo.org

Further Reading

Berlin, Edward A. *King of Ragtime: Scott Joplin and His Era*. New York: Oxford University Press, 1995. Reprint. Oxford University Press, 2016.
Curtis, Susan. *Dancing to a Black Man's Tune: A Life of Scott Joplin*. Columbia: University of Missouri Press, 2004.

Joplin, Scott. *Treemonisha Vocal Score.* Mineola, NY: Dovers Publications, 2001.

White, H. Loring. *Ragging It: Getting Ragtime into History (and Some History into Ragtime).* Lincoln, NE: iUniverse, Inc., 2005.

Sistrunk Parade and Festival

Date Observed: February
Location: Fort Lauderdale

T he Sistrunk Parade and Festival celebrates the culture and accomplishments of the people of African descent and is amongst the oldest African-American promotional events in the Broward County area.

Historical Background

African-American festivals have been taking place on a widespread scale in the United States since the 1980s. Many of these festivals have been initiated to connect the past with the present in black communities and to foster understanding of the African diaspora and the contributions people of African descent have made worldwide. Festivals also provide opportunities for local black communities to display their talents and highlight their accomplishments.

Creation of the Festival

The two-day festival was founded in 1979 by the City of Fort Lauderdale and the Northwest Business Association with a view to promote economic development in the community and educate youth and tourists about the ethnodiversity of Broward County and the South Florida region. The festival showcases the history and heritage of the region through educational programs and cultural events, and attracts participants and spectators from the tri-county area and other parts of Florida.

Named after pioneering doctor, James Franklin Sistrunk (1891–1966), World War veteran and the first African-American physician who practiced in Fort Lauderdale (for 44 years), the annual Sistrunk festival celebrates the culture and accomplishments of African Americans in the region. Sistrunk was born in Midway, Florida (near Tallahassee) and graduated from Meharry Medical College in Nashville, Tennessee. He served in the U.S. Armed Forces during World War I, after which he relocated to Fort Lauderdale to practice medicine. Although a qualified surgeon, Sistrunk was forbidden from performing surgeries in local white hospitals. In 1938, he established Provident Hospital, Fort Lauderdale's first medical facility for treating black patients. In the course of an illustrious practice spanning 44 years, Doctor Sistrunk made house calls throughout Broward County and attended over 5,000 deliveries.

The city honored the doctor by naming a street and the bridge over the North Fork River after him.

Observance

The Sistrunk Parade, with its multicultural nuances, school marching bands, step teams, and decorated floats, is the highpoint of the festival, kicking off at Lincoln Park and winding its way along the historic Sistrunk boulevard. The culmination of the parade is the Sistrunk street festival. On this day, the boulevard fills up with patrons and attendees who gather to enjoy music concerts featuring popular artists, sporting contests, and recreational activities. The festival also provides a platform for community activities, such as health checkups, voter registration, and information booths. Street food vendors offer local fare, and themed activities and fun events provide family entertainment. Sistrunk Scholarship Programs are awarded to less-privileged students in Broward County to provide financial assistance for higher education. Establishing art centers in low socioeconomic communities and collaborating with other ethnic cultural organizations have also remained an important focus of this historic festival.

Contacts and Websites

Sistrunk Historical Festival, Inc.
P.O. Box 1122,
Fort Lauderdale, FL 33302
754-779-4376
E-mail: info@sistrunkfestival.org
https://www.sistrunkfestival.org

African American Research Library And Cultural Center
2650 Sistrunk Blvd.
Fort Lauderdale, FL 33311
954-357-6282

Further Reading

http://www.fortlauderdaleobserver.com/sistrunk/DrSistrunk.htm

Slaves' Christmas

Date Observed: Several days on and around December 25
Location: Slave states

efore the Civil War, the Christmas season was one time that slaves could
take a break from hard labor. Although some slaveowners allowed only
a day of rest, others permitted celebrations that began on Christmas Eve
and continued over a period of several days to more than a week.

Historical Background

From colonial times to emancipation, slaves in North America had little to
celebrate. However, in spite of the horrors of slavery, the Christmas festivities
were some of the most lively events for enslaved people (*see also* **Junkanoo**).
Former slave Booker T. Washington (1856–1915), who became an educator and
founded the Tuskegee Institute in Alabama (now Tuskegee University), considered the holiday a favorite among slaves. On the other hand, escaped slave
and famed abolitionist Frederick Douglass (1818–1895) believed slaveowners
used the Christmas holidays to prevent slave rebellions by encouraging them
to feast and drink to excess (*see also* **Frederick Douglass Day**).

Some holiday experiences can be found in the slave narratives collected by
the Federal Writers Project of the Works Progress Association established
during the Great Depression of the 1930s. Memories and oral stories from the
last living generation of African Americans born into slavery were collected,
transcribed, and published. Other historical Christmas accounts are found in
books written by escaped slaves such as Harriet Jacobs, who wrote under the
assumed name "Linda Brent" to hide her identity.

Christmas was a time when many slaves attempted to escape because slaveholders were busy celebrating and paid little attention to what was going on
in the slave quarters. In some cases, slaveowners took their slaves with them

to other plantations during the holidays, which also presented opportunities to run away. William and Ellen Craft, who wrote *Running a Thousand Miles for Freedom* (1860), describe their daring escape from a Southern plantation and how they reached Pennsylvania, a free state, on Christmas Day in 1848.

Creation of the Observance

Slaves have observed Christmas since colonial times, although the celebrations varied depending on where the slaves were located. Some colonists ignored Christmas or condemned celebrations of the holiday as a pagan event. For other colonists, particularly in the South, Christmas on the plantation was a festive event that lasted from several days to weeks.

On some plantations, the Christmas holiday for slaves lasted as long as the yule log burned in the main fireplace of the planter's home. Slaves cut the log from a large tree and sometimes soaked it in a swamp so that it would burn slowly. When the log burned and broke into two parts, the holiday was officially over.

Observance

The Christmas season on some plantations began early in December and frequently included a harvest event known as **corn shucking**. The event involved the labor of many slaves who husked corn all night long. After the work was done, slaves danced to the music of fiddles and handmade instruments.

Although corn husking ended with festivities, it was not comparable to having several days or more than a week off from hard labor for the Christmas holidays. During that time, some slaves received passes that allowed them to visit relatives or friends on nearby plantations. Others spent the time quilting or making items such as corn brooms and baskets.

On Christmas morning, it was the custom on many plantations for slaves to gather outside the manor house to receive gifts. Southern planters usually gave their slaves a jug of whiskey, new clothes, and extra food for feasts. This food included meats such as chicken and ham, which were seldom part of their regular rations, and ingredients needed to bake cakes and pies. Along with feasting and drinking, Christmas celebrations in slave quarters included dancing, singing, and general merrymaking. However, when the holiday was over, slaves went back to the drudgery of sunup-to-sundown labor, and often, the brutality of slave owners and overseers.

Contact and Website

The Colonial Williamsburg Foundation
P.O. Box 1776
Williamsburg, VA 23187-1776
757-229-1000 (or) 855-756-9516
E-mail: cwres@cwf.org
https://www.history.org/Almanack/life/Af_Amer/aalife.cfm

Further Reading

Craft, William, and Ellen Craft. *Running a Thousand Miles for Freedom; or, The Escape of William and Ellen Craft from Slavery.* London: William Tweedie, 1860. Electronic Text Center. University of Virginia Library, Charlottesville, 1999. https://docsouth.unc.edu/neh/craft/summary.html

Gulevich, Tanya. "Slaves' Christmas." In *Encyclopedia of Christmas and New Year's Celebrations.* 2nd ed. Detroit: Omnigraphics, 2003.

Jacobs, Harriet. *Incidents in the Life of a Slave Girl. Written by Herself.* CreateSpace Independent Publishing Platform, 2016.

Washington, Booker T. *Up from Slavery: An Autobiography.* Garden City, NY: Doubleday & Company, 1901. Documenting the American South. University Library, University of North Carolina at Chapel Hill, 1997. Reprint. Blurb Inc., 2019.

Sugar Grove Underground Railroad Convention

Date Observed: Third weekend in June
Location: Sugar Grove, Pennsylvania

The two-day Sugar Grove Underground Railroad Convention in Sugar Grove, Pennsylvania, commemorates the Sugar Grove Anti-Slavery Convention of June 1854, which the famed abolitionist Frederick Douglass called "the crowning convention of them all." The event also celebrates **Juneteenth** on June 19, the day in 1865 when, two-and-a-half years after the Emancipation Proclamation was issued, slaves in Texas learned they were free (*see also* **Emancipation Day; Frederick Douglass Day** *and* **Juneteenth**).

Historical Background

From the 1830s to the time of the Civil War, anti-slavery conventions were common throughout the northern states. Women from several states formed anti-slavery societies and held the first Anti-Slavery Convention of American Women in 1837. Other conventions included men and women, with both black and white abolitionists in attendance.

One anti-slavery convention was held in 1854 in Sugar Grove, Pennsylvania, on the border between Pennsylvania and New York, near Lake Erie. Settled in 1797 by an abolitionist family, Sugar Grove was a place where many abolitionists lived, and it became a safe haven for fugitive slaves on their way to Canada via the Underground Railroad (*see also* **August Quarterly; Emancipation Day** *and* **Harriet Tubman Day**). Prominent abolitionists Frederick Douglass, Rev. Jermain Loguen, and Lewis Clark addressed the Sugar Grove Convention at an outdoor meeting with more than 500 people in attendance. Before speaking, Douglass had tea in the home of Cynthia Catlin Miller, who was active in the

Frederick Douglass at Sugar Grove

Frederick Douglass described the Sugar Grove event in his *Frederick Douglass' Paper* published June 23, 1854:

The crowning Convention was held Saturday and Sunday, in a beautiful grove in Sugar Grove, Warren County, Pennsylvania, about three miles from Busti. The responsibility of getting up this meeting rested upon the Storom family at Busti—an enterprising family of farmers, well to do on the world and when I tell you that these industrious and well to do farmers are of the color of you and me, you will . . . draw from it the right hopes for our whole people.

I observed that this family (it is a large one) had so deported itself, that white people among whom they moved, appeared to regard and treat them precisely as respectable people ought to be treated. . . .

But a word of the Convention; it was, as I have said, the crowning one of all. . . . The meeting was strictly a religious Anti-Slavery meeting, and left a most favorable impression for the cause (*see also* **Frederick Douglass Day**).

Sugar Grove Fugitive Aid Society, and sewed clothes for escaping slaves. On the eve of Veterans Day, the Black History Museum and Cultural Center of Virginia unveiled a statue honoring the Tuskegee Airmen, as embodied by one of the group's most distinguished members. The bronze life-size likeness of Lt. Col. Howard Lee Baugh, a Petersburg native, greeted visitors at the entrance to the museum in Jackson Ward at the site of the former Leigh Street Armory, originally the home of an African-American militia in the late 1800s.

Creation of the Observance

The first reenactment of the Sugar Grove Convention took place in 2004, under the leadership of creator Gregory Wilson, director of Underground Railroad programs for the Warren County Historical Society. After reading

Douglass's account of the first anti-slavery convention in Sugar Grove, Wilson was inspired to recreate it. He and other residents of Sugar Grove were proud of their anti-slavery heritage and wanted to share their stories and activities of their past.

Observance

The annual Sugar Grove event features presentations by historians performing as Frederick Douglass, Rev. Jermain Loguen, and other well-known figures from the abolitionist movement. Many Sugar Grove residents in this town of 9,000 appear in period costumes and help set the stage for reenactment of the abolitionists' speeches.

Offspring of the town's early abolitionists take part, among them a descendant of Cynthia Catlin Miller, who had tea with Douglass at her home in Sugar Grove during the 1854 convention. Activities also include guided tours and history workshops for students and educators.

Contact and Website

Warren County Historical Society
210 Fourth Ave.
P.O. Box 427
Warren, PA 16365
814-723-1795
E-mail: warrencountyhistory@aol.com
http://www.warrenhistory.org

Further Reading

Bordewich, Fergus M. *Bound for Canaan: The Underground Railroad and the War for the Soul of America.* New York: HarperCollins/Amistad Press, 2005.

Buckmaster, Henrietta. *Let My People Go: The Story of the Underground Railroad and the Growth of the Abolition Movement.* Columbia: University of South Carolina Press, 1992.

Burgan, Michael. *Escaping to Freedom: The Underground Railroad.* New York: Facts on File, 2006. (young adult)

Douglass, Frederick. Letter to W. J. Watkins, Esq. Appearing in the *Frederick Douglass' Paper*, Rochester, New York, June 23, 1854.

Parker, John P. *His Promised Land: The Autobiography of John P. Parker, Former Slave and Conductor on the Underground Railroad*. Edited by Stuart Seely Sprague. New York: W. W. Norton, 1996. Reprint. W. W. Norton, 1998.

Sweet Auburn Springfest

Date Observed: May, mostly over Mother's Day Weekend
Location: Auburn Avenue District, Downtown Atlanta

R egarded as the largest outdoor festival in the Southeast, the Sweet Auburn Springfest attracts thousands of festivalgoers each year to a two-day celebration of the rich culture of the people of African descent.

Historical Background

The historic district of Sweet Auburn in Atlanta, popularly known as "the cradle of the civil rights movement," plays host to the annual Sweet Auburn Spring festival. Charles E. Johnson, a settler of Sweet Auburn, who goes by the monicker "The mayor of Sweet Auburn Avenue," is credited with founding the spring festival. A native of Philadelphia, Johnson realized the potential of the district in the mid-nineties and went on to found the Springfest in its present form, transforming it from a glorified flea market to a large-scale event. Auburn Avenue, which *Forbes Magazine* once called "the richest Negro street in the world," is the heart of the spring festival. The avenue boasts more celebrities, successful professionals, politicians, and financial institutions than any other African American avenue in the South and stands as testimony to the tenaciousness of African Americans in their struggle against economic and racial segregation.

Creation of the Festival

The festival is a celebration of the history and cultural heritage of the African-Americans in the Sweet Auburn district through literature, art, food, and entertainment. Over the years, it has grown in stature and provided an impetus to local talent and commerce. People come from distant places to participate as vendors or to hang out with friends and family and enjoy the rich and varied cultural experience.

Observance

Entry is free and over a dozen stages offer live music of diverse genres and a variety of entertainment. From fun zones for kids to a pavilion for women, there is something for all ages. There's even a booth for seniors. Vendors lining the 1.5-mile avenue sell clothes and fashion accessories, food, and art work. Car and bike shows, technology expos, and artists' markets offer a wide range of merchandise. Festival Goers can also sign up for walking tours of the historic landmarks, the most important being the Martin Luther King Jr. National Historical Park. The park consists of several buildings closely associated with the life of Rev. Dr. Martin Luther King Jr. and his legacy as a leader of the U.S. Civil Rights Movement. These landmarks bear testimony to the systemic racism against African Americans and to the perseverance and tenacity with which the community fought back to achieve equality for all people irrespective of color, race, religion, or gender. Among the iconic landmarks is the Ebenezer Baptist Church where Dr. King preached and is interred alongside his wife, Coretta Scott King. Another equally important piece of history is the Walk of Fame, which honors some of the courageous activists of the American Civil Rights Movement. An interactive visitor center offers multimedia exhibits that trace the parallel paths of Dr. King and the Civil Rights Movement.

Contacts and Websites

Sweet Auburn Spring Festival
230 John Wesley Dobbs Ave.
Atlanta, GA 30303
678-667-1375
https://www.sweetauburn.com

Tuskegee Airmen Convention

Date Observed: A week in August
Location: Varies

The renowned World War II Tuskegee airmen, who inspired revolutionary reform in the U.S. armed forces, have reunited at an annual convention since 1972. During the convention, Tuskegee airmen are honored for their service and heroism in spite of many social barriers and the racially segregated military at the time.

Historical Background

Before U.S. involvement in World War II, many U.S. military officials were under the false and prejudicial assumption that African Americans were not physically or psychologically suited for combat, and particularly for flight training with the U.S. Army Air Corps (which later became the U.S. Air Force). But in 1941, President Franklin D. Roosevelt launched an experiment to determine "colored" suitability for combat air service. The military expected the experiment to fail and believed that the so-called colored were not capable of operating complex combat aircraft. However, men in the program proved them wrong.

In 1880 the Alabama State Legislature authorized the founding of Tuskegee Institute in Tuskegee, Alabama (it became Tuskegee University in 1985). On July 4, 1881, Booker T. Washington—the first teacher and principal of Tuskegee—opened the school, which grew into a major center for African-American education. There, for the first time in the history of the U.S. Army Air Corps, African-American men were trained as pilots, meteorologists, intelligence and engineering officers, flight surgeons, mechanics, control-tower operators, and many other positions that support an air force squadron.

443

Benjamin O. Davis Jr. (third from left) and other Tuskegee pilots in March 1942.

A full squadron completed training by 1942, but it remained at Tuskegee until 1943, under the leadership of Captain Benjamin O. Davis Jr., who became the first African-American general of the U.S. Air Force. The squadron received additional training to help it prepare for combat. Under Davis's command, African-American fighter pilots fought in aerial battles over North Africa, Sicily, and Europe, flying in 15,553 sorties and 1,578 missions. From June 1944 to April 1945, the airmen flew 200 bomber escort missions, over most of central and southern Europe, without losing a single bomber to the enemy. To white American bomber crews, they were reverently known as "Black Redtail Angels" because of the bright red paint on the tail assemblies of their aircraft. German pilots both feared and respected the Tuskegee Airmen, calling them the "Schwartze Vogelmenschen," or "Black Birdmen."

In 1948 President Harry S. Truman issued an executive order that integrated the military. In 2005 the U.S. Congress passed a resolution honoring the Tuskegee airmen for their bravery in World War II and their role in creating an integrated U.S. Air Force. In 2006 Congress voted unanimously to present the Tuskegee airmen with the Congressional Gold Medal. Monuments and memorials in several states—including Colorado, Georgia, and Iowa—have been dedicated in honor of the airmen, too.

Creation of the Convention

After several well-attended reunions of retired Tuskegee airmen during the post-World War II years, the Tuskegee Airmen, Inc. (TAI) was founded in Detroit, Michigan. The organization held its first convention in 1972. Since that time, the convention has helped to call attention to the airmen's heroic missions and provide an opportunity to share their experiences with youth.

Tuskegee Airment, Inc. is a non-military and non-profit organization, which has 56 chapters nationwide. Through its conventions and activities during the year, the TAI has conducted local and national programs that have introduced young people to the world of aviation and science. TAI also has provided awards to "deserving cadets" in the Air Force Reserve Officer Training Corps.

Observance

Convention events include general sessions/workshops, military forums/presentations, special events, an exhibition hall. and a grand banquet. This convention offers a wonderful opportunity for current and future aviators as well as aviation enthusiasts to historical accounts firsthand from American aviation pioneers.

Contacts and Websites

Tuskegee Airmen, Incorporated
P.O. Box 830060
Tuskegee, AL 36083
334-725-8200; fax: 334-725-8205
E-mail: mthomas@tuskegeeairmen.org
http://tuskegeeairmen.org

Tuskegee Institute National Historic Site
1212 W. Montgomery Rd.
Tuskegee, AL 36088
334-727-3200; fax: 334-727-1448
https://www.nps.gov/tuin/index.htm

Further Reading

Francis, Charles E. *The Tuskegee Airmen: The Men Who Changed a Nation.* Edited by Adolph Caso. Wellesley, MA: Branden Books, 1997. Reprint. Branden Books, 2008.

Homan, Lynn M., and Thomas Reilly. *Black Knights: The Story of the Tuskegee Airmen.* Gretna, LA: Pelican Publishing, 2002.

McKissack, Patricia C., and Fredrick L. McKissack. *Red-Tail Angels: The Story of the Tuskegee Airmen of World War II.* New York: Walker and Company, 1995. (young adult)

Mills, William G. *Combat Edge,* February 2005.

Umoja Karamu

Date Observed: Fourth Sunday in November
Location: African-American Communities

Umoja Karamu (oo-MOH-jah kah-RAH-moo) is a celebration of unity within the African-American family, community, and nation. "Umoja Karamu" is a Swahili term meaning "unity feast." Many African Americans celebrate this day as an alternative to the national Thanksgiving Day holiday. The unity feast may also be observed during **Kwanzaa** celebrations in late December.

Historical Background

The concept of African and African-American unity is centuries old. But during the 1960s and 1970s, it was a major focus of black nationalists. During the 1980s and 1990s, Afrocentric scholars such as Ishakamusa Barashango (lecturer, author, and founder of Philadelphia's Temple of the Black Messiah), drew further attention to the theme. Barashango, who died in 2004, argued that African Americans and black people of the diaspora should reject such European-American holidays as Thanksgiving and concentrate instead on understanding Africa's culture and values that are the distinctive heritage of black people.

Creation of the Holiday

In 1971 Brother Edward Simms Jr. of the Temple of the Black Messiah in Philadelphia developed Umoja Karamu to celebrate the African-American family and home. According to Barashango, Simms defined the purpose of Umoja Karamu as "an effort to inject new meaning and solidarity into the Black Family through ceremony and symbol." The date for the holiday, the fourth Sunday of November, was established by the Temple of the Black

Messiah in Washington, D.C. African Americans in other cities, including Philadelphia, Baltimore, and Chicago, soon followed the example.

Observance

The feast itself is centered on five symbolic colors: black, white, red, green, and gold/orange, which represent five historical periods in African-American history. Black represents African-American family strength before slavery; white symbolizes the effects of slavery on black families; red stands for liberation from slavery; green signifies the struggle for civil rights and equality; and gold, or orange, signals the African-American family's hope for the future.

Each symbolic color also corresponds with certain foods, such as:

Black—black-eyed peas, black olives, black beans
White—rice, potatoes, yucca
Red—cranberry juice, red peppers, tomatoes
Green—greens, celery, lettuce
Gold/Orange—cornbread, cheese, squash.

The meal begins with a prayer and libation—that is, pouring a drink to honor ancestors, an African tradition. As foods are passed and shared, an appointed person reads historical narratives appropriate for each represented period in the African-American family.

Many African-American churches hold services before individual families celebrate Umoja Karamu. The feast and ceremony are also part of multicultural programs on university campuses. Many black student unions sponsor such events in November or as part of annual Kwanzaa celebrations.

Further Reading

Anyike, James C. *African American Holidays: A Historical Research and Resource Guide to Cultural Celebrations.* Chicago: Popular Truth, 1991.

Barashango, Ishakamusa. *Afrikan People and European Holidays: A Mental Genocide, Book 2.* Afrikan World Books, 1983.

Eklof, Barbara. *For Every Season: The Complete Guide to African American Celebrations, Traditional to Contemporary.* New York: HarperCollins, 1997.

W. C. Handy Music Festival

Date Observed: From second week till last week of July
Location: Florence, Alabama

The W. C. Handy Music Festival, sponsored by the Music Preservation Society of the Alabama Shoals, is held in the Shoals area of Florence, Alabama, near the famous musical town of Muscle Shoals. The week-long event honors the man known as the "Father of the Blues."

Historical Background

Born in a log cabin on November 16, 1873, in Florence, Alabama, William Christopher Handy was the son of Charles Bernard Handy and Elizabeth Brewer Handy, former slaves. William's father and grandfather were African Methodist Episcopal (AME) ministers.

While growing up, Handy often heard spirituals at the AME church and the chants of black field or dock workers along the Tennessee River, which added to his innate interest in music. He noted in his autobiography that, at the young age of 10,

> I could catalogue almost any sound that came to my ears, using the tonic *sol-fa* system. I knew the whistle of each of the river boats on the Tennessee. . . . I could tell what the birds in the orchards and woodlands were singing. . . .

> Whenever I heard the song of a bird and the answering call of its mate, I could visualize the notes in the scale. Robins carried a warm alto theme. Bobolinks sang contrapuntal melodies. Mocking birds trilled cadenzas. Altogether, as I fancied, they belonged to a great outdoor choir.

449

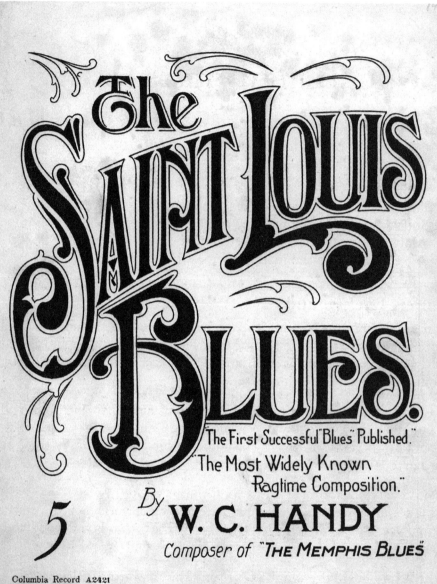

Sheet music cover for W. C. Handy's "The Saint Louis Blues," published in 1918.

Handy saved money that he earned at various jobs to buy a guitar. But when he brought the guitar home, his father was incensed, claiming the instrument was used to play secular music, which he considered part of the devil's work. Rev. Handy ordered his son to take the guitar back to the store, and then provided organ lessons for him.

The organ music did not appeal to young Handy, and the lessons did not last long. But as a teenager, Handy heard a trumpeter who visited Florence, and he decided to buy a cornet and learn to play it. Under the guidance of a Fisk University professor, he mastered the fundamentals of music and began performing with a local band. He also sang first tenor with a quartet.

Handy left Alabama in 1892 and traveled with various bands for several years. He married Elizabeth Price in 1898, and from 1900 to 1902, he taught music at a college in Huntsville, Alabama. He left teaching to establish his own jazz band, which was common for professional musicians of the time.

Once, while performing in Mississippi, a local blues band played during a break, and Handy saw that the audience loved the music, which had what has been called a "raw, primitive" sound, reflecting the hardship of blacks in America. He also realized that the blues could be commercially successful, and he began to compose his own renditions.

By this time—about 1905—Handy had made his home in Memphis, Tennessee, where he met Harry Pace, a lyricist. The two collaborated in writing songs, eventually forming the Pace and Handy Music Company. In 1909 Handy was asked to write a campaign song for a mayoral candidate, Edward Crump. The song, titled "Mr. Crump," was later published with new lyrics as "Memphis Blues." Thus, Handy introduced the blues style to national—and then worldwide—audiences. Other compositions followed, such as "Beale Street Blues," "Yellow Dog Blues," "Mississippi Blues," and the world-renowned "St. Louis Blues," which jazz vocalist Bessie Smith recorded in the mid-1920s, helping to popularize the tune (*see also* **Bessie Smith Strut**).

In 1918 the Pace and Handy Music Company moved to New York, but the company disbanded in 1920. Pace established a record company, and the Handy family maintained the publishing firm. During the 1920s, Handy continued to compose music and lead his band. He also supported numerous other black musicians and wrote *Blues: An Anthology*, published in 1926. Several other books by Handy about African-American music and composers

451

were issued in the 1930s. In 1941 his autobiography, *Father of the Blues*, was published.

Handy was honored in many ways during his lifetime as well as after his death in 1958. In Florence, Alabama, Handy's home and museum memorialize him, and across the United States his name graces schools, streets, parks, and other public places. A statue of Handy stands in Wilson Park in downtown Florence.

Creation of the Festival

In 1982 the Music Preservation Society of the Alabama Shoals—a quad-city area that includes Florence, Muscle Shoals, Sheffield, and Tuscumbia—staged its first W. C. Handy Music Festival to celebrate the life of the Florence native. Since then, an increasing number of musicians attract thousands of visitors to the Shoals area for the festival. An estimated 150,000 people come from across the United States and other countries.

Observance

In July 2019, the W.C. Handy Music Festival featured Dizzy Gillespie as the headline artist. It was a ten-day festival with nearly 300 events and music at locations throughout northwest Alabama, including parks, restaurants, stores, libraries, museums, art galleries, sidewalks, parking lots, and lawns The Festival continued to serve as an opportunity to preserve, promote, and present the musical heritage of northwest Alabama. Other legendary entertainers included Miki Howard, and The Manhattans, featuring Gerald Alston and special guest saxophonist Dee Lucas. Along with musical events, the festival offered such activities as a street strut, golf tournament, fishing tournament, and a "walk-and-run" foot race.

Contacts and Websites

Florence/Lauderdale Convention & Visitors Bureau
200 Jim Spain Dr.
Florence, AL 35630
256-740-4141 or 888-356-8687
http://www.visitflorenceal.com/about-florence/contact

W. C. Handy Music Festival
215 E Tuscaloosa St.
Florence, AL 35630
256-766-7642
http://www.wchandymusicfestival.org

W. C. Handy Home, Museum, and Library
620 W College St.
Florence, AL 35630
256-760-6434
https://www.visitflorenceal.com/
things_to_do/w-c-handy-birthplace-museum-library

Further Reading

Carlin, Richard. "Handy, W. C." In *African American Lives*, edited by Henry Louis Gates Jr. and Evelyn Brooks Higginbotham. New York: Oxford University Press, 2004.

Handy, D. Antoinette. "W. C. Handy." In *Black Heroes*, edited by Jessie Carney Smith. Foreword by Nikki Giovanni. Canton, MI: Visible Ink Press, 2001.

Southern, Eileen. *The Music of Black Americans: A History*. 3rd ed. New York: W. W. Norton and Company, 1997.

Watch Night

Date Observed: December 31
Location: African-American Communities

In many African-American communities across the United States, the last day of the year is observed as Watch Night, also known as "Freedom's Eve." Church services commemorate the night before President Abraham Lincoln's Emancipation Proclamation became effective January 1, 1863, freeing slaves in Confederate-controlled areas. Once the news was received, there were prayers, shouts, and songs of joy as many people fell to their knees and thanked God. Slaves in other places did not gain their freedom until 1865 with the ratification of the 13th amendment (*see also* **Emancipation Day** *and* **National Freedom Day**).

Historical Background

On September 22, 1862, in the midst of the Civil War, U.S. President Abraham Lincoln issued a preliminary proclamation to free slaves in Confederate states and parts of states that had joined the Confederates. Lincoln declared that he would sign the proclamation making it official on January 1, 1863, if the Confederates did not rejoin the Union. The South continued the fight, and free blacks and slaves alike waited anxiously for the proclamation to become effective.

When December 31, 1862, arrived, slaves on some plantations met in praise houses, or if they were not allowed to congregate, they gathered secretly in cabins or in the woods to pray for freedom. In the North, African Americans and prominent abolitionists—white and black—gathered in churches to pray, sing, and wait hopefully for news from Washington, D.C.

According to one legend, in Boston, Massachusetts, where abolitionists had congregated at the Tremont Temple Baptist Church, a man came running

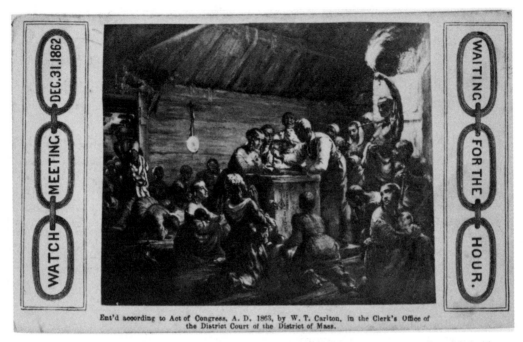

DEC.31.1862 WATCH MEETING
WAITING FOR THE HOUR.

Ent'd according to Act of Congress, A. D. 1863, by W. T. Carlton, in the Clerk's Office of the District Court of the District of Mass.

This 1863 illustration depicts a watch meeting of December 31, 1862. The man at the table holds a watch as the group awaits news of the Emancipation Proclamation.

down the aisle five minutes before midnight, crying out that the news was on the wire and emancipation was coming.

Creation of the Observance

After the original December 31 Watch Night, or Freedom's Eve, in 1862, annual commemorations took place, but they were sometimes dangerous events until slavery was fully abolished in 1865. Watch Night remains an important observance each year in countless black churches, although in recent decades some pastors have had to review the significance of the event for congregations unfamiliar with its historical background.

Observance

Before Watch Night services in African-American churches begin, there may be a feast that includes soul food—black-eyed peas, collard or turnip greens, chicken, and other traditional dishes. African drummers and dancers might perform.

455

A Tragic New Year's Eve Ritual

Before New Year's Eve became a celebratory event, slave families dreaded the occasion. On the next day slaveowners would balance their accounts. Some owners would sell their slaves in order to pay down debts, and that could mean breaking up families. Thus New Year's Eve would be a heart-wrenching time, because there was always the possibility that family members would never see each other again.

Harriet Jacobs, who wrote *Incidents in the Life of a Slave Girl Written by Herself*, published for the author in 1861, described a mother's anguish on New Year's Eve:

> She sits on her cold cabin floor, watching the children who may all be torn from her the next morning; and often does she wish that she and they might die before the day dawns. She may be an ignorant creature, degraded by the system that has brutalized her from childhood; but she has a mother's instincts, and is capable of feeling a mother's agonies.
>
> On one of these sale days, I saw a mother lead seven children to the auction-block. She knew that *some* of them would be taken from her; but they took *all*. The children were sold to a slave-trader, and their mother was bought by a man in her own town. Before night her children were all far away. She begged the trader to tell her where he intended to take them; this he refused to do. How *could* he, when he knew he would sell them, one by one, wherever he could command the highest price? I met that mother in the street, and her wild, haggard face lives to-day in my mind. She wrung her hands in anguish, and exclaimed, "Gone! All gone! Why *don't* God kill me?" I had no words wherewith to comfort her. Instances of this kind are of daily, yea, of hourly occurrence.

In many African-American churches, the service on December 31 normally begins anywhere from 7 p.m. to 10 p.m. and features prayer, singing, testimonies, and a sermon, and ends at midnight at the beginning of the New Year. A pastor or member of the congregation may recall the original Freedom's

Eve. Just before midnight, the lights in a church may be dimmed or turned off for prayer. As the new year comes in, the Emancipation Proclamation may be read. In places where ties to Africa are recognized, the service may include greeting the spirit, an ancient ritual in which a watchman keeps track of the movements of the moon for the exact time when midnight arrives.

Because Watch Night occurs during the seven-day **Kwanzaa** celebration, some services recognize the sixth principle of Kwanzaa, *kuumba*. Both Watch Night and Kwanzaa celebrate freedom and looking to the future.

Another type of ritual on Watch Night takes place in Bolden, Georgia, an African-American community near Eulonia. There, members of the Mt. Calvary Baptist Church, known as the "McIntosh County Shouters," take part in the ring shout, a tradition that can be traced back to slavery and West African culture. The ring shout is a religious ceremony with holy dancing and shouts of praise to the Lord.

Many historians believed that the ring shout had died out completely in the United States, but the McIntosh County Shouters brought the tradition to light when they performed at the **Georgia Sea Island Festival** in 1980. The group includes African-American elders who have passed on the tradition from their enslaved forebears and are committed to preserving the practice.

Since its first public appearance in 1980, the group has been featured at many other venues around the United States, including the Lincoln Center in New York City and the Smithsonian Institution in Washington, D.C. The Shouters also have appeared in documentaries, and their songs have been recorded on CDs.

For their stage performances, the McIntosh County Shouters recreate the ring shout as close to their traditional practice as possible. The group begins the dance with shuffling movements in a counterclockwise circle, never lifting or crossing their feet—foot-crossing is considered unholy. The *New Georgia Encyclopedia* describes the performance this way:

A "songster" will "set" or begin a song, slowly at first, then accelerating to an appropriate tempo. These lines will be answered by a group of singers called "basers" in call-and-response pattern. The stick-man, sitting next to the leader, will beat a simple rhythm with a broom or other wood stick, and the basers will add rhythm with hand clapping and foot patting. The songs are special shout songs, at one time called "running spirituals." For the most part they form a separate repertoire from spirituals, jubilees, and later gospel songs. Ranging from light-spirited to apocalyptic, at times they carry coded references to slavery. Sometimes participants pantomime the meaning of the verses being sung—for example, extending their arms in the "eagle wing" gesture to evoke friends urging a slave, Daniel, to fly from the master's whip.[1]

Contact and Website

Georgia Humanities
50 Hurt Plz. S.E., Ste. 595
Atlanta, GA 30303
404-523-6220; fax: 404-523-5702
https://www.georgiahumanities.org

Further Reading

Gulevich, Tanya. "Watch Night." In *Encyclopedia of Christmas and New Year's Celebrations.* 2nd ed. Detroit: Omnigraphics, 2003.

Henderson, Helene. "Emancipation Day." In *Patriotic Holidays of the United States.* Detroit: Omnigraphics, 2006.

Jacobs, Harriet. *Incidents in the Life of a Slave Girl. Written by Herself.* Edited by L. Maria Child. 1861. Reprint. OK Publishing, 2017.

Joyner, Marsha. "Gathering Place." *Honolulu Star-Bulletin,* January 1, 2006.

Kachun, Mitch. *Festivals of Freedom: Memory and Meaning in African American Emancipation Celebrations, 1808–1915.* 2003. Reprint. Amherst: University of Massachusetts Press, 2006.

---

[1] Reprinted with permission from The New Georgia Encyclopedia, http://www.georgiaencyclopedia.org, a project of the Georgia Humanities Council.

Watts Summer Festival

Date Observed: Second weekend in August
Location: Watts neighborhood, Los Angeles, California

The Watts Summer Festival is held each year during the month of August. It is held partly to commemorate 34 residents of Watts (an African-American neighborhood in Los Angeles, California) who died during the August 1965 revolt, which is sometimes referred to as a riot. The festival also serves as a vehicle for bringing a positive focus on the community.

Historical Background

Between August 11 and 17, 1965, the relatively unknown community of Watts in Los Angeles, California, made a major impression on the rest of the United States. The Watts uprising resulted from racial tensions that had been brewing in the Los Angeles metropolitan area for decades.

Ironically, Los Angeles is the only major city in the United States founded by settlers largely of African descent. According to the 1900 census, 2,100 African Americans resided in the city in that year and, within a decade, the number would grow to 15,000. During the early part of the 20th century, many African Americans owned homes in the city. But housing bans (which at first were intended for Asians, Mexicans, and Jews) eventually were applied against blacks who were relegated to South Los Angeles communities such as Watts. These notorious areas were on the bottom rung for delivery of civic services. Not only was housing substandard, but medical care was spotty, schools under par, and employment opportunities few and far between.

All of this laid the groundwork for what erupted in August of 1965. On the evening of August 11, a white California Highway Patrol Officer, Lee Minkus, pulled over Marquette Frye, a young black man, for erratic driving. A crowd gathered as Frye and his brother, Ronald, were questioned. Their mother Rena arrived, after which accounts vary; however, there is no dispute that at some point a struggle ensued and the three Frye family members were taken into custody. Subsequently, a bottle was thrown at a police vehicle.

Later on that evening, and into the late-night and early-morning hours of the next day, sporadic incidents of violence began to occur. Concerned community leaders called a meeting in Athens Park at midday on the 12th, hoping to quell the growing fury. Instead, television cameras broadcast an angry black youth proclaiming his intent to "burn" the neighborhood—which helped to incite others who shared his rage. The 13th brought thousands of African-American residents to the streets; by that evening, thousands of National Guardsmen were deployed and the first deaths had occurred.

Over the course of the next few days, Americans watched in disbelief as buildings burned and businesses were looted. The tally of devastation by the time a curfew was lifted on August 17 was stunning: 34 Watts residents dead, 1,100 people were injured, 4,000 arrests, 600 buildings were damaged or destroyed across a 100-block area, and an estimated $200 million in damages.

Creation of the Festival

A number of Watts community activists came together after the incendiary events of that August 1965 summer. They were intent on changing the city's, the nation's, and even the world's impression of their corner of the globe. The activists believed that the television cameras that had been focused on their neighborhood for those few, short days had captured limited, biased, uninformed, and prejudicial impressions of their community. Therefore, these Watts residents were anxious to find a way to convey a more realistic, positive, and human view of their lives. And so the idea for the Watts Summer Festival was born.

The first festival was held in 1966 as a fairly free-form event. Booths were set up on the streets, and there were no charges for vendors who exhibited. All energies were devoted to making the festival an upbeat event, one where the community could begin to feel a sense of pride and belonging.

As time has passed, the festival has grown and become more organized and structured—to the dismay of some and the delight of others. The festival attracts many people, year after year, and also continues to receive the support of famous African Americans, from top musicians to prominent movie stars.

In 1972, *Wattstax*, a concert offshoot of the festival's entertainment events, was held at L.A.'s Memorial Coliseum, the first time an African-American organization ever sold out that venue, and an accompanying album *Wattstax, the Living World* was recorded. The following year, a spin-off Wattstax film was produced and a special restoration version was released with much fanfare in June 2003.

Observance

Over the second weekend in August, festivalgoers look forward to such activities and displays as art and business exhibits, a carnival, a children's village, a sports village, a senior citizens' pavilion, various concerts and performing arts shows, food and beverage concession stands, a custom car/bike/van show, a fashion show, and a film festival. The festival also includes a remembrance of activist Halifu Tommy Jacquette and a screening of "Wattstax," the concert documentary film.

"Spirit of Watts Tours" also are given during the festival to make certain that the neighborhood's history is not forgotten, as well as to ensure that misconceptions about the area's past are dispelled and positive views about its development are represented.

A variety of social-service needs are also tended to during the festival, with representatives from numerous civic and other groups on hand to offer assistance and information.

Finally, the festival's community forum provides a place for debate and exchange of ideas about issues that affect African Americans at the local, state, national, and international levels.

Contact and Website

Watts Neighborhood Council
1703 Santa Ana Blvd. N.
Los Angeles, CA 90002
323-564-0260
E-mail: info.wattsnc@gmail.com
https://wattsnc.org

Further Reading

Diver-Stamnes, Anne C. *Lives in the Balance: Youth, Poverty, and Education in Watts.* Albany: State University of New York Press, 1995.

Horne, Gerald. *Fire This Time: The Watts Uprising and the 1960s.* Charlottesville: University of Virginia Press, 1995.

Hunt, Darrell M. *Screening the Los Angeles 'Riots': Race, Seeing, and Resistance.* Edited by Jeffrey C. Alexander and Steven Seidman. New York: Cambridge University Press, 1997.

Jacobs, Ronald N. *Race, Media, and the Crisis of Civil Society: From Watts to Rodney King.* Edited by Jeffrey C. Alexander and Steven Seidman. New York: Cambridge University Press, 2000.

West Indies Emancipation Day

Date Observed: August 1
Location: West Indies and U.S. cities

Slavery was abolished on Great Britain's island possessions in the West Indies on August 1, 1834, but slaves were not totally free until four years later, on August 1, 1838. The day has been celebrated in the West Indies, South America, and some U.S. and Canadian communities. Emancipation Day is a public holiday in the former British colonies of Barbados, Jamaica, Trinidad and Tobago, and Guyana.

Historical Background

Like thousands of enslaved people in the North American colonies and states, most slaves in the British territories of the West Indies came from West African countries such as Nigeria. After decades of anti-slavery efforts in Great Britain, the nation banned the slave trade in 1807. But slaveholders within the British Empire still kept people in bondage. Public pressure to abolish slavery continued, with more than 200 branches of the British Anti-Slavery Society active by 1824. At the same time, pro-slavery planters in the British Caribbean and their supporters in Parliament fought to maintain the status quo. As was true in the U.S., the controversy sometimes led to violence and slave rebellions.

In 1833, the British Slavery Abolition Act, which became effective August 1, 1834, abolished slavery throughout England and all British possessions. West Indian island governments were allowed to determine whether or not emancipation would occur immediately or gradually. Only Antigua and Bermuda released their slaves in 1834.

Other British West Indian colonies in the Caribbean followed the provisions of the Abolition Act. The law granted complete freedom to children under six years of age, but any slave older than six was required to serve an

IMMEDIATE EMANCIPATION

This engraving by S. H. Gimber was based on a painting by Alexander Rippingille. The engraving of celebrating West Indians was created sometime between 1838 and 1862.

apprenticeship. The Act declared slaves were "entitled to be registered as apprenticed labourers and to acquire thereby all rights and privileges of freedom." Their so-called entitlement included working without pay for 45 hours each week for their former owners. In addition, ex-slaves were supposed to learn how to function in a free society.

As apprentices, agricultural workers had to labor for a period of six years; domestics and other non-field workers had to apprentice for four years. Their compensation was no different from slave provisions: food, clothing, housing, and medical treatment. Former owners, on the other hand, were compensated for their loss of "property." The British government paid West Indian planters a total of 20 million pounds.

At first, when slaves in the British West Indies learned about their free status, they celebrated on August 1, 1834, by dancing in the streets, attending religious services, and expressing their happiness in many ways. But joy soon turned to anger and resentment when the new "apprentices" were forced the next day to go back to work for their former owners. People who had hoped for and anticipated freedom gathered in protests on the islands and in Guyana. Militia and special guards put down the protests and rebellions, and many "apprentices" were jailed and flogged in public squares. Some were hanged. Others ran away and found safety in maroon communities—settlements of escaped slaves in remote forest or mountainous areas.

During the next few years, island governments individually granted complete emancipation. All apprenticed laborers throughout the British West Indies were legally free by August 1, 1838. On that day, ex-slaves in the West Indies, as well as free African Americans and American abolitionists—black and white—celebrated. Americans marked the day with speeches and prayers expressing hope that West Indian emancipation would lead to freedom for slaves everywhere.

Creation of the Observance

A few American celebrations of West Indian Emancipation Day took place on August 1, 1834, when abolitionists and free blacks believed that slaves on the Caribbean islands were actually freed. For several years afterward, occasional anniversary commemorations took place, but the number of commemorations increased after August 1, 1838.

What to the Slave Is the Fourth of July?

In 1852, the Rochester (New York) Ladies' Anti-Slavery Society invited Frederick Douglass to deliver a speech about the Fourth of July. Douglass agreed, and appeared before the group on the 5th of July. He began what is now considered one of his most famous and eloquent speeches by recounting the colonists' fight to be free of British rule. Then he launched into the reasons why asking a slave to celebrate independence was hypocritical. Speaking as an escaped slave and for enslaved African Americans, he asked his audience:

> What have I, or those I represent, to do with your national independence? Are the great principles of political freedom and of natural justice, embodied in that Declaration of Independence, extended to us? and am I, therefore, called upon to bring our humble offering to the national altar, and to confess the benefits and express devout gratitude for the blessings resulting from your independence to us?

> Would to God, both for your sakes and ours, that an affirmative answer could be truthfully returned to these questions! Then would my task be light, and my burden easy and delightful. . .

> But, such is not the state of the case. I say it with a sad sense of the disparity between us. I am not included within the pale of this glorious anniversary! Your high independence only reveals the immeasurable distance between us. The blessings in which you, this day, rejoice, are not enjoyed in common. The rich inheritance of justice, liberty, prosperity and independence, bequeathed by your fathers, is shared by you, not by me. The sunlight that brought life and healing to you, has brought stripes and death to me. This Fourth [of] July is yours, not mine. You may rejoice, I must mourn

Some free West Indians left the Caribbean for the United States, settling in New Bedford, Massachusetts, known for its anti-slavery movement and a stop on the Underground Railroad. West Indians who settled there made Emancipation Day an annual event, beginning about 1838 or 1839.

Free blacks and abolitionists in other U.S. and Canadian cities also initiated Emancipation Day celebrations. Providence, Rhode Island, for example, first commemorated the abolition of West Indian slavery in 1849, and after 1863, the annual Emancipation Day on August 1 recognized the freedom of some U.S. slaves (*see also* **Emancipation Day**). In Nicodemus, Kansas, an annual Emancipation Day on the last weekend in July originally celebrated the freeing of slaves in the West Indies. It is now also a homecoming celebration for descendants of African Americans who settled the town (*see also* **Homecoming Emancipation Celebration**).

Observance

From the 1840s to the end of the Civil War, the First of August Emancipation Day, sometimes called "Freedom Day," was celebrated in North America from the east to the west coasts, in Canadian provinces, and, of course, in the West Indies. Celebrations took place in churches, government buildings, or outdoors in plazas, public squares, or wooded picnic areas. These anniversary celebrations provided public forums for African Americans, black and white abolitionists, and others to demonstrate their belief in human liberty.

At first, U.S. celebrations were small, but by the 1840s they had grown and spread to a variety of locations. The Massachusetts Anti-Slavery Society reported that the 1844 festivities in Boston and other cities included processions, speeches, singing, and "elegant collations" (feasts). In its report, the Society noted that the First of August anniversary "was fast taking the place of the Fourth of July in the hearts of the true lovers of Liberty."

Indeed, for African Americans of the 1800s, July 4th had little meaning, as former slave, abolitionist leader, and orator Frederick Douglass pointed out in his 1852 speech "What to the Slave Is the Fourth of July?" (*see also* **Frederick Douglass Day**). That holiday celebrated the nation's independence but ignored the fact that thousands of black people did not enjoy freedom and were still enslaved. The August 1st Emancipation Day, on the other hand, was an opportunity to bring African Americans together for a celebration they could call their own and enjoy a sense of community. Also, it was a way to seek public support for abolition and the larger cause of universal human rights.

After the 13th Amendment to the Constitution abolished slavery in the United States in 1865, First of August commemorations were overshadowed by Emancipation Day, **Juneteenth**, and similar observances celebrating the end of slavery in the United States. However, in some U.S. locations, August 1st Emancipation Day observances continued or were restored.

There was an annual festival in Albion, Michigan, for example, into the early decades of the 20th century. In a 1927 celebration, more than 3,000 blacks from across the state gathered. They watched a parade, listened to speeches, enjoyed a barbecue lunch, attended a boxing match, and in the evening danced at an Emancipation Day Ball. The actual celebration of Emancipation Day begins on 31 July. There is an all-night vigil, church services, parades, patriotic speeches, cultural performances, and more. After the parade, there was a free concert at Freedom Plaza, featuring musical acts such as Faith Evans, Mya, Doug E. Fresh, Kenny Lattimore, Master Gee of the Sugar Hill Gang, Ayanna Gregory, Spur of the Moment Band, and several more acts.

Further Reading

Bowers, Detine L. "A Place to Stand: African-Americans and the First of August Platform." *The Southern Communication Journal*, Summer 1995.

Douglass, Frederick. "The Meaning of the Fourth of July for the Negro, Speech at Rochester, New York, July 5, 1852." In *The Life and Writings of Frederick Douglass, Volume II: Pre-Civil War Decade, 1850–1960,* by Philip S. Foner. New York: International Publishers Co., 1950. Kachun, Mitch. *Festivals of Freedom: Memory and Meaning in African American Emancipation Celebrations, 1808–1915.* Amherst: University of Massachusetts Press, 2003. Massachusetts Anti-Slavery Society. *Thirteenth Annual Report of the Massachusetts Anti-Slavery Society*, January 22, 1845. Reprint. 1853. In *The Negro American: A Documentary History*, edited Leslie H. Fishel Jr. and Benjamin Quarles. Glenview, IL: Scott Foresman.

Roberts, David. "Forgotten American Observance: Remembering the First of August." *Ex Post Facto Journal of the History Students at San Francisco State University*, 2002. https://history.sfsu.edu/sites/default/files/EPF/2002_David%20Roberts-ilovepdf-compressed.pdf

Women's Day Celebrations

Date Observed: Varies
Location: Churches nationwide

W omen's Day celebrations are dedicated to honoring the women in a church's congregation, raising funds for women's church missions, and recognizing the contributions of women in all areas of life. Women's Day originated within the National Baptist Convention, but is now observed by churches of many different denominations throughout the United States.

Historical Background

In the late 1800s, women lived with many restrictions and lacked opportunities that were available to men. Women were often discouraged from getting an advanced education or pursuing serious studies, and they were not yet allowed to vote. It was commonly believed that women were incapable of making important contributions to society. Social norms dictated that women should limit their activities to raising children and performing household chores. It was considered inappropriate for a woman to participate in many activities, including intellectual pursuits or any sort of leadership position. Women were limited in the kind of jobs they could hold, and they often had only two options: domestic servant or elementary-school teacher. During this time, opportunities for African-American women were even more constrained, and most who held jobs worked as servants.

As a young girl growing up in Virginia during the late 19th century, Nannie Helen Burroughs wanted to change things for women. After graduating from high school, Burroughs attempted to become a teacher, but no school would hire an African-American woman. After many endeavors to find a job other than domestic service, Burroughs took a position as corresponding secretary of the Women's Convention Auxiliary to the National Baptist Convention from 1900 to 1909. She became a tireless advocate for women and devoted her life to issues surrounding women's education and personal development.

Creation of the Observance

In 1906 Burroughs proposed the creation of Women's Day to the Baptist Convention leadership as a way of remedying the exclusion of women from participating in most church and other social activities.

At that time, the main goal of the Women's Convention Auxiliary was to raise money for foreign missionary work. Burroughs envisioned the national Women's Day as a focused fundraising project in support of that goal. In order to raise awareness among women and get them interested in participating in Women's Day, Burroughs wanted to create a program of prayer, worship, music, and inspirational speeches. These program materials were to be distributed to local churches for the purpose of energizing women in the congregation. Burroughs believed that women were an untapped resource within the church, and that they could be just as successful as men in the areas of public speaking, motivation, fundraising, and informed leadership. After some discussion, the National Baptist Convention approved Burroughs's plan and she proceeded to organize materials for Women's Day.

On the last Sunday in July 1907, the first Women's Day observance was held in Nashville, Tennessee. Women's Day quickly grew in popularity, and many churches began observing the day using the materials created by Burroughs. These Women's Day events marked the first time that women had been allowed to speak in Baptist churches, and many took advantage of the opportunity. Early Women's Day events included groups of women who went from church to church, speaking to the congregation at each location and soliciting donations to support foreign missionary work. Significant funds were raised in support of the various missionary programs sponsored by the national Baptist church.

The focus of Women's Day has evolved since the first observances took place in the early 1900s. The day has become important as a time to honor women in the congregation and acknowledge the many contributions made by women in all areas of life. African-American churches still use the day to raise money for charitable causes, but many have expanded the focus of Women's Day to include social and educational programs of interest to women. Women's Day remains a primary fundraising day in many gatherings, though its main focus upon foreign missions has expanded or diminished to add other concerns.

Women's Day offerings have, as proposed in the 2009 Lectionary Cultural Resource, "insured the economic stability of many churches, supported missions to Africa and other countries and also offered financial support for pastors and members to denominational conventions and meetings."

Observance

Churches observe Women's Day in many different ways. Some churches bring in visiting speakers or preachers, usually women, to deliver a special sermon on that day. Others provide an afternoon luncheon or tea honoring the women of the congregation, or a special mother-daughter event is held. Still other churches plan elaborate day-long programs in honor of Women's Day, sometimes held at a local restaurant or banquet facility instead of at the church itself. These programs provide women with an opportunity to get away from their normal routines for a day of relaxation, fun, and spiritual renewal. Women's Day observances such as these usually include guest speakers, workshops and seminars, health education, and sometimes even fashion shows.

The date, location, and schedule for Women's Day celebrations are determined by individual churches. Although Women's Day was originally observed in late July, churches now designate different days throughout the year as Women's Day. Activities related to Women's Day continue to be successful fundraisers. Many church leaders also credit the day with expanding the opportunities available for women in leadership positions within the church.

Contact

Nannie Helen Burroughs School
601 50th St., N.E.
Washington, DC 20019
202-883-0141

Further Reading

Gantt, Alice. "Women's Day." Black Congregational Ministries Committee, National Council of Churches USA, October 1995.
Smith, Jesse Carney. *Black Firsts: 4,000 Ground-Breaking and Pioneering Historical Events.* 3rd ed., revised and expanded. Canton, MI: Visible Ink Press, 2013.

Zora Neale Hurston Festival of the Arts and Humanities

Date Observed: Last week in January
Location: Eatonville, Florida

Anthropologist, folklorist, and writer Zora Neale Hurston is honored in a festival of the arts and humanities in Eatonville, Florida, which Hurston claimed as her birthplace. The ZORA!™ annual festival is organized by the Association to Preserve Eatonville and is held during the last week in January. It is a multiday event that includes museum exhibitions, theatrical productions, arts education programming, public talks and a three-day Outdoor Festival of the Arts.

Historical Background

Throughout her lifetime, Zora Neale Hurston called Eatonville, Florida, her hometown—the place where she was born—and she gave the year of her birth as 1901. Yet records show she was born in Alabama in 1891. When she was one or two years old, however, her family moved to Eatonville, one of the nation's first all-black incorporated towns. Eatonville had a strong influence on her writing and life choices.

When Hurston was 13 years old, her mother died, and her father, a preacher, carpenter, and farmer in Eatonville, sent her to Jacksonville to attend a boarding school, the Florida Baptist Academy, where two of her siblings also were enrolled. Hurston did well in her studies, but did not respond with deference to authority figures—in fact, she was called "sassy."

After less than five months at the Academy, Hurston learned that her father had remarried, which distressed her and the other children. She had never been close to her father, whose many marital infidelities disturbed her, and

Zora Neale Hurston, at the New York Times *Book Fair in November 1937.*

his remarriage to a much younger woman upset her even further. She also learned that her father had not paid for her stay at the boarding school.

In order to complete her freshman year, Hurston did domestic work at the school. When the school term ended, she expected her father to come for her, but he did not, and a school administrator paid her way home—which turned out to be a disaster. She had a brutal fight with her stepmother, and Hurston again left home, forced out by her father.

Hurston spent the next few years staying with various family members and working as a domestic. About 1915, she got a job as a maid for one of the stars in a touring Gilbert & Sullivan theater company, and stayed with the traveling troupe for 18 months. When she left the group in Baltimore, Maryland, she found menial jobs and hoped to go back to school.

Hurston on Eatonville

In Zora Neale Hurston's autobiography, *Dust Tracks on a Road* (1942), she wrote about Eatonville as her birthplace:

Like the dead-seeming, cold rocks, I have memories within that came out of the material that went to make me. Time and place have had their say.

So you will have to know something about the time and place where I came from, in order that you may interpret the incidents and directions of my life.

I was born in a Negro town. I do not mean by that the black back-side of an average town. Eatonville, Florida, is, and was at the time of my birth, a pure Negro town—charter, mayor, council, town marshal and all. It was not the first Negro community in America, but it was the first to be incorporated, the first attempt at organized self-government on the part of Negroes in America. . . .

On August 18, 1886, the Negro town, called Eatonville, after Captain Eaton, received its charter of incorporation from the state capital at Tallahassee, and made history by becoming the first of its kind in America, and perhaps in the world. So, in a raw, bustling frontier, the experiment of self-government for Negroes was tried. White Maitland and Negro Eatonville have lived side by side for fifty-five years without a single instance of enmity. The spirit of the founders has reached beyond the grave.

In 1917, after much frustration trying to save money for tuition, Hurston enrolled in a free public night school. Even though she was actually 26 years old, she looked like a teenager and gave her age as 16 and birth date as 1901, a myth she continued to perpetuate for the rest of her life.

Because she did well academically, Hurston gained confidence to enroll in a black preparatory school, Morgan Academy, connected with Morgan College (now Morgan State University). The dean of Morgan helped her find a job with the family of a trustee in order to pay her tuition.

Cover of a 2006 edition of Zora Neale Hurston's classic novel, originally published in 1937.

After graduating from Morgan, Hurston became a part-time student at Howard University in Washington, D.C. Again, she worked at menial jobs to support herself. At Howard, she began her writing career, publishing her first short story (set in Eatonville) in the university's literary magazine *Stylus*.

Over the next few years, Hurston found publishing outlets for more of her short stories, also based on Eatonville. After winning an award in 1925 for a story titled "Spunk," she moved to New York and became associated with the Harlem Renaissance, a literary and artistic movement. Hurston also was granted a scholarship to Barnard, where she combined studies in anthropology with her writing. She earned her Bachelor of Arts degree in 1928, becoming the first African American to graduate from Barnard.

From the time of her years at Barnard through the 1930s, Hurston conducted fieldwork in African-American folklore in the South and the Caribbean, collecting songs, sermons, legends, children's games, and staying in labor camps, all of which contributed to some of her best writing. She was the first African American to publish black folklore, and much of her published work includes tales in dialect and descriptions of everyday black culture. She also wrote novels, plays, anthropological studies, poetry, and magazine articles.

During the 1940s, Hurston's literary output was irregular, and not necessarily well-received, although her autobiography, *Dust Tracks on a Road* (1942), sold well. Yet her income from writing was not enough to cover expenses, so she again became a domestic to support herself.

Controversy surrounded Hurston during the 1950s when she opposed, or failed to support, civil rights efforts. She also was involved in ultraconservative political issues and wrote for magazines that espoused conservative views. She argued that black people should not feel sorry for themselves but should be strong individuals and work steadfastly to reach their goals. Hurston spoke in a letter to Countee Cullen about facing hardships through the quote "I have the nerve to walk my own way, however hard, in my search for reality, rather than climb upon the rattling wagon of wishful illusions."

In 1959, she suffered a severe stroke, and in 1960 died in a Fort Pierce, Florida, welfare home. Not until years after her death did Hurston's work come to the fore once more. In 1975, Alice Walker, who later became well known for her literary work, wrote an article describing her visit to a cemetery where she placed a marker near what was thought to be Hurston's grave. Walker's article helped rekindle interest in Hurston, as did the 1977 publication of Robert D. Hemenway's *Zora Neale Hurston: A Literary Biography*. Since then, Hurston's work has caught the attention of many new readers, writers, storytellers, filmmakers—and festival goers.

Creation of the Festival

The idea for the Zora Neale Hurston Festival was sparked in 1989 when Orange County officials in central Florida wanted to expand a main road that ran through Eatonville, 10 miles north of Orlando. In response, residents formed the Association to Preserve the Eatonville Community and organized a festival to raise funds to stop the road project and maintain the town. The first festival was held in 1990. Today the Association's goals include celebrating Hurston, Eatonville, and the larger cultural contributions of African Americans.

Observance

The week-long festival, also known as Zora!, takes place at a variety of venues. There is a "HATitude" luncheon with a style show to celebrate Hurston's fondness for hats. A concert choir performance and ecumenical Christian service at a church in Eatonville; a bus tour of Hurston's favorite places in Eatonville, Maitland, and the surrounding area; a smorgasbord of international foods; art exhibits; cultural programs; and public forums with notable guest speakers are all part of the celebration.

Contact and Website

The Hurston Museum
227 E. Kennedy Blvd.
Eatonville, FL 32751
407-647-3188
http://zorafestival.org

Further Reading

Boyd, Valerie. *Wrapped in Rainbows: The Life of Zora Neale Hurston.* 2008. Reprint. New York: Scribner, 2011.

Deck, Alice A. "Zora Neale Hurston." In *Black Heroes,* edited by Jessie Carney Smith. Foreword by Nikki Giovanni. Canton, MI: Visible Ink Press, 2001.

Hemenway, Robert E. *Zora Neale Hurston: A Literary Biography.* Foreword by Alice Walker. Urbana: University of Illinois Press, 1977.

Kaplan, Carla, ed. *Zora Neale Hurston: A Life in Letters.* New York: Doubleday, 2002.

Luker, Ralph E. "Hurston, Zora Neale." In *African American Lives,* edited by Henry Louis Gates Jr. and Evelyn Brooks Higginbotham. New York: Oxford University Press, 2004.

Appendices

Appendix 1: Chronology

This appendix lists significant events in the history of the African-American holidays, festivals, and celebrations covered in this volume. It includes dates of the first observance of events as well as significant dates relating to the people and historical events that are memorialized during the holiday or festival. Although historical events are included, this chronology is not intended to serve as a comprehensive list of events in African-American history.

1624

Dutch immigrants bring enslaved Africans to New York. *See* **Pinkster**

1711

October 17—Poet Jupiter Hammon is born a slave on Long Island, New York. *See* **Black Poetry Day**

1760

February 14—Richard Allen, founder of the African Methodist Episcopal Church, is born a slave in Philadelphia, Pennsylvania. *See* **Founder's Day/Richard Allen's Birthday**

December 25—Jupiter Hammon composes poem considered to be the first published by an African American. *See* **Black Poetry Day**

1767

September 29—Kunta Kinte, enslaved Gambian and ancestor of writer Alex Haley, arrives in Annapolis, Maryland. *See* **Kunta Kinte Heritage Festival**

1770

March 5—Crispus Attucks is the first American to die during the Boston Massacre, an event precipitating the Revolutionary War. *See* **Crispus Attucks Day**

1771

March 5—Boston Massacre and Crispus Attucks's death are commemorated in Boston, and each year thereafter. *See* **Crispus Attucks Day**

1775

First American abolitionist society is founded by Quakers in Pennsylvania. *See*
Emancipation Day

April 19—The Revolutionary War between the American colonies and Great
Britain begins with the Battle of Lexington and Concord in Massachusetts. *See*
Crispus Attucks Day

1777

July 12—Vermont is the first state to outlaw slavery. *See* **Emancipation Day**

1782

Peter Spencer, founder of the African Union Methodist Church, is born in Kent
County, Maryland. *See* **August Quarterly**

1787

April 12—The Free African Society is organized by Absalom Jones and Richard
Allen in Philadelphia, Pennsylvania. *See* **Emancipation Day**; **Founder's Day/
Richard Allen's Birthday**

November—Richard Allen and other black members of St. George's Methodist
Church in Philadelphia, Pennsylvania, are forced to leave a church service; Allen
later founds the first blackcontrolled church in America. *See* **Founder's Day/
Richard Allen's Birthday**

1792

May 8—U.S. Congress passes law prohibiting people of color from serving in the
military. *See***Battle of Olustee Reenactment**

1794

July 29—Church founded by Richard Allen is dedicated as Bethel African
Methodist Episcopal Church in Philadelphia, Pennsylvania. *See* **Founder's Day/
Richard Allen's Birthday**

1799

Celia Mann, a freed slave and midwife, is born in Charleston, South Carolina. *See*
Jubilee: Festival of Black History & Culture

March 29—New York state legislation gives freedom to children of slaves born
after July 1799. *See* **African American Day Parade**

1803

One of the first documented revival meetings is held on Shoulderbone Creek in
Hancock County, Georgia. *See* **Church Revivals**

A group of Igbos from west Africa is brought to St. Simons Island, from Savannah, Georgia. Rather than become slaves, they drown themselves in Dunbar Creek, later known as Ebo Landing. *See* **Georgia Sea Island Festival**

May 18—The first Haitian flag is flown by revolutionaries fighting for independence from France. *See* **Haitian Flag Day**

January 1—The United States legally prohibits the slave trade. *See* **Emancipation Day**

1811

Town council of Albany, New York, passes law banning Pinkster, a primarily African-American festival. *See* **Pinkster**

1813

Peter Spencer and others found the African Union Methodist Church in Wilmington, Delaware. *See* **August Quarterly**

1814

August 28—African Union Methodist Church holds its first annual conference, called the August Quarterly. *See* **August Quarterly**

1818

February—Frederick Douglass is born into slavery near Easton, Maryland. *See* **Frederick Douglass Day**

1820

Harriet Tubman is born in Dorchester County, Maryland. *See* **Harriet Tubman Day**

1821

African Grove Theater, the first African-American theater company, is formed in New York City. *See* **National Black Theatre Festival**

1827

July 4—State of New York abolishes slavery. *See* **African American Day Parade**

1831

March 26—Richard Allen dies in Philadelphia, Pennsylvania. *See* **Founder's Day/ Richard Allen's Birthday**

1833

The American Anti-Slavery Society is established by black and white abolitionists in Philadelphia, Pennsylvania. *See* **Emancipation Day**

1834

August 1—Slavery is abolished throughout the British Empire, including its Caribbean territories; emancipation becomes effective on August 1, 1838. *See* **West Indies Emancipation Day**

1838

September—Frederick Douglass escapes slavery in Maryland, makes his way north to freedom, and settles in New Bedford, Massachusetts. *See* **Frederick Douglass Day**

1843

July 25—Peter Spencer dies in Wilmington, Delaware. *See* **August Quarterly**

1844

Celia Mann moves into a one-room house (later known as the Mann-Simons Cottage) in Columbia, Georgia; the First Calvary Baptist Church meets in the basement. *See* **Jubilee: Festival of Black History & Culture**

1848

December 25—William and Ellen Craft, after escaping from a Georgia plantation, reach freedom in Pennsylvania. *See* **Slaves' Christmas**

1849

Harriet Tubman escapes slavery in Maryland and travels alone to freedom in Pennsylvania. *See***Harriet Tubman Day**

1850

September 18—As part of the Compromise of 1850, U.S. Congress revises the Fugitive Slave Act of 1793, mandating that escaped slaves be returned to their former states or territories. *See* **Emancipation Day; Jerry Rescue Day**

1851

October 1—William Jerry Henry, a fugitive slave captured and arrested in Syracuse, New York, is freed from jail by abolitionists. *See* **Jerry Rescue Day**

1852

July 5—Frederick Douglass delivers speech "What to the Slave Is the Fourth of July?" at the Ladies' Anti-Slavery Society in Rochester, New York. *See* **West Indies Emancipation Day**

1854

June—Anti-slavery convention is held in Sugar Grove, Pennsylvania, an event later described in *Frederick Douglass' Paper* on June 23, 1854. *See* **Sugar Grove Underground Railroad Convention**

June—Cowboy Nate "Nat" Love, also known as "Deadwood Dick," is born a slave in Tennessee. *See* **Black Cowboy Parade**

1857

New Orleans holds its first Mardi Gras parade. *See* **Mardi Gras in African-American Traditions**

March 6—Supreme Court rules in *Dred Scott v. Sanford* that blacks cannot become citizens and that Congress cannot limit the spread of slavery in U.S. territories. *See* **Emancipation Day**

1858

March 5—Black abolitionists in Boston designate the anniversary of the Boston Massacre as Crispus Attucks Day. *See* **Crispus Attucks Day**

1860

William and Ellen Craft's *Running a Thousand Miles for Freedom* is published. *See* **Slaves' Christmas**

1861

Harriet Jacobs's *Incidents in the Life of a Slave Girl Written by Herself* is published. *See* **Watch Night**

January 29—Kansas is admitted to the Union as a free state after violent confrontations between pro-slavery and anti-slavery forces. *See* **Emancipation Day**

April 12—U.S. Civil War begins with attack on Fort Sumter in Charleston, South Carolina. *See* **Battle of Olustee Reenactment**; **Emancipation Day**

1862

Penn Center, one of the first schools for emancipated slaves, is established on St. Helena Island in South Carolina. *See* **Penn Center Heritage Days**

April 16—President Abraham Lincoln signs the Compensated Emancipation Act, freeing enslaved persons in the District of Columbia. *See* **Emancipation Day in Washington, D.C.**

May 20—President Lincoln signs the Homestead Act of 1862, prompting thousands of blacks to move to Kansas in hopes of owning land. *See* **Emancipation Day in Hutchinson, Kansas**; **Homecoming Emancipation Celebration**

July 17—U.S. Congress passes the Second Confiscation Act, freeing slaves who are able to cross Union lines, as long as they were owned by supporters of the Confederacy. *See* **Battle of Olustee Reenactment**

July 17—U.S. Congress repeals 1792 law prohibiting people of color from serving in the military. *See* **Battle of Olustee Reenactment**

September 22—President Lincoln issues preliminary emancipation proclamation to free slaves in Confederate states. *See* **Emancipation Day**; **Watch Night**

December 31—African Americans and white abolitionists await the announcement of the signing of the Emancipation Proclamation. *See* **Watch Night**

1863

January 1—The Emancipation Proclamation, freeing slaves in Confederate states, takes effect. *See* **Emancipation Day**; **Juneteenth**

July—Frederick Douglass meets with President Lincoln at the White House to protest discrimination against black troops. *See* **Frederick Douglass Day**

1864

George Washington Carver, inventor and botanist, is born in Diamond, Missouri. *See* **George Washington Carver Day**

February 20—U.S. Civil War Battle of Olustee is fought in Florida. *See* **Battle of Olustee Reenactment**

1865

February 1—President Lincoln signs the 13th Amendment to the Constitution, abolishing slavery. *See* **Emancipation Day**; **National Freedom Day**

April 9—General Robert E. Lee surrenders his Confederate troops in Richmond, Virginia, bringing an end to the U.S. Civil War. *See* **Battle of Olustee Reenactment**

June 19—Slaves in Texas learn they have been freed by the Emancipation Proclamation of January 1, 1863. *See* **Emancipation Day**; **Juneteenth**

1866

April 19—First Emancipation Day celebration is held in Washington, D.C., commemorating the Compensated Emancipation Act of 1862. *See* **Emancipation Day in Washington, D.C.**

June 19—First commemoration of Juneteenth is held in Texas. *See* **Juneteenth**

July 28—U.S. Congress creates six Army regiments of African-American soldiers. *See* **Buffalo Soldiers Commemorations**

1868

Composer Scott Joplin is born in Texas. *See* **Scott Joplin Ragtime Festival**

February 23—W. E. B. Du Bois, writer and activist, is born in Great Barrington, Massachusetts. *See* **Martin Luther King Jr.'s Birthday**

1870

February 3—U.S. Congress ratifies 15th Amendment, granting black men the right to vote. *See* **Bridge Crossing Jubilee**

July 9—Emanuel Stance is the first African American in the post-Civil War period to receive a Congressional Medal of Honor. *See* **Buffalo Soldiers Commemorations**

December 5—William "Bill" Pickett, cowboy and rodeo performer, is born in Travis County, Texas. *See* **Bill Pickett Invitational Rodeo**

November 16—W. C. Handy, known as the father of the blues, is born in Florence, Alabama. *See* **W. C. Handy Music Festival**

1878

August 1—Settlers in Nicodemus, Kansas, hold first celebration of the 1834 emancipation of slaves throughout the British Empire. *See* **Homecoming Emancipation Celebration; West Indies Emancipation Day**

1880

Meeting of Baptist pastors in Montgomery, Alabama, takes place, initiating the National Baptist Convention, USA, Annual Session. *See* **National Baptist Convention, USA, Annual Session**

1881

July 4—Tuskegee Institute opens with Booker T. Washington as its principal. *See* **Tuskegee Airmen Convention**

1885

First professional black baseball team is formed in New York City. *See* **Jackie Robinson Day**

1887

August 17—Marcus Garvey, founder of the Universal Negro International Association, is born in St. Ann's Bay, Jamaica. *See* **Haile Selassie's Birthday; Marcus Garvey's Birthday**

1889

April 15—A. Philip Randolph, civil rights activist and founder of the Brotherhood of Sleeping Car Porters, is born in Crescent City, Florida. *See* **Martin Luther King Jr.'s Birthday**

August—The first Emancipation Day celebration in Hutchinson, Kansas, is held. *See* **Emancipation Day in Hutchinson, Kansas**

1891

January 7—Writer Zora Neale Hurston is born in Eatonville, Florida. *See* **Zora Neale Hurston Festival of the Arts and Humanities**

1892

August 23—Haile Selassie, ruler of Ethiopia, is born in Ejarsagoro, Harar, Ethiopia. *See* **Haile Selassie's Birthday**

1894

April 15—Singer Bessie Smith is born in Chattanooga, Tennessee. *See* **Bessie Smith Strut**

1895

February 20—Frederick Douglass dies at Cedar Hill, his home in Washington, D.C. *See* **Frederick Douglass Day**

1896

Booker T. Washington invites George Washington Carver to join the faculty of Tuskegee Institute. *See* **George Washington Carver Day**

May 18—U.S. Supreme Court upholds a Louisiana statute in *Plessy v. Ferguson*, which allows segregation as long as facilities for blacks are not inferior to those of whites. *See* **Martin Luther King Jr.'s Birthday**

November 20—Sallie Martin, known as the mother of gospel music, is born in Pittfield, Georgia. *See* **Chicago Gospel Music Festival**

1898

April 9—Paul Robeson, singer, actor, and activist, is born in Princeton, New Jersey. *See* **Paul Robeson's Birthday**

1899

July 1—Thomas Andrew Dorsey, known as the father of gospel music, is born in Villa Rica, Georgia. *See* **Chicago Gospel Music Festival**

1900

July 23—First Pan-African Congress is held in London, England. *See* **Pan African Bookfest and Cultural Conference**

1901

First African-American parade during Mardi Gras in New Orleans is organized by the Zulu Social Aid and Pleasure Club (Krewe of Zulu). *See* **Mardi Gras in African-American Traditions**

August 4—Louis Armstrong, musician and singer, is born in New Orleans, Louisiana. *See* **Satchmo SummerFest**

1904

Sigma Pi Phi, thought to be the oldest African-American fraternity, is founded in Philadelphia, Pennsylvania. *See* **Greek Organizations' Conventions**

1905

May 6—Robert S. Abbott produces the first issue of the *Chicago Defender*, which becomes one of the most important African-American newspapers in the country. *See* **Bud Billiken Parade and Picnic**

July 28—First Women's Day observance is held in Nashville, Tennessee. *See* **Women's Day Celebrations**

1908

Alpha Kappa Alpha, the first African-American sorority, is formed at Howard University in Washington, D.C. *See* **Greek Organizations' Conventions**

November 29—Adam Clayton Powell Jr., Harlem's first black congressman, is born in New Haven, Connecticut. *See* **African American Day Parade**

1909

February 12—The National Association for the Advancement of Colored People (NAACP) is founded. *See* **Martin Luther King Jr.'s Birthday**

1912

One of the earliest African-American resorts is founded on the island of Idlewild, north of Grand Rapids, Michigan. *See* **Idlewild Music Festival**

1913

February 4—Rosa Parks, often referred to as the mother of the civil rights movement, is born in Tuskegee, Alabama. *See* **Martin Luther King Jr.'s Birthday**; **Rosa Parks Day**

March 10—Harriet Tubman dies in Auburn, New York, at the Harriet Tubman Home for Aged and Indigent Colored People. *See* **Harriet Tubman Day**

1915

Carter Goodwin Woodson and others organize the Association for the Study of Negro Life and History in Chicago. *See* **African-American History Month**

March 13—*The Birth of a Nation*, a film that portrays post-Civil War anarchy in a black-ruled South, is released. *See* **Hollywood Black Film Festival**

1916

January—First issue of the *Journal of Negro History* is published by Carter Goodwin Woodson and the Association for the Study of Negro Life and History. *See* **African-American History Month**

1917

April 1—Scott Joplin dies in New York City. *See* **Scott Joplin Ragtime Festival**

1919

January 31—Baseball player Jackie Robinson is born in Cairo, Georgia. *See* **Jackie Robinson Day**

1920

First professional black baseball league is founded by Andrew Foster. *See* **Jackie Robinson Day**

August 29—Musician Charlie Parker is born in Kansas City, Kansas. *See* **Charlie Parker Jazz Festival**

1921

Nate "'Nat" Love dies. *See* **Black Cowboy Parade**

August 11—Alex Haley, author of *Roots*, is born in Ithaca, New York. *See* **Kunta Kinte Heritage Festival**

1923

The *Chicago Defender* is first newspaper in the country to include a special page for children. It is named for the fictional character, Bud Billiken. *See* **Bud Billiken Parade and Picnic**

February 17—Bessie Smith's first record, "Downhearted Blues," is released, selling over 750,000 records in its first month. *See* **Bessie Smith Strut**

June 21—Marcus Garvey is convicted of mail fraud. *See* **Marcus Garvey's Birthday**

1924

November 27—First Turkey Day Classic is held in Montgomery, Alabama, when Alabama State College plays Tuskegee. *See* **Football Classics**

1925

May 19—Malcolm X is born Malcolm Little in Omaha, Nebraska. *See* **Malcolm X's Birthday**

1926

Second week in February—First Negro History Week, created by Carter Goodwin Woodson and the Association for the Study of Negro Life and History, is observed. *See* **African-American History Month**

1927

April 27—Coretta Scott, wife of Martin Luther King Jr., is born in Heiberger, Alabama. *See* **Martin Luther King Jr.'s Birthday**

December—Marcus Garvey is deported to Jamaica. *See* **Marcus Garvey's Birthday**

1929

January 15—Martin Luther King Jr., civil rights leader, is born in Atlanta, Georgia. *See* **Martin Luther King Jr.'s Birthday**

August 11—First Bud Billiken Parade and Picnic for children is held in Chicago, Illinois. *See* **Bud Billiken Parade and Picnic**

November 2—Haile Selassie I is named ruler of Ethiopia. *See* **Haile Selassie's Birthday**

1932

Sallie Martin and Thomas A. Dorsey found the National Convention of Gospel Choirs and Choruses. *See* **Chicago Gospel Music Festival**

1933

Orange Blossom Classic begins as a football contest between Florida A&M and Howard University. *See* **Football Classics**

1936

January 6—Haile Selassie is named *Time* magazine's Man of the Year for 1935. *See* **Haile Selassie's Birthday**

1937

Katherine Dunham establishes Negro Dance Group in Chicago. *See* **DanceAfrica**

September 26—Bessie Smith dies in Clarksdale, Mississippi. *See* **Bessie Smith Strut**

1940

Sallie Martin and Kenneth Morris start a gospel publishing company in Chicago. Martin and Morris, Inc., goes on to become the most prominent publisher of gospel music in the country. *See* **Chicago Gospel Music Festival**

June 10—Marcus Garvey dies in London, England. *See* **Marcus Garvey's Birthday**

1941

The 99th Fighter Squadron, known as the "Tuskegee Experiment," is formed at Alabama's Tuskegee Institute. *See* **Tuskegee Airmen Convention**

W. C. Handy's autobiography, *Father of the Blues*, is published. *See* **W. C. Handy Music Festival**

1942

Zora Neale Hurston's autobiography, *Dirt Tracks on a Road*, is published. *See* **Zora Neale Hurston Festival of the Arts and Humanities**

February 1—First National Freedom Day celebration takes place in Philadelphia, Pennsylvania. *See* **National Freedom Day**

1943

January 5—George Washington Carver dies in Tuskegee, Alabama. *See* **George Washington Carver Day**

1946

Pearl Primus founds a dance company in New York City. *See* **DanceAfrica**

January 12 —Malcolm Little is arrested for burglary in Boston. *See* **Malcolm X's Birthday**

1947

April 15—Jackie Robinson plays in his first major league baseball game. *See* **Jackie Robinson Day**

1948

June 30—President Harry S. Truman signs legislation designating February 1 as National Freedom Day. *See* **Emancipation Day**; **National Freedom Day**

July 26—President Truman issues executive order integrating the military. *See* **Tuskegee Airmen Convention**

1949

April 25—State of New Jersey designates Crispus Attucks Day as a day of observance. *See* **Crispus Attucks Day**

1952

August 7—Malcolm Little is paroled from prison. *See* **Malcolm X's Birthday**

1954

May 17—U.S. Supreme Court declares "separate but equal" educational facilities to be unconstitutional in the decision of *Brown v. Board of Education of Topeka* (Kansas). *See* **African-American History Month**; **Martin Luther King Jr.'s Birthday**

June—Malcolm X becomes minister of New York Temple No. 7 in Harlem. *See* **Malcolm X's Birthday**

October 31—Martin Luther King Jr. becomes pastor of Dexter Avenue Baptist Church in Montgomery, Alabama. *See* **Martin Luther King Jr.'s Birthday**

1955

March 12—Charlie Parker dies in New York City. *See* **Charlie Parker Jazz Festival**

December 1—Rosa Parks is arrested in Montgomery, Alabama, when she refuses to give up her bus seat to a white man. *See* **Martin Luther King Jr.'s Birthday; Rosa Parks Day**

December 5—Black residents of Montgomery, Alabama, led by Martin Luther King Jr., begin a 381-day boycott of city buses. *See* **Martin Luther King Jr.'s Birthday; Rosa Parks Day**

1956

November 13—U.S. Supreme Court upholds ruling that segregation on city bus lines is unconstitutional. *See* **Martin Luther King Jr.'s Birthday; Rosa Parks Day**

December 21—Montgomery bus boycott ends. *See* **Martin Luther King Jr.'s Birthday; Rosa Parks Day**

1957

Malcolm X becomes the national representative for the Nation of Islam. *See* **Malcolm X's Birthday**

1958

Alvin Ailey starts a dance company in New York City. *See* **DanceAfrica**

The Negro American League plays its last games. *See* **Jackie Robinson Day**

March 28—W. C. Handy dies in New York City. *See* **W. C. Handy Music Festival**

1960

January 28—Zora Neale Hurston dies in Fort Pierce, Florida. *See* **Zora Neale Hurston Festival of the Arts and Humanities**

July 17—The George Washington Carver National Monument near Diamond, Missouri, is dedicated. *See* **George Washington Carver Day**

1961

The *Ebony* Museum (later renamed DuSable Museum of African American History) is founded by Margaret and Charles Burroughs and other artists in Chicago, Illinois. *See* **DuSable Museum Arts & Crafts Festival**

The Historic Columbia Foundation is established in Columbia, South Carolina. *See* **Jubilee: Festival of Black History & Culture**

1962

July 23—Jackie Robinson is first African American elected to the Baseball Hall of Fame. *See* **Jackie Robinson Day**

September 22—A centennial celebration of the preliminary emancipation proclamation is held at the Lincoln Memorial in Washington, D.C. *See* **Emancipation Day**

October 22—First NAACP performing arts awards ceremony and fundraiser (later named NAACP Image Awards) is held at the Coconut Grove nightclub in Hollywood, California. *See* **NAACP Image Awards**

1963

April 16—After being jailed for participating in a sit-in, Martin Luther King Jr. appeals to fellow pastors in his "Letter from Birmingham City Jail." *See* **Martin Luther King Jr.'s Birthday**

August 27—W. E. B. Du Bois dies in Accra, Ghana. *See* **Martin Luther King Jr.'s Birthday**

August 28—Martin Luther King Jr. delivers his "I Have a Dream" speech during the March on Washington, which draws over 250,000. *See* **Martin Luther King Jr.'s Birthday**

1964

Malcolm X resigns from the Nation of Islam and founds the Organization of Afro-American Unity and the Muslim Mosque, Inc. *See* **Malcolm X's Birthday**

January 23—The 24th Amendment to the Constitution, ending the poll tax, is ratified by 38 states. *See* **Bridge Crossing Jubilee**

April 3—Malcolm X delivers "The Ballot or the Bullet" speech in Cleveland, Ohio. *See* **Malcolm X's Birthday**

Late April—Malcolm X makes the Hajj, the Muslim pilgrimage to Mecca, Saudi Arabia. *See* **Malcolm X's Birthday**

July 2—U.S. Congress passes the Civil Rights Act of 1964, outlawing discrimination based on a person's color, race, religion, sex, or national origin. *See* **Martin Luther King Jr.'s Birthday**

December 10—Martin Luther King Jr. receives the Nobel Peace Prize in Oslo, Norway. *See* **Martin Luther King Jr.'s Birthday**

1965

February 14—Malcolm X is assassinated by three Nation of Islam members at the Audubon Ballroom in Harlem. *See* **Malcolm X's Birthday**

March 7—Civil rights leaders and others are attacked by police while conducting a peaceful voting rights march at Edmund Pettus Bridge in Selma, Alabama. *See* **Bridge Crossing Jubilee; Martin Luther King Jr.'s Birthday**

March 15—President Lyndon B. Johnson asks Congress to pass a voting rights bill. *See* **Bridge Crossing Jubilee**

March 21—Martin Luther King Jr. and other civil rights activists lead a five-day voting rights march from Selma to Montgomery, Alabama. *See* **Bridge Crossing Jubilee**

August 6—President Johnson signs into law the Voting Rights Act of 1965, which outlaws discriminatory voting practices, such as literacy tests. *See* **Martin Luther King Jr.'s Birthday**

1966

Maulana Karenga, professor of black studies at California State University at Long Beach, creates Kwanzaa. *See* **Kwanzaa**

August 12–14—First Watts Summer Festival is held in Los Angeles, California. *See* **Watts Summer Festival**

1967

Chuck Davis forms dance company in New York. *See* **DanceAfrica**

1968

April 4—Martin Luther King Jr. is assassinated in Memphis, Tennessee. *See* **Martin Luther King Jr.'s Birthday**

April 8—Representative John Conyers of Michigan introduces a bill to create a federal holiday honoring Martin Luther King Jr. *See* **Martin Luther King Jr.'s Birthday**

1969

Abe Snyder and others organize the first African American Day Parade in Harlem. *See* **African American Day Parade**

1970

First Ifa Festival and Yoruba National Convention is held at Oyotunji African Village near Sheldon, South Carolina. *See* **Ifa Festival and Yoruba National Convention**

Indiana Black Expo is founded in Indianapolis. *See* **Indiana Black Expo's Summer Celebration**

First Olokun Festival is held in Oyotunji African Village near Sheldon, South Carolina. *See* **Olokun Festival**

October 17—Stanley Ransom, library director in New York, promotes first national observance of Black Poetry Day. *See* **Black Poetry Day**

1971

May 19—First Malcolm X birthday observance is held at the new Malcolm X Cultural Education Center in Washington, D.C. *See* **Malcolm X's Birthday**

June 19–20—First Indiana Black Expo Summer Celebration is held in Indianapolis. *See* **Indiana Black Expo's Summer Celebration**

July 6—Louis Armstrong dies in Queens, New York. *See* **Satchmo SummerFest**

August 21—Prisoner and activist George L. Jackson, known as one of the Soledad Brothers, is killed by prison guards during an apparent escape attempt. *See* **Black August Benefit Concert**

November 28—First African-American unity celebration of Umoja Karamu is held in Philadelphia, Pennsylvania. *See* **Umoja Karamu**

December 9—William "Bill" Pickett is first black man inducted into the Rodeo Hall of Fame in Oklahoma City. *See* **Bill Pickett Invitational Rodeo**

1972

Tuskegee Airmen, Inc., holds its first convention in Detroit, Michigan, where the group is founded. *See* **Tuskegee Airmen Convention**

Ohio State University establishes a Black Studies Department. *See* **African American Heritage Festival**

October 24—Jackie Robinson dies in Stamford, Connecticut. *See* **Jackie Robinson Day**

1973

December 23—The movie *The Sting* opens in Chicago, sparking the popularity of Scott Joplin's score, "The Entertainer." *See* **Scott Joplin Ragtime Festival**

1974

The DuSable Museum holds its first arts and crafts festival in Chicago. *See* **DuSable Museum Arts & Crafts Festival**

First Harlem Day celebration is held in the Harlem district of New York City. *See* **Harlem Week**

First Scott Joplin Ragtime Festival is held in Sedalia, Missouri. *See* **Scott Joplin Ragtime Festival**

December 2—The campus of Penn Center, on St. Helena Island, South Carolina, is designated anational historical landmark. *See* **Penn Center Heritage Days**

1975

First Oshun Festival (later renamed the Odunde Festival) is held in Philadelphia, Pennsylvania. *See* **Odunde Festival**

August 27—Haile Selassie dies in Ethiopia. *See* **Haile Selassie's Birthday**

October—First Black Cowboy Parade is held in Oakland, California. *See* **Black Cowboy Parade**

1976

Alex Haley's book, *Roots*, is published and becomes a bestseller. *See* **Kunta Kinte Heritage Festival** for

January 23—Paul Robeson dies in Philadelphia, Pennsylvania. *See* **Paul Robeson's Birthday**

February 10—Gerald R. Ford is the first president of the U.S. to issue a proclamation calling the observance of Black History Month. *See* **African-American History Month**

February 20—Robert Hayden is appointed Poet Laureate by the Librarian of Congress and serves until 1978. *See* **Black Poetry Day**

May 4—The Pulitzer committee honors Scott Joplin with a Special Award in Music. *See* **Scott Joplin Ragtime Festival**

1977

February 20—First reenactment of the Battle of Olustee takes place. *See* **Battle of Olustee Reenactment**

June—First DanceAfrica festival is held in Brooklyn, New York. *See* **DanceAfrica**

August—First Goombay Festival takes place in the Coconut Grove neighborhood of Miami, Florida. *See* **Miami Bahamas Junakoo Festival**

August 21–22 —First Georgia Sea Island Festival is held on St. Simons Island. *See* **Georgia Sea Island Festival**

August 28—The city council of Berkeley, California, passes an ordinance designating Malcolm X's birthday as a public holiday. The law becomes effective in 1979. *See* **Malcolm X's Birthday**

1978

First Jubilee Festival of Heritage takes place in Columbia, South Carolina. *See* **Jubilee: Festival of Black History & Culture**

Kenny Gamble and Ed Wright create Black Music Month. *See* **Black Music Month**

September 8—First Mississippi Delta Blues and Heritage Festival is held in Greenville. *See* **Mississippi Delta Blues and Heritage Festival**

1979

May—A block party is held by students at Ohio State University; it continues each year and is later organized as the African-American Heritage Festival. *See* **African American Heritage Festival**

May 16—A. Philip Randolph dies in New York City. *See* **Martin Luther King Jr.'s Birthday**

June 7—President Jimmy Carter declares the first Black Music Month. *See* **Black Music Month**

June 7—Texas legislature passes act making Juneteenth an official state holiday. *See* **Juneteenth**

1981

Walter King, African-American initiate into the Yoruban religious society of Ifa, is crowned a king in Ife, Nigeria. *See* **Ifa Festival and Yoruba National Convention**

February 14–16—First Festival Sundiata is held in Seattle, Washington. *See* **Festival Sundiata**

June 14, 21, 28 and August 4, 11—First Bessie Smith Strut takes place as part of the Five Nights in Chattanooga (later Riverbend Festival) in downtown Chattanooga, Tennessee. *See* **Bessie Smith Strut**

November—Penn Center Heritage Days festival is revived, after a hiatus of over 30 years. *See* **Penn Center Heritage Days**

1982

First Goombay! celebration is held in Asheville, North Carolina. *See* **Goombay!**

Mary Carter Smith of Baltimore, Maryland, and Linda Goss of Philadelphia, Pennsylvania, found the National Association of Black Storytellers. *See* **National Black Storytelling Festival and Conference**

August—First African World Festival in Milwaukee, Wisconsin, takes place. *See* **African World Festival in Milwaukee**

August—First W. C. Handy Music Festival takes place in Florence, Alabama. *See* **W. C. Handy Music Festival**

September 10—First African Street Festival is held in Nashville, Tennessee. *See* **African Street Festival**

1983

First National Black Storytelling Festival takes place in Baltimore, Maryland. *See* **National Black Storytelling Festival and Conference**

Scott Joplin Ragtime Foundation is established. *See* **Scott Joplin Ragtime Festival**

July 1–3—First Rondo Days Celebration is held in St. Paul, Minnesota. *See* **Rondo Days Celebration**

August 26–28—First African World Festival in Detroit, Michigan, takes place. *See* **African World Festival in Detroit**

November 2—U.S. Congress passes legislation to establish a federal holiday to honor Martin Luther King Jr. *See* **Martin Luther King Jr.'s Birthday**

1984

First Chicago Gospel Music Festival is held in Grant Park. *See* **Chicago Gospel Music Festival**

September—First Bill Pickett Invitational Rodeo is held in Denver, Colorado. *See* **Bill Pickett Invitational Rodeo**

Late September to early October—First annual MOJA Festival is held in Charleston, South Carolina. *See* **MOJA Arts Festival**

1985

First Fillmore Jazz Festival is held in San Francisco, California. *See* **Fillmore Jazz Festival**

May—Gwendolyn Brooks is appointed Poet Laureate by the Librarian of Congress and serves until 1986. *See* **Black Poetry Day**

1986

Dorothy I. Height, civil-rights activist, organizes the first Black Family Reunion Celebration in Washington, D.C. *See* **National Black Family Reunion Celebration**

1987

First Kunta Kinte Heritage Festival is held in Crownsville, Maryland. *See* **Kunta Kinte Heritage Festival**

July 26—First Ga-Dangme Homowo Festival of Thanksgiving (later renamed Ghanafest) is held in Chicago. *See* **Ghanafest**

August 21–22—First Denver Black Arts Festival is held. *See* **Colorado Black Arts Festival**

1988

June 13–14, 20–21—First DanceAfrica festival in Washington, D.C., takes place. *See* **DanceAfrica**

June 18—Sallie Martin dies in Chicago. *See* **Chicago Gospel Music Festival**

July—First National Black Arts Festival is held in Atlanta, Georgia. *See* **National Black Arts Festival**

1989

First Kuumba Festival is held in Knoxville, Tennessee. *See* **Kuumba Festival**

January—First Pan African Bookfest is held in Fort Lauderdale, Florida. *See* **Pan African Bookfest and Cultural Conference**

July—First National Black Theatre Festival is held in Winston-Salem, North Carolina. *See* **National Black Theatre Festival**

August—First Harambee Festival is held at Benedict College in Columbia, South Carolina. *See* **Harambee Festival**

December 15—The film *Glory*, which portrays the U.S. Civil War's first all-black volunteer company, is released. *See* **Battle of Olustee Reenactment**

1990

First Homowo Festival is held in Portland, Oregon. *See* **Homowo Festival**

January 26–27—First Zora Neale Hurston Festival of the Arts and Humanities is held in Eatonville, Florida. *See* **Zora Neale Hurston Festival of the Arts and Humanities**

March 13—U.S. Congress passes law designating March 10 as a day to honor Harriet Tubman. *See* **Harriet Tubman Day**

1991

The Elegba Folklore Society begins the annual Down Home Family Reunion in Richmond, Virginia. *See* **Down Home Family Reunion**

May 25—First Black Pride Festival is held in Washington, D.C., to raise money for AIDS patients. *See* **DC Black Pride**

September 28 October 5—First DanceAfrica festival in Chicago takes place. *See* **DanceAfrica**

1992

The Malcolm X Grassroots Movement is formed in Brooklyn, New York. *See* **Black August Benefit Concert**

January 3—Julie Dash's *Daughters of the Dust*, the first feature-length film by an AfricanAmerican woman to receive a wide theatrical release, opens in Chicago. *See* **African American Women in Cinema Film Festival**

February—First Pan African Film & Arts Festival is held in Los Angeles, California. *See* **Pan African Film & Arts Festival**

February 10—Alex Haley dies in Seattle, Washington. *See* **Kunta Kinte Heritage Festival**

July 24—U.S. Congress passes bill designating July 28 as Buffalo Soldiers Day. *See* **Buffalo Soldiers Commemorations**

September 12–13—First African/Caribbean International Festival of Life is held in Chicago. *See* **African/Caribbean International Festival of Life**

1993

May 18—Rita Dove is appointed Poet Laureate by the Librarian of Congress and serves until 1995. *See* **Black Poetry Day**

June 6—First DC Caribbean Carnival is held in Washington, D.C. *See* **DC Caribbean Carnival**

July through August—First African Film Festival is held in New York City. *See* **African Film Festival**

August 29—First Charlie Parker Jazz Festival is held in New York City. Avenue B is renamed "Charlie Parker Place." *See* **Charlie Parker Jazz Festival**

1995

September—First Maafa Commemoration is held in New York City. *See* **Maafa Commemoration**

October 16—Hundreds of thousands of African-American men gather at the National Mall in Washington, D.C., for the Million Man March. *See* **Millions More Movement March**

1996

February—First Native Islander Gullah Celebration is held on Hilton Head Island, South Carolina. *See* **Hilton Head Island Gullah Celebration**

March—First Bridge Crossing Jubilee reenactment in Selma, Alabama, is organized by the National Voting Rights Museum and Institute. *See* **Bridge Crossing Jubilee**

October 20—President Bill Clinton signs law directing U.S. Mint to create a coin honoring Crispus Attucks. *See* **Crispus Attucks Day**

November 12—The town of Nicodemus, Kansas, is designated a national historic site. *See* **Homecoming Emancipation Celebration**

1997

Acapulco Black Film Festival (later renamed the American Black Film Festival) is established by Jeff Friday and others. *See* **American Black Film Festival**

May—First Pan African Festival of Georgia takes place in Macon. *See* **Pan African Festival of Georgia**

1998

First African American Women in Cinema Film Festival is held in New York City. *See* **African American Women in Cinema Film Festival**

August—The Malcolm X Grassroots Movement holds its first concert in New York City. *See* **Black August Benefit Concert**

August 12—U.S. Congress designates February 1 as National Freedom Day. *See* **National Freedom Day**

1999

Fillmore Jazz Preservation District is dedicated in San Francisco, California. *See* **Fillmore Jazz Festival**

First Kwanzaa stamp is issued by the U.S. Postal Service. *See* **Kwanzaa**

Tuskegee University holds first George Washington Carver Convocation, celebrating his life and legacy. *See* **George Washington Carver Day**

February 19–21—First Hollywood Black Film Festival is held. *See* **Hollywood Black Film Festival**

March 27—Charlie Parker is honored during a three-day tribute in his hometown of Kansas City, including the dedication of a memorial statue. *See* **Charlie Parker Jazz Festival**

June 15—Rosa Parks is awarded the Congressional Gold Medal of Honor. *See* **Rosa Parks Day**

2000

St. Simons African-American Heritage Coalition is formed in attempt to stem loss of blackowned historic property on the island. *See* **Georgia Sea Island Festival**

April 27–30—First Denver Pan African Film Festival is held. *See* **Denver Pan African Film Festival**

October 16—Million Families March is held in Washington, D.C., commemorating the fifth anniversary of the Million Man March. *See* **Millions More Movement March**

2001

August 2–5—First Satchmo SummerFest is held in New Orleans, Louisiana. *See* **Satchmo SummerFest**

October 1—A reenactment of the Jerry Rescue takes place in Syracuse, New York, on its 150th anniversary. *See* **Jerry Rescue Day**

2002

Ebo Landing on St. Simons Island, Georgia, is consecrated as holy ground. *See* **Georgia Sea Island Festival**

Acapulco Black Film Festival is renamed the American Black Film Festival and moves to the Miami/South Beach area of Florida. *See* **American Black Film Festival**

August—Georgia Sea Island Festival is revived after a hiatus of several years. *See* **Georgia Sea Island Festival**

August 10–11—First Idlewild Jazz Festival is held in Idlewild, Michigan. *See* **Idlewild Music Festival**

2003

August—AFRAM Festival in Seaford, Delaware, resumes after a four-year hiatus (festival began in the 1990s). *See* **Eastern Shore AFRAM Festival**

2004

First reenactment of the 1854 Sugar Grove Convention takes place in Sugar Grove, Pennsylvania. *See* **Sugar Grove Underground Railroad Convention**

April 15—Major League Baseball designates this day as Jackie Robinson Day. *See* **Jackie Robinson Day**

2005

February 10—Walter King, founder of the Oyotunji African Village near Sheldon, South Carolina, dies. *See* **Ifa Festival and Yoruba National Convention**

March 2—Rachel Robinson accepts Congressional Gold Medal on behalf of her deceased husband, Jackie Robinson. *See* **Jackie Robinson Day**

April 14–17—First observance of Emancipation Day in Washington, D.C., as an official public holiday. *See* **Emancipation Day in Washington, D.C.**

May 10—U.S. Congress passes resolution honoring Tuskegee airmen for bravery during World War II. *See* **Tuskegee Airmen Convention**

May 19—Audubon Ballroom in Harlem is reopened as the Malcolm X and Dr. Betty Shabazz Memorial and Education Center. *See* **Malcolm X's Birthday**

October 14—The Millions More March is held in Washington, D.C., on the 10th anniversary of the Million Man March. *See* **Millions More Movement March**

October 24—Rosa Parks dies in Detroit, Michigan. *See* **Rosa Parks Day**

2006

January 6—Pilgrim Baptist Church in Chicago, considered the birthplace of gospel music, is severely damaged in a fire. *See* **Chicago Gospel Music Festival**

January 30—Coretta Scott King dies in Baja California, Mexico. *See* **Martin Luther King Jr.'s Birthday**

February 28—New Orleans celebrates the 150th anniversary of Mardi Gras observances in the city. *See* **Mardi Gras in African-American Traditions**

March 28—U.S. Congress votes to present Tuskegee airmen with Congressional Gold Medal of Honor. *See* **Tuskegee Airmen Convention**

2007

April 15—President Bush Pays Tribute to Baseball Great Jackie Robinson. *See* **Jackie Robinson Day**

2008

June 17—President Bush Honors Black Music Month. *See* **Black Music Month**

July 30—United States Congress apologizes for slavery and "Jim Crow." *See* **DanceAfrica**

2009

The U.S. Postal Service issues a commemorative stamp in celebration of Kwanzaa. *See* **Kwanzaa**

2013

June 25—The U.S. Supreme Court overturns part of the 1965 Voting Rights Act in Shelby County. *See* **Martin Luther King Jr.'s Birthday**

July 13—George Zimmerman acquitted, provoking nationwide protests. The Black Lives Matter movement is created by Alicia Garza, Patrisse Cullors, and Opal Tometi, in response to the ongoing racial profiling of and police brutality against young black men.. *See* **Watts summer festival**

2015

June 17—Nine African Americans are killed in the Charleston Church Shooting at Emanuel African Methodist Episcopal Church in downtown Charleston, S.C.*See* **Founder's Day/Richard Allen's Birthday**

November 1— Michael Bruce Curry becomes the first African-American Presiding Bishop of the Episcopal Church, having been elected by an overwhelming margin on the first ballot of the 78th General Convention the preceding June. *See* **Founder's Day/Richard Allen's Birthday**

Appendix 2: Calendar of Holidays, Festivals, and Celebrations

This appendix lists each currently observed event in calendar order, followed by the event's location. Events that do not include a location are those that are widely observed around the U.S. Within each month, events that annually occur on the same fixed date are listed irst. These are followed by events that occur throughout the month or events that take place during the month on varying dates each year.

January

Fixed Dates
Jan 1—Emancipation Day
Jan 5—George Washington Carver Day

Non-Fixed Dates
3rd Mon—Martin Luther King Jr.'s Birthday
Last week—Zora Neale Hurston Festival of the Arts and Humanities, Eatonville, FL

February

Fixed Dates
Feb 1—National Freedom Day
Feb 14—Frederick Douglass Day
Feb 20—Buffalo Soldiers Commemorations, MD

Non-Fixed Dates
Month-long—African-American History Month
Month-long—Hilton Head Island Gullah Celebration, Hilton Head Island, SC
Sun closest to or on Feb 14—Founder's Day/Richard Allen's Birthday
Mid-Feb—Battle of Olustee Reenactment, Olustee, FL
3rd weekend—Festival Sundiata, Seattle, WA
Last Sat—Harambee Festival, Columbia, SC
Last weekend—Olokun Festival, Sheldon, SC
Date varies—Pan African Film & Arts Festival, Los Angeles, CA
Date varies—Sistrunk Parade and Festival, Fort Lauderdale, FL

Date varies—AfroSolo Arts Festival, San Francisco, CA
Date varies—IFE-ILE's Afro-Cuban Dance Festival, Miami, FL

March

Fixed Dates
Mar 5—Crispus Attucks Day, Boston, MA; NJ
Mar 10—Harriet Tubman Day

Non-Fixed Dates
1st weekend—Bridge Crossing Jubilee, Selma, AL
Last week—NAACP Image Awards, Los Angeles, CA
Last week—African American Heritage Festival, Columbus, OH
Last week—African American Women in Cinema Film Festival, New York, NY

April

Fixed Dates
Apr 15, on or around—Jackie Robinson Day
Apr 16—Emancipation Day in Washington, DC

Non-Fixed Dates
Last week—Denver Pan African Film Festival, Denver, CO
Last week—Pan African Festival of Georgia, Macon, GA
10 days in Apr or May—Pan African Bookfest and Cultural Conference, Fort
    Lauderdale, FL
Apr through May—African Film Festival, New York, NY

May

Fixed Dates
May 18—Haitian Flag Day
May 20—Emancipation Day, Tallahassee, FL
May 29—Emancipation Day, Upson County, GA

Non-Fixed Dates
Last weekend—DC Black Pride, Washington, DC
Last weekend—DanceAfrica, Brooklyn, NY
10 days in May or Apr—Pan African Bookfest and Cultural Conference, Fort
    Lauderdale, FL
Apr through May—African Film Festival, New York, NY
Date varies—Pinkster, Sleepy Hollow, NY
Last week— Scott Joplin Ragtime Festival, Sedalia, MO
Mother's Day weekend— Sweet Auburn Springfest, Atlanta, GA

June

Fixed Dates
June 19—Juneteenth

Non-Fixed Dates
Month-long—Black Music Month
1st weekend—Chicago Gospel Music Festival, Chicago, IL
2nd Sun—Odunde Festival, Philadelphia, PA
3rd Mon—Bessie Smith Strut, Chattanooga, TN
1st weekend—Georgia Sea Island Festival, St. Simons Island, GA
3rd weekend—Sugar Grove Underground Railroad Convention, Sugar Grove, PA
Date varies—Hollywood Black Film Festival, Hollywood, CA
Date varies—Kuumba Festival, Knoxville, TN
Date varies—Pinkster, Brooklyn, NY
Last weekend—Miami Bahamas Junakoo Festival, Miami, FL

July

Fixed Dates
July 4, five days including—African/Caribbean International Festival of Life, Chicago, IL
July 4, weekend nearest—Fillmore Jazz Festival, San Francisco, CA
July 5—Emancipation Day, Rochester, NY
July 23—Haile Selassie's Birthday
July 28—Buffalo Soldiers Commemorations

Non-Fixed Dates
1st weekend—Ifa Festival and Yoruba National Convention, Sheldon, SC
Mid-July—Colorado Black Arts Festival, Denver, CO
Mid-July—Indiana Black Expo's Summer Celebration, Indianapolis, IN
2nd weekend—DuSable Museum Arts & Crafts Festival, Chicago, IL
2nd weekend, 10 days beginning—National Black Arts Festival, Atlanta, GA
2nd weekend, 10 days beginning— W. C. Handy Music Festival, Florence, AL
3rd weekend—Rondo Days Celebration, St. Paul, MN
Last Sat—Ghanafest, Chicago, IL
Last week in odd-numbered years—National Black Theatre Festival, Winston-Salem, NC
Last weekend—Homecoming Emancipation Celebration, Nicodemus, KS
Date varies—American Black Film Festival, Miami/South Beach, FL
2nd weekend—DC Caribbean Carnival, Washington, DC
2nd weekend—Idlewild Music Festival, Idlewild, MI

August

Fixed Dates

Aug 1—West Indies Emancipation Day
Aug 17—Marcus Garvey's Birthday

Non-Fixed Dates

Month-long—Harlem Week, New York, NY
Early Aug—Emancipation Day in Hutchinson, KS
Early Aug—Satchmo SummerFest, New Orleans, LA
1st weekend—African World Festival in Milwaukee, WI
2nd Sat—Bud Billiken Parade and Picnic, Chicago, IL
2nd weekend—Eastern Shore AFRAM Festival, Seaford, DE
2nd weekend—Watts Summer Festival, Los Angeles, CA
3rd weekend—African World Festival in Detroit, MI
3rd weekend—Down Home Family Reunion, Richmond, VA
Last weekend—August Quarterly, Wilmington, DE
Last weekend—Charlie Parker Jazz Festival, New York, NY
Date varies—Black August Benefit Concert, New York, NY
Date varies—Homowo Festival, Portland, OR
Date varies—National Black Family Reunion Celebration, Rockford, IL
First weekend—Black Arts Fest MKE, Milwaukee, WI

September

Fixed Dates

Sep 17—Frederick Douglass Day, New Bedford, MA

Non-Fixed Dates

1st Mon—J'Ouvert Celebration and West Indian-American Day Carnival, Brooklyn, NY
1st week—National Baptist Convention, USA, Annual Session
2nd weekend—National Black Family Reunion Celebration, Washington, DC
3rd Sat—Mississippi Delta Blues and Heritage Festival, Greenville, MS
3rd Sun—African American Day Parade, New York, NY
2nd and 3rd week—Maafa Commemoration, Brooklyn, NY
3rd weekend—African Street Festival, Nashville, TN
Late Sep—Kunta Kinte Heritage Festival, Crownsville, MD
Late Sep to early Oct—MOJA Arts Festival, Charleston, SC
Date varies—Goombay!, Asheville, NC
Last weekend—Jubilee: Festival of Black History & Culture, Columbia, SC
First weekend—The African American Cultural Festival of Raleigh and Wake County, Raleigh, NC

October
Fixed Dates
Oct 1—Jerry Rescue Day, Syracuse, NY

Non-Fixed Dates
1st Sat—Black Cowboy Parade, Oakland, CA
Late Oct—DanceAfrica, Chicago, IL

November
Fixed Dates
Nov 1—Emancipation Day, MD

Non-Fixed Dates
Mid-Nov—National Black Storytelling Festival and Conference
2nd weekend—Penn Center Heritage Days, St. Helena Island, SC
4th Sun—Umoja Karamu
Nov through Feb—Bill Pickett Invitational Rodeo

December
Fixed Dates
Dec 1—Rosa Parks Day
Dec 26 to Jan 1—Kwanzaa
Dec 31—Watch Night

Appendix 3: Geographical List of Holidays, Festivals, and Celebrations

This appendix lists currently observed events by the state(s) in which they take place, as discussed in this volume. Under each state, events that are official state holidays or observances are listed first, followed by events observed in cities within the state.

Alabama

Florence—W. C. Handy Music Festival, last week in July
Selma—Bridge Crossing Jubilee, four days in Mar, including 1st weekend
Tuskegee—George Washington Carver Day, Jan 5

Alaska

Official state observance—Juneteenth, June 19

Arkansas

Official state observance—Juneteenth, June 19

California

Official state observance—Juneteenth, June 19

Berkeley—Malcolm X's Birthday, May 19
Hollywood—Hollywood Black Film Festival, one week in June
Los Angeles—Kwanzaa, Dec 26 – Jan 1
Los Angeles—NAACP Image Awards, Feb
Los Angeles—Pan African Film & Arts Festival, Feb
Los Angeles—Watts Summer Festival, 2nd weekend in Aug
Oakland—Black Cowboy Parade, 1st Sat in Oct
Oakland—Malcolm X's Birthday, May 19
Sacramento—Martin Luther King Jr.'s Birthday, 3rd Mon in Jan
San Francisco—AfroSolo Arts Festival, February
San Francisco—Fillmore Jazz Festival, weekend nearest July 4

Colorado

Denver—Colorado Black Arts Festival, five days in July
Denver—Denver Pan African Film Festival, last week in Apr

Connecticut

Official state observance—Juneteenth, June 19

Delaware

Official state observance—Juneteenth, June 19

Seaford—Eastern Shore AFRAM Festival, 2nd weekend in Aug
Wilmington—August Quarterly, Third weekend in Aug

District of Columbia

Official district holiday—Emancipation Day in Washington, D.C., Apr 16

Black Music Month, June
DC Black Pride, Last weekend in May
Church Homecomings, Sep
DanceAfrica, 2nd week in June
DC Caribbean Carnival, 2nd week of July
Frederick Douglass Day, Feb 14
Juneteenth, June 19
Malcolm X's Birthday, May 19
Martin Luther King Jr.'s Birthday, 3rd Mon in Jan
National Black Family Reunion Celebration, 2nd weekend in Sep

Florida

Official state observance—Juneteenth, June 19

Buena Vista—Black Music Month, June
Delray Beach—Haitian Flag Day, May 18
Eatonville—Zora Neale Hurston Festival of the Arts and Humanities, last week in Jan
Fort Lauderdale—Haitian Flag Day, May 18
Fort Lauderdale—Pan African Bookfest and Cultural Conference, 10 days in Apr or May
Fort Lauderdale—Sistrunk Parade and Festival, February
Fort Myers—Haitian Flag Day, May 18
Miami—American Black Film Festival, five days in July
Miami—Haitian Flag Day, May 18
Miami—IFE-ILE's Afro-Cuban Dance Festival, February

Miami—Miami Bahamas Junakoo Festival, last weekend in June
Olustee—Battle of Olustee Reenactment, mid-Feb
St. Petersburg—Martin Luther King Jr.'s Birthday, 3rd Mon in Jan
Tallahassee—Emancipation Day, May 20
Tampa—Haitian Flag Day, May 18

Georgia

Atlanta—Martin Luther King Jr.'s Birthday, 3rd Mon in Jan
Atlanta—National Black Arts Festival, 10 days beginning 3rd weekend in July
Atlanta—Sweet Auburn Springfest, Mother's day weekend in May
Bolden—Watch Night, Dec 31
Macon—Pan African Festival of Georgia, last week in Apr
St. Simons Island—Georgia Sea Island Festival, First week of June
Savannah—Founder's Day/Richard Allen's Birthday, Sun closest to or
    on Feb 14
Upson County—Emancipation Day, May 29

Idaho

Official state observance—Juneteenth, June 19

Illinois

Official state observance—Juneteenth, June 19

Chicago—African/Caribbean International Festival of Life, five days
    including July 4
Chicago—Bud Billiken Parade and Picnic, 2nd Sat in Aug
Chicago—Chicago Gospel Music Festival, 1st weekend in June
Chicago—DanceAfrica, late Oct
Chicago—DuSable Museum Arts & Crafts Festival, 2nd weekend in July
Chicago—Ghanafest, last Sat in July
Chicago—Kwanzaa, Dec 26 to Jan 1
Rockford—National Black Family Reunion Celebration, Aug

Indiana

Bloomington—Juneteenth, June 19
Indianapolis—Indiana Black Expo's Summer Celebration, mid-July
Roberts Settlement—Church Homecomings, July 4

Iowa

Official state observance—Juneteenth, June 19

Kansas

Hutchinson—Emancipation Day in Hutchinson, Kansas, early Aug
Kansas City—Juneteenth, June 19
Nicodemus—Homecoming Emancipation Celebration, last weekend in July
Topeka—Juneteenth, June 19
Wichita—Juneteenth, June 19

Kentucky

Official state observance—Juneteenth, June 19

Louisiana

Official state observance—Juneteenth, June 19

New Orleans—Mardi Gras in African-American Traditions, two weeks before the beginning of Lent
New Orleans—Satchmo SummerFest, Three days in early Aug

Maryland

Official state observance—Buffalo Soldiers Commemorations, July 28

Official state observance—Emancipation Day, January 1, September 22, and Other Dates
Annapolis—Kunta Kinte Heritage Festival, late Sep
Dorchester County—Harriet Tubman Day, Mar 10
Rockville—Martin Luther King Jr.'s Birthday, 3rd Mon in Jan

Massachusetts

Boston—Crispus Attucks Day, Mar 5
Boston—Haitian Flag Day, May 18
New Bedford—Frederick Douglass Day, Feb 14; Sep 17

Michigan

Official state observance—Juneteenth, June 19

Detroit—African World Festival in Detroit, 3rd weekend in Aug
Detroit—Black Music Month, June
Detroit—Martin Luther King Jr.'s Birthday, 3rd Mon in Jan
Detroit—Rosa Parks Day, Dec 1
Idlewild—Idlewild Music Festival, Second weekend of July

Minnesota

St. Paul—Rondo Days Celebration, 3rd weekend in July

Mississippi

Greenville—Mississippi Delta Blues and Heritage Festival, 3rd Sat in Sep
Natchez—Juneteenth, June 19

Missouri

Official state observance—Juneteenth, June 19

Sedalia—Scott Joplin Ragtime Festival, Last week of May

New Jersey

Official state observance—Crispus Attucks Day, Mar 5
Official state observance—Juneteenth, June 19

New Mexico

Official state observance—Juneteenth, June 19

New York

Official state observance—Juneteenth, June 19

Albany—Martin Luther King Jr.'s Birthday, 3rd Mon in Jan
Auburn—Harriet Tubman Day, Mar 10
Brooklyn—DanceAfrica, Memorial Day weekend in May
Brooklyn—J'Ouvert Celebration and West Indian-American Day Carnival, 1st Mon
in Sep
Brooklyn—Maafa Commemoration, 3rd week in Sep
Brooklyn—Pinkster, June
New York—African American Day Parade, 3rd Sun in Sep
New York—African American Women in Cinema Film Festival, three days
in late Oct
New York—African Film Festival, Apr through May
New York—Black August Benefit Concert, Aug
New York—Black Music Month, June
New York—Charlie Parker Jazz Festival, weekend in late Aug
New York—Haitian Flag Day, May 18
New York—Harlem Week, July through Aug
New York—Kwanzaa, Dec 26 to Jan 1
New York—Malcolm X's Birthday, May 19

New York—Marcus Garvey's Birthday, Aug 17
New York—Rosa Parks Day, Dec 1
Rochester—Emancipation Day, July 5
Sleepy Hollow—Pinkster, May
Syracuse—Jerry Rescue Day, Oct 1

North Carolina

Asheville—Goombay!, Sep
Raleigh—Martin Luther King Jr.'s Birthday, 3rd Mon in Jan
Raleigh—The African American Cultural Festival of Raleigh and Wake County, 1st weekend in Sep
Winston-Salem—National Black Theatre Festival, last week in July during odd-numbered years

Ohio

Cincinnati—National Black Family Reunion Celebration, 2nd weekend in Sep
Columbus—African American Heritage Festival, last week in March
Gallia County—Emancipation Day, Sep 22

Oklahoma

Official state observance—Juneteenth, June 19

Oregon

Portland—Homowo Festival, one day in Aug

Pennsylvania

Philadelphia—Founder's Day/Richard Allen's Birthday, Sun closest to or on Feb 14
Philadelphia—National Freedom Day, Feb 1
Philadelphia—Odunde Festival, 2nd Sun in June
Philadelphia —Umoja Karamu, 4th Sun in Nov
Sugar Grove—Sugar Grove Underground Railroad Convention, 3rd weekend in June

South Carolina

Charleston—MOJA Arts Festival, late Sep to early Oct
Columbia—Harambee Festival, last Sat in Feb
Columbia—Jubilee: Festival of Black History & Culture, last weekend in Sep
Hilton Head Island—Hilton Head Island Gullah Celebration, Feb

St. Helena Island—Penn Center Heritage Days, 2nd weekend in Nov
Sheldon—Ifa Festival and Yoruba National Convention, 1st weekend in July
Sheldon—Olokun Festival, last weekend in Feb

Tennessee

Chattanooga—Bessie Smith Strut, 3rd Mon in June
Knoxville—Kuumba Festival, three days in early June
Nashville—African Street Festival, 3rd weekend in Sep
Nashville—Black Music Month, June

Texas

Official state observance—Juneteenth, June 19

Austin—Juneteenth, June 19
Denton—Juneteenth, June 19
Galveston—Juneteenth, June 19

Virginia

Richmond—Down Home Family Reunion, 3rd weekend in Aug
Richmond—Kwanzaa, Dec 26 to Jan 1

Washington

Seattle—Festival Sundiata, mid-June

Wisconsin

Milwaukee—African World Festival, 1st weekend in Aug
Milwaukee—Black Arts Fest MKE, 1st weekend in Aug
Milwaukee—Marcus Garvey's Birthday, Aug 17

Wyoming

Official state observance—Juneteenth, June 19

Bibliography

Bibliography

This Bibliography lists books and articles consulted in the preparation of this volume.

Aberjhani, and Sandra L. West. *Encyclopedia of the Harlem Renaissance*. New York: Facts on File, 2003.

Abernethy, Francis Edward, ed. *Juneteenth Texas: Essays in African American Folklore*. Denton: University of North Texas Press, 1996.

Abrahams, Roger D. *Singing the Master*. New York: Penguin Books, 1992.

Acosta, Teresa Palomo. "Juneteenth." *Handbook of Texas Online*. Austin: The General Libraries at the University of Texas at Austin and the Texas State Historical Association, 1999. http://www.tsha.utexas.edu/handbook/online/articles/JJ/lkj1.html.

Adams, Virginia M., ed. *On the Altar of Freedom: A Black Soldier's Civil War Letters from the Front*. New York: Warner Books, 1991.

Adero, Malaika. *Up South: Stories, Studies, and Letters of This Century's African American Migrations*. New York: The New Press, 1994.

"African American Religious Leaders." *New York Public Library African American Desk Reference*. New York: John Wiley & Sons, 1999.

Albee, Edward. *The American Dream, The Death of Bessie Smith and Fam & Yam*. New York: Dramatists Play Service Inc., 1962.

Albertson, Chris. *Bessie*. New Haven, CT: Yale University Press, 2003.

Albertson, Chris, and Gunther Schuller. *Bessie Smith: Empress of the Blues*. New York: Schirmer Books, 1975.

Allen, Ray, and Lois Wilcken, eds. *Island Sounds in the Global City: Caribbean Popular Music and Identity in New York*. Urbana: University of Illinois Press, 2002.

Allen, Richard. *The Life, Experience, and Gospel Labours of the Rt. Rev. Richard Allen. To Which is Annexed the Rise and Progress of the African Methodist Episcopal Church in the United States of America. Containing a Narrative of the Yellow Fever in the Year of Our Lord 1793: With an Address to the People of Colour in the United States. Written by Himself*. Philadelphia: Martin & Boden, 1833.

521

Anderson, S. E. *The Black Holocaust for Beginners.* New York: Writers and Readers Publishing, 1995.

Annual Report: Indiana Black Expo, Inc.: Continuing the Legacy, 2005. http://www.indianablackexpo.com/pdf/Annual%20Report%202005%20Final.pdf.

Anthony, Michael. "The First Emancipation Day." *Trinidad Guardian,* August 27, 1998. http://www.nalis.gov.tt/Festivals/emancipation_day.html.

Anyike, James C. *African American Holidays: A Historical Research and Resource Guide to Cultural Celebrations.* Chicago: Popular Truth, 1991.

Appiah, Kwame Anthony, and Henry Louis Gates Jr., eds. *Africana: The Encyclopedia of the African and African American Experience: The Concise Desk Reference.* Philadelphia: Running Press, 2003.

———. *The New Africana: Encyclopedia of the African and African American Experience.* 5 vols. New York: Oxford University Press, 2005.

Aptheker, Herbert. *American Negro Slave Revolts.* 5th ed. New York: International Publishers, 1987.

Arching, Gerard. *Masking and Power: Carnival and Popular Culture in the Caribbean.* Minneapolis: University of Minnesota Press, 2002.

Armes, Roy. *Postcolonial Images: Studies in North African Film.* Bloomington: Indiana University Press, 2005.

Armstrong, Louis. *Satchmo: My Life in New Orleans.* New York: Prentice-Hall, 1954.

———. *Swing That Music.* Introduction by Rudy Vallee. New York: Longmans, Green and Company, 1936.

Arnesen, Eric J. *Black Protest and the Great Migration: A Brief History with Documents.* Boston: Bedford Book/St. Martin's, 2002.

Asante, Melefi K., and Mark T. Mattson. *The African-American Atlas: Black History and Culture—An Illustrated Reference.* New York: Simon & Schuster/Macmillan, 1998.

Attoun, Marti. "The Spirit of Nicodemus." *American Profile,* January 26–February 1, 2003. http://www.americanprofile.com/issues/20030126/20030126_2765.asp.

Auguste, Wilner. "Gearing Up for a Month-Long Celebration of Haitian Pride." *Dorchester Reporter* (Boston, MA), April 9, 2005. http://www.bostonneighborhoodnews.com/comment.html.

Baldwin, Lewis V. *"Invisible" Strands in African Methodism: A History of the African Union Methodist Protestant and Union American Methodist Episcopal Churches, 1805–1980.* Metuchen, NJ, and London: The American Theological Library Association and The Scarecrow Press, 1983.

———. *The Mark of a Man: Peter Spencer and the African Union Methodist Tradition.* Lanham, MD: University Press of America, 1987.

Banham, Martin, Errol Hill, and George Woodyard, eds. *Cambridge Guide to African and Caribbean Theatre*. New York: Cambridge University Press, 2005.

Banks, William H., Jr. *Beloved Harlem: A Literary Tribute to Black America's Most Famous Neighborhood, From the Classics to the Contemporary*. New York: Doubleday-Broadway/Harlem Moon, 2005.

Banner, Ellen M. "Festival Sundiata Brings African-American Community Together." *The Seattle Times*, February 20, 2006. http://seattletimes.nwsource.com/html/home/

"Baptists." In *Encyclopedia of Black America*, edited by W. Augustus Low and Virgil A. Clift. New York: McGraw-Hill Book Company, 1981.

Barashango, Ishakamusa. *African People and European Holidays: A Mental Genocide, Book 1*. Washington, DC: IVth Dynasty Publishing Company, 1979.

Barlas, Robert. *Cultures of the World: Bahamas*. New York: Marshall Cavendish, 2000.

Barnes, Sandra T. *Africa's Ogun: Old World and New*. 2nd ed. Bloomington: Indiana University Press, 1997.

Barr, Cameron W. "DC Rally a Tribute to the Passion of a Million." *Washington Post*, October 16, 2005. http://www.washingtonpost.com/wp-dyn/content/article/2005/10/15/AR2005101501496.html.

Barret, Leonard E. *The Rastafarians*. Boston: Beacon Press, 1997.

Bates, Angela. "The Kansas African-American History Trail." Reprinted courtesy of the Kansas Department of Commerce. *Kansas Magazine, 3rd Issue*, 1994. http://crm.cr.nps.gov/archive/19–2/19-2-13.pdf.

Bates-Rudd, Rhonda. "Rhythms of the African World: Detroit Brings Out the Best of Art, Music, Clothing and Food to Celebrate Cultures." *The Detroit News*, August 18, 1999.

Bell, Bernard W., Emily R. Grosholz, and James B. Stewart, eds. *W. E. B. Du Bois on Race and Culture: Philosophy, Politics, and Poetics*. New York: Routledge, 1996.

Bellecourt, Vernon. "The Glorification of Buffalo Soldiers Raises Racial Divisions between Blacks, Indians." *Indian Country Today*, May 4, 1994.

Bellenir, Karen, ed. *Religious Holidays and Calendars: An Encyclopedic Handbook*. 3rd ed. Detroit: Omnigraphics, 2004.

Bennett, Lerone, Jr. "Harriet Tubman's Private War: Iconic Freedom Fighter Waged Unremitting Struggle Against the Slave System." *Ebony*, March 2005.

Bentley, Judith. *Harriet Tubman*. New York: Franklin Watts, 1990. (young adult)

Berlin, Edward A. *King of Ragtime: Scott Joplin and His Era*. New York: Oxford University Press, 1996.

Berlin, Ira, Mark Favreau, and Steven Miller, eds. *Remembering Slavery: African Americans Talk about Their Personal Experiences of Slavery and Freedom*. New York: The New Press, 1998.

Best, Wallace. "Bud Billiken Day Parade." *Encyclopedia of Chicago*. Chicago: Chicago Historical Society, Newberry Library, and Northwestern University, 2005. http://www.encyclopedia.chicagohistory.org/pages/175.html.

Bibbs, Rebecca. "Looking Up – IBE President Joyce Rogers Sets Her Sights on a Higher Level." *Indianapolis Woman Magazine*, October 2005. http://www.indianapoliswoman.com/covergallery/05/oct.html.

Biden, Joseph R., Jr. Floor Statement: The Big Quarterly, August 1, 2002. http://biden.senate.gov/newsroom/details.cfm?id=188532&&.

Billington, Monroe Lee. *New Mexico's Buffalo Soldiers, 1866–1900*. Boulder: University Press of Colorado, 1991.

Black, Albert W. *The Other Holocaust: The Sociology and History of African Americans, Vol. I.*Boston: Pearson Custom Publishing, 2002.

"Black Men Converge on Washington for Rally." *USA Today*, updated February 16, 1996. http://www.usatoday.com/news/index/nman010.htm.

"Black Poetry Day." In *Holidays, Festivals, and Celebrations of the World Dictionary*, edited by Helene Henderson. 3rd ed. Detroit: Omnigraphics, 2005.

Blatt, Martin Henry, Thomas J. Brown, and Donald Yacovone, eds. *Hope and Glory: Essays on the Legacy of the 54th Massachusetts Regiment*. Amherst: University of Massachusetts Press, 2000.

Blight, David W. "Emancipation." In *The African-American Experience: Selections from the Five-Volume Macmillan Encyclopedia of African-American Culture and History*, edited by Jack Salzman. New York: Macmillan, 1998.

"Blues." In *Encyclopedia of Black America*, edited by W. Augustus Low and Virgil A. Clift. New York: McGraw-Hill Book Company, 1981.

Bordewich, Fergus M. *Bound for Canaan: The Underground Railroad and the War for the Soul of America*. New York: HarperCollins/Amistad Press, 2005.

Bowers, Detine L. "A Place to Stand: African-Americans and the First of August Platform." *The Southern Communication Journal*, Summer 1995.

Boyd, Melissa D. "Remembering Rondo." *Star Tribune* (Minneapolis, MN), July 20, 2001.

Boyd, Valerie. *Wrapped in Rainbows: The Life of Zora Neale Hurston*. New York: Scribner, 2003.

Boyer, Horace Clarence. "Gospel Music." In *The African-American Experience: Selections from the Five-Volume Macmillan Encyclopedia of African-American Culture and History*, edited by Jack Salzman. New York: Macmillan, 1998.

Brachear, Manya A. "Black Baptists Forge Agenda: Focus on Schools, Jobs, Health Care." *Chicago Tribune*, January 28, 2005.

Bradford, Sarah H. *Harriet Tubman: The Moses of Her People*. Auburn, NY: W. J. Moses, Printer, 1869.

Bradley, Patricia. *Slavery, Propaganda, and the American Revolution.* Jackson: University Press of Mississippi, 1999.

Branch, Muriel Miller. *The Water Brought Us: Story of the Gullah Speaking People.* Orangeburg, SC: Sandlapper Publishing Company, 2005. (young adult)

Branch, Taylor. *At Canaan's Edge: America in the King Years, 1965–68.* New York: Simon & Schuster, 2006.

———. *Parting the Waters: America in the King Years, 1954–63.* New York: Simon & Schuster, 1988.

———. *Pillar of Fire: America in the King Years, 1963–65.* New York: Simon & Schuster, 1998.

Brandon, George. *Santería from Africa to the New World: The Dead Sell Memories.* Bloomington: Indiana University Press, 1997.

Breitman, George, ed. *Malcolm X Speaks.* New York: Grove Press, 1966.

Brinkley, Douglas G. *Rosa Parks.* New York: Viking Penguin, 2000.

Brothers, Thomas. *Louis Armstrong's New Orleans.* New York: W. W. Norton & Company, 2006.

Broussard, Antoinette. *African-American Celebrations and Holiday Traditions: Celebrating with Passion, Style, and Grace.* New York: Citadel Press, 2004.

Brown, Luther. "The Image Awards Turn 30." *The New Crisis,* December 1998. http://www.findarticles.com/p/articles/mi_qa3812/is_199812/ai_n8817192.

Brown, Scot. *Fighting for US: Maulana Karenga, the US Organization, and Black Cultural Nationalism.* New York: New York University Press, 2003.

Buckmaster, Henrietta. *Let My People Go: The Story of the Underground Railroad and the Growth of the Abolition Movement.* Columbia: University of South Carolina Press, 1992.

Burchard, Peter. *One Gallant Rush: Robert Gould Shaw and His Brave Black Regiment.* New York: St. Martin's Press, 1990.

Burgan, Michael. *Escaping to Freedom: The Underground Railroad.* New York: Facts on File, 2006. (young adult)

Burger, Mark. "Behind the Scenes: Technical Crew Prepares Path for the National Black Theater Festival." *Winston-Salem Journal,* July 31, 2005.

Burns, Ken C., and Geoffery C. Ward. *Jazz: A History of America's Music.* New York: Knopf, 2002.

Burroughs, Tony. *Black Roots: A Beginner's Guide to Tracing the African American Family Tree.* New York: Simon & Schuster, 2001.

Butler, Anne. "Historic African-American Church in West Feliciana Still Making a Joyful Noise Unto the Lord." Town of Francisville, LA, 2005. http://www.stfrancisville.net/town/news/afton2005.html.

Butler, Ron. "The Buffalo Soldier, A Shining Light in the Military History of the American West." *Arizona Highways,* March 1972.

Cannon, Angie. "Secret Paths to Freedom." *Philadelphia Inquirer*, February 24, 2002.

Cantor, George. *Historic Landmarks of Black America*. Detroit: Gale Research, 1991.

Carlin, Richard. "Handy, W. C." In *African American Lives*, edited by Henry Louis Gates Jr. and Evelyn Brooks Higginbotham. New York: Oxford University Press, 2004.

Carr, Robert T. *Black Nationals in the New World: Reading the African-American and West Indian Experience*. Durham, NC: Duke University Press, 2002.

Chambers, Melanie. "The History of the Black Family Reunion." *The Hilltop-Metro* (Howard University, Washington, DC), September 6, 2005. http://www.thehilltoponline.com.

Charles, Jacqueline. "Parties, Protests Mark Haiti Flag." *Miami Herald*, May 18, 2005. "Charlie Parker Memorial Issue." *Down Beat*, March 11, 1965.

Chieni, Susan Njeri. *The Harambee Movement in Kenya: The Role Played By Kenyans and the Government in the Politics of Education and Other Social Services*. Department of Educational Foundations, Moi University, Kenya, Institute of Distance Education, 1998, last modified April 26, 1999. http://boleswa97.tripod.com/chieni.htm.

Christian, Charles M., ed. *Black Saga: The African American Experience—A Chronology*. Washington, DC: Counterpoint, 1999.

Chu, Daniel, and Bill Shaw. *Going Home to Nicodemus: The Story of an African American Frontier Town and the Pioneers Who Settled It*. Parsippany, NJ: J. Messner, 1994. (young adult)

Clarke, Kamari Maxine. *Mapping Yoruba Networks: Power and Agency in the Making of Transnational Communities*. Durham, NC: Duke University Press, 2004.

Clayborne, Carson. "King, Martin Luther, Jr." In *African American Lives*, edited by Henry Louis Gates Jr. and Evelyn Brooks Higginbotham. New York: Oxford University Press, 2004.

Clinton, Catherine. *Harriet Tubman: The Road to Freedom*. New York: Little, Brown and Company, 2004.

———. "On the Road to Harriet Tubman: She Has Become One of the Most Famous of All American Women, But to the Biographer She Is a Tantalizingly Elusive Quarry." *American Heritage*, June–July 2004.

Coakley, Joyce. *Sweetgrass Baskets and the Gullah Tradition*. Mount Pleasant, SC: Arcadia Publishing, 2006.

Colaiaco, James A. *Martin Luther King, Jr.: Apostle of Militant Nonviolence*. New York: St. Martin's Press, 1988.

Coleman, Stan. "Sharing the Legacy: Reservists Connect with the Past at Tuskegee Airmen Gathering." *Citizen Airman*, October 2004.

Collier, Adore. "The Man Who Invented Kwanzaa." *Ebony*, January 1998.

Cone, James H. *Martin and Malcolm and America: A Dream or a Nightmare.* Maryknoll, NY: Orbis Books, 1992.

Cooper, Desiree. "Black Sorority Sisters Epitomize Citizenship." *Detroit Free Press*, July 11, 2006.

Cose, Ellis. *Bone to Pick: Of Forgiveness, Reconciliation, Reparation, and Revenge.* New York: Simon & Schuster, 2005.

Cox, Clinton. *Undying Glory: The Story of the Massachusetts 54th Regiment.* New York: Scholastic, 1993. (young adult)

Craft, William, and Ellen Craft. *Running a Thousand Miles for Freedom; or, The Escape of William and Ellen Craft from Slavery.* London: William Tweedie, 1860. Electronic Text Center. University of Virginia Library, Charlottesville, 1999. http://etext.lib.virginia.edu/toc/modeng/public/CraThou.html.

Cronon, E. David. *Black Moses: The Story of Marcus Garvey and the Negro Improvement Association.* Foreword by John Hope Franklin. Madison: University of Wisconsin Press, 1969.

Cunningham, Michael, and Craig Marbarry. *Spirit of Harlem: A Portrait of America's Most Exciting Neighborhood.* New York: Doubleday, 2003.

Curry, Mary Cuthrell. *Making the Gods in New York: The Yoruba Religion in the African American Community.* New York: Garland, 1997.

Curtis, Nancy C. *Black Heritage Sites: The North.* New York: The New Press, 1996.

———. *Black Heritage Sites: The South.* New York: The New Press, 1996.

Curtis, Susan. *Dancing to a Black Man's Tune: A Life of Scott Joplin.* Columbia: University of Missouri Press, 2004.

Darden, Robert. *People Get Ready: A New History of Black Gospel Music.* Chicago: Continuum International Publishing Group, 2004.

Dash, Julie, with Toni Cade Bambara and bell hooks. *Daughters of the Dust: The Making of an African American Woman's Film.* New York: The New Press, 1992.

Davis, Angela Y. *Blues Legacies and Black Feminism: Gertrude 'Ma' Rainey, Bessie Smith, and Billie Holiday.* New York: Random House, 1998.

De La Torre, Miguel A. *Santería: The Beliefs and Rituals of a Growing Religion in America.* Grand Rapids, MI: William B. Eerdmans Publishing Company, 2004.

Deck, Alice A. "Zora Neale Hurston." In *Black Heroes*, edited by Jessie Carney Smith. Foreword by Nikki Giovanni. Canton, MI: Visible Ink Press, 2001.

Degiglio-Bellemare, Mario. "Cuba: Santería, Scarcity, and Survival." *Catholic New Times*, February 13, 2005.

Demaline, Jackie. "Black Theater Festival Organizers Aim Higher." *The Cincinnati Enquirer*, August 19, 2001. http://www.enquirer.com/editions/2001/08/19/tem_black_theater.html.

Denenberg, Barry. *Stealing Home: The Story of Jackie Robinson.* New York: Scholastic, 1990. (young adult)

Denvergov.org. "Denver Black Arts Festival Celebrates Heritage," press release, July 9, 2001. http://www.denvergov.com/newsarticle.asp?id=2821.

———. "Daring, Fresh Films Featured at Pan African Festival," press release, April 10, 2002. http://www.denvergov.org/newsarticle.asp?id=4032.

Dernerstein, Robert. "Award, Family Await Cheadle in Denver." *Rocky Mountain News* (Denver), April 29, 2005. http://www.rockymountainnews.com/drmn/spotlight_columnists/article/0,2777,DRMN_23962_3740612,00.html.

Dewan, Shaila. "A Six-Day Bash Celebrates Black Theater." *The New York Times,* August 6, 2005.

Dickerson, Amina J. "DuSable Museum." *Encyclopedia of Chicago.* Chicago: Chicago Historical Society, Newberry Library, and Northwestern University, 2005. http://www.encyclopedia.chicagohistory.org/pages/398.html.

Diver-Stamnes, Anne C. *Lives in the Balance: Youth, Poverty, and Education in Watts.* Albany: State University of New York Press, 1995.

Dodson, John. "Religion and Dry Fork." Bland County (Virginia) History Archives, 2000. http://www.bland.k12.va.us/bland/rocky/dryfork/dfreligion.html.

Douglass, Frederick. *Life and Times of Frederick Douglass.* Hartford, CT: Park Publishing Company, 1881.

———. *Narrative of the Life of Frederick Douglass, An American Slave, Written by Himself.* Boston: Anti-Slavery Office, 1845.

———. "The Meaning of the Fourth of July for the Negro, Speech at Rochester, New York, July 5, 1852." In *The Life and Writings of Frederick Douglass, Volume II: Pre-Civil War Decade, 1850–1960,* by Philip S. Foner. New York: International Publishers Co., 1950.

———. Letter to W. J. Watkins, Esq. Appearing in the *Frederick Douglass' Paper,* Rochester, New York, June 23, 1854.

Duberman, Martin. *Paul Robeson.* New York: The New Press, 1995.

Dudley, Shannon. *Carnival Music in Trinidad: Experiencing Music, Expressing Culture.* New York: Oxford University Press, 2003.

Edgar, Walter. *South Carolina: A History.* Columbia: University of South Carolina Press, 1998.

Edward, Gary, and John Mason. *Black Gods: Orisa Studies in the New World.* Brooklyn, NY: Yoruba Theological Archministry, 1998.

Edwards, Holly. "African Festival 'Feels Like Family'." *The Tennessean,* September 19, 2004.

Ehrenstein, David. "Sisters with Cameras: Director Yvonne Welbon Talks about Discovering the Advantage Lesbian Directors Have Over Their Straight Counterparts, While Tracing the History of Female African-American Filmmakers in *Sisters in Cinema*." *The Advocate*, February 17, 2004.

Eichholz, Alice, and James M. Rose. *Black Genesis: A Resource Book for African-American Genealogy*. Baltimore, MD: Genealogical Publishing Company, 2003.

Eklof, Barbara. *For Every Season: The Complete Guide to African American Celebrations, Traditional to Contemporary*. New York: HarperCollins, 1997.

Ellerson, Beti. *Sisters of the Screen: Women of Africa on Film, Video and Television*. Lawrenceville, NJ: Africa World Press, 2000.

Ellis, A. B. *Yoruba-Speaking Peoples of the Slave Coast of West Africa*. 1894. Internet Sacred Text Archive, 1999. http://www.sacred-texts.com/afr/yor/yor04.htm.

Emilio, Luis F. *A Brave Black Regiment: The History of the Fifty-Fourth Regiment of Massachusetts Volunteer Infantry, 1863–1865*. 1894. Reprint. Cambridge, MA, and New York: Da Capo Press, 1995.

Emmons, Natasha. "Same Themes, New Dreams." *Variety*, February 23, 2006. http://www.variety.com/ac2006_article/VR1117938786?nav=naacp.

Ershine, Noel Leo. *From Garvey to Marley: Rastafari Theology*. Gainesville: University Press of Florida, 2005.

Ewart, Jane, ed. *Eyewitness Travel Guide*. New York: DK Publishing, 2003.

"A Fair to Remember: Throngs Shop, Eat, Bounce Along to Jazz at the Fifteenth Annual Festival Despite Cold." *San Francisco Examiner*, July 2, 2000.

Fairbanks, Evelyn. *The Days of Rondo*. St. Paul: Minnesota Historical Society Press, 1990.

Fairclough, Adam. *Martin Luther King, Jr*. Athens: University of Georgia Press, 1995.

Farley Emery, Lynn. *Black Dance: From 1619 to Today*. 3rd ed. Hightstown, NJ: Princeton Book Company, 2005.

Farrakhan, Louis. "An appeal to all those who would be a part of the Millions More Movement," undated. http://www.millionsmoremovement.com/news/open_letter.htm.

Federal Writers' Project of the Works Progress Administration for the State of Maryland. *Slave Narratives: A Folk History of Slavery in the United States From Interviews with Former Slaves. Vol. VIII. Maryland Narratives*. Washington, DC, 1941. http://memory.loc.gov/ammem/snhtml/snhome.html.

Feldman, Eugene Pieter Romayn. *The Birth and the Building of the DuSable Museum*. Chicago: DuSable Museum Press, 1981.

Fields, Gary, and Maria Puente. "A Movement or Just a Moment?" *USA Today*, undated (updated October 10, 1996). http://www.usatoday.com/news/index/nman001.htm.

"Filmmaker Spike Lee and Actress Rosario Dawson Honored at American Black Film Festival."*Jet,* August 16, 2004.

Fine, Elizabeth C. *Soulstepping: African American Step Shows.* Champaign: University of Illinois Press, 2003.

Fishel, Leslie H., Jr., and Benjamin Quarles, eds. *The Negro American: A Documentary History.* Glenview, IL: Scott, Foresman and Company, 1967.

Fitts, Leroy. "National Baptist Convention, U.S.A." In *The African-American Experience: Selections from the Five-Volume Macmillan Encyclopedia of African-American Culture and History,* edited by Jack Salzman. New York: Macmillan, 1998.

Floyd, Samuel A., Jr. *The Power of Black Music: Interpreting Its History from Africa to the United States.* New York: Oxford University Press, 1995.

Foner, Philip S. *Paul Robeson Speaks: Writings, Speeches, and Interviews, a Centennial Celebration 1918–1974.* Secacus, NJ: Lyle Stuart/Citadel Press, 1982.

Ford, Omar. "Heritage Days Return Thursday." *Beaufort Gazette,* November 4, 2001. http://www.beaufortgazette.com/local_news/story/1092088p-1136468c.html.

———. "Heritage Days Celebration Begins." *Beaufort Gazette,* November 12, 2004. http://www.beaufortgazette.com/local_news/story/4174245p-3947804c.html.

Foster, Gwendolyn Audrey. *Women Filmmakers of the African and Asian Diaspora: Decolonizing the Gaze, Locating Subjectivity.* Carbondale: Southern Illinois University Press, 1997.

Francis, Charles E. *The Tuskegee Airmen: The Men Who Changed a Nation.* Edited by Adolph Caso. Wellesley, MA: Branden Books, 1997.

Franklin, John Hope. *The Emancipation Proclamation.* Garden City, NY: Doubleday & Company, 1963.

———. "The Emancipation Proclamation: An Act of Justice." *Prologue,* a quarterly publication of the National Archives and Records Administration, Summer 1993. http://www.archives.gov/publications/prologue/1993/summer/emancipation-proclamation.html.

Frazier, E. Franklin. *The Negro Church in America.* New York: Schocken Books, 1971.

Frohock, Fred M. "Free Exercise of Religion: Lucumi and Animal Sacrifice." Occasional Paper Series, Institute for Cuban and Cuban-American Studies, University of Miami, November 2001. http://www.latinamericanstudies.org/religion/santeria.pdf.

Frommer, Harvey. *Rickey and Robinson: The Men Who Broke Baseball's Color Barrier.* Boulder, CO: Taylor Trade Publishing Company, 2003.

Gantt, Alice. "Women's Day." Black Congregational Ministries Committee, National Council of Churches USA, October 1995. http://www.ncccusa.org/nmu/mce/womens_day.pdf.

Garvey, Marcus, and Bob Blaisdell, ed. *Selected Writings and Speeches of Marcus Garvey.* Mineola, NY: Dover Publications, 2004.

Gates, Henry Louis, Jr., and Evelyn Brooks Higginbotham, eds. *African American Lives.* New York: Oxford University Press, 2004.

Gay, Kathlyn. *I Am Who I Am: Speaking Out about Multiracial Identity.* New York: Franklin Watts, 1995.

———. *Religion and Spirituality in America: The Ultimate Teen Guide.* Lanham, MD: Scarecrow Press, 2006. (young adult)

Gay, Kathlyn, and Martin K. Gay. *Heroes of Conscience: A Biographical Dictionary.* Santa Barbara, CA: ABC-CLIO, 1996.

Georgia Writers Project, Work Projects Administration. *Drums and Shadows: Survival Studies Among the Georgia Coastal Negroes.* Athens: University of Georgia Press, 1986.

Gerlach, Larry R. "Robeson, Paul." In *African American Lives,* edited by Henry Louis Gates Jr. and Evelyn Brooks Higginbotham. New York: Oxford University Press, 2004.

"Ghanafest 2002 in Chicago." GhanaHomePage Diasporan News, August 1, 2002. http://www.ghanaweb.com/GhanaHomePage/NewsArchive/artikel.php?ID=26116.

Gibbs, C. R., and Dayo Akinsheye, ed. *Black Inventors: From Africa to America, Two Million Years of Invention and Innovation.* Silver Spring, MD: Three Dimensional Publishing, 1995.

Giblin, James. "Introduction: Diffusion and Other Problems in the History of African States." Art & Life in Africa Project of the School of Art and Art History, University of Iowa. Revised March 7, 1999. http://www.uiowa.edu/~africart/toc/history/giblinstate.html.

Gissen, Jesse. "Mos Def, Black Moon, & More Hit Black August Concert for HIV/AIDS Awareness." SOHH.com, July 11, 2005. http://www.sohh.com/articles/article.php/7299.

Glazier, Stephen D., ed. *Encyclopedia of Africa and African-American Religions.* New York: Routledge, 2001.

Gleason, Judith. *Oya: In Praise of an African Goddess.* New York: HarperCollins, 1992.

Gocking, Rogers. *History of Ghana.* Westport, CT: Greenwood Publishing Group, 2005.

Goines, Leonard. "Jazz." In *The African-American Experience: Selections from the Five-Volume Macmillan Encyclopedia of African-American Culture and History,* edited by Jack Salzman. New York: Macmillan, 1998.

González-Wippler, Migene. *Santería: The Religion.* St. Paul, MN: Llewellyn Publications, 2004.

Goodman, Amy. Interview with Manning Marable. *Democracy Now!*, February 21, 2005. http://www.democracynow.org/article.pl?sid=05/02/21/1458213ED.

Goodwine, Marquetta L., ed. *The Legacy of Ibo Landing: Gullah Roots of African American Culture*. Atlanta, GA: Clarity Press, 1998.

Gourse, Leslie. *Louis' Children: American Jazz Singers*. Lanham, MD: Rowman & Littlefield Publishers, 2001.

Gugler, Joseph. *African Film: Re-Imagining a Continent*. Bloomington: Indiana University Press, 2004.

Gulevich, Tanya. "Jonkonnu," "Slaves' Christmas," and "Watch Night." In *Encyclopedia of Christmas and New Year's Celebrations*. 2nd ed. Detroit: Omnigraphics, 2003.

Gutiérrez, Ramon A., and Geneviève Fabre. *Feasts and Celebrations in North American Ethnic Communities*. Albuquerque: University of New Mexico Press, 1995.

Hajdusiewicz, Babs Bell. *Mary Carter Smith: African-American Storyteller*. Berkeley Heights, NJ: Enslow Publishers, 1995. (young adult)

Hale, Thomas A. *Griots and Griottes: Masters of Words and Music*. Bloomington: Indiana University Press, 1998.

Haley, Alex. *Roots*. Garden City, NY: Doubleday, 1976.

Hamilton, Charles V. *Adam Clayton Powell, Jr.: The Political Biography of an American Dilemma*. Lanham, MD: Rowman & Littlefield/Cooper Square Press, 2002.

Handy, D. Antoinette. "W. C. Handy." In *Black Heroes*, edited by Jessie Carney Smith. Foreword by Nikki Giovanni. Canton, MI: Visible Ink Press, 2001.

Handy, W. C. *Blues: An Anthology*. 1926. Reprint. Bedford, MA: Applewood Books, 2001.

———. *Father of the Blues: An Autobiography*. 1941. Reprint edited by Arna Wendell Bontemps. Foreword by Abbe Niles. London: Sidgwick and Jackson, 1957.

Hanes, Bailey C. *Bill Pickett, Bulldogger: The Biography of a Black Cowboy*. Norman: University of Oklahoma Press, 1977.

Harley, Sharon. *The Timetables of African-American History: A Chronology of the Most Important People and Events in African-American History*. New York: Simon & Schuster/ Touchstone, 1996.

Harris, Leslie M. *In the Shadow of Slavery: African Americans in New York City, 1626–1863.*Chicago: University of Chicago Press, 2004.

Harris, Michael W. *The Rise of Gospel Blues: The Music of Thomas Andrew Dorsey in the Urban Church*. New York: Oxford University Press, 1992.

Harris, Milton M., with Morris Levitt, Roger Furman, and Ernest Smith. *The Black Book*. New York: Random House, 1974.

Haviser, Jay B., ed. *African Sites: Archeology in the Caribbean.* Princeton, NJ: Marcus Wiener Publishers, 1999.

Height, Dorothy I. *Open Wide the Freedom Gates: A Memoir.* New York: PublicAffairs, 2003.

Hemenway, Robert E. *Zora Neale Hurston: A Literary Biography.* Urbana: University of Illinois Press, 1977.

Henderson, Helene. "Emancipation Day." In *Patriotic Holidays of the United States.* Detroit: Omnigraphics, 2006.

Henze, Paul B. *Layers of Time: A History of Ethiopia.* New York: Macmillan/Palgrave, 2000.

Hepner, Randal L. "Rastafari in the U.S." In *Encyclopedia of African and African-American Religions,* edited by Stephen D. Glazier. New York: Routledge, 2001.

Heron, W. Kim. "A World of Africa in Detroit." *Detroit Free Press,* August 26, 1983.

Hill, Laban Carrick. *Harlem Stomp!: A Cultural History of the Harlem Renaissance.* New York: Little, Brown/Megan Tingley, 2004. (young adult)

Hill, Martin J. *The Harambee Movement in Kenya.* Oxford: Berg Publishers, 1991.

Hill, Ruth Edmonds. "Rosa Parks." In *Black Heroes,* edited by Jessie Carney Smith. Foreword by Nikki Giovanni. Canton, MI: Visible Ink Press, 2001.

Hine, Darlene Clark. "Parks, Rosa." In *African American Lives,* edited by Henry Louis Gates Jr. and Evelyn Brooks Higginbotham. New York: Oxford University Press, 2004.

Hodeir, Andre, and Jean-Louis Pautrot, eds. *Andre Hodeir Jazz Reader.* Ann Arbor: University of Michigan Press, 2006.

Holdcroft, Leslie. "Festival Sundiata: It's a Fun Time of African and African American Culture Appreciation." *Seattle Post-Intelligencer,* February 17, 2006. http://seattlepi.nwsource.com/lifestyle/259786_fam17.html.

Homan, Lynn M., and Thomas Reilly. *Black Knights: The Story of the Tuskegee Airmen.* Gretna, LA: Pelican Publishing, 2001.

Horne, Gerald. *Fire This Time: The Watts Uprising and the 1960s.* Charlottesville: University of Virginia Press, 1995.

Horton, James Oliver, and Lois E. Horton, eds. *A History of the African American People: The History, Traditions & Culture of African Americans.* Detroit: Wayne State University Press, 1997.

Hull, Arthur. *Drum Circle Spirit: Games, Exercises and Facilitation.* Northampton, MA: White Cliffs Media, Inc., 1998.

Hunt, Darrell M. *Screening the Los Angeles 'Riots': Race, Seeing, and Resistance.* Edited by Jeffrey C. Alexander and Steven Seidman. New York: Cambridge University Press, 1997.

Hurley, Anthony E., Renee Larrier, and Joseph McLarren, eds. *Migrating Words and Worlds: PanAfricanism Updated*. Trenton, NJ: Africa World Press, 1998.

Hurston, Zora Neale. *Dust Tracks on a Road*. 1942. Reprinted with a foreword by Maya Angelou. New York: HarperPerennial, 2006.

———. *Go Gator and Muddy the Water: Writings by Zora Neale Hurston from the Federal Writers' Project*. Edited and with a biographical essay by Pamela Bordelon. New York: W. W. Norton & Company, 1990.

———. *Moses, Man of the Mountain*. 1938. Reprinted with a foreword by Deborah E. McDowell. New York: HarperPerennial, 1991.

———. *Tell My Horse*. 1938. Reprinted with a foreword by Ishmael Reed. New York: HarperPerennial, 1990.

———. *Their Eyes Were Watching God*. 1939. Reprinted with a foreword by Mary Helen Washington. New York: HarperPerennial, 1990.

"Indiana Black Expo." *The Indianapolis Star*, Indystar.com Library Factfiles, July 2005. http://www2.indystar.com/library/factfiles/organizations/black_expo/black_expo.html.

"An Interview with Oba Osijeman Adefunmi I of Oyotunji, South Carolina." *Isokan Yoruba Magazine*, Fall 1996-Winter 1997. http://www.yoruba.org/Magazine/Winter97/Win9706.htm.

Isom, Wendy. "Tent Revival Brings Old-Time Religion to Jackson Fairgrounds." *The Jackson (TN) Sun*, July 2, 2006. http://www.jacksonsun.com/apps/pbcs.dll/article?AID=/20060702/NEWS01/607020314/1002.

"Jackson, George Lester." In *Africana: The Encyclopedia of the African and African American Experience, A Concise Reference*, edited by Kwame Anthony Appiah and Henry Louis Gates Jr. Philadelphia: Running Press, 2003.

Jackson, Jerma A. *Singing in My Soul: Black Gospel Music in a Secular Age*. Chapel Hill: University of North Carolina Press, 2004.

Jackson, Kenneth T., ed. *The Encyclopedia of New York City*. New Haven, CT: Yale University Press, 1995.

Jacobs, Harriet. *Incidents in the Life of a Slave Girl. Written by Herself*. Edited by L. Maria Child. Boston: Published for the Author, 1861.

Jacobs, Ronald N. *Race, Media, and the Crisis of Civil Society: From Watts to Rodney King*. Edited by Jeffrey C. Alexander and Steven Seidman. New York: Cambridge University Press, 2004.

James, Winston. *Holding Aloft the Banner of Ethiopia: Caribbean Radicalism in Early Twentieth-Century America*. New York: Verso, 1998.

Jasen, David A., and Gene Jones. *Black Bottom Stomp: Eight Masters of Ragtime and Early Jazz*. New York: Routledge, 2002.

Jeffrey, Julie Roy. "Religious Revivals." Lincoln/Net: Abraham Lincoln Historical Digitization Project, undated. http://lincoln.lib.niu.edu/digitalrevival.html.

Jenkins, Everett. *Pan-African Chronology III: A Comprehensive Reference to the Black Quest for Freedom in Africa, the Americas, Europe and Asia, 1914–1929.* Jefferson, NC: McFarland & Company Publishers, 2001.

Jenkins, Olga Culmer. *Bahamian Memories: Island Voices of the Twentieth Century.* Gainesville: University Press of Florida, 2000.

Johnson, Lynn d. "The Distribution of Black Films." *Bright Lights Film Journal*, April 2002. http://www.brightlightsfilm.com/36/distribution1.html.

Joiner, Lottie L. "NAACP Honors the Arts." *The Crisis*, May/June 2003. http://www.findarticles.com/p/articles/mi_qa4081/is_200305/ai_n9179619.

Jones, Absalom, and Richard Allen. *A Narrative of the Proceedings of the Black People, during the Late Awful Calamity in Philadelphia, in the Year 1793: And a Refutation of some Censures, Thrown upon them in some late Publications.* Philadelphia: Printed for the authors, by William W. Woodward, 1794.

Joplin, Scott. *Treemonisha Vocal Score.* Mineola, NY: Dovers Publications, 2001.

Joyner, Marsha. "Gathering Place." *Honolulu Star Bulletin*, January 1, 2006. http://starbulletin.com/2006/01/01/editorial/commentary.htm.

"Jubilee: Festival of Heritage in Columbia, SC, Promotes Diversity and Cultural Awareness." *Carolina Arts*, August 2003. http://www.carolinaarts.com/803jubilee.html.

"Jubilee! Historic Columbia Celebrates African-American Heritage This Weekend with Singing, Art, Dance, Drama." *Leisure Magazine, The Times and Democrat* (Columbia, SC), August 25, 2004. http://www.timesanddemocrat.com/articles/2004/08/25/pm/pm1.txt.

Kachun, Mitch. *Festivals of Freedom: Memory and Meaning in African American Emancipation Celebrations, 1808–1915.* Amherst: University of Massachusetts Press, 2003.

Kanneh, Kadiatu. *African Identities: Race, Nation, and Culture in Ethnography, Pan-Africanism and Black Literatures.* New York: Routledge, 1998.

Kaplan, Carla, ed. *Zora Neale Hurston: A Life in Letters.* New York: Doubleday, 2002.

Kaplan, Sydney, and Emma Nogrady Kaplan. *The Black Presence in the Era of the American Revolution.* Amherst: University of Massachusetts Press, 1989.

Karenga, Maulana. *Kwanzaa: A Celebration of Family, Community and Culture.* Los Angeles: University of Sankore Press, 1998.

Kashatus, William C. "54th Massachusetts Regiment: A Gallant Rush for Glory." *American History*, October 2000.

Kasinitz, Philip. *Caribbean New York: Black Immigrants and the Politics of Race.* Ithaca, NY: Cornell University Press, 1992.

Kathryn. "The Mariel Boatlift of 1980," October 5, 2017. https://www.floridamemory.com/blog/2017/10/05/the-mariel-boatlift-of-1980/

Katz, William Loren. *Black Indians: A Hidden Heritage.* New York: Atheneum, 1986.

———. *The Black West.* New York: Broadway Books, 2005.

———. *Eyewitness: A Living Documentary of the African American Contribution to American History.* Revised and updated. New York: Simon & Schuster/Touchstone, 1995.

Kelley, Robin D. G. "Into the Fire: 1970 to the Present." In *To Make Our World Anew: A History of African Americans,* edited by Robin D. G. Kelley and Earl Lewis. New York: Oxford University Press, 2000.

Kennedy, Lisa. "A Festival Filled with Powerful Moments." DenverPost.com, November 25, 2005. http://www.denverpost.com/search/ci_3247160.

Kilson, Marion. "Homowo: Celebrating Community in Ga Culture." Online version of a paper presented at the Society for Applied Anthropological Annual Meeting in 1991, published in *Sextant: The Journal of Salem State College,* 1993. http://www.salemstate.edu/sextant/v4n1/kilson.html.

King, Coretta Scott. *My Life with Martin Luther King, Jr.* Revised edition. New York: Henry Holt, 1993.

King, Martin Luther, Jr. *Letter from Birmingham City Jail.* Philadelphia: American Friends Service Committee, May 1963.

———. Nobel Prize Acceptance Speech. http://www.nobelprizes.com/nobel/peace/MLKnobel.html.

———. *Stride Toward Freedom.* New York: Harper & Row, 1958.

———. *A Testament of Hope: The Essential Writings and Speeches of Martin Luther King, Jr.* Edited by James M. Washington. San Francisco: HarperSanFrancisco, 1986.

———. *Where Do We Go from Here: Chaos or Community?* New York: Harper & Row, 1967.

Kofi Acree, Eric. "Message from the Africana Librarian." *Sankofa Africana Library Newsletter* (Cornell University Library), February 2003. http://www.library.cornell.edu/africana/newsletter/feb2003.htm.

Kofskey, Frank. *Black Music, White Business: Illuminating History and Political Economy of Jazz.* New York: Pathfinder Press, 1997.

Kremer, Gary B., ed. *George Washington Carver: In His Own Words.* Columbia: University of Missouri Press, 1987.

Lamb, Chris. *Blackout: The Untold Story of Jackie Robinson's First Spring Training.* Lincoln: University of Nebraska Press, 2004.

Landau, Elaine. *Bill Pickett: Wild West Cowboy.* Berkeley Heights, NJ: Enslow Publishers, 2004. (young adult)

Lanning, Michael Lee. *The African-American Soldier: From Crispus Attucks to Colin Powell.* New York: Kensington/Citadel Press, 2004.

Lawrence, Lee. "Chronicling Black Lives in Colonial New England." *Christian Science Monitor,* October 29, 1997. http://csmonitor.com/cgi-bin/durableRedirect. pl?/durable/1997/10/29/feat/feat.1.html.

Leckie, William H. *The Buffalo Soldiers: A Narrative of the Negro Cavalry in the West.* Norman: University of Oklahoma Press, 1967.

Lee, Chisun. "Taking the Rap." *The Village Voice,* September 6–12, 2000. http://www. villagevoice.com/news/0036,lee,17912,1.html.

Lehman, Jeffrey, ed. *The African American Almanac.* 9th ed. Detroit: Gale, 2003.

Leonnig, Carol D. "Celebrating the Day Freedom Arrived." *Washington Post,* April 17, 2005.

Lewis, Monica. "10 Years after Million Man March, Conveners Announce the Millions More Movement." BlackAmericaWeb.com, May 2, 2005. http://www. blackamericaweb.com/site.aspx/bawnews/march503.

Lindberg, Rich. *Passport's Guide to Ethnic Chicago.* New York: McGraw-Hill, 1997.

Lindberg, Richard C. "DuSable, Jean Baptiste Pointe." In *African American Lives,* edited by Henry Louis Gates Jr. and Evelyn Brooks Higginbotham. New York: Oxford University Press, 2004.

Loguen, Jermain Wesley. *The Rev. J. W. Loguen, as a Slave and as a Freeman. A Narrative of Real Life.* Syracuse, NY: J. G. K. Truair & Co.: Stereotypers and Printers, 1859. Documenting the American South. University Library, University of North Carolina at Chapel Hill, 1999. http://docsouth.unc.edu/neh/loguen/ loguen.html.

Lomax, Alan. *The Land Where the Blues Began.* New York: The New Press, 2002.

Lornell, Kip. "Dorsey, Thomas Andrew." In *African American Lives,* edited by Henry Louis Gates Jr. and Evelyn Brooks Higginbotham. New York: Oxford University Press, 2004.

Love, Nat. *The Life and Adventures of Nat Love, Better Known in the Cattle Country as "Deadwood Dick," By Himself.* 1907. Reprint. New York: Arno Press, 1968.

Low, W. Augustus, and Virgil A. Clift, eds. *Encyclopedia of Black America.* New York: McGrawHill, 1981.

Lubell, Dee C. "Heritage Giving Birth to Cultures. Cultures Reuniting Heritage Through History." *High Tide's Guide to St. Simons Island,* Spring 2005.

———. "Sea Island Festival." *Upscale Magazine,* May 2005.

Luker, Ralph E. "Hurston, Zora Neale." In *African American Lives,* edited by Henry Louis Gates Jr. and Evelyn Brooks Higginbotham. New York: Oxford University Press, 2004.

Lush, Tamara. "Haitian Roots Deepening." *St. Petersburg Times*, May 6, 2002.

MacKintosh, Barry. "George Washington Carver: The Making of a Myth." *The Journal of Southern History*, November 1976.

Major League Baseball. "Major League Baseball Declares April 15 Jackie Robinson Day," March 3, 2004. http://mlb.mlb.com/NASApp/mlb/mlb/news/mlb_press_release.jsp?ymd=20040303&content_id=644548&vkey=pr_mlb&fext=.jsp.

Malcolm X. "The Ballot or the Bullet." Speech delivered April 3, 1964, in Cleveland, OH. http://www.americanrhetoric.com/speeches/malcolmxballot.htm.

Malcolm X with Alex Haley. *The Autobiography of Malcolm X: As Told to Alex Haley.* New York: Grove Press, 1966.

Mamiya, Lawrence H. "Farrakhan, Louis Abdul." In *The African-American Experience: Selections from the Five-Volume Macmillan Encyclopedia of African-American Culture and History*, edited by Jack Salzman. New York: Macmillan, 1998.

Marable, Manning. "By Any Means Necessary: The Life and Legacy of Malcolm X." Speech at Metro State College, Denver, Colorado, February 21, 1992. http://www.zmag.org/zmag/articles/barmarable.htm.

Marable, Manning, ed. *Souls: A Critical Journal of Black Politics, Culture and Society*, Winter 2005. (Malcolm X issue).

Mason, John. *Olookun: Owner of Rivers and Seas.* Brooklyn, NY: Yoruba Theological Archministry, 1996.

Massachusetts Anti-Slavery Society. *Thirteenth Annual Report of the Massachusetts AntiSlavery Society*, January 22, 1845. In *The Negro American: A Documentary History*, edited by Leslie H. Fishel Jr. and Benjamin Quarles. Glenview, IL: Scott Foresman and Company, 1967.

Maxwell, Louise P. "Gullah." In *The African-American Experience: Selections from the FiveVolume Macmillan Encyclopedia of African-American Culture and History*, edited by Jack Salzman. New York: Macmillan, 1998.

Mbithi, Philip M., and Rasmus Rasmusson. *Self-Reliance in Kenya: The Case of Harambee.* New York: Homes & Meier Publishers, 1978.

McCurdy, Michael, ed. *Escape from Slavery: The Boyhood of Frederick Douglass in His Own Words.* New York: Alfred A. Knopf, 1994. (young adult)

McFeely, William S. *Frederick Douglass.* New York: W. W. Norton & Company, 1991.

McKinney, Lora-Ellen. *Christian Education in the African American Church: A Guide for Teaching Truth.* Foreword by Johnny Ray Youngblood. Valley Forge, PA: Judson Press, 2003.

McKissack, Patricia C., and Fredrick L. McKissack. *Days of Jubilee: The End of Slavery in the United States.* New York: Scholastic, 2003. (young adult)

———. *Red-Tail Angels: The Story of the Tuskegee Airmen of World War II*. New York: Walker and Company, 1995. (young adult)

McNeil, Lydia. "Peter Spencer." In *The Encyclopedia of African American Culture and History*, edited by Jack Salzman, David Lionel Smith, and Cornel West. Vol. 5. New York: Macmillan, 1996.

Meckna, Michael. *Satchmo: The Louis Armstrong Encyclopedia*. Westport, CT: Greenwood Publishing Group, 2004.

"'The Meeting Continued All Night, Both by the White and Black People': Georgia Camp Meeting, 1807." History Matters: The U.S. Survey Course on the Web, undated. http://historymatters.gmu.edu/d/6518/.

Miles, Johnnie H., Juanita J. Davis, Sharon E. Ferguson-Roberts, and Rita G. Giles. *Almanac of African American Heritage*. Foreword by Clara L. Adams-Ender. San Francisco: Wiley/JosseyBass, 2001.

Miller, Edward A. *Gullah Statesman: Robert Smalls from Slavery to Congress, 1839–1915*. Columbia: University of South Carolina Press, 1995.

Mills, Frederick V. "Allen, Richard." In *African American Lives*, edited by Henry Louis Gates Jr. and Evelyn Brooks Higginbotham. New York: Oxford University Press, 2004.

Mills, William G. "The Tuskegee Experience." *Combat Edge*, February 2005.

Mohl, Raymond A. "Black Immigrants: Bahamians in Early Twentieth-Century Miami." *Florida Historical Quarterly*, January 1987.

Moody, Shelah. "JEFFERSON AWARD: Presented to Thomas Robert Simpson / Arts to educate, inspire, provoke." ———, October 15, 2006. https://www.sfgate.com/living/article/JEFFERSON-AWARD-Presented-to-Thomas-Robert-2468226.php

Moore, Carman. *Somebody's Angel Child: The Story of Bessie Smith*. New York: Thomas Y. Crowell Co., 1969.

Moore, Eric. "Black College Football Classic Games: A Taste of the HBCU Athletic Experience." CollegeView.com, undated. http://www.collegeview.com/articles/CV/hbcu/classic_games.html.

Morris, Robert C. "Wright, Richard Robert, Sr." In *African American Lives*, edited by Henry Louis Gates Jr. and Evelyn Brooks Higginbotham. New York: Oxford University Press, 2004.

Moss, Marilyn. "Sisters in Cinema." *Hollywood Reporter*, February 6, 2004.

Mottesheard, Ryan. "Urban Heats Up with ABFF; Miami-based Festival Increases Awareness for Segment." *Daily Variety*, July 11, 2005.

Mugleston, William F. "Garvey, Marcus." In *African American Lives*, edited by Henry Louis Gates Jr. and Evelyn Brooks Higginbotham. New York: Oxford University Press, 2004.

———. "Love, Nat." In *African American Lives*, edited by Henry Louis Gates Jr. and Evelyn Brooks Higginbotham. New York: Oxford University Press, 2004.

Muhammad, Elijah. "What Is Islam? What Is a Muslim?" *Muhammad Speaks Newspaper*, July 17, 1970. http://www.muhammadspeaks.com/about.html.

Murphy, Joseph M. *Santería: African Spirits in America*. Boston: Beacon Press, 1993.

———. *Working the Spirit: Ceremonies of the African Diaspora*. Boston: Beacon Press, 1994.

"Music." In *Encyclopedia of Black America*, edited by W. Augustus Low and Virgil A. Clift. New York: McGraw-Hill Book Company, 1981.

"Music: Major African American Musical Forms." *New York Public Library African American Desk Reference*. New York: John Wiley & Sons, 1999.

Muwakkil, Salim. "Black History Month Matters." *In These Times*, January 2006. http://www.inthesetimes.com/site/main/article/2476/.

Myers, Walter Dean. *Malcolm X: By Any Means Necessary*. New York: Scholastic, 1994. (young adult)

Nash, Gary B. "Allen, Richard." In *The African-American Experience: Selections from the FiveVolume Macmillan Encyclopedia of African-American Culture and History*, edited by Jack Salzman. New York: Macmillan, 1998.

National Council of Negro Women. *The Black Family Reunion Cookbook: Recipes and Food Memories from the National Council of Negro Women*. New York: Fireside/Simon & Schuster, 1993.

New York Public Library. *The New York Public Library African American Desk Reference*. New York: Wiley/Stonesong Press, 1999.

Newton, James E., and Harmon Carey. "Diamonds of Delaware and Maryland's Eastern Shore: Seven Black Men of Distinction." In *A History of African Americans of Delaware and Maryland's Eastern Shore*, edited by Carole Marks. Newark: University of Delaware, 1997. http://www.udel.edu/BlackHistory/diamonds.html.

"1904–2004: The Boulé at 100: Sigma Pi Phi Fraternity Holds Centennial Celebration." *Ebony*, September 2004.

Norton, Eleanor Holmes. "Honoring the 13th Annual DC Black Pride Celebration and Earl D. Fowlkes." *Congressional Record*, May 14, 2003.

Núñez, Luis Manuel. *Santería: A Practical Guide to Afro-Caribbean Magic*. Dallas, TX: Spring Publications, 1992.

O'Brien, David M. *Animal Sacrifice and Religious Freedom: Church of the Lukumi Babalu Aye v. City of Hialeah*. Lawrence: University Press of Kansas, 2004.

Olatunji, Babatunde, with Robert Atkinson. *Beat of My Drum: An Autobiography*. Foreword by Joan Baez. Philadelphia: Temple University Press, 2005.

Osofsky, Gilbert. *Harlem: The Making of a Ghetto.* Chicago: Ivan R. Dee, Publisher, 1996.

Ostwalt, Conrad. "Camp Meetings." The Tennessee Encyclopedia of History and Culture, 1998. http://tennesseeencyclopedia.net/imagegallery.php?EntryID=C011.

Ottley, Roi. *The Lonely Warrior: The Life and Times of Robert S. Abbott.* Chicago: H. Regnery, 1955.

Painter, Nell Irvin. *Exodusters: Black Migration to Kansas after the Reconstruction.* New York: Knopf, 1977.

"Pan Africanism." In *Encyclopedia of Black America*, edited by W. Augustus Low and Virgil A. Clift. New York: McGraw-Hill, 1981.

Parker, John P. *His Promised Land: The Autobiography of John P. Parker, Former Slave and Conductor on the Underground Railroad.* Edited by Stuart Seely Sprague. New York: W. W. Norton, 1996.

Parks, Rosa, with Jim Haskins. *Rosa Parks: My Story.* New York: Puffin Books, 1992.

Patrick, Diane. *The New York Public Library Amazing African American History: A Book of Answers for Kids.* New York: Wiley/Stonesong Press, 1998. (young adult)

———. "The Celebration Continues." *Publishers Weekly*, February 26, 2001.

Patrick, K. C. "Chuck Davis and Dance Africa." *Dance Magazine*, April 2004.

Patton, June O. "'And the truth shall make you free': Richard Robert Wright, Sr., Black Intellectual and Iconoclast, 1877–1897. (Vindicating the Race: Contributions to African-American Intellectual History)." *The Journal of Negro History*, January 1996.

Patton, Sharon F. *African-American Art.* New York: Oxford University Press, 1998.

Pemberton, Doris Hollis. *Juneteenth at Comanche Crossing.* Austin, TX: Eakin Press, 1983.

Pepin, Elizabeth, and Lewis Watts. *Harlem of the West: The San Francisco Fillmore Jazz Era.* San Francisco: Chronicle Books, 2005.

Pershing, Linda. "'You can't do that, you're the wrong race': African American Women Storytellers at a Contemporary Festival." *Women and Language*, Spring 1996.

Peterson, Robert W. *Only the Ball Was White: A History of Legendary Black Players and All-Black Professional Teams.* New York: Oxford University Press, 1992.

Pfaff, Francoise. *Focus on African Films.* Bloomington: Indiana University Press, 2004.

Phillips, Braden. "A Fresh Face: Revamp Hopes to TV Aud's, Org's Vision." *Variety*, March 1, 2001. http://www.variety.com/index.asp?layout=naacp2001&articleID=VR1117794483.

Pickard, Carey. "Pan African Festival of Georgia." *New Georgia Encyclopedia.* Athens: University of Georgia Library, 2002. http://www.georgiaencyclopedia.org/nge/Article.jsp?id=h-760.

Pierre, Robert E., and Hamil R. Harris. "A Decade Later, Marchers Look for More." *Washington Post*, October 16, 2005. http://www.washingtonpost.com/wp-dyn/content/article/2005/10/15/AR2005101501588.html.

Piersen, William. *Black Legacy: America's Hidden Heritage*. Amherst: University of Massachusetts Press, 1993.

———. *Black Yankees: The Development of an Afro-American Sub-Culture in EighteenthCentury New England*. Amherst: University of Massachusetts Press, 1988.

Pinkney, Andrea Davis. *Bill Pickett—Rodeo Ridin' Cowboy*. New York: Harcourt Children's Books, 1999. (young adult)

Pollitzer, William S. *The Gullah People and Their African Heritage*. Athens: University of Georgia Press, 1999.

Potter, Joan. *African American Firsts: Famous Little-Known and Unsung Triumphs of Blacks in America*. New York: Kensington Publishing, 2002. (young adult)

Powledge, Fred. *Free At Last? The Civil Rights Movement and the People Who Made It*. Boston: Little, Brown and Company, 1991.

Prah, Kwesi Kwaa. *Beyond the Color Line: Pan-Africanist Disputations, Selected Sketches, Letters, Papers and Reviews*. Trenton, NJ: Africa World Press, 1998.

Prescott, Jean. "Tent Revival: Katrina Survivors, Take Heart." *The Sun Herald* (Biloxi, MS), July 7, 2006. http://www.sunherald.com/mld/sunherald/living/14984210.htm.

Preston, Dickson J. *Young Frederick Douglass: The Maryland Years*. Baltimore: Johns Hopkins University Press, 1980.

Price, Richard. "Maroons: Rebel Slaves in the Americas." Originally published in the *1992 Festival of American Folklife* catalogue; reprinted with permission from the Center for Folklife and Cultural Heritage of the Smithsonian Institution. http://www.folklife.si.edu/resources/maroon/educational_guide/23.htm.

Priestly, Brian. *Chasin' the Bird: Life & Legend of Charlie Parker*. New York: Oxford University Press, 2005.

Pyatt, Sherman E., and Alan Johns. *A Dictionary and Catalog of African American Folklife of the South*. Westport, CT: Greenwood Press, 1999.

Ramdanie, Tanesha. "The Road to Freedom." Ministry of Education, Jamaica Information Service, August 2, 2002. http://www.jis.gov.jm/education/html/20020731T150000–0500_327_JIS_THE_ROAD_TO_FREEDOM.asp.

Ramos-Zayas, Ana Y. *National Performances: The Politics of Class, Race, and Space in Puerto Rican Chicago*. Chicago: University of Chicago Press, 2003.

Rampell, Ed. "Ayuko Babu" (interview). *Los Angeles City Beat*, February 10, 2006. http://www.lacitybeat.com/article.php?id=1654&IssueNum=88.

Rampersad, Arnold, ed. *The Oxford Anthology of African-American Poetry*. New York: Oxford University Press, 2005.

Ramsey, Guthrie P., Jr. *Race Music: Black Cultures from Bebop to Hip-Hop*. Berkeley: University of California Press, 2003.

Ransom, Stanley A. *America's First Negro Poet*. Port Washington, NY: Kennikat Press, 1970.

Ras, Nathaniel. *50th Anniversary of His Imperial Majesty Emperor Haile Selassie I First Visit to the United States (1954–2004)*. Oxford: Trafford Publishing, 2004.

"Rastafarians." In *Africana: The Encyclopedia of the African and African American Experience: The Concise Desk Reference*, edited by Kwame Anthony Appiah and Henry Louis Gates Jr. Philadelphia: Running Press, 2003.

Reed, Christopher Robert. *"All the World Is Here!": The Black Presence at White City*. Bloomington: Indiana University Press, 1999.

———. *Black Chicago's First Century, Volume 1, 1833–1900*. Columbia: University of Missouri Press, 2005.

Reed, Ishmael. *Blues City: A Walk in Oakland*. New York: Crown Publishing Group, 2003.

Reich, Howard. "Gospel Music Loses Its Storied Birthplace." *Chicago Tribune*, January 8, 2006.

Reuben, Paul P. "Chapter 2: Early American Literature— 1700–1800: Jupiter Hammon." *PAL:Perspectives in American Literature—A Research and Reference Guide—An Ongoing Project*. January 4, 2003. http://www.csustan.edu/english/reuben/pal/chap2/hammon.html.

Rich, Wilbur C. "Detroit, Michigan." In *The African-American Experience: Selections from the Five-Volume Macmillan Encyclopedia of African-American Culture and History*, edited by Jack Salzman. New York: Macmillan, 1998.

Richardson, Karen, and Steven Green, eds. *T-Dot Griots: An Anthology of Toronto's Black Storytellers*. Victoria, British Columbia, Canada: Trafford Publishing, 2004.

Richman, Josh. "A Lone Cowboy Rides Roughshod Over Racism." *Forward* (New York, NY), October 17, 2003. http://www.forward.com/issues/2003/03.10.17/faces.html.

Rickford, Russel John. *Betty Shabazz: Her Life with Malcolm X and Fight to Preserve His Legacy*. Naperville, IL: Sourcebooks, 2004.

Riley, Dorothy Winbush. *The Complete Kwanzaa: Celebrating Our Cultural Harvest*. New York: Perennial, 1996.

Roberts, David. "Forgotten American Observance: Remembering the First of August." *Ex Post Facto Journal of the History Students at San Francisco State University*, 2002. http://userwww.sfsu.edu/~epf/2002/roberts.html.

Robeson, Paul. *Here I Stand*. 1958. Reprint. Boston: Beacon Press, 1998.

Robinson, Jackie. *Baseball Has Done It*. Introduction by Spike Lee. Brooklyn, NY: Ig Publishing, 2005.

Robinson, Jackie, with Alfred Duckett. *I Never Had It Made: An Autobiography of Jackie Robinson.* New York: Harper Collins Publishers, 2003.

Robinson, Sharon. *Promises to Keep: How Jackie Robinson Changed America.* New York: Scholastic, 2004. (young adult)

Root, Maria P. P., ed. *Racially Mixed People in America.* Newbury Park, CA: Sage Publications, 1992.

Rosenbaum, Art. "McIntosh County Shouters." *New Georgia Encyclopedia.* Athens: University of Georgia Library, 2005. http://www.georgiaencyclopedia.org/nge/Article.jsp?id=h-520.

Ross, Leon T., and Kenneth A. Mimms. *African American Almanac: Day-By-Day Black History.* Jefferson, NC: McFarland & Company, 1997.

Rummel, Jack. *Malcolm X.* New York: Chelsea House, 2004. (young adult)

Russell, Daniel James. *History of the African Union Methodist Protestant Church.* 1920. Documenting the American South. University Library, The University of North Carolina at Chapel Hill, 2001. http://docsouth.unc.edu/church/russell/russell.html.

"Russell Simmons and Gabrielle Union Saluted at American Black Film Festival." *Jet,* August 4, 2003.

Rutkoff, Peter M., ed. *Cooperstown Symposium on Baseball and American Culture 1997: Jackie Robinson.* Jefferson, NC: McFarland & Company Publishers, 2000.

Sagan, Miriam. *Malcolm X.* San Diego: Lucent Books, 1997. (young adult)

Salm, Steven J., and Toyin Falola. *Culture and Customs of Ghana.* Westport, CT: Greenwood Publishing Group, 2002.

Salzman, Jack, ed. *The African-American Experience: Selections from the Five-Volume Macmillan Encyclopedia of African-American Culture and History.* New York: Macmillan, 1998.

Sanchez, Jonathan. "The MOJA Index." *Charleston City Paper,* September 28, 2005. http://archive.charlestoncitypaper.com/layout.asp?id=47686&action=detail&catID=1254&parentID=1254.

Sanchez, Marta E. *Shakin' Up Race and Gender: Intercultural Connections in Puerto Rican, African American, and Chicano Narratives and Culture (1965–1995).* Austin: University of Texas Press, 2006.

Sanchez, Sara M. "Afro-Cuban Diasporan Religions: A Comparative Analysis of the Literature and Selected Annotated Bibliography." Occasional Paper Series, Institute for Cuban and Cuban-American Studies, University of Miami, August 2000. http://www.miami.edu/iccas/AFRO2.pdf.

Sanders McCutcheon, Gloria. "George Washington Carver: A Blend of Business and Science, He Left Legacy of Agricultural Research Still Applicable Today." *The Times and Democrat* (Orangeburg, SC), February 17, 2003. http://www.thetandd.com/articles/2003/02/17/features/features1.t.

Savage, Beth. *African American Historic Places.* Hoboken, NJ: John Wiley & Sons, 1994.

Schlissel, Lillian. *Black Frontiers: A History of African-American Heroes in the Old West.* New York: Simon & Schuster Books for Young Readers, 1995. (young adult)

Schubert, Irene, and Frank Schubert. *On the Trail of the Buffalo Soldier 2: New and Revised Biographies of African Americans in the U.S. Army, 1866–1917.* Lanham, MD: Scarecrow Press, 2004.

Selassie, Haile. "Address Delivered by His Imperial Majesty Haile Selassie 1st at the Conference of the Heads of States and Governments." Speech delivered at Addis Ababa, May 25, 1963. United Nations Economic Commission for Africa. http://www.uneca.org/adfiii/riefforts/ref/speech/Ethiopia.pdf.

Selassie I, Haile, and Edward Ullendorff, trans. *The Autobiography of Emperor Haile Selassie I: King of Kings and Lord of All Lords; My Life and Ethiopia's Progress 1892–1937 (Vol. 1).* New York: Frontline Books, 1999.

Shakelton, Paula G. "Revivals and Camp Meetings." *New Georgia Encyclopedia.* Athens: University of Georgia Library, updated November 23, 2003. http://www.georgiaencyclopedia.org/nge/Article.jsp?id=h-759.

Simmons, Charles A. *The African American Press: A History of News Coverage During National Crises, with Special Reference to Four Black Newspapers, 1827–1965.* Jefferson, NC: McFarland and Company, 2006.

Simon, Darran. "Haitians to Raise Flags for Unity." *Miami Herald,* May 17, 2004.

Slatta, Richard W. *The Cowboy Encyclopedia.* New York: W. W. Norton, 1996.

Smalls, Irene. "Roots of an African-American Christmas. "http://www.melanet.com/johnkankus/roots.html.

Smith, Gerrit. Letter to John Thomas, chairman of the Jerry Rescue Committee, August 27, 1859. Gerrit Smith Broadside and Pamphlet Collection, Syracuse University Library. http://libwww.syr.edu/digital/collections/g/GerritSmith/521.htm.

Smith, Jessie Carney. *Black Firsts: 4,000 Ground-Breaking and Pioneering Historical Events.* 2nd ed., revised and expanded. Canton, MI: Visible Ink Press, 2003.

Smith, Jessie Carney, ed. *Black Heroes.* Foreword by Nikki Giovanni. Canton, MI: Visible Ink Press, 2001.

Smith, Linell. "Memories from the Mall." *Baltimore Sun,* October 2, 2005. http://www.baltimoresun.com/features/custom/unisun/bal-un.march02oct02,1,5009773.story?coll=bal-unisun-headlines.

Smith, Michael P. *Mardi Gras Indians.* Gretna, LA: Pelican Publishing Co., 1994.

Smith, Rhonda. "Back in the Day: Former Clubhouse Patrons Reminisce about Popular Black Club." *Washington Blade,* May 27, 2005. http://www.aegis.com/News/WB/2005/WB050527.html.

Smith, Thomas G. "Football." In *The African-American Experience: Selections from the FiveVolume Macmillan Encyclopedia of African-American Culture and History*, edited by Jack Salzman. New York: Macmillan, 1998.

Sobania, Neal. *Culture and Customs of Kenya.* Westport, CT: Greenwood Publishing Group, 2003.

Southern, Eileen. *The Music of Black Americans: A History.* 3rd ed. New York: W. W. Norton and Company, 1997.

Southgate, Martha. "Memorializing the Middle Passage: How a Brooklyn Church Is Starting a Movement to Honor Our Ancestors Lost in the Slave Trade." *Essence,* February 2000.

Soyer, Daniel. "Fraternities and Sororities." In *The African-American Experience: Selections from the Five-Volume Macmillan Encyclopedia of African-American Culture and History*, edited by Jack Salzman. New York: Macmillan, 1998.

Spratling, Cassandra. "African World Festival." *Detroit Free Press,* August 15, 2001.

Stanton, Junious Ricardo. "Odunde Celebrates 27th Year: One of America's Largest Street Festivals." *Chicken Bones: A Journal,* n.d. http://www.nathanielturner.com/odundefestival2003.htm.

Stephens, Michelle A. *Black Empire: The Masculine Global Imaginary of Caribbean Intellectuals in the United States, 1914–1962.* Durham, NC: Duke University Press, 2005.

Stevens, Ronald. *Idlewild: Black Eden of Michigan.* Charleston, SC: Arcadia Publishers, 2001.

Stewart, Osamuyimen Thompson. "The Edo of Benin, Nigeria." Edo Nation Online. http://www.edo-nation.net/stewart1.htm.

Sutter, Mary. "Black Fest Picks 'One' (American Black Film Festival 'On the One')." *Daily Variety,* July 18, 2005.

Sykes, Leonard, Jr. "Garvey Celebration Represents a Call for Peace and Unity in Community." *Milwaukee Journal Sentinel Online,* August 20, 2005. http://www.jsonline.com/story/index.aspx?id=349763.

Sylvester, Melvin. "African-Americans in Motion Pictures: The Past and the Present." Schwartz Memorial Library, Long Island University, 1999 (updated 2005). http://www.liu.edu/cwis/cwp/library/african/movies.htm.

Tanenbaum, Barry. "Living History." *Shutterbug,* October 2003. http://shutterbug.com/features/1003sb_living/.

Taylor, Charles A. *Juneteenth: A Celebration of Freedom.* Greensboro, NC: Open Hand Publishing, 2002. (young adult)

———. "The Black Church and Juneteenth." *Madison (WI) Times Weekly Newspaper,* June 1723, 2005. http://www.madtimes.com/archives/june2005_3/madtimes_063.htm.

Taylor, Quintard. *In Search of the Racial Frontier: African Americans in the American West, 1528–1990*. New York: W. W. Norton, 1998.

Terrill, Robert E. *Malcolm X: Inventing Radical Judgment*. East Lansing: Michigan State University Press, 2004.

Thomas, Laurence Mordekhai. *Vessels of Evil: American Slavery and the Holocaust*. Philadelphia: Temple University Press, 1994.

Thurnbauer, Marcia. "Try Out African World Festival." *Milwaukee Journal Sentinel Online*, August 8, 2005. http://www.jsonline.com/news/editorials/aug05/346953.asp.

Tibbetts, John H. "Living Soul of Gullah." *Coastal Heritage,* Spring 2000. http://www.scseagrant.org/library/library_coaher_spring_2000.htm.

Titon, Jeff Todd. "Blues, The." In *The African-American Experience: Selections from the FiveVolume Macmillan Encyclopedia of African-American Culture and History*, edited by Jack Salzman. New York: Macmillan, 1998.

Torres, Ailene. "African Street Festival Aims to Bring Together People and Share Cultures." *The Tennessean*, September 18, 2005.

Travis, Dempsey J. *An Autobiography of Black Politics.* Introduction by U.S. Senator Paul Simon. Chicago: Urban Research Press, 1987.

Tyehimba, Cheo. "African Gods in South Carolina." *Essence*, December 1995.

Tygiel, Jules. *Baseball's Great Experiment: Jackie Robinson and His Legacy*. New York: Oxford University Press, 1997.

Ukadike, Nwachukwu Frank. *Black African Cinema.* Berkeley: University of California Press, 1994.

Vernon-Jackson, Hugh O., and Patricia Wright. *West African Folk Tales*. Mineola, NY: Dover Publishing, 2003.

Walker, Lewis, and Benjamin C. Wilson. *Black Eden: The Idlewild Community*. East Lansing: Michigan State University Press, 2002.

Ward, Geoffrey C., and Ken Burns. *Jazz: A History of America's Music*. New York: Knopf, 2002.

Washington, Booker T. *Up from Slavery: An Autobiography*. Garden City, NY: Doubleday & Company, 1901. Documenting the American South. University Library, University of North Carolina at Chapel Hill, 1997. http://docsouth.unc.edu/washington/washing.html.

Weber, Bruce. "Black Theater: Beyond Definition." *The New York Times*, August 8, 2003.

Webster, Raymond B. *African American Firsts in Science & Technology*. Farmington Hills, MI: Gale, 1999.

Welsh-Ashante, Kariamu, ed. *African Dance: An Artistic, Historical and Philosophical Inquiry*. Trenton, NJ: Africa World Press, 1994.

West, Cornel. *Race Matters.* Boston: Beacon Press, 1993.

Wheeler, B. Gordon. *Black California, A History of African-Americans in the Golden State.* New York: Hippocrene Books, 1993.

White, H. Loring. *Ragging It: Getting Ragtime into History (and Some History into Ragtime).* Lincoln, NE: iUniverse, Inc., 2005.

White, Shane. "Pinkster: Afro-Dutch Syncretization in New York City and the Hudson Valley." *Journal of American Folklore,* January–March 1989.

———. "'It Was a Proud Day': African American Festivals and Parades in the North, 1741–1834." *Journal of American History,* June 1994.

White, Shane, and Graham White. *The Sounds of Slavery.* Boston: Beacon Press, 2005.

Widner, Jennifer A. *The Rise and Fall of a Party State in Kenya: From Harambee! to Nyayo!* Berkeley: University of California Press, 1993.

Wiggins, William H., Jr. *O Freedom! Afro-American Emancipation Celebrations.* Knoxville: University of Tennessee Press, 2000.

———. "The Emancipation of Nicodemus." *Natural History,* July–August, 1998.

Wilkie, Laurie A., and Paul Farnsworth. *Sampling Many Pots: An Archaeology of Memory and Tradition at a Bahamian Plantation.* Gainesville: University Press of Florida, 2005.

Willett, Frank. *African Art.* 3rd ed. New York: Thames & Hudson, 2003.

Williams, Colleen Madonna Flood, and James Henderson, eds. *The Bahamas* (Discover the Caribbean Series). Broomall, PA: Mason Crest Publishers, 2002. (young adult)

Williams, John. "Re-creating Their Media Image: Two Generations of Black Women Filmmakers." *Black Scholar,* Spring 1995.

Williams, Juan, with the Eyes on the Prize Production Team. *Eyes on the Prize: America's Civil Rights Years, 1954–1965. A Companion Volume to the PBS Television Series.* Introduction by Julian Bond. New York: Viking Penguin, 1987.

Williams, Paige. "Gullah, A Vanishing Culture." *Charlotte (NC) Observer,* February 7, 1993. http://faculty.ed.umuc.edu/~jmatthew/articles/gullah.html.

Williams-Myers, Albert James. *Long Hammering: Essays on the Forging of an African-American Presence in the Hudson River Valley to the Early Twentieth Century.* Trenton, NJ: Africa World Press, 1994.

Willis, W. Bruce. *The Adinkra Dictionary: A Visual Primer on the Language of Adinkra.* Washington, DC: Pyramid Complex, 1998.

Wilson, Joseph T. *The Black Phalanx: A History of the Negro Soldiers of the United States in the Wars of 1775–1812, 1861–'65.* 1890. Reprint. Manchester, NH: Ayer, 1992.

Wintz, Cary D., and Paul Finkelman, eds. *Encyclopedia of the Harlem Renaissance.* 2 vols. New York: Routledge, 2004.

Wonndrich, David. *Stomp and Swerve: American Music Gets Hot, 1843–1924.* Chicago: Chicago Review Press, 2003.

Woodson, Carter. *The Mis-Education of the Negro.* 1933. Reprint. New York: AMS Press, 1977.

Wright, Kai, ed. *The African-American Archive: The History of the Black Experience in Documents.* New York: Black Dog & Leventhal Publishers, 2001.

Zobel, Hiller B. *Boston Massacre.* New York: W. W. Norton, 1996.

Zook, Jim. "Sea Grass Roots." *Coastal Living,* May 2005.

———. "Celebrating 10 Years! Labor Day Weekend, August 31st and September 1st, 2019."

———. "Sistrunk Historical Festival, Inc.'s Events in Fort Lauderdale, FL."

Organizations—
Contact Information
and Websites

Organizations—Contact Information and Websites

This section includes all websites, including available contact information, listed in the entries in alphabetical order by the name of the sponsoring organization.

African American Cultural Alliance
1215 9th North Ave., Ste. 210
P.O. Box 22173
Nashville, TN 37202
615-942-0706; Hotline: 329-521-4038
http://www.aacanashville.org

African American Cultural Center
3018 W. 48th St.
Los Angeles, CA
323-299-6124; fax: 323-299-0261
http://www.officialkwanzaawebsite.org/
    index.shtml

African-American Day Parade, Inc.
P.O. Box 1860
New York, NY 10027
917-294-8107
http://www.aacanashville.org

African American Research Library and
    Cultural Center
2650 Sistrunk Blvd.
Fort Lauderdale, FL
954-357-6282

African American Women in Cinema
    Organization, Inc.
545 Eighth Ave., Ste. 401
New York, NY 10018
212-769-7949
http://www.aawic.org

African Film Festival, Inc.
154 W. 18th St., Ste. 2A
New York, NY 10011
212-352-1720
http://www.africanfilmny.org

African Heritage Cultural Arts
    Center
6161 N.W. 22nd Ave.
Miami, FL 33142
305-638-6771

"African American History Month"
https://www.africanamericanhistorym
    onth.gov

African Methodist Episcopal Church
500 8th Ave., S.
Nashville, TN 37203
615-254-0911; fax: 615-254-0912
http://www.ame-church.com

African Studies Center
10244 Bunche Hall
405 Hilgard Ave.
P.O. Box 951310
Los Angeles, CA 90095
310-825-3686; fax: 310-206-2250
http://www.international.ucla.edu/
    africa/mgpp

African World Festival
315 E. Warren Ave.
Detroit, MI 4820
313-494-5800
http://thewright.org/african-world-festival

Alpha Kappa Alpha
5656 S. Stony Island Ave.
Chicago, IL 60637
773-684-1282
http://www.aka1908.com

Alpha Phi Alpha Fraternity, Inc.
2313 St. Paul St.
Baltimore, MD
410-554-0040; fax: 410-554-0054
https://apa1906.net

American Black Film Festival
http://www.abff.com

Malcolm X College
American Museum of Natural History
Central Park W. at 79th St.
New York, NY 10024
212-769-5000; fax: 212-496-3605
http://www.amnh.org

American Public Transportation Association
1300 I St N.W., Ste. 1200 E.
Washington, DC 20005
202-496-4800; fax: 202-496-4324;
http://www.apta.com

Asbury United Methodist Church
926 11th St., N.W.
Washington, DC 20001
202-628-0009; fax: 202-783-0519
http://www.asburyumcdc.org

Asheville Convention & Visitors Bureau
39 S. Market St.
Asheville, NC 28801
828-258-6129
http://www.exploreasheville.com

Association for the Study of African-American Life and History
301 Rhode Island Ave., N.W.
Washington, DC 20059
202-238-5910
http://www.asalh.org

Atlanta Convention & Visitors Bureau
233 Peachtree St. N.E., Ste. 1400
Atlanta, GA 30303
404-521-6600
https://www.atlanta.net

Avery Research Center
125 Bull St.
Charleston, SC 29424
843-953-7609; fax: 843-953-7607
https://avery.cofc.edu

Baptist World Center Headquarters
1700 Baptist World Center Dr.
Nashville, TN 37207
866-531-3054; 615-228-6292;
fax: 615-262-3917
http://www.nationalbaptist.com

Bayou Classic
1433 N. Claiborne Ave.
New Orleans, LA 70112
504-827-1892; fax: 504-455-7103
http://www.mybayouclassic.com

Beaufort County Black Chamber of Commerce
Visitors Information
711 Bladen St.
Beaufort, SC 29902
843-986-1102
https://bcbcc.org

Benedict College
1600 Harden St.
Columbia, SC 29204
803-705-4519; fax: 803-705-6654

Bill Pickett Invitational Rodeo
National Office
5829 S Quintero Cir.
Centennial, CO 80015
303-373-1246
http://www.billpickettrodeo.com

Black American West Museum and
    Heritage Center
3091 California St.
Denver, CO 80205
720-242-7428
https://bawmhc.org

Black Hollywood Education & Resource
    Center
1875 Century Park E., Ste. 6th Fl.
Los Angeles, CA
323- 957-4656; fax: 310-284-3169
http://www.bherc.org

Brooklyn Academy of Music, Inc.
Bldg. 30, Lafayette Ave.
Brooklyn, NY 11217
http://www.bam.org

Brooklyn Tourism and Visitors Center
Brooklyn Borough Hall
209 Joralemon St.
Brooklyn, NY 11201
718-802-3700; fax: 718-802-3778
https://www.brooklyn-usa.org

Buffalo Soldier Monument
290 Stimson Ave.
Fort Leavenworth, KS 33027
913-682-4113
http://kansastravel.org/
    buffalosoldiermonument.htm

Buffalo Soldiers National Museum
713-942-8920
http://www.buffalosoldiermuseum.com

"Buffalo soldiers" online exhibit at the
    International Museum of the Horse
Kentucky Horse Park
4089 Iron Works Pkwy.
Lexington, KY 40511
859-233-4303; 800-678-8813; fax: 859-
    254-0253
http://www.imh.org/imh/buf/buftoc.
    html

Center for Contemporary Black
    History
760 Schermerhorn Extension—MC 5512
Columbia University
1200 Amsterdam Ave.
New York, NY 10027
212-854-1489; fax: 212-854-7060
http://www.columbia.edu/cu/ccbh/
    mxp/index.html

Charles H. Wright Museum of African
    American History
315 E. Warren Ave.
Detroit, MI 48201
313-494-5800
http://thewright.org

Charleston Area Convention and
    Visitors Bureau
423 King St.
Charleston, SC 29403
843-853-8000; 800-868-8118
http://www.charlestoncvb.com

Chattanooga African-American
    Museum
200 E. Martin Luther King Blvd.
Chattanooga, TN 37403
423-266-8658; fax: 423-267-1076
http://www.bessiesmithcc.org

Chattanooga Chamber of Commerce
811 Broad St., Ste. 100
Chattanooga, TN 37402
423-756-2121
http://www.chattanoogachamber.com

Chattanooga Area Convention &
　Visitors Bureau
736 Market St., 18th Fl.
Chattanooga, TN 37402
423-756-8687; 800-322-3344
http://www.chattanoogafun.com

Chicago Convention and Tourism
　Bureau
301 E. Cermak Rd.
Chicago, IL 60616
312-567-8500
http://www.choosechicago.com

Chicago Defender
4445 S. Martin Luther King Dr.
Chicago, IL 60653
312-225-2400; fax: 312-225-9231
http://www.chicagodefender.com

Chicago Defender Charities, Inc.
700 E. Oakwood Blvd., 5th Fl.
Chicago, IL 60616
773-536-3710
http://www.budbillikenparade.org

Chicora Foundation, Inc.
P.O. Box 8664
861 Arbutus Dr.
Columbia, SC 29202
803-787-6910
http://www.sciway.net/hist/chicora/
　mitchelville-6.html

Church of the Lukumi Babalu Aye
436 Palm Ave.
Hialeah, FL 33012
http://www.churchofthelukumi.com

City of Charleston Office of Cultural
　Affairs
75 Calhoun St., Ste. 3800
Charleston, SC 29401
843-724-7305
http://www.mojafestival.com/home

City of Hutchinson
125 E. Ave. B
P.O. Box 1567
Hutchinson, KS 67501
620-694-2611; fax: 620-694-2673
http://www.hutchgov.com

City of Seaford
414 High St.
P.O. Box 1100
Seaford, DE 19973
302-629-9173; fax: 302-629-9307
http://www.seafordde.com

City Park Foundation
830 Fifth Ave.
New York, NY 10021
212-360-1399
https://cityparksfoundation.org

CMG Worldwide
429 N. Pennsylvania St., Ste. 204
Indianapolis, IN 46204
317-570-5000
https://www.cmgworldwide.com/
　malcolm-x

Coastal Discovery Museum
P.O. Box 23497
Hilton Head Island, SC 29925
843-689-6767
http://www.coastaldiscovery.org

Colorado Black Arts Festival
1700 City Park Esp.
Denver, CO 80205
303-306-8672
https://www.denver.org/listing/city-
　park/6822

Company B, 54th Massachusetts
 Volunteer Infantry Regiment
54th Mass
P.O. Box 116
Kensington, MD
http://www.54thmass.org

Connecticut State Library
231 Capitol Ave.
Hartford, CT 6106
860-757-6500; 866-886-4478
https://libguides.ctstatelibrary.org/hg/
 africanamerican/blackgovernors

DanceAfrica in Washington, DC
3225 8th St., N.E.
Washington, DC 20017
202-269-1600; fax: 202-269-4103
http://www.danceplace.org

DC Black Pride Black Lesbian and Gay
 Pride Day, Inc.
http://www.dcblackpride.org

DC Caribbean Carnival, Inc.
4809-A Georgia Ave., N.W., Ste. 112
Washington, DC 20011
202-726-2204
http://www.dccarnival.com

Delta Sigma Theta Sorority, Inc.
1707 New Hampshire Ave., N.W.
Washington, DC 20009
202-986-2400; fax: 202-986-2513
http://www.deltasigmatheta.org

Denton Juneteenth Committee
P.O. Box 51291
Denton, TX 76206
940-349-8575
http://www.juneteenthdentontx.org

Denver Film Society
1510 York St.
Denver, CO 80206
303-595-3456
http://www.denverfilm.org

Destination DC
901 7th St., N.W., 4th Fl.
Washington, DC
202-789-7000; fax: 202-789-7037
http://www.washington.org

District of Columbia Mayor's Office
John A. Wilson Bldg.
1350 Pennsylvania Ave., N.W.
Washington, DC 20004
202-727-2643
https://mayor.dc.gov/release/mayor-
 bowser-announces-2019-dc-
 emancipation-day-festivities

Dorchester County Office of Tourism
2 Rose Hill Pl.
Cambridge, MD 21613
410-228-1000; 800-522-TOUR (8687)
https://visitdorchester.org

Dunbar-Jupiter Hammon Public
 Library
the largest African-American book
 collection in southwest Florida
3095 Blount St.
Fort Myers, FL 33916
239-533-4150; fax: 239-485-1194
https://www.leegov.com/library/
 branches/db

DuSable Museum of African American
 History
740 E. 56th Pl.
Chicago, IL 60637
773-947-0600
http://www.dusablemuseum.org

Eastside Arts Alliance
Malcolm X Jazz Festival
2277 International Blvd.
P.O. Box 17008
Oakland, CA 94601
510-533-6629
https://www.eastsideartsalliance.org/
    contact

Eastern Shore AFRAM Festival
P.O. Box 687
Seaford, DE 19973
302-628-1908
https://www.easternshoreafram.org

Elegba Folklore Society's Cultural
    Center
101 E. Broad St.
Richmond, VA 23219
804-644-3900
http://www.elegbafolkloresociety.org

Eubie Blake National Jazz Institute and
    Cultural Center
847 N. Howard St.
Baltimore, MD 21201
410-225-3130
http://www.eubieblake.org

Franklin Square/Emancipation Day
    Parade
8601 Adelphi Rd.
College Park, MD 20740
866-272-6272; 301-837-2000
https://www.archives.gov/college-
    park

Frederick Douglass National Historic
    Site
1411 W St., S.E.
Washington, DC
202-426-5961
http://www.nps.gov/frdo

French Quarter Festivals, Inc.
400 N. Peter, Ste. 205
New Orleans, LA 70130
504-522-5730; fax: 504-522-5711
http://www.fqfi.orgorhttp://www.
    satchmosummerfest.com

George Washington Carver National
    Monument
5646 Carver Rd.
Diamond, MO 64840
417-325-4151
http://www.nps.gov/gwca

Ghana National Council of
    Metropolitan Chicago
http://www.ghananationalcouncil.org

Government of the Bahamas Ministry of
    Youth Sports and Culture
Thompson Blvd.
P.O. Box 4891
Nassau, Bahamas
242-502-0600; fax: 242-322-6546
http://www.bahamas.gov.bs

Greater Fort Lauderdale Convention &
    Visitors Bureau
101 NE Third Ave., Ste. 100
Fort Lauderdale, FL 33301
800-227-8669; fax: 954-765-4466
http://www.sunny.org

Greater Harlem Chamber of
    Commerce
200A W. 136th St.
New York, NY
212-862-7200; fax: 212-862-8745
http://www.harlemdiscover.com

Greater Miami Convention & Visitors
  Bureau
701 Bricknell Ave., Ste. 2700
Miami, FL 33131
800-933-8448; fax: 305-539-3000
http://www.gmcvb.com

Greater Milwaukee Convention and
  Visitors Bureau
648 N. Plankinton Ave., Ste. 425
Milwaukee, WI
800-231-0903; 414-273-3950;
fax: 414-273-5596
http://www.milwaukee.org

Haitian Americans United
10 Fairway St., Ste. 218
Mattapan, MA 2126
617-298-2976
http://www.hauinc.org/html/programs/
  indexFlag.asp

Harmony Gold USA, Inc.
7655 W. Sunset Blvd.
Los Angeles, CA 90046
323-851-4900; fax: 928-447-2127

Harriet Tubman National Holiday
P.O. Box 832127
Stone Mountain, GA 30083
302-762-8010
http://www.harriettubman.com/index.
  html

Hartmann Studios
1150 Brickyard Cove Rd., Ste. 202
Richmond, CA 94801
http://www.fillmorestreetjazzfest.com

Hilton Head Island-Bluffton Chamber
  of Commerce and Visitor &
  Convention Bureau
1 Chamber of Commerce Dr.
P.O. Box 5647
Hilton Head Island, SC 29938
843-785-3673; 800-523-3373

Historic Columbia Foundation
1601 Richland St.
Columbia, SC 29201
803-252-7742;
fax: 803-929-7695
http://www.historiccolumbia.org

The HistoryMakers, an organization
  that collects videos, oral histories,
  and other materials on African-
  American heritage
1900 S. Michigan Ave.
Chicago, IL 60616
312-674-1900; fax: 312-674-1915
http://thehistorymakers.com

Homowo African Arts & Cultures
7725 N. Fowler Ave.
Portland, OR 97211
503-288-3025
http://www.homowo.org/festival.html

Hutchinson Emancipation Day
  Committee, Inc.
P.O. Box 701
Hutchinson, KS 67504-0701
620-663-6673
http://www.shopkansas.net/eday/misc.
  html

Hutchinson/Reno County Chamber of
  Commerce
117 N. Walnut
P.O. Box 519
Hutchinson, KS 67504
620-662-3391; fax: 620-662-2168
http://www.hutchchamber.com/
  community/index.htm

Idlewild African American Chamber of
  Commerce
P.O. Box 435
Idlewild, MI 49642
678-492-6814
http://www.iaacc.com

Idlewild Historic & Cultural Center
7025 Broadway Ave.
Idlewild, MI 49642

In The Life Atlanta, Inc.
1530 Dekalb Ave.
Atlanta, GA 30357
404-872-6410; fax: 404-506-9730
http://www.inthelifeatl.com

Independence Hall Visitor Center
520 Chestnut St.
Philadelphia, PA 19106
215-965-2305; fax: 215-597-1548
http://www.nps.gov/inde

Indiana Black Expo, Inc.
3145 N. Meridian St.
Indianapolis, IN 46208
317-925-2702; fax: 317-925-6624
http://www.indianablackexpo.com

Indiana University–Purdue University
   at Indianapolis
Frederick Douglass Papers
902 W. New York St.
Indianapolis, IN 46202
317-274-5834
http://www.iupui.edu/~douglass/index.
   htm

International Association of African
   American Music
413 S Broad St.
Philadelphia, PA 19147
215-664-1677; fax: 610-664-5940
http://www.iaaam.com/home.html

International Festival of Life
c/o Martin's Inter-Culture, Ltd.
1325 S. Wabash Ave., Ste. 307
Chicago, IL 60605
312-427-0266; fax: 312-427-0268
https://www.internationalfestivaloflife.
   co

Jefferson Street United Merchants
   Partnership, Inc.
1215 9th Ave. N., Ste. 201
Nashville, TN 37208
615-726-5867; fax: 615-726-2078
http://www.jumptojefferson.com

Juneteenth.com
P.O. Box 871750
New Orleans, LA 70187
504-245-7800
http://www.juneteenth.com

Kappa Alpha Psi Fraternity, Inc.
2322-24 N. Broad St.
Philadelphia, PA 19132
215-228-7184; fax: 215-228-7181
http://www.kappaalphapsi1911.com

King County Courthouse
516 Third Ave.
Seattle, WA 98104
206-296-0100; 800-325-6165
http://www.metrokc.gov/exec/robeson/
   about.htm

Kingdom of Oyotunji African Village
56 Bryant Ln.
Seabrook, SC 29941
843-846-8900
http://www.oyotunjivillage.net/
   oyo2_007.htm

Kunta Kinte-Alex Haley Foundation,
   Inc.
Asbury United Methodist Church
87 West St., 2nd Fl.
Annapolis, MD 21401
410-295-9395; fax: 410-295-9396
http://www.kintehaley.org

Kwanzaa Heritage Foundation
One Kwanzaa Circle
Los Angeles, CA 90060

Library of Congress
101 Independence Ave, S.E.
Washington, DC 20540
202-707-5000

Louis Armstrong Archives
Queens College
332-338 Rosenthal Library
Flushing, NY 11367-1597
http://www.satchmo.net

Louis Armstrong House
34-56 107th St.
Corona, NY 11368
718-997-3670; fax: 718-997-3677
http://www.satchmo.net

Madam C. J. Walker Building
617 Indiana Ave.
Indianapolis, IN 46202
317-236-2099
http://www.walkertheatre.com/walker_
    building.htm

Major League Baseball Advanced Media
c/o MLB Advanced Media, L.P.
75 Ninth Ave., 5th Fl.
New York, NY 10011
212-485-8959; fax: 212-485-3456
http://mlb.mlb.com/NASApp/mlb/mlb/
    events/jrd/index.jsp

Malcolm X College
1900 W. Van Buren
Chicago, IL 60612
312-850-7000
http://malcolmx.ccc.edu

Malcolm X Grassroots Movement
https://www.mxgm.org

Marcus Garvey Cultural Center
    University of Northern Colorado
928 20th St., Campus Box 41
Greeley, CO 80639
970-351-2351; fax: 970-351-2337
https://www.unco.edu/marcus-garvey-
    cultural-center

The Martin Luther King, Jr. Research
    and Education Institute
Cypress Hall D-Wing
466 Via Ortega
Stanford, CA
650-723-2092; fax: 650-723-2093

Miami/Bahamas Goombay Festival in
    Coconut Grove, Inc.
4716 Brooker St.
Miami, FL 33133
305-446-0643; fax: 305-446-6265
http://www.
    goombayfestivalcoconutgrove.com

Million Man March 1995, Inc.
7351 S. Stony Island Ave.
Chicago, IL 60649
773-324-6000
http://www.millionsmoremovement.com

Minnesota Historical Society
345 W. Kellogg Blvd.
St. Paul, MN 55102
651-259-3000; 800-657-3773
http://www.mnhs.org

Mississippi Action for Community
    Education, Inc.
119 Theobald St.
Greenville, MS 38701
662-335-3523; fax: 662-334-2939
http://www.deltamace.org

Montgomery County Historical Society
111 W. Montgomery Ave.
Rockville, MD 20850
301-340-2825; fax: 301-340-2871
https://montgomeryhistory.org

Mother Bethel A.M.E. Church and
    Richard Allen Museum
419 Richard Allen Ave.
South 6th St.
Philadelphia, PA 19147
215-925-0616; fax: 215-925-1402
https://www.motherbethel.org/content.
    php?cid=13

National Association of Black
    Storytellers, Inc.
1601-03 E. North Ave.
P.O. Box 67722
Baltimore, MD 21215
410-947-1117
http://www.nabsinc.org/home.asp

The National Association of Buffalo
    Soldiers & Troopers Motorcycle Club
http://www.buffalosoldiersnational.com

National Black Arts Festival
Peachtree Center, North Tower
235 Peachtree St., Ste. 1725
Atlanta, GA 30303
404-730-7315; fax: 404-7300-7104
http://www.nbaf.org

National Civil Rights Museum
450 Mulberry St.
Memphis, TN 38103
901-521-9699; fax: 901-521-9740
http://www.civilrightsmuseum.org

National Council of Negro Women, Inc.
633 Pennsylvania Ave., N.W.
Washington, DC 20004
202-737-0120
http://ncnw.org

National Cowboy and Western Heritage
    Museum
1700 N.E. 63rd St.
Oklahoma City, OK 73111
405-478-2250
http://www.nationalcowboymuseum.org

National Great Blacks in Wax Museum
1601-03 E. North Ave.
Baltimore, MD 21213
410-563-3404; fax: 410-563-7806
http://www.greatblacksinwax.org

National Multicultural Western
    Heritage Museum
2029 N Main St.
Ft. Worth, TX 76164
817-922-9999; 817-534-8801; fax: 817-
    923-9304
http://www.cowboysofcolor.org

National Voting Rights Museum &
    Institute
P.O. Box 1366, Selma, AL
334-526-4340; fax: 334-418-1991
http://www.nvrmi.org

Neal-Marshall Black Culture Center
Indiana University
275 N. Jordan Ave.
Bloomington, IN 47405
812-855-9271; fax: 812-855-9148
https://blackculture.indiana.edu

Negro Leagues Baseball Museum
1616 E. 18th St.
Kansas City, MO 64102
816-221-1920; fax: 816-221-8424
http://www.nlbm.com

New Orleans Convention & Visitors
Bureau
2020 St. Charles Ave.
New Orleans, LA 70130
800-672-6124; 504-566-5011; fax: 504-
566-5046
https://www.neworleans.com/contact-us

Nicodemus Historical Society &
Museum
611 S. 5th St.
Nicodemus, KS 67625
785-839-4280
https://www.
nicodemushistoricalsociety.org

North Carolina Black Repertory
Company
P.O. Box 95
Winston-Salem, NC
336-723-2266; fax: 336-723-2223
https://ncblackrep.org

Oakland Black Cowboy Association
P.O. Box 4889
Oakland, CA
http://www.blackcowboyassociation.org

"ODUNDE Exhibition"
Philadelphia Folklore Project
735 S. 50th St.
Philadelphia, PA 19143
215-726-1106
http://www.folkloreproject.org

ODUNDE Inc.
P.O. Box 21748
2308 Grays Ferry Ave.
Philadelphia, PA 19146
215-732-8510
https://www.odundefestival.org/contact.
html

Olustee Battlefield Citizens Support
Organization
P.O. Box 382
Glen St. Mary, FL 32040
https://battleofolustee.org/what_is_cso.
htm

Olustee Battlefield Historic State Park
Citizens Support Organization
C/O Stephen Foster FCC State Park
11016 Lillian Saunders Dr.
White Springs, FL 32096
https://www.floridastateparks.org

Omega Psi Phi Fraternity, Inc.
3951 Snapfinger Pkwy.
Decatur, GA 30035
404-284-5533; fax: 404-284-0333
http://www.oppf.org

Onondaga Historical Association
Museum & Research Center
321 Montgomery St.
Syracuse, NY 13202
315-428-1864; fax: 315-471-2133
http://www.cnyhistory.org

Penn School National Historic
Landmark District
P.O. Box 126
16 Penn Center Circle W.
St. Helena Island, SC 29920
843-838-2432; fax: 843-838-8545
http://www.penncenter.com

Phi Beta Sigma
145 Kennedy St., N.W.
Washington, DC 20011
202-726-5434; fax: 202-882-1681
http://www.pbs1914.org

Philadelphia Black Gay Pride, Inc.
http://www.phillyblackpride.org

Philipsburg Manor
381 N Broadway
Sleepy Hollow, NY 10591
https://hudsonvalley.org/historic-sites/
philipsburg-manor

Real Cowboy Association
1010 Maledon Dr.
Longview, TX 75602
903-753-3165

Rhode Island Black Storytellers
393 Broad St.
P.O. Box 14
Providence, RI
401-312-4347
https://www.nabsinc.org/affiliate

Richmond Region Tourism
401 N. 3rd St.
Richmond, VA 23219
800-370-9004
https://www.visitrichmondva.com

Riverbend Festival Friends of the
Festival
200 Riverfront Pkwy.
Chattanooga, TN 37402
423-756-2211; fax: 423-756-2719
http://www.riverbendfestival.com

Montgomery County Historical Society
111 W. Montgomery Ave.
Rockville, MD 20850
301-340-2825; fax: 301-340-2871
https://montgomeryhistory.org

Nicodemus National Historic Site
304 Washington Ave.
Nicodemus, KS
785-839-4233; fax: 785-839-4323
https://www.nps.gov/nico/contacts.htm

Nicodemus Historical Society &
Museum
611 S. 5th St.
Nicodemus, KS 67625
785-839-4280
https://www.nicodemushistoricalsociety
.org

Rondo Avenue, Inc.
1360 University Ave.
P.O. Box 140
St. Paul, MN 55104
651-315-7676; fax: 651-538-6511
http://rondoavenueinc.org

Rutgers University
600 Bartholomew Rd.
Piscataway, NJ
848-445-3545; fax: 732-445-3151
http://prcc.rutgers.edu

Sisters in Cinema, a resource guide
provided by Yvonne Welbon's Our
Film Works, Inc.
http://www.sistersincinema.com

St. Paul Community Baptist Church
859 Hendrix St.
Brooklyn, NY 11207
718-257-1300; fax: 718-257-2988
https://www.spcbc.com/
commemoration-of-the-maafa

St. Petersburg/Clearwater Area
Convention and Visitors Bureau
13805 58th St. N., Ste. 2-200
Clearwater, FL 33760
877-352-3224; fax: 727-464-7200
https://www.visitstpeteclearwater.com

St. Simons African American Heritage
    Coalition
P.O. Box 20145
291 S. Harrington Rd.
St. Simons Island, GA 31522
912-634-0330
http://ssiheritagecoalition.org

Schomburg Center for Research in Black
    Culture
New York Public Library
"Malcolm X: A Search for Truth"
515 Malcolm X Blvd. (135th St. and
    Malcolm X Blvd.)
New York, NY 10037
917-275-6975

Scott Joplin International Ragtime
    Foundation
P.O. Box 1244
Sedalia, MO 65302
660-826-2271
http://www.scottjoplin.org

Sedalia Convention and Visitors Bureau
600 E. Third St.
Sedalia, MO 65301
800-827-5295; 660-826-2932

Sigma Gamma Rho Sorority, Inc.
1000 Southhill Dr., Ste. 200
Cary, NC 27513
888-747-1922; 919-678-9720; fax: 919-
    678-9721;
http://www.sgrho1922.org

Sigma Pi Phi Fraternity
260 Peachtree St., N.W., Ste. 1604
Atlanta, GA 30303
404-529-9919
https://www.sigmapiphi.org

Sundiata African American Cultural
    Association
P.O. Box 24723
Seattle, WA
866-505-6006; fax: 206-420-6184
http://www.festivalsundiata.org

The Colonial Williamsburg Foundation
"African American Experience"
P.O. Box 1776
Williamsburg, VA
757-229-1000; 855-756-9516
https://www.history.org/Almanack/life/
    Af_Amer/aalife.cfm

The Harriet Tubman Home
180 South St.
Auburn, NY 13201
315-252-2081
http://www.nyhistory.com/
    harriettubman

The Harriet Tubman Organization, Inc.
424 Race St.
Cambridge, MD 21613
410-228-0401
http://www.intercom.net/npo/tubman

The Hurston Museum
227 E. Kennedy Blvd.
Eatonville, FL 32751
407-647-3188
http://zorafestival.org

The Jackie Robinson Foundation
One Hudson Sq.
75 Varick St., 2nd Flr.
New York, NY 10013-1917
fax: 212-290-8081

The Shabazz Center
3940 Broadway
New York, NY 10032

Tuskegee Airmen, Incorporated
P.O. Box 830060
Tuskegee, AL 36083
334-725-8200; fax: 334-725-8205
http://tuskegeeairmen.org

Tuskegee Institute National Historic
Site
1212 W. Montgomery Rd.
Tuskegee, AL 36088
334-727-3200; fax: 334-727-1448;
http://www.nps.gov/tuin

Tubman Museum
310 Cherry St.
Macon, GA 31201
478-743-8544; fax: 478-743-9063

Universal Negro Improvement
Association and African
Communities League
Thomas W. Harvey Memorial
Division
1609-11 Cecil B. Moore Ave., Ste. 121
Philadelphia, PA 19121
215-236-0782
http://www.unia-acl.org

Warren County Historical Society
210 Fourth Ave.
P.O. Box 427
Warren, PA 16365
814-723-1795; 814-723-1795
http://www.warrenhistory.org

W. C. Handy Home, Museum, and
Library
620 W. College St.
Florence, AL 35630
256-760-6434
https://www.visitflorenceal.com/
things_to_do/w-c-handy-birthplace-
museum-library

W. C. Handy Music Festival
217 E. Tuscaloosa St.
Florence, AL 35630
256-766-7642
http://www.wchandymusicfestival.org

West Indian-American Day Carnival
Association
323-325 Rogers Ave.
Brooklyn, NY 11225
718-467-1797
http://wiadcacarnival.org

Wisconsin Black Historical Society/
Museum
2620 W. Center St.
Milwaukee, WI 53206
414-372-7677
http://www.wbhsm.org

Wyckoff House Museum
5816 Clarendon Rd.
Brooklyn, NY 11203
718-629-5400
https://wyckoffmuseum.org

YMI Cultural Center
39 S. Market St.
Asheville, NC 28801
828-257-4540
https://ymiculturalcenter.org

Zeta Phi Beta Sorority, Inc.
1734 New Hampshire Ave., N.W.
Washington, DC 20009
202-387-3103
http://www.zphib1920.org

Zulu Social Aid and Pleasure Club, Inc.
732 N. Broad St.
New Orleans, LA 70119
504-827-1661
http://www.kreweofzulu.com/contact-
us

Photo and Illustration Credits

Photo and Illustration Credits

All Library of Congress images are from the Prints and Photographs Division unless otherwise indicated.

All Library of Congress images are from the Prints and Photographs Division unless otherwise indicated.

Cover photos: Library of Congress (parade); Comstock/Milestones (Kwanzaa); Donald Uhrbrock/Time Life Pictures/Getty Images (MLK, Jr.); Idlewild Foundation/Landmine Design (poster).

Page xiii: Thomas B. Morton/courtesy of the Philadelphia Folklore Project.

African American Day Parade: AP Images (p. 6).

African American Women in Cinema Film Festival: DAUGHTERS OF THE DUST copyright © 1991 Geechee Girls Productions. DVD package design copyright © 1999 Kino International Corp. (p. 12).

African World Festival in Detroit: AP Images (p. 20).

African-American History Month: all Library of Congress (p. 30) - Bethune Gordon Parks, photographer, LC-USW3-013518-C; Bunche Carl Van Vechten Collection, LC-USZ62-91184; Jordan *U.S. News & World Report* Magazine Collection, LC-U9-32937, frame 32A/33; Marshall *U.S. News & World Report* Magazine Collection, LC-U9-1027B, frame 11; Randolph Gordon Parks, photographer, LC-USW3-011696- C; Wilkins *U.S. News & World Report* Magazine Collection, LC-U9-9522, frame 6.

August Quarterly: Methodist collections of Drew University Library (p. 45).

Battle of Olustee Reenactment: State Archives of Florida (p. 50).

Bessie Smith Strut: Library of Congress, Carl Van Vechten Collection, LC-USZ62-100863 (p. 55).

Bill Pickett Invitational Rodeo: Library of Congress (p. 59).

Black Cowboy Parade: Denver Public Library, Western History Collection/X-21563 (p. 71).

Bridge Crossing Jubilee: Library of Congress (p. 85); Library of Congress, NYWT&S Collection, LC-USZ62-135695 (p. 86).

Bud Billiken Parade and Picnic: Library of Congress, FSA/OWI Collection, LC-USW3-000698-D (p. 90).

Buffalo Soldiers Commemorations: Library of Congress (p. 93).

Charlie Parker Jazz Festival: Metronome/Getty Images (p. 98).

Church Homecomings: Library of Congress, FSA/OWI Collection, LC-USF33-030967-M4 (p. 108).

Crispus Attucks Day: United States Mint (p. 119).

DC Caribbean Carnival: AP Images (p. 131).

Emancipation Day: Library of Congress (p. 145); State Archives of Florida (p. 152).

Emancipation Day in Washington, D.C.: Library of Congress (p. 161).

Festival Sundiata: SUNDIATA: AN EPIC OF OLD MALI copyright © Longman Group Ltd. (English version) 1965. Fourteenth impression 2005. Cover photograph: Senegalese glass painting from private collection (p. 164).

Football Classics: NewsCom.com (p. 171).

Founder's Day/Richard Allen's Birthday: Library of Congress (p. 174).

Frederick Douglass Day: Library of Congress (p. 181).

George Washington Carver Day: Library of Congress (p. 186).

Greek Organizations' Conventions: AP Images (p. 201).

Haile Selassie's Birthday: Library of Congress, FSA/OWI Collection, LC-USW33-019078-C (p. 206).

Harlem Week: Library of Congress, FSA/OWI, LC-USW3-031102-C (p. 217).

Harriet Tubman Day: Library of Congress (p. 220).

Homecoming Emancipation Celebration: courtesy of the National Park Service/Nicodemus National Historic Site (p. 233).

Honoring Santerįa Orishas: AP Images (p. 240).

J'Ouvert Celebration and West Indian-American Day Carnival: Mario Tama/Getty Images (p. 260).

Jackie Robinson Day: Library of Congress (pp. 265, 269).

Juneteenth: PICA 05476, Austin History Center, Austin Public Library (p. 279); courtesy of the Gavelston Island Convention and Visitors Bureau (p. 280); AP Images (p. 284).

Kunta Kinte Heritage Festival: courtesy, Enoch Pratt Free Library, Central Library/State Library Resource Center, Baltimore, Md. (p. 294).

Kwanzaa: Adobe® Image Library/Festive Icons (p. 299); Stephen Chernin/Getty Images (pp. 303, 304).

Malcolm X's Birthday: *Detroit News* Collection/Walter P. Reuther Library, Wayne State University (p. 313); AP Images (p. 316); MALCOLM X (1972) copyright © 1972/Renewed copyright © 2000. MALCOLM X (1992) copyright © 1992. Package design copyright © 2005 Warner Bros. Entertainment Inc. (p. 318).

Marcus Garvey's Birthday: Library of Congress (p. 322).

Mardi Gras in African-American Traditions: Shutterstock.com/Natalia Bratslavsky (p. 327).

Martin Luther King Jr.'s Birthday: Donald Uhrbrock/Time Life Pictures/Getty Images (p. 332); AFP/Getty Images (p. 339); Stephen Chernin/Getty Images (p. 341); photo by M.T. Harmon, Office of Public Affairs, Corporation of National and Community Service (p. 343).

Millions More Movement March: AP Images (p. 350); Andrew Council/AFP/Getty Images (p. 351).

National Baptist Convention, USA, Annual Session: Paul J. Richard/AFP/Getty Images (p. 363).

National Black Storytelling Festival and Conference: AP Images (p. 372).

National Freedom Day: National Archives/www.ourdocuments.gov (p. 380).

Odunde Festival: Thomas B. Morton/courtesy of the Philadelphia Folklore Project (p. 388).

Pan African Film & Arts Festival: Nancy Ostertag/Getty Images (p. 400).

Paul Robeson's Birthday: NewsCom.com (p. 403).

Rosa Parks Day: California African-American Museum (p. 417); Mario Tama/Getty Images (p. 419).

Satchmo SummerFest: AFP/Getty Images (p. 422).

Tuskegee Airmen Convention: Library of Congress, FSA/OWI Collection, LC-USZ62-107498 (p. 444).

W. C. Handy Music Festival: Library of Congress/Brown University Library (p. 450).

Watch Night: Library of Congress (p. 455).

West Indies Emancipation Day: Library of Congress (p. 464).

Zora Neale Hurston Festival of the Arts and Humanities: Library of Congress (p. 474); THEIR EYES WERE WATCHING GOD (HarperPerennial/HarperCollins Publishers) copyright © 1937 by Zora Neale Hurston. Renewed 1965 by John C. Hurston and Joel Hurston. First HarperPerennial Modern Classics edition published 2006. Cover design by Robin Bilardello derived from a photograph by Brad Wilson/Photonica. (p. 476).

Index

Index

The Index lists holidays, festivals, people, places, organizations, customs, symbols, foods, musical and literary works, and other subjects mentioned in the entries. Names of entries in this volume appear in bold-faced type. Illustrations are denoted by the abbreviation (ill.).

creole, 211, 225, 328–9, 406, 423
Creole Wild West, 328–9
Crisis, 331, 369
Crispus Attucks Day, 118, 121
Crispus Attucks Monument (Boston, Massachusetts), 120
Crispus Attucks Parade (Newark, New Jersey), 121
Crowder, Baba, 388 (ill.)
Crozer Theological Seminary (Chester, Pennsylvania), 333
Crump, Edward, 451
Cuba, 67, 94, 239, 253–4, 381, 389
Cuban Giants, 266
Cuban Rap Festival, 67
Cuffe, Paul, 314
Cullen, Countee, 216, 477
Cummings, James C., Jr., 256

D

Daley, Richard, 193
dance, 72, 114, 254–5, 287, 303–4, 329, 353, 388, 410, 428
  Caribbean, 123
  See also Ballin' the Jack; cakewalk; Charleston; DanceAfrica; jitterbug; ring dance ceremony; ring shout; step shows; Vola Shuffle
DanceAfrica, 123–6, 133
Dance Center of Columbia College (Chicago, Illinois), 125
Dance Place (Washington, D.C.), 125
Dances and Drums of Africa, 125
Dash, Julie, 12
Daughters of the Dust, 12
Daughtry, Herbert, 303 (ill.)
Davis, Angela, 66
Davis, Benjamin O., Jr., 94, 444 (ill.)
Davis, Chuck, 124
Davis, Edward, 29
Davis, Miles, 167
Dawson, Rosario, 43

DC Black Lesbian Gay Pride Day, Inc., 128
DC Black Pride, 127–9
DC Caribbean Carnival, 130–2
Deadwood Dick, 70
Delany, Martin Robinson, 28
De La Torre, Miguel A., 240, 242
Delaware, 44–8, 173, 282
  AFRAM Festival, 141
Delta Sigma Theta, 201
Denton, Texas, Juneteenth observances in, 281
Denver, Colorado, 134
  Denver Black Arts Festival, 113
  Denver Pan African Film Festival, 133
Denver Film Society, 133
Denver Pan African Film Festival, 133–4, 229
Dessalines, Jean Jacques, 211
Detroit, Michigan, 128, 133, 247, 373
  African World Festival, 19
  Martin Luther King Jr.'s Birthday, 418
  Rosa Parks Day, 417
  Tuskegee Airmen Convention, 445
Devlin, George, 214
Dielman, Frederick, 161 (ill.)
Dinizulz, Nana, 125
dinner-on-the-grounds, 108 (ill.)
  See also barbecues; picnics
Disney World. *See* Downtown Disney Pleasure Island, Walt Disney World Resort
Domino, Fats, 76
Dorchester County, Maryland, 219, 222
Dorsey, Thomas A., 102–3
Douglass, Frederick, 183–4, 273, 437–8, 466–7
  and Christmas, 433
  Frederick Douglass Day, 27
  National Historic Site, 33
  speeches of, 182
  and Sugar Grove Anti-Slavery Convention, 436

Wyckoff Farmhouse Museum (Brooklyn,
New York), 410
Wyoming, 62, 282

X

X, Malcolm, 66, 292, 300, 312, 336, 341
See also Malcolm X's Birthday

Y

"Yellow Dog Blues," 451
YMICC. 196–7 *See* Young Men's
Institute Cultural Center, Inc.
Yokonomo. 287 *See* Junkanoo
Yoruba, 135, 239–42, 250, 302, 387, 391
See also Ifa Festival and Yoruba
National Convention; Odunde
Festival; Olokun Festival

Youngblood, Johnny, 310
Young Men's Institute Cultural Center,
Inc. (YMICC; Asheville, North
Carolina), 196

Z

zawadi, 301, 305
Zawditu, Empress, 205
Zeta Phi Beta, 201
*Zora Neale Hurston: A Literary
Biography,* 477
**Zora Neale Hurston Festival of the Arts
and Humanities,** 11, 216, **473–8**
See also Hurston, Zora Neale
Zulu Krewe, 327
Zulu parade, Mardi Gras, 329
Zulu Social Aid and Pleasure
Club, 327

9/23